# Media Economics

## Theory and Practice

# Media Economics

## Theory and Practice

### Third Edition

*Edited by*

**Alison Alexander**
*University of Georgia*

**James Owers**
*Georgia State University*

**Rod Carveth**
*Rochester Institute of Technology*

**C. Ann Hollifield**
*University of Georgia*

**Albert N. Greco**
*Fordham University*

Routledge
Taylor & Francis Group
New York   London

First published by Lawrence Erlbaum Associates, Inc., Publishers
10 Industrial Avenue
Mahwah, New Jersey 07430

*Transferred to digital printing 2010 by Routledge*
Routledge

270 Madison Avenue
New York, NY 10016

2 Park Square, Milton Park
Abingdon, Oxon OX14 4RN, UK

Cover design by Sean Sciarrone

**Library of Congress Cataloging-in-Publication Data**

Media economics : theory and practice / edited by Alison
Alexander ... [et al.].—3rd ed.
    p.  cm.

Includes bibliographical references and index.
ISBN 0-8058-4580-1 (pbk. : alk. paper)
1. Mass media—Economic aspects. I. Alexander, Alison.
P96.E25M4   2003
338.4'730223—dc21
                                    2003045401
                                          CIP

# Contents

# Preface

The importance of media economics became apparent as the massive business reorganizations of the 1980s and 1990s became the failures of the new century. Due to regulatory, technological, and financial changes, media became the target of takeovers, breakups, mergers, and acquisitions. Media economics became much more than understanding cash flow within a single business organization. This book is designed to focus on the principle of economics in the business sector and to apply it to specific media industries.

This volume examines the process of decision making in media economics through an exploration of such topics as industrial restructuring, regulatory constraints on media operations, and changing economic value. Because the structure and value of media industries have changed so rapidly over the last decade, it is important to understand the mechanics of such change so as to provide insight into the processes reproducing contemporary trends in media economics, rather than simply documenting historical patterns.

Part I of this book focuses on the concerns of media economics, the techniques of economic and business analysis, and overall characteristics of the rapidly changing media environments. Chapter 1, by James Owers, Rod Carveth, and Alison Alexander, is designed to provide a framework of reference in economics and business. This chapter should enable the reader without a background in these areas to appreciate the overall structure, conceptual content, and application of economics to media business. For the reader with a strong background in economic and business studies, this chapter serves as a brief review and introduction to the application of these disciplines to media firms. Chapter 2, by Robert Corn-Revere and Rod Carveth, provides a context for understanding the recent regulatory changes for media industries, particularly the Telecommunications Act of 1996. From the vantage point of Corn-Revere, a communications lawyer for more than a decade, the authors produce a view of the legal structures that guide public policy toward electronic media. Chapter 3, by Gary Ozanich and Michael Wirth, considers business combinations in the media industries through an analysis of the amount and types of restructuring within the communications industries and as related to the whole of the U.S. economy. The authors closely detail those transactions to consider thoroughly how mergers and acquisitions are employed in changing the structure of media firms. The final chapter in Part I reviews changes in international media economic practices. Ann Hollifield argues that the 1990s were a decade of globalization as co-ventures and global integration of media industries became the norm.

Part II examines economic practice within specific media industries. Chapter 5 (Robert Picard), chapter 6 (Al Greco), chapter 7 (Doug Ferguson), chapter 8 (Ben Bates and Todd Chambers), chapter 9 (Doug Gomery), chapter 10 (Al Albarran), chapter 11 (Eric Rothenbuhler and Tom McCourt), chapter 12 (Mary Alice Shaver), and chapter 13 (Rod Carveth) illustrate contemporary business practices in the newspaper, book, magazine, television, cable, movie, radio, advertising, music, and online industries. Picard predicts that despite a decline in readership, newspaper companies will remain healthy by adopting technological innovations in adapting to the lifestyle changes of their readers. Greco outlines the health and challenges of both the book and magazine industries. Ferguson argues that if the current television networks are to remain financially viable, they are going to have to find a market niche with their programming rather than continuing their present strategy of attempting to reach a mass market. Bates and Chambers note that the cable industry is at a crossroads, with impending competition creating new opportunities and new dangers. By contrast, Gomery sees no end to the domination of the movie industry by the current Hollywood oligopoly, noting that the industry has successfully adapted to recent changes. Albarran explores the interdependence of media economic resources, noting the changes that have occurred historically with the advent of new technologies, and their implications for the contemporary radio industry. Rothenbuhler and McCourt overview the recorded music industry, with particular attention to the structure of the industry and the strategic decision-making techniques that record companies use to address the characteristic uncertainty in the music business. Shaver details the operation of the advertising industry, with particular attention to function of agencies. Carveth assesses the challenges of the online industry in the era after the dot-com crash.

For those who wish to pursue issues further, suggested readings are provided at the end of each chapter. A glossary is also provided. Two appendices are provided online for those interested in financial media management.

## ACKNOWLEDGMENTS

A project such as this would not be possible without the efforts of many people. We particularly thank our authors for their patience and expertise. We also acknowledge the editors of this series and the reviewers and readers of the previous edition who have given us helpful feedback.

*—Alison Alexander*
*—James Owers*
*—Rod Carveth*
*—C. Ann Hollifield*
*—Al Greco*

# I

# Economic Value and Structure

# Chapter 1

# An Introduction to Media Economics Theory and Practice

JAMES OWERS
*Georgia State University*

ROD CARVETH
*Rochester Institute of Technology*

ALISON ALEXANDER
*University of Georgia*

## MEDIA ECONOMICS AS A FIELD OF STUDY

Media economics may never have been more important for the industry than at the present time. The past several years have been a tumultuous period for media firms. In addition to the financial stresses and volatility faced by firms in general, media firms have been encountering the forces of technological and organizational change as they seek ways to maintain viability in a rapidly changing business and social environment. Perhaps the most prominent example of the challenges manifests itself in the ongoing travails of AOL Time Warner, Inc. Heralded by its proponents in January 2000 as a masterful organizational development to address the challenges of technological change and the financial demands of investors, within 2 years this combination was considered to be a failure from most perspectives. Many of the key players are gone, and further exits and organizational change, some of which may essentially "undo" the combination, will likely continue. Many of the ongoing series of strategic initiatives announced by the firm are greeted with skepticism and investor evaluation of the firm is pessimistic.

The widely cited example of AOL Time Warner, Inc. reflects the challenges faced by media firms in general. The changing technological, economic, and organizational environments and demands of the various constituencies of media firms place such firms under tremendous pressure. This clearly implies the need for ever-more efficient management of such firms. Practices that may have sufficed in less challenging times might now lead to untenable levels of operating and financial stress for media firms. The material on media economics addressed in this book appears to have reached a new level of importance for those involved in the operation and management of media firms.

## What Is Media Economics?

The field of media economics is often seen as a subspecialty of both media and economics. However, as events over the past two decades have indicated, media economics has become an identifiable new field of study and practice. It combines principles of both the study of media and communications with the examination of economic principles and their application in managing firms in the sector.

The study of media and communications concerns itself with issues of freedom of speech, access to the media, the social impact of media content, and the effects of new communication technology. All these areas involve a discussion of economic principles to some degree. The introduction of TiVo technology provides a classic example of the interaction between media and economics attributes of an activity. From media and communication perspectives TiVo technology provides the powerful potential for more efficient personal viewing and content management by parents for their children. But the implication for an advertising-based medium such as TV is dramatic. TV executives are on record as noting the seismic implication for the present economic model of widespread adoption of such technologies. In the music industry, the Napster example has clearly illustrated how media economics often plays out with guidelines from the legal establishment when conflicts arise and regulatory guidelines are silent in an area.

Whether most or all citizens will enjoy universal access to the new telecommunications technologies will depend on how information service providers are able to recover their costs and make a profit within the confines of the contemporaneous legal framework. A. J. Leibling once said, "Freedom of the press belongs to whomever owns one." Although this may be a cynical quote, ownership of a mass-media vehicle requires substantial capital investment, linking economic means to the information in the media environment.

Economic principles must be embraced by media sector industries if viable firms are to continue in an ever more demanding economic context. In his landmark introductory text, Samuelson (1976) defined economics as:

1. AN INTRODUCTION TO MEDIA ECONOMICS THEORY AND PRACTICE    5

The study of how people and society end up choosing, with or without the use of money, to employ scarce productive resources that could have alternative uses, to produce various commodities and distribute them for consumption, now or in the future, among various persons and groups in society. (p. 3)

Thus, economics is concerned with *what* is produced, the technology and organization of *how* it is produced, and *for whom* it is produced. For example, a firm produces outputs it expects will sell to its target client groups (*what*) and it will employ the most efficient technology and effective organization as possible (*how*). The proceeds of selling the output will be distributed to employees, suppliers, and (if there remains a profit) owners and shareholders (*for whom*).

Media economics is a term employed to refer to the business operations and financial activities of firms producing and selling output into the various media industries.[1] Firms in particular industries have obvious similarities, and when an industry reaches sufficient scale it typically spawns a field of study focusing on the unique operating and financial attributes of firms in that industry. There are fields of study examining the unique attributes of banking, real estate, airlines, dot-coms and high technology, and almost all major lines of business. It is within this context that media economics reflects an industry that has long since reached the scale where it has its own field of specialized industry analysis and knowledge regarding firms operating in the various media industries. The operations of these firms are undertaken in the context of given market conditions, technological alternatives, the regulatory and legal environment, and their anticipated financial implications. Media economics is concerned with how the media industries allocate resources to create information and entertainment content to meet the needs of audiences, advertisers, and other societal institutions (Picard, 1990).

The context of scarce resources, technological and organizational constraints, responses to preferences of consumers, and the distributional aspects of whose tastes and preferences will dominate is pervasive in all economic analysis. Media economics focuses on the consideration of the genre of goods and services comprising the media segment of the economy. The media industries are generally very visible segments of the economy. The major firms in these industries are known to almost all adults as a result of their pervasive products. Viacom/CBS, Disney, Gannett, and AOL Time Warner are examples of well-known media firms. Although the general nature of prominent firms is familiar, structurally the media industries are complex. Many media firms have interests in several major media industries. For example, the 1996 merger of Turner Broadcasting with Time Warner resulted in a company with major interests in film and television production, magazine and book publishing, pay-cable programming, and cable TV system ownership. Subsequently, the AOL Time Warner merger in 2000 added the overlay of online services. It is an interesting fact of very large-scale firms that they frequently generate structural conflicts such as when some of their units (in distribution) compete with firms that might also be customers (for the production units). It is attributes such as this that underlie the economic and organizational attribute of firms where by bigger is not always better. Nevertheless, in the media industries there has been a general trend toward larger firms integrating production assets and distribution. This is well illustrated by Rupert Murdock's News Corp, Disney, AOL Time Warner, and Viacom/CBS. However, the financial travails and dismal investment performance of Disney and AOL Time Warner in the new millennium illustrate that the trend toward larger organizations is not a guarantee of subsequent economic and financial success.

In addition to the classic media companies, some firms not usually categorized as involved in media industries nevertheless have major media interests (e.g., General Electric, the corporate owner of the NBC television network). These attributes are not unique to the media industries—they are longstanding features of industrial organization in most well-established industries. Questions related to "who owns the media" are substantially complicated by this ubiquitous characteristic of industrial organization.

This chapter of the book identifies and describes the basic principles of micro- and macroeconomics. Without considering the detailed particular focus of specific types of media firms, the overall relation of each function to media operations is outlined. Specific examination of how they apply to particular media industries is in subsequent chapters. Two appendices are provided online for those interested in accounting and financial management in the media industries. The URL for the book is: https://www.erlbaum.com/shop/tek9.asp?pg=products&specific=0-08058-4580-1. Directly above the description of the book will be a link that says View Appendices for the Book.

Thus it is the role of this chapter to develop first the economic and then the corporate contexts within which media economics is practiced. The economics section first considers *macroeconomics*—the overall functioning of the economy as a context for all industries and firms. The second part of the economics section considers the specific economic functions and behaviors of firms and individuals, an analysis known as *microeconomics*. The functional dimensions of all firms are identified and described in the third section, and the dynamics of how firms change is the subject of the final section.

The remaining chapters in Part I of this book explore in more detail important economic elements such as structure, value, resources, utility, and regulation. Part II considers the application of media economic principles to particular media industries.

## MACROECONOMICS

As indicated previously, macroeconomics refers to aggregates in the economy and how the economy works as a system. An important macroeconomic aggregate is gross domestic product (GDP). This refers to the total output of goods and services (in a particular year). The components of GDP are consumption (C), investment (I), and government expenditures (G).[2] Hence

$$GDP = C + I + G$$

### Consumption

Not surprisingly, the consideration of what influences the amount of consumption of a particular product or service is labeled *demand analysis*. Such factors are analyzed under microeconomics. In macroeconomics, the primary influences on aggregate consumption are the level of income, growth in income, the inclination (*propensity*) to save, and expectations regarding the future course of the economy.[3] The marginal propensity to save refers to how much of an extra dollar of income will be saved. Consumption expenditures are those outlays for which there is little realizable (saleable) remnant at the end of the year. In contrast to the macroeconomic use of the term *investment* considered in the following section, consumption is an intuitively straightforward concept. Some income goes toward meeting nondiscretionary expenses such as income taxes and social security taxes. The component of our income that is not subject to legal disposition by way of charges such as taxes is known as disposable income (DI).[4] An important aspect of total consumption expenditure is the division of disposable income into consumption and saving (S):

$$DI = C + S$$

The consumption expenditures of households (a term that includes any domestic unit, regardless of the nature or size of the "family")[5] on media products and services is part of consumption expenditures. In an overall manner, the proportion of consumption dollars going to media expenditures has increased. In 1920, the percentage of DI spent on broadcast media was 0. The relation between technology, product development, and patterns of consumption expenditures is important. When a new media product or service becomes technologically feasible, it competes with other potential uses of consumer purchasing power. The outcome of such a competition turns on whether the new products are substitutes or complements for existing products in the marketplace. TV has significantly reduced the market potential for radio (they are partially substitutes), whereas the availability of VCRs has increased the potential for film studios (they are complementary products in the marketplace). Cable news programs are obvious substitutes for the traditional broadcast evening news programs and the long-term decline in audience for the traditional broadcast news programs was to be anticipated.[6] Implications regarding the need for adaptability to changed technological and regulatory contexts are clear.

The contribution of the media industries to GDP is substantial. In 1982, the contribution of these industries to GDP was 2.6%. By 1986, it had grown to be 2.9% of GDP. The increasing role continued into the late 1980s. Although the economy as a whole grew at an average compound rate of 7.4% in the 1981–1986 interval, media industry spending grew at an average rate of 11.2%. It should be noted that these growth rates are high relative to historical growth rates which are typically in the range of 3% to 4%. After the recession of the early 1991s, the U.S. (and many other world economies) experienced a prolonged boom until 2000. Again, the growth rates were, by historical standards, unsustainable. Growth rates of the order of 5% to 7% per year were experienced for much of the decade of the 1990s. This halcyon interval was of course followed by a prolonged downturn starting in 2000. During the booming 1990s, new technology meant that in aggregate the media industries grew at rates even above the economy as a whole, increasing both their absolute size and relative importance in the economy. It is not inevitable that the share of the economy held by the media industries will continue to grow, as evidenced by the dramatic reversal of fortunes for those media firms in the so-called "dot-com" segment.[7]

One of the most important factors affecting consumption (C) is demography. From the period of 1946 to 1964, the United States underwent a major demographic shift commonly referred to as the "baby boom," the oldest members of which are now in their mid-50s . During this period, live births in this country reached 4 million per year. Following 1964, the birth rate leveled off to slightly more than 2 million births per year, with a significant rise during the 1980s and the peak of the baby "boomlet" at 4.2 million births in 1990.[8] Hence, although the youth market drove marketing and media decisions during the 1970s, the 1980s witnessed a dramatic decline in that cohort group. For example, the number of teenagers amounted to almost 21 million in 1980, and declined to about 16.5 million in 1995. This decline in the youth market meant changes in terms of program content (*Happy Days* replaced by *thirtysomething*) and media consumption (teens represent about 50% of theatrical box-office receipts). But demographic cycles are very predicable and must be managed. As the 1980s baby boomlet progresses, it will result in the largest ever high school class in 2009. Clearly demographics are both important and changing. There is also a regional element as the sun-belt gains in relative (and in some areas absolute) terms vis-à-vis the snowbelt.

There were 74.9 million baby boomers born from 1946 to 1964. The Generation Xers (1965–1981) numbered 58.5 million. The Millennials or Generation Ys number 78.2 million from 1982 through 2001. The cyclical patterns are marked and will affect society in a major way. Nevertheless, the baby boomers will affect directly and indirectly many of the media decisions for the next 4 decades (until around the year 2039, when the youngest "boomer" will be 75). If recent trends hold, entertainment expenditures will continue to remain at approximately their current levels into the 21st century. Individuals aged 35 to 44 historically spend approximately 50% above average on entertainment and twice the average for video accessories and audio equipment. If the presently 25- to 34-year-old cohort group (the "gen-Xers") spend in a similar manner, then entertainment expenditures might well decline in the coming decade. This would be due to the impact of a smaller group of then 35- to 44-year-olds spending less on entertainment.

Thus demographics in the United States have some interesting patterns that will provide significant challenges to media and other industries. Although the number of teens in the United States had declined somewhat, there is now an increase in the number of younger children and early teens, resulting in a median age in the United States of 26 years. Yet the longevity factor means that the fastest growing age group in the United States is the elderly. From 13% of the population in 1980, people over the age of 55 will constitute 20% of the U.S. population by the year 2005.[9] This means that between 1990 and 2020 the number of people over the age of 50 will increase by 74%, whereas the number of those under 50 will grow by 1%. This shift will be meaningful in terms of media content and marketing, as older people tend to read more and consume television more than other age groups.

In addition, an increasing number of women continued to enter the workforce. By the year 2000, more than 80% of women aged 25 to 54 were in the labor force, and most of the rest will be out of the workforce only temporarily. At the same time, decisions to have children are being put off to a later date, and the number of households with married couples is declining.[10] For television, this means a decreasing number of viewers for daytime television, both for adult shows (soap operas) and children's program (such as Sesame Street and cartoons).

The demographics also show that society has become more multicultural. Immigration is growing at a greater rate than the "natural increase" (growth defined as the number of births minus the number of deaths). Currently, 1 in 10 baby boomers were born outside the United States. By the year 2000, one employee in four was from a minority group. The Hispanic market has already become increasingly important to advertisers, as approximately 37 million Americans can be considered to belong to this ethnic group.[11] This growing market has significant implications for advertisers, as well as Hispanic directed broadcast and cable services and print media. Clearly there are geographic patterns, with Hispanic groups focused in Miami, New York, Los Angeles, Texas and Chicago.[12]

## Investment

In the context of macroeconomics, investment refers to the acquisition of capital goods—those with a life of several years. Thus, in contrast to the intuitively appealing definition of consumption, the economic definition of investment in the context of GDP is more complex. It refers to *new* investment in "real" (in contrast to financial) assets—*new* plant and equipment, the creation of *new* business units, additional inventory, and *new* construction. This provides a good example of the difference between the real and financial aspects of the economy. When a household buys a new bond issued by a (media) firm, it is a financial investment (typically possible because of savings) for the household, but it is not an investment that becomes part of GDP. Only real-asset expenditures are considered investment for the sake of GDP. Thus, if the media firm uses the money from the bond to develop a new product (e.g., a new movie) or build a new studio, that expenditure is investment in the macroeconomic context.

Thus, the majority of GDP investment is typically undertaken by firms. Households undertake GDP investment when they acquire *new* homes, cars, consumer "durables" (e.g., dishwashers). Household investment is important, but typically not dominant. Nevertheless, as experienced in the U.S. economy in the early years of the 21st century, when firms are pessimistic and are holding back on investment, the ongoing purchase of new homes and cars can be important in avoiding recession in the economy.

Investment plays a very important role in influencing fluctuations in the business cycle. Later coverage on valuation and investment decisions (see chap. 3, this volume) formalize the well-founded intuition that both households and firms are more likely to make investments if they have relatively optimistic expectations regarding the future. Real-asset investment expenditures such as new houses, autos, and big screen TVs by households and new studios, equipment, and products by firms have a multiplier effect in the economy (GDP). For each dollar spent on investment items, there is a multiple increase in GDP. This is a double-edged sword. It tends to add to the momentum on upward swings in the economy, but the failure to spend on investment exacerbates a recession.

As an illustration of the multiplier effect, consider the case of a production studio deciding to invest in a new film. If it spends, for example, $20 million on the movie production, then that is a direct increase of the same amount in the "I" component of GDP. However, the $20 million it invests is paid to actors, other employees, returns to investors, and other business firms supplying necessary inputs. In turn, the employees will consume some of their wages and salaries (i.e., increase the C component of GDP) and the other business firms will pay (most of) their receipts out to their employees or make other business expenditures. Clearly the $20 million invested in the new film increases the GDP by an amount greater than the expenditure itself. Investment has a multiplied effect. Economists have examined the multiplier in great detail and estimates of its numerical value are made. Numerical estimates of the multiplier often fall in the range of four to six. If it is, say, five, then the incremental investment (I) of $20 million in the film would increase the GDP by $100 million after all the incremental cycles had worked their way through the economy.

The multiplier effect makes the level of investment a critical factor in determining the level of economic activity (GDP). The motivation for states and cities to have films shot in their locales is apparent from this consideration of the multiplier effect. Economists have long been aware of the multiplier effect and government policy frequently seeks to influence the level of investment.[13]

## Government Expenditure (G), Monetary Policy, and Regulation

*Fiscal Policy (G).*    The two primary economic functions of government policy are *fiscal policy* and *monetary policy*. Fiscal policy deals with the raising of revenues by government and the level and type of government expenditures. The raising of revenues by government is generally conceived of as coming from taxes. However, in addition to income and business taxes, most Western European governments receive revenues from the Value Added Tax (VAT).

Clearly, the appropriate level of taxation and how it is spent is subject to political perspectives and debate on fiscal policy is inevitable. Regardless of personal perspectives on taxes and government expenditures, the important economic consequences of different policies should not be overlooked. For example, increasing taxes reduces disposable income (DI) and this typically reduces consumption (C). If the taxes do not result in increased government expenditure (G), then, all other things being equal, GDP will decline. The 1980s saw a lowering of the marginal tax rates in the United States and Great Britain. The "supply-side" perspective proposes that there is an optimal tax rate that maximizes tax revenues. This rate is conceived of as being relatively low and there is thus strong incentive to be productive. The perspective was widely emulated in the policies of other economies. There is understandably fierce debate regarding the merits of different levels of taxation and government expenditure. This debate reflects different perspectives on the "for whom" allocation issue discussed previously. Advocates of lower taxes favor increased disposable income (DI) and letting individuals make the choices. The rationale in support of higher taxes is associated with greater influence of the government on how society's resources are allocated.

Analysis of the levels and types of taxes and government expenditures requires a consideration of both economic policy and issues of political philosophy. The different perspectives of tax rates and level of government expenditure reflect varying interpretations of the role of government in society and these are manifested in party affiliation and other political activity. For example, considerable debate in the United States concerns the impact of running large domestic deficits. Some critics call for a constitutional amendment to require that the federal budget be balanced; other critics see the deficits as unfortunate, but not critical for the economy.[14]

For media managers, understanding the economic motivation for, and consequences of, government fiscal policy further improves management in that the impact of present conditions on future fiscal policy can be better anticipated. This is well illustrated by debate as to how to avoid recession and stimulate the economy given the economic challenges being faced in the new millennium following the bursting of the technology and stock market bubble and the impact of global terrorism.

The importance of fiscal policy is reflected in the substantial lobbying efforts that are brought to bear in attempts to influence tax codes and fiscal policy. For example, broadcasters have long lobbied Congress not to impose spectrum fees for ownership of broadcast licenses.

Fiscal policy, governmental revenue, and expenditure decision making, is part of the total economic environment affecting firms. Awareness of such policy is essential for both understanding what is occurring in the broad economic environment and determining normative strategies for viable and proactive media management. A widely admired quality in effective managers is the ability to prosper regardless of what party and set of policies is in political power. This ability is critically contingent on an understanding of particular politicians and parties and the associated economic policies with their implications for media firms.

*Monetary Policy.*    Monetary policy refers to the government's influence over the banking system, money supply, and the level of interest rates. Countries with dynamic media industries all have central banks that serve important functions. In the United States, the Federal Reserve Bank System (the "Fed") is the central bank. In the United Kingdom, it is the Bank of England. These banks are the instruments of government monetary policy via several mechanisms.

Although the modern system of banking with one central banking system functions quite similarly in the various mixed-capitalist economies, the details of the banking systems vary considerably. In the United States, there are approximately 9,500 commercial banks, whereas in the United King-

dom and Canada there are approximately 10 to 12 large banks w
branches throughout the respective countries.

Although there is debate on just how powerful the Fed is, most economists and financial practitioners consider its capabilities to be extensive. For
example, the Fed, under the chairmanship of Paul Volker (who came into the
position in October 1979), placed an emphasis on reducing inflation. The Fed
did this by maintaining "tight money" conditions, which manifest themselves in scarce credit, high interest rates, and lower levels of economic activity (GDP). This confluence of factors often come together late in an expansion
cycle. The Fed can slow down an "overheated" economy.

In contrast, when the economy is in a recession, the Fed typically increases the supply of money (through government bond transactions in the
financial markets and discount rate changes) and this reduces interest rates
(as it did in the 2001 and 2002 under the leadership of Fed chairman Alan
Greenspan). A reduced cost of borrowing typically increases investment (I)
and economic activity so long as business confidence has not dropped too
far. If business confidence is below a certain threshold, then even an increase in the money supply may not be effective—"The Fed cannot push on
a string." That is when the government typically steps in with direct spending stimulus.[15]

Because of the importance of matters affected by central bank policy,
following the course of monetary policy is necessary for the proficient
management of any firm. In international comparative analyses of economics of long-term growth and low inflation rates, the Fed gets very high
ratings. The strong growth of the U.S. economy in 1994–1999, and the con-
current low inflation and interest rates is a reflection of this. The Fed has
been criticized for making money too available in the late 1990s and having contributed to the bubble that developed. However, the primary responsibility and concern of the Fed is inflation and that has not been a
problem in recent times.

*Regulation.*    Beyond fiscal and monetary policy, there are other means
by which the government can affect business. The political philosophy governing such policy is a critical issue. Despite differing political philosophies, there has been a general trend to deregulation and reduction of direct
controls over the past 25 years. Changes in the specific policies of various
administrations have played out within this overall trend. The Carter administration started deregulation, and that process was generally followed
by subsequent administrations. Politically and ideologically, the shift signaled that Americans were tired of "big" government, and wanted government to be less intrusive in matters of the business. Generally the Reagan
and George H. Bush years resulted in fewer restrictions on the media industries. In broadcasting, practices such as audience ascertainment, program-

ming logs, commercial time restrictions, and even the Fairness Doctrine were eliminated. In addition, the number of broadcast stations an individual or company could own increased from 7 per class (AM, FM, or TV) to 12, and the 3-year mandatory period for owning a station was eliminated. With FCC chairman Mark Fowler leading the way, the marketplace rather than regulation became the operating principle for media operations.[16] With some variations reflecting political philosophy, this trend was generally continued in the Clinton and George W. Bush administrations. The decisions of FCC Chairman Powell's (George W. Bush) administration are having major implications for media and telecommunications firms.

Additionally, the concept of what constituted antitrust was shifted from a within-industry perspective to an interindustry perspective. Hence, the rationale for eliminating the Fairness Doctrine was that with so many media outlets, any bias of one outlet would be more than offset by the fairness and objectivity of others. This is a direct reflection of the impact of technology and competing delivery systems on industry structure and competitive concerns. In addition, the Cable Act of 1984 signaled that the federal government would relax restrictions on the cable industry, such as control over rates. Although cable franchises exist as local monopolies, the Act specified that cable systems would be exempt from municipal regulation if there was effective competition in the market. In 1985, the FCC defined effective competition as the existence of three over-the-air broadcast signals. However, this was not a particularly powerful counter to cable and as a result, costs increased for consumers and cable franchises became more profitable. Cable companies also began to create tiers of service, splitting basic cable service into two or more levels to subscribe to, with each level costing a bit more per month. As cable became more attractive as an investment, the number of services proliferated.[17] In the classic manner of monopolies being vulnerable over time, competition from a new technology has been a source of discipline for the cable industry. Satellite TV is growing much more rapidly than cable, and beginning to address issues wherein it has had a competitive disadvantage (e.g., local content).

In recent years there have been a spate of large mergers in the media industries. These reflect a notably relaxed regulatory environment. The acquisition of Capital Cities ABC by Disney in 1995 paved the way for other production- and distribution-motivated mergers and acquisitions and neither the Justice Department or FCC provided much challenge. Other transactions that followed included Viacom's acquisition of CBS in 1999, and the AOL-Time Warner combination in 2000. Other major conglomerates within the media industries include Sony Corp., Vivendi Universal SA, and Bertelsmann. These have had decidedly mixed outcomes, with the majority being unsuccessful. This topic is examined later in this chapter under *Restructuring*. The notion that "bigger is better" is not always correct and the degree of difficulty in running these behemoths is a major lesson for the industry.

The acquisition and conglomeration process in the media (and other) industries has in recent times been facilitated by another effective form of deregulation. In an attempt to promote economic growth, starting in the 1980s the government began to loosen the controls and regulations on the financial markets in pursuit of the policy goal of increasing the level of investment and triggering the multiplier effect. These changes and the associated greater flexibility were generally welcomed by the business community but there have been some unintended negative consequences. The increased availability of capital and financing has increased the potential to make dramatic mistakes. For example, the destruction of wealth (decrease in shareholder total wealth[18]) associated with the AOL Time Warner merger was approximately $200 billion in the 2 years following its formation. Of course the freedom to not make large deals remains and the AOL Time Warner transactions illustrates how even initiatives approved by stockholders can go very wrong if there is unsatisfactory execution of the vision motivating a merger.

Despite the government actions in response to the junk bond and S&L crises of the 1990s, and the stock market crash of 2000–2003, the financial markets remain relatively free of controls in the 21st century. Market forces remain the primary determinant of trends and transactions. The lack of aggressive antitrust actions in response to transactions such as the Capital Cities/ABC/Disney, Viacom/CBS and AOL/Time Warner media mergers illustrate that there has not been a substantial revision of government policy on such matters under the Clinton administration. The George W. Bush administration has not changed the trend to letting free market forces determine primary directions. Since the mid-1990s it has the joint forces of (a) the market and (b) the ongoing evolution of industrial organization (illustrated by the formation of the film and TV production company DreamWorks SKG), rather than government policy, that determined major developments in the media (and most other) industries.

## International Economics

There are two overall balances that are of particular significance for an economy. The first is the internal government budget—government revenues minus expenditures. The other balance is the difference between imports and exports—the *external accounts*. Consideration of the external accounts introduces complex issues of international economics, substantial coverage of which is outside the scope of this book. Government policy is critical for the practice of foreign trade and commerce. Although there are some notable instances of protectionism, tariffs, and quotas, in recent years, U.S. policies have been to maintain relatively open markets for foreign goods. The generally well-reasoned motivation for this set of policies is that it will make goods available on the domestic market at competitive prices and keep domestic producers efficient. In the theory of Ricardo, if all countries have free trade, then *comparative advantage* will see each country specializing in the production of goods and services for which it is best suited and most competitive. This creates the optimal outcome—Pareto optimality—the state where no economic unit can be made better off as a result of reallocation of production and distribution without another unit becoming worse off.

The film industry has provided some prominent examples of this principle in action in recent years. Some countries have promoted themselves as having cost advantage in the production of movies. Reflecting this competitive advantage, parts of *Lord of the Rings* were filmed in New Zealand.

When international trade is taken into consideration, the basic model of GDP needs to be modified. Interpreting consumption (C), investment (I) and government (G) to be purely domestic expenditures, then exports (X) and imports (M) must be accounted for. Thus:

$$GDP = C + I + G + (X - M)$$

The current account balance is what is referred to as all exports (including many media products) minus all imports $(X - M)$. Both exports and imports include physical trade, as well as "invisibles" such as interest and insurance premiums from transactions with nonresidents ("foreigners").

The strength of currencies affects foreign trade. A strong currency makes it expensive to foreigners and they purchase fewer exports from a country with a strong currency. Exporters based in the United States were challenged by a strong dollar in the 1990s. The converse effect is that a strong currency makes other currencies and imports less expensive. Changes in currencies are thus the theoretical source of "international competitiveness" adjustments for economies. In practice things get complicated by factors such as runs of currencies running high deficits and/or with high levels of inflation.

Media products are a major export from the United States. Media exports greatly exceed media imports, making a substantial net positive contribution to the balance of payments.[19] As is frequently the case, exports are good for both the individual exporting company, and the country's economy. Export sales play a major role in the success of many U.S. movies that are not major box-office successes in the domestic marketplace.

## MICROECONOMICS: CONSUMERS, FIRMS, AND MARKETS

Microeconomics deals with how individual economic units (households and firms) make decisions regarding their economic activity. As discussed at the beginning of this chapter, each society must address the economic questions of (a) *what* goods and services will be produced (scarcity choices); (b) *how* they will be produced (technology and industrial organization issues); and (c) *for whom* they will be produced (distribution). There is a close relation between macro- and microeconomics. The macroeconomic environment is the context within which microeconomic decisions are made, and government policy also influences microeconomic issues. For example, income distribution is substantially influenced by taxation policies and distributional policies such as welfare and unemployment programs.

Economic analysis typically assumes that individual economic units (households and firms) make their respective economic decisions in a "rational" manner. The "rational economic unit" is presumed to maximize its goal or "objective function" (utility or satisfaction for households, profits and value for firms) within the constraints of their resources, and the economic and legal environment.[20] This stresses the important responsibility of the government to create economic, legal and regulatory environments and incentive systems whereby the pursuit of individual economic goals is also conducive to the maximization of aggregate economic well-being (generally equivalent to maximizing GDP). For example, if a firm can maximize profits by using an inexpensive but polluting technology, then that firm's optimization will not be conducive to society's maximization if it is not forced to incur the costs associated with its polluting. When the correlation between individual maximization and aggregate, societal maximization is not present, the notion of "fallacy of composition" is employed to refer to economic activity that maximizes the goal attainment of individual economic units but does not maximize overall social welfare. When government policies have the effect of creating such a divergence, serious misallocation of scarce economic resources can, and often does, result.

One application of the "fallacy of composition" to the media industries is the issue of violent and sexually suggestive media content. Many successful (e.g., profitable) films and television programs are action-oriented and contain a significant amount of violent and suggestive portrayals. Critics, backed by a substantial amount of social science research evidence, contend that although media firms maximize profit potential with this form of media content, such content may lead to unfavorable societal consequences, such as antisocial behavior on the part of its audiences. Only when "activists" took direct action did Time Warner divest its interests in its "gangsta rap" music operations in 1995. Technology such as TiVo is partially motivated by being a response to the associated concerns.

Given *that* individual households and firms maximize within an existing economic context and related incentive structure, we now turn to a consideration of the decision-making processes of households or individuals and firms, and the economic mechanisms by which their economic activities are coordinated.

## Households and Individuals: "Consumers"

Economists assume that individuals maximize utility. Utility refers to satisfaction and enjoyment from the consumption (today or in the future) of a particular good or service. The economic analysis of utility examines why particular choices are made. For example, declining network viewership is readily explained in terms of microeconomic theory of consumer choice, and the increasing range of choices.

Consumer choice is a broader consideration than comparison of substitutes. Not only does it consider such questions as "Why do I purchase CDs instead of audiocassettes?" but also "Why do I not buy a large-screen TV even if I can afford one?" There are two key attributes to answering questions relating to choice and demand for particular items: resources and individual preferences.

Resources generally refer to purchasing power. Individuals generate purchasing power from their assets—marketable skill sets produce wages and salaries, financial assets yield interest and dividends, and other assets such as real estate and businesses yield profits (or losses). The returns from our various assets are determined in the labor and financial markets and in the fortunes of businesses directly owned.

As defined, *resources* include the stock of assets owned and the flow of income they generate. This means that an individual's purchasing power includes the possibility of spending all financial and business assets (and possibly borrowing against future earnings) in any one period, and having only wages and salary income in future periods. That possibility is present, and, given a presumption of the desirability of free choice, should be. The key point is that preferences are the province of individuals. This is not inconsistent with "rational-person" economic behaviors. In the full and rigorous development of the economics of choice, rational behavior requires only decisions consistent with economic scarcity, not a particular set of preferences. Rational economic behavior has individuals always preferring more income to less, and not paying higher prices than necessary for pure substitute packages of goods and services.

Economists have an equilibrium condition for the optimal outcome of individual purchase decisions whereby the last (i.e., marginal) dollar spent on each different type of good and service ("i," "j," "k," etc.) generates the same "marginal utility." Expressed formally, with each MUi indicating the marginal utility from the consumption of an additional unit of good "i," and Pi indicating the price of that unit:

$$\frac{MUi}{Pi} = \frac{MUj}{Pj} = \frac{MUk}{Pk} = \text{for all consumption choices (i, j, k, etc.)}$$

Given that the marginal utility from the last unit of a particular good or service declines as more units are purchased, typically additional units will be purchased only if the price declines.[21] Given the equilibrium condition expressed in the equation just given, for individual consumers there will be a "downward-sloping" demand curve for any particular good or service. Starting from a given optimal position, more will be purchased only if the price declines. This relationship is depicted in Fig. 1.1.

Although preferences vary from one individual consumer to another, the "law" of diminishing marginal utility applies to all consumers and the aggregate demand relationship for a particular good or service at a particular point in time will also be downward sloping. It will have the same general shape as the individual demand curve in Fig. 1.2 although the scale units on the X-axis will be different—perhaps thousands or millions rather than single-digit numbers.

As in all areas of marketing, the downward sloping demand curve relationship provides many insights into the operation of media industries. Although we have couched the discussion in terms of consumer demand, the cost analysis relating to firms' maximizing decisions means that the demand for inputs into the production and marketing process is also downward sloping. For example, in softening markets for advertising, the networks are able to place "floaters" (advertisements that can be, within limits, aired at a time of the network's choice) only by substantially reduc-

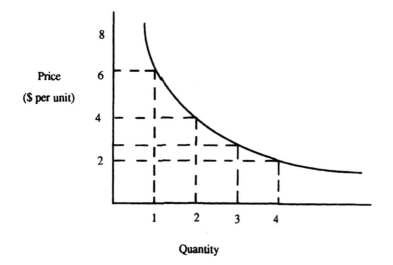

FIG. 1.1.   Individual consumer's downward sloping demand curve.

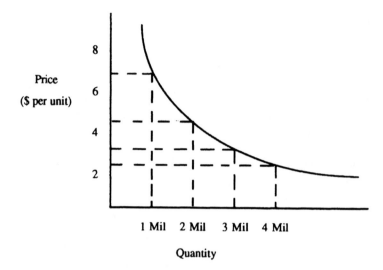

FIG. 1.2.    Aggregate market's downward sloping demand curve.


ing the rate. In the 1990s, some print advertisers began to face competition from Internet advertisers (see chap. 5, this volume).

### Firms' Decisions—"Producers"

Firms purchase inputs (land, labor, and capital) in resource markets, and transform these inputs into outputs (products and services), employing the technological and industrial organizational choices considered to be the most efficient of those available. Marketing and distribution costs are incurred in attaining the final sale of the output. Generally, the goal is the maximizing of economic profits.[22]

The "theory of the firm" is a large and complex body of knowledge that is important for a full examination of the coverage of supply of goods and services. Here we take an overview of decisions made by firms and leave the interested reader to seek further coverage in the referenced materials (cf. Picard, 1990).

Firms have varying degrees of influence in their input markets as far as affecting prices is concerned. For example, a small firm seeking to purchase less than 1% of the offering in a particular market will have little opportunity to influence the price by exercising its option (or threatening to do so) to not make a purchase at the going price. In contrast, a large firm will have considerable potential in this arena. In summary, some firms will be "price takers" in the inputs/factor-of-production markets, whereas others will be "price influencers."

Just how input prices relate to the cost of production will be significantly influenced by the production process and form of organization employed in the transformation of inputs into outputs. These issues are referred to by economists as the "production function." Technology clearly plays a key role in determining potential production techniques and their relative efficiency. A prominent media example is the role of electronic typesetting in the newspaper industry. Although many workers were understandably resistant to this technology, fearing loss of jobs, the potential of electronic typesetting to make the newspaper industry more efficient is clear.

Another dimension of the production function is the set of choices and features that determine the partition of costs into fixed and variable. The "dot-com" firm had high fixed costs and relatively low variable costs, a structure that proved fatal when "eyeballs" could not be translated into revenue producing transactions or subscriptions.

For a given price and volume, maximizing profits requires minimum production cost. As noted above, total costs of production include both fixed costs and variable costs. Examples of fixed costs include depreciation on the plant and the wages of staff employees (as contrasted to production-line employees). Variable costs include the materials directly used in producing output and the wages of production line employees. The fixed–variable cost relationships are depicted in Fig. 1.3.

Some costs are neither purely fixed nor purely variable in nature. In particular, several costs have a *step-function* nature—they take discrete steps up, but do not vary in direct proportion to units of output. For example, a plant may have the capacity to produce 250,000 newspapers per day. When circulation demand requires that a second plant be built, the introduction of the second plant would significantly increase fixed costs at the 250,000 level of production in a step-like manner.

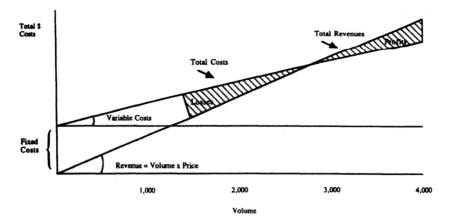

FIG. 1.3.     Cost and revenue relationships.

These cost structures will vary considerably from one type of media industry to another. Once a decision to make a film is taken, most costs become fixed. By contrast, for a publishing firm printing a book that does not have a large advance, a significant portion of its costs will be variable, determined largely by the number of books produced. The cost relationships depicted in Fig. 1.3 are the simplest; in practice, complexities such as nonlinearities are encountered. Recent refinements in cost measurement systems such as Activity Based Costing (ABC) have provided critical additional information to managers. Activity Based Costing provides an opportunity for better understanding and measurement of costs. It has particular relevance for industries engaged in repetitive production processes, a feature that is found in many media firms.

A key factor in determining the competitive structure of industries in terms of the number of competitors and relative efficiency is what happens to the average cost of production as volume increases. The average cost of a unit of production for a given level of production is:

$$\frac{\text{Fixed costs} + (\text{Variable Cost Per Unit} \times \text{Number of Units Produced})}{\text{Number of Units Produced}}$$

The simplest models of production assume that initially the average cost of production decreases as scale economies are realized. However, after some level of output, average costs of production begin to increase, typically because of some limited resource that makes other factors/inputs less productive. The scarce factor can be as clear-cut as the physically limited size of a key location site (e.g., a production studio) or as complex as the ability (or lack thereof) of a particular management team to efficiently manage an increasingly large enterprise. If there is managerial limitation in terms of span of control or coordinating incompatible managers, then doubling all inputs may result in an increase in production that is less than double and so-called "diseconomies of scale."[23] If a doubling of inputs results in more than a doubling of units of output, then generally economies of scale are still being realized. It is such synergy that motivates managers. However, approximately 75% of all mergers are later considered unsuccessful. The hubris of managers rather than the consistent delivery of synergies is considered to provide the key explanation for the ongoing series of mergers and acquisitions in the face of such poor average outcomes.

For these reasons, the "theory of the firm" assumes that firms' costs of producing units increase, as a result of having exhausted opportunities for economies of scale and encountering nonreplicable resources. Economists capture these inclinations in an upward sloping supply curve, as in Fig. 1.4. Because firms are operating at levels of output such that unit costs are increasing as volume increases, they can supply more to a market only at the higher prices necessary to meet their increasing unit cost of production.

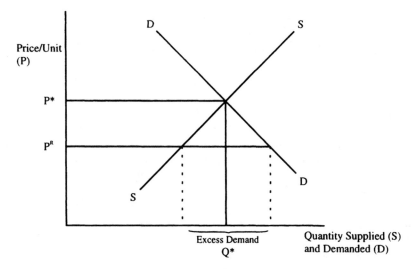

FIG. 1.4.   Supply and demand relationships and market outcomes.

The competitive structure of media industries reflects different levels of efficiency, economies of scale, technology, and industrial organization. For example, the broadcast television industry has relatively few firms, reflecting both the technology of production (channel/license availability) and the scale of operations necessary to achieve most efficient cost relationships. By contrast, the book and magazine publishing industries have literally thousands of firms, albeit dominated by a few major companies. The technology of print publishing is such that the fixed costs of physical production are typically not the major factor in the overall cost structure since much of the printing is outsourced to specialty print shops. Perhaps the critical factor in the profitable operation of smaller scale publishing houses is the availability of an efficient and effective distribution channel. Effective refers to getting the task accomplished, whereas efficiency refers to the cost competitiveness of doing so. As introductory business texts often note, "killing a housefly with a sledgehammer is effective, but not efficient."

## Markets

For a given good or service, the superimposition of demand and supply curves on the same diagram leads to an analysis as depicted in Fig. 1.4. The "theory of the consumer" sustains the downward sloping demand "curve," which can take the shape of either a curve or a line, and the "theory of the firm" the upward sloping demand curve. What will be the outcome in the marketplace?

At point P*, Q* in Fig. 1.4, the curves coincide. This indicates the "marketing clearing" price (P*), and corresponding quantity (Q*) transacted. If this intersection of supply and demand is resolved in this manner, the market is said to be in "equilibrium." Buyers will want to demand Q* units, and firms will want to supply Q* units. As economists say, "there will be a coincidence of wants, not a want of coincidence."

The depiction of "the Market" as in Fig. 1.4 is a powerful analytical framework. For example, if a regulatory authority sets a price PR less than the market clearing P*, then at that regulatory price quantity demanded will exceed the quantity firms choose to supply at that price, and there will "excess demand"—leading to nonprice allocation, such as "queuing" and "rationing coupons."

The impact of additional suppliers in a market will move the supply curve "out/down," generally with the impact of a decrease in price. The relevance of this to media markets is direct. For example, the much of the deregulatory process is motivated by leading to increased supply. The Telecommunications Act of 1996 is a widely cited example of this motivation.

Supply and demand curves are not easily measured for any given market. Firms often try to determine the "shape" of the demand curve they "face" (or supply) by such techniques as market surveys and experimenting with the impact of price changes. And of key relevance to the media industries is the fact that advertising is motivated by the potential to influence demand curves. Advertising attempts to "raise" the demand curves.

## Conditions of Supply and Demand—Elasticity

As before, the familiar upward-sloping supply curve reflects combinations of price and quantity supplied. As price increases, producers make a higher profit and wish to place more product on the market. When one or more of the factors previously held constant changes, this shifts the supply curve outward (increase in supply) or inward (decrease in supply), depending on which factor changed and its positive or negative relationship to supply. The shape of the supply curve is known as its elasticity and reflects the relative responsiveness of quantity supplied to changes in prices. Elasticity depends primarily on the closeness of substitutes in production and the amount of time available for producers to respond.

If a supplier faces a "steep" (inelastic) demand curve, then a price increase imposed by the supplier (being a jump in the supply curve) will lead to a large price increase, and a little decrease in market-clearing quantities.[24] Conversely, if a supplier facing elastic demand curves increases prices that supplier will lose a large part of the demand, and the price increase will be only partly "passed on." Again, numerous applications of these relationship can be observed in the media markets.

These considerations are also of direct relevance to government policy. If a tax is added to a good or service, the effect is equivalent to raising the supply curve. Who really "absorbs" the tax? In the formal terminology of tax theory, what is the "incidence" of the tax? It is determined by the relative elasticities of demand and supply. In the extreme case of a completely inelastic demand curve (i.e., a price has no impact on quantity demanded), all the burden (incidence) is borne by buyers. The price goes up by the full amount of the tax per unit.[25]

However, a discussion of elasticity highlights a feature of demand curves—they change over time. Although a demand curve may look very inelastic, the availability of substitutes will have an impact over time; so will the impact of technology. For example, the increase in automobile fuel efficiency significantly reduced the demand curve for gasoline, although the gas lines of 1974 and 1979 indicated clearly the short-run inelasticity of demand. Satellite TV has significantly increased the elasticity cable TV providers are facing.

### Market Imperfections

The ideal case depicted earlier is a reflection of the conditions economists call "perfect markets." This assumes knowledgeable consumers, many competing suppliers, and an upward-sloping supply curve. There are many instances where such ideal conditions are not met, and many of these are encountered in the media industries.

For example, if there is only one supplier, there is the potential for monopolist behaviors. Duopolies are two-competitor markets, as are sometimes the case in large-city newspapers. These are examples of market conditions that provide the potential for strategies and behaviors that are to the detriment of consumers. A "pure" monopolist can change very high prices, at least in the short run before substitutes get established. This explains the regulations on cable-TV rates, in order to prevent a single supplier from "acting like a monopolist."

Another market condition that can have related implications is where the per-unit cost continues to decrease as volume increases, which is different from the assumptions underlying the upward-sloping supply curve in the preceding analysis. An efficient large-scale producer will be able to drive out other competitors, or prevent them reaching profitability, and become a monopolist.

Thus the notion of an ideal competitive marketplace is closely tied to the wide dispersal of market power associated with the perfectly competitive market structure. When firms become large and command significant market control, the supply, demand, and price functions of the market are disrupted and consumer sovereignty is diminished. On a local market level, this is what has happened with the newspaper and cable industries, as most areas have only one local newspaper and one local cable system. Similarly, when the market fails to adequately provide public goods or take account of products with harmful byproducts (externalities), then the government may have to step in and play a role as well. Of course this conclusion is subject to vociferous debate. The recent debates over violent and suggestive content in television shows are an excellent example of such issues.

## THE FUNCTIONAL DIMENSIONS OF MEDIA FIRMS

Awareness of microeconomic principles provides a conceptual framework for understanding the operations of media firms. These principles directly apply to such dimensions as industrial organization, production and distribution, technology use, promotion, marketing and distribution, accounting and information systems, financial management, and transactions in the financial system. These are now considered in turn.

### Organization

Business firms of any substantial size are what sociologists term *complex organizations*. The sophistication of contemporary technology and the size of operation necessary to release the economies of scale often associated with its implementation mean that many business firms are indeed very complex organizations. Certainly many media firms fit this profile. It is difficult to envisage the functions of a television network being accomplished without a large and complex structure.

An organization can be defined as two or more people working together to achieve a common goal, and most media and other business organizations require the coordination of many individuals and activities. The coordination of activities requires a structured interrelationship between the various functions and subtasks that are required to achieve the overall organizational goals. The primary representation of this in the typical business firm is the organization chart. The organization chart formalizes the grouping of tasks, areas of responsibility, and reporting channels. A typical organization chart of a U.S. media corporation is shown in the following illustration.

### Organizational Structure

A typical organization chart reflects the legal and functional structure of the corporation in the so-called mixed capitalist economy. Members of the board of directors are appointed (at least technically and legally) by the stockholders. The chief executive officer (CEO) is responsible for the ongoing operations across all the functional areas within the policy guidelines provided by the Board of Directors.[26] Primary functional areas range from production (e.g., movie) to financial (e.g., raising monies for movie production). In addition to these primary functional areas, there is an increasing role of international operations.

Just how the responsibility for each functional area is allocated is determined by the type of organizational structure employed. The type reflected earlier is a combination of line and staff organizational format. *Line* refers to the actual production of the goods and services that the firm primarily exists to produce, whereas *staff* describes those functions that do not directly produce the primary good or service, but which are necessary for the overall functioning of the firm. The functional areas of accounting and personnel are typical of staff functions in media firms. The matrix form of organization has both vertical and horizontal (in the context of the organization chart shown earlier) areas of responsibility. Quite often the organization of international operations employs the matrix arrangement. The manager of a foreign branch will often have responsibility for all the functional areas in his territory, but will work closely with the home office functional vice presidents in each area for major decisions in the respective arena. For example, the marketing of television programs in multiple foreign markets is handled by one vice president of international programming, who coordinates her activities with other relevant vice presidents within the network.

## Production

In the terminology of economics, production refers to the creation of the good or service being provided by the firm. In the media industries, the pro-

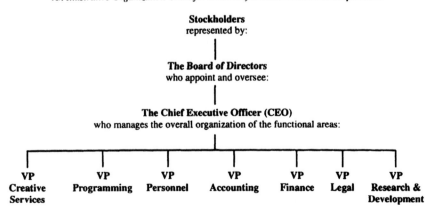

*An Illustrative Organization Chart for a Publicly Owned U.S. Media Corporation*

**Stockholders**
represented by:

**The Board of Directors**
who appoint and oversee:

**The Chief Executive Officer (CEO)**
who manages the overall organization of the functional areas:

| VP Creative Services | VP Programming | VP Personnel | VP Accounting | VP Finance | VP Legal | VP Research & Development |

duction varies from the physical products of print media (e.g., newspapers, magazines) to the transient products of broadcast media (e.g., broadcast news and entertainment programs). Much of this book is devoted to consideration of the specifics of the production undertakings of the various media industries. Thus the line function receives more general attention here.

The process of creating a product to distribute to market varies widely across the media industries. In the case of newspapers, for example, production is by necessity compressed into a few hours. Most processes—assembling newsworthy items from reporters and wire services, layout and typesetting, the physical availability of the product for distribution—must take place in a compressed time frame. In contrast, the time frame for a book may be months or years.

Within particular segments of the industry, there have been some notable changes in the production process in recent years. For example, few book and magazine publishers now physically undertake their own printing, as major commercial printers such as R.R. Donnelley & Sons Co. do the majority of book and magazine printing on an ongoing basis. Technological developments have facilitated efficient operations for firms that require geographically dispersed facilities locations. For example, the availability of satellite communications improves the efficiency of the production process for publications where there is a standard product that is printed (with minor variations reflecting regional editions) in several locations. Prominent examples include *The Wall Street Journal* and *USA Today*.

### Marketing & Distribution

The channels of distribution, market coverage, use of intermediaries, and techniques of physical distribution clearly vary markedly according to the specific media industry being considered, and the significance of distribution management varies. For the TV networks, the pattern of owned and affiliated stations provides a relatively stable pattern and distribution is not perceived to be an area of that business requiring continual attention. In contrast, for small-scale book publishers, channels of marketing and distribution generate repetitive problems and the search for a "better" solution is in some ways ongoing.

One of the most notable changes in distribution that occurred as a result of technology was the growth of the number of homes that have VCRs and remote controls. The number of homes with VCRs increased from 1% in 1980 to more than 65% in 1989. They are now close to ubiquitous. The impact of VCRs is twofold. First, VCRs led to a whole new "ancillary" market for theatrical films. Motion picture companies now derive revenues from video sales to either video rental outlets or direct sales (*sell through*) to consumers. Film companies now often obtain greater profits from home video sales than from box-office receipts. Home video viewing has also had an impact on pay-cable viewer-ship, broadcast TV viewer-ship, and theater movie-going. Second, VCRs have resulted in a whole new way for people to view television. Viewers can now *time shift*, that is, tape programs to watch at another time, rather than at the time a broadcast or cable network airs its programs. The most popular type of program that is recorded is the daytime soap opera, a direct result of the increasing number of working women in this country. Viewers can also "graze," or sample programs across the dial at any one time. More importantly for advertisers, viewers can zip through commercials by fastforwarding or zap them by not recording them.

The expansion of fiber optics in the cable industry during the 1980s resulted in consumers having the potential of receiving hundreds of channels. Even more importantly, the development of the addressable converter meant that cable companies could more easily implement pay-per-view (PPV) services. So far, PPV has been used for major event types of broadcasts (e.g., heavyweight championship fights, concerts, etc.) and as movie services. The expansion of fiber optics also means there is the potential for more narrowly targeted cable services. In the future, sports fans may be able to view electronic media channels dedicated to football, basketball, or baseball. The narrowness of the market will only be limited by the potential revenue (either through advertising or by subscription) of that market.

## Marketing & Promotion

*Marketing* is an inclusive term involving market identification and research, evaluation and standardization of products and services, and the promotion and selling of the product or service. Over time and frequently in a cyclical manner, most of the media industries both benefit and suffer from changes in the markets served and changes brought about by technological developments. For example, the beeper industry grew as a result of the technological developments facilitating its operation, and now faces challenging competition from the cellular telephone technology and industry. Clearly broadcast TV is exposed to new competitive challenges with the pervasive availability of cable television, direct broadcast satellite services, VCRs, and high-definition television technology.

The nature of the competitive arena varies widely within the media industries. Book publishing includes literally thousands of firms in the United States, and there are few barriers to entry. Although structural challenges such as distribution channels explain why the industry is dominated by a relatively small number of firms, nevertheless many small, specialized firms continue to prosper. In some ways, this approximates the economist's notion of a fully competitive market. In contrast, until the widespread availability of cable television, the networks operated under approximately oligopolistic market conditions, under which a small number of firms dominate and control the market. Now, however, the technological and distributional developments mean that many TV consumers see numerous substitutes to network TV available. Reflecting full awareness of these trends, there is now considerable investment by networks in those additional services (e.g., ABC and ESPN) although such investment is monitored by the FCC.

## Accounting and Information Systems

Some familiarity with the essentials of financial accounting is necessary for a full awareness of what is involved in media management. Accounting must process many types of data as a functional area of activity. Whereas the general presentation of accounting focuses on the types of accounting data found in financial statements, a broader interpretation of the role of accounting is to perceive the accounting function as part of the total information system within the firm.

Accounting as a profession has two primary branches—financial accounting, and cost and management accounting. The head accountant (often referred to as the *Controller*) is in many firms considered to have overall information technology (IT) responsibility.

The accounting functions and accounting statements (Balance Sheet, Income Statement/Profit & Loss Statement, and Statement of Cash Flows) are considered in Appendix A online at https://www.erlbaum.com/shop/tek9.asp?pg=products&specific=0-8058-4580-1. Directly above the description of the book will be a link that says View Appendices for the Book. After identifying the main concerns of cost and management accounting, this appendix focuses on financial accounting.

## Financial Management of Media Operations

Many of the numbers reported in the balance sheet and income statement are the result of operating and financial decisions made by the firm. For example, the level of debt is typically determined at least partly by management's interpretation of what is an optimal level of debt. The results of the firm's operating decisions also have an impact on the firm financial statements. Clearly, whether sales are profitable will have a major impact on the overall financial performance. Analysis and interpretation of accounting statements thus includes an examination of past results and an anticipation of likely future results.

## Financial Decisions

Modern financial management perceives the challenges of this functional responsibility to be selecting worthwhile investments in media assets and managing existing assets, acquiring the necessary funds to finance the assets, and providing returns to the sources of funds (interest to lenders, dividends and capital gains to stockholders).

These investments, financing, and distribution decisions are considered in turn in Appendix B. The essential elements are describes in what follows.

## Rate of Return

The rate of return (ROR) is a primary metric in finance. It is a generally simple concept, and can be introduced by way of a numerical example. If a security was purchased a year ago for $100, today it is worth $110, and the security paid a $5 dividend throughout the year, then an intuitively appealing (and correct) rate of return is 15% over the year. Formally:

$$ROR = \frac{PRICEend - PRICEbeginning}{PRICEbeginning} + \frac{INCOMEduring}{PRICEbeginning}$$

or

$$= \frac{110 - 100}{100} + \frac{5}{100} = \frac{15}{100} = 15\%$$

**ROR = Captial Gain component of ROR + Income component of ROR**

## Risk and Return

Rate of return is a central focus for both managers and investors, and there is a fundamental relationship between *risk* and Required Rate of Return (RROR). The actual Rate of return (ROR as mentioned earlier) is historical, reflecting the return in the past. The RROR is what investors need in order to be enticed to undertake or continue an investment. For example, many investors liked the high ROR from owning stocks in the 1990s, but, when then came to expect negative or low returns in the new millennium they chose to withdraw from stocks. Their expected ROR was not equal to (or in excess of) what they required to undertake the risk.

Without going through the intricate mathematical derivation of the relevant models from economics and finance, it is intuitively appealing that the higher the perceived risk, the greater the required return. In compensation for a greater potential downside, investors must be paid (in the form of higher expected return) for taking on more risk.

The formal model of risk/return most widely used in finance is the Capital Asset Pricing Model (CAPM).[27] Verbally, the required ROR on security "j" is the sum of a risk-free rate of return (the "price of time" earned on completely safe Treasury bills) plus a return for risk bearing. Risk compensation depends on the price of risk per unit of time and the amount of risk. Reflecting this, the return for risk is the product of two components:

- The *Market Premium*, or the price per unit of risk. It is the amount by which the average return on the overall stock market (i.e. the index fund) exceeds the risk free rate earned by Treasury bills. The market premium typically falls in the range of 6% to 9%.
- The risk measure *beta*, or the variation relative to a portfolio of well-diversified stocks (the market portfolio, which is what an index fund aims to be). The metric for beta is such that investments for which the ROR varies more than the market have a beta of more than 1. Those that vary less than the market have betas of less than 1.

Media firms exhibit a variety of beta coefficients. Large, diversified media firms typically have beta coefficients in the range of 1.05 to 1.25, whereas the stocks of small specialty media firms can exhibit beta coefficients in the range of 1.5 to 2.0. These beta coefficients are widely used in the practice of media management and investments.

## The Financial System

Financial decisions are made within the context of the overall financial system. The financial system includes: (a) financial markets (e.g., the New York Stock Exchange, American Stock exchange and NASDAQ); (b) financial instruments (e.g., stock and bonds); (c) financial institutions and intermediaries (e.g., banks); (d) financial practices and procedures; and (e) financial laws and regulations. The primary functions of the financial system are to transfer savings to productive investments, provide efficient means of making payments, retain confidence in the currency, and enable law-abiding economic units to acquire such necessary financial services as risk management (via the insurance industry) in cost-efficient ways. Confidence in the integrity of the financial system is critical for its effective functioning. We concentrate here on the financial markets.

## Financial Markets

The fundamental partition in stock markets is between primary markets and secondary markets Primary markets are where new securities are issued, whereas secondary markets are where existing ("used") securities are traded.

### Primary Markets

These are the various markets and processes by which new securities are issued by firms (stocks and bonds), government and government agencies (bonds), and households (e.g., mortgages). This category includes many segments and market processes. For firms, investment banking plays a critical role in the primary markets. The prices paid when new securities are issued reflect current interest rates and required rates of return.

Firms issue new stocks in one of two ways: (a) the first public offering of a firm's stock (Initial Public Offerings—IPOs), and (b) additional issue of an already publicly traded firm (seasoned issue offerings). This market involves the marketing and distribution functions of investment bankers. The volume of trading in the primary markets is but a small fraction of that in secondary markets. The media produced some of the more prominent IPOs during the boom years of the late 1990s with examples such as Netscape's (where the issue price of $28 rose to $75 within 3 hours of trading beginning in August 1997) and Pixar's. In the early years of the new millennium, IPOs became rare. In a time of lowered expectations of business performance, investors *expected* Rate of Return (ROR) seldom met their required ROR.

### Secondary Markets

In these markets, existing ("used") financial securities are traded. The transactions in these markets do not directly provide new capital to firms although prices in secondary markets are important because they affect the rates of return firms must pay when they do make new security issues in the primary markets. These markets include the well-known stock markets—the New York Stock Exchange (NYSE) and the American Stock Exchange (AMEX). In addition to these exchange markets, the secondary markets also include the NASDAQ and over-the-counter (OTC) markets. The OTC stock market uses the National Association of Securities Dealers Automatic Quotation (NASDAQ) system to make markets for securities. The securities traded OTC are typically those of smaller public companies, although some of the companies traded OTC on the National Market System (NMS) segment of that market are sufficiently large to trade on the NYSE and AMEX if they choose. Examples of such firms include Apple Computer and Microsoft. The OTC market is a major market for the trading of bonds.

### Other Markets

There are many other financial markets, including those for options, forward and futures contracts, foreign exchange, and such specialized securities as commercial paper. A media manager who comes to be involved in the financial management of a firm will require formal courses in both corporate financial management and the processes and practices of the financial markets.

## THE DYNAMICS OF MEDIA ECONOMICS

### Corporate Goals

In the corporate form of organization, the shareholders are legally considered the constituents with the ultimate authority for the conduct of the firm's affairs within the given legal context. The goal assumed for corporate management is "the maximization of shareholder/owner wealth," which is equivalent to pursuing the goal of maximizing the stock price of publically traded firms. This goal of maximizing shareholder wealth has prompted a significant number of U.S. firms to adopt measures to trim costs (downsize), increase revenues (expand) or both. These measures tend to fall into two categories, *incremental changes* and *corporate restructuring*.[28] We will employ this dichotomy in examining how media firms change in their pursuit of better financial results.

### Organizational Change in the Pursuit of Goals

#### Incremental Changes

Companies engaging in incremental changes are attempting to become more effective and efficient firms without massive modifications of their structure, function and culture. The more common type of incremental changes are identified here.

*Creating Cost Efficiencies.*    In general, firms always seek cost efficiencies. However, corporate owners/stockholders have become ever more demanding over the past two decades. Their demand for ongoing improvement in their return on investment have forced companies to operate as efficiently as possible. Achieving these efficiencies can take on a variety of forms. For example, one such way may be a shift in accounting practices from traditional cost accounting techniques to Activity-Based Costing (ABC), a method created by Robert S. Kaplan of Harvard Business School (along with others). Traditional accounting practices identify costs according to the category of expense (i.e., salaries, fringe benefits, fixed costs, etc.) and allocate them on the basis of volume. Activity-based costing spreads costs over the tasks that are performed (i.e., processing orders, buying component parts, assembling parts, etc.). This type of accounting provides a more accurate assessment of costs, and allows companies to analyze "cost drivers." For example, when Advanced Micro Devices (AMD), a semiconductor manufacturer, used traditional accounting procedures, it overestimated the cost of high-volume chips and underestimated the cost of low-volume chips. By switching to activity-based costing, the company discovered that the low-volume chips were 75% more costly than they had estimated. AMD was then able to alter its product mix. Another prominent example is typesetting in the newspaper industry. That process was a dominant factor in determining production costs rather than variations in the number of newspapers produced. Of course electronic typesetting changed that cost structure markedly and was controversial at the time of its introduction.

One of the problems facing entertainment companies is that success in the marketplace tends to fluctuate more widely than for other industries. In addition, many costs must be incurred before the product gets feedback as to its current appeal to the marketplace. For example, after a decade where situation comedies did well in the syndication marketplace, programmers discovered that public tastes shifted to more expensive hour-long adventure shows, such as *Highlander: The Series* and *Xena: Warrior Princess.* Such a shift is not only related to cost, but is a complete production changeover (situation comedies are generally videotaped using interior sets; whereas, dramatic shows are filmed using more exterior shots).

A frequently examined area for cost reduction is through personnel layoffs. "Raiders" and other potential acquirers (domestic or foreign) can make offers for firms considered to be inefficiently operated. This puts considerable pressure on management teams for dramatic short-term improvement in the bottom-line. This pressure was felt by both incumbent managers and those who acquired media firms (motivated either by improving cost efficiencies or generating "synergy"). The cuts in broadcast network employee ranks often associated with the restructuring of the 1980s have been widely documented. Further cuts may come from advances in the mechanization of media production, such as the replacement of camera operators at NBC News by robotic cameras. The 1990 *New York Daily News* management–labor struggle, and the 1995–1996 strike at the *Detroit Free Press* were very visible manifestations of the pressures that can build in the quest to hold down costs.

***Pursuing Additional Revenue Streams.***    The generation of incremental revenues from existing legacy assets is an obvious area for generating incremental profits. The experience of the cable industry with the emergence of the internet is an excellent example of this potential. The Cable Act of 1984 freed cable systems from most local rate control. Cable systems raised pay cable prices, thereby increasing their earning potential. Municipalities, however, retained rate control over basic cable services. Consequently, many cable systems began to break their basic service into tiers, redefining *basic* as carriage of local over-the-air broadcast signals and low-profit cable networks. More popular cable networks were then carried on a "premium basic" or "basic plus" tier, not covered by local rate control. During the late 1980s, cable companies had their sale value pegged at $2,500 per subscriber, up from $1,000 per subscriber in 1980. These rates continued to increase in some major transactions in the 1990s.

In 1992, Congress again passed legislation to control cable rates, especially basic cable rates. As a result, costs for tiers above basic cable rose dramatically. The Telecommunications Act of 1996 eliminated federal control over cable rates. However, because of slowing cable penetration rates, and potential competition from other technologies (e.g., direct broadcast satellite—DBS), key players in the cable industry (e.g., TCI) moved to raise revenue by providing Internet access and phone service. The success of the cable in generating incremental revenues from hard-wired Internet access (in contrast to dial-up) has been considerable and cable provides serious competition to the IDSL services offered by telephone companies.

Media firms have been aggressive in the pursuit of "Niche" Marketing to add to, or preserve, revenue streams. A classic example is provided by the earlier experience of the major networks. From the period of 1978 to 1997, broadcast network share of the audience dropped from 90% to just under 50%, thus raising the question of the role that networks will play in the future. From 1988 to 1992, CBS tried to carve an identity as a sports programming broadcast network. CBS Sports acquired rights to baseball, exclusivity to the NCAA college basketball tournament, and the 1992 Olympics, paying out some $2 billion. It billed 1990 as the "Dream Season" for sports. Although that CBS effort proved to be a costly failure, others (e.g., Fox) have been more successful as youth-oriented and culturally diverse networks. In magazine publishing, many of the 12,000 titles available on newsstands are niche titles. This includes many titles owned by large media enterprises. The rapidly expanding Internet publishing is leading to further niche-pursuit, limited-interest titles. However, the general lack of success in generating sufficient monetary revenues from these pursuits is well known.

### Corporate Restructuring—Overall Motivations

Some of the largest media firms are experiencing crises in the new millennium. Within a matter of weeks in late 2002 and early 2003 top executives of AOL Time Warner, Vivendi Universal SA, Bertelsmann, and Sony were removed. Many of these crises are associated with problems related to corporate structure. These are very large firms, often put together by way of mergers and acquisitions (M&A). Given that approximately 75% of mergers and acquisitions are considered to be unsuccessful, why did media firms go so forcefully into down this hazardous path? These are the issues addressed in this section.

Corporate organizations have been changing rapidly in recent years. Many attributes of the corporate form of organization involve tradeoffs on issues such as span of control, economies of scale, and the bureaucratic structures often associated with large and complex organizations. In the

1980s, there emerged an increasing awareness of the potentially inefficient structure of some large corporate organizations. The associated first wave of downsizing restructuring saw many firms reduce in size or substantially change the set of operations encompassed under the one corporate organization. Yet concurrently, other firms increased in size and added to their range of activities and operations. In many instances, the respective changes can be reasoned to be efficient in the given circumstances. The circumstances include the nature of the particular firms, current market conditions for both inputs and outputs, the technology involved in operations and distribution, and the contracting arrangements necessary for its operations. Media conglomerates were supposedly going to be very efficient in the production and distribution of media content. For example, AOL subscribers were supposedly going to use the AOL Internet unit's services to serve as delivery path for an increased volume of Time Warner content. The strategy clearly did not work.

The primary motivation behind much of the M&A activity is to achieve more efficient organizational forms. However, there are a variety of potential motivations for mergers, not all of which generate more efficient organizations. For example, managers may seek to maximize the size of their empire and acquire other firms even if is not an efficient process. They may engage in mergers that are unlikely to be efficient, even if their stated goal is profitability improvement and enhanced shareholder value. Such dysfunctional behavior is examined under agency theory whereby it is well known that the *agents* (top managers) may act in their own best interests rather than that of the *principal* (the stockholders). This agency problem is partially solved ("aligning incentives") by giving top managers stock options whereby they loose along with stockholders if decisions reduce rather than increase the stock price. This type of arrangement made Michael Eisner one of the top-paid executives during the heyday of Disney Corp. However, stockholders are now complaining that with the stock price less than one half its previous level, whereas managers' options may be out of the money (i.e., the *exercise price* is higher than the stock price) the managers have not suffered actual monetary losses (as have stockholders). In addition, they curiously often remain in office. In the case of Disney, top management has remained in place even after a 5-year slump. The ongoing incumbency is often considered a governance deficiency whereby there are not sufficient consequences for poor performance after a run of success.

An exception to the ongoing incumbency is the example of Steve Case with AOL Time Warner. He cashed out more than $100 million of profits on company stock when it was at high levels around the time of the merger and on those holdings avoided the disastrous subsequent losses in value. Investor fury at this situation contributed to his ouster as Chairman in early 2003. Time Warner is the quintessential example of a firm where managerial hubris rather then harshly objective rational analysis best explains major mergers and acquisitions. The business fiasco associated with the AOL acquisition of Time Warner is recent and well known. Essentially, Time Warner top management (with the curious approval of the board of directors who supposedly look after the interests of stockholders) accepted inflated AOL "Internet-bubble" stock for the more durable "old-media" assets of Time Warner. The subsequent losses to stockholders are in the order of $200 billion.

Yet, interestingly this was not the first curious M&A related controversy in the company's recent history. Although now overshadowed by the AOL transaction, Time Inc. was also in a controversial M&A situation about a decade before. In the summer of 1989, Paramount offered stockholders in Time, Inc. $175 (and then $200) per share, but the offer was rejected by Time, Inc. management and its board of directors. It was never put to a stockholder vote, a controversial attribute of some corporate takeover battles ("control contests," see Grundfest, 1990). Time and Warner merged to create Time Warner Inc. By October 1990, Time Warner shares sold for less than $70. For Time Inc. shareholders this was approximately one third of what one party (Paramount) was willing to pay for the shares in the summer of 1989.

A key attribute associated with restructuring is valuation. As noted in chapter 3 of this volume, valuation combines scientific tools of analysis (e.g., present value mathematics) with estimates of future sales levels and cash flows. Clearly the estimation of future flows is an inexact process, and different sets of expectations and varying degrees of hubris/delusion will result in different individuals and firms having individual valuations for a given property or business. Typically, if a business is being transacted, it goes to the highest bidder. This is why businesses sell even their best divisions (sometimes called *cash cows* or *crown jewels*). If a business receives an offer for a good property and the bid reflects a valuation above what the firms considers to be the value of the division or unit, accepting the offer is rational.

It is different valuations (based on different sets of expectations of future sales, profits and cash flows) that generated much of the restructuring activity of the past decade. In this valuation process, the potential for a division to be worth different amounts to different corporate owners should be recognized. For example, a firm with international operations may be able to generate more incremental cash flows from the rights to publish the lines of a domestic publisher overseas than could the domestic publisher needing to establish a new international division. Although this notion of synergy is particularly pleasing conceptually, empirical research often fails to identify material evidence that it is realized, particularly in domestic mergers. In fact, much of the downsizing restructuring activity in recent years has been the undoing of earlier mergers that did not work out. Studies indicate that approximately 75% of all mergers are (at least partially) reversed by divestitures in the following decade. The actual (in contrast to anticipated) synergies can be negative if dysfunctional bureaucracies become necessary to control very large corporate organizations. The infighting between the various divisions of AOL Time Warner are infamous and widely reported. As in production, there can be both economies and, past a certain scale, diseconomies of organization.

## Restructuring Strategies

Major restructuring involves the following categories of changes (see Hite & Owers, 1983):

- business combinations (mergers and acquisitions),
- business separations (downsizing divestitures such as sell-offs and spin-offs), and
- substantial realignment of the financing and ownership of a given business (e.g., leveraged buyouts [LBOs] and recapitalizations).

Although the sell-off is the most frequently used form of restructuring, this section also describes the other forms that restructuring may take, in order to give the reader a broader perspective and familiarity with the terminology.

### Business Combinations—Mergers, Acquisitions, (M&A) and Joint Ventures

There have been five "waves" of business combination activity in the U.S. economy. The first occurred in the early years of the 20th century, the era of the large trusts (and triggered the early antitrust regulations); the second occurred in the 1920s; and the third in the late-1960s. However, all of these previous merger waves were overshadowed in magnitude by the conglomerate formation merger and acquisition wave of the 1980s, which itself was been exceeded by the 1990's merger wave. There has been a dramatic reduction in M&A activity in the new millennium. Mergers and acquisitions can be implemented by friendly mergers or contested changes in control (*takeover battles*) such as hostile tender offers wherein the firm being bought (the *target*) does not want to be acquired. There is a role for proxy contests in this process.

The term *business combination* typically conjures up notions of whole-firm combinations, such as mergers and acquisitions. A discussion of mergers and acquisitions is found in chapter 3, this volume. However, an important category of business combination occurs when two or more firms selectively combine parts of their operations and form joint ventures. Joint venture formation in the U.S. economy (and internationally) is extensive, and is playing a growing role in the media industries. Strategic alignments via joint ventures are increasingly a means of achieving improved results without formally merging firms. Formal mergers involve many complexities and raise sensitive issues such as who will manage the combined firm and how differing corporate cultures will be integrated. Joint ventures avoid many of these issues and are more readily undone if they are not successful. Moreover, by selectively combining only those parts of two firms where the potential for synergy is greatest, the likelihood of efficiency gains may be greatest. Research findings are generally supportive such as those of each of these hypotheses.

Joint ventures are widely used in certain media industries. For example, the production of a major movie involves the coordinated activities of several businesses (as the lengthy credits attest to). This also illustrates another advantage of the joint venture form of organization. It can have an intentionally limited life. After collaborating for a specific purpose, the venturing entities terminate the joint venture in an orderly and anticipated manner. This is in marked contrast top the often messy undoing of whole-firm mergers and acquisitions.

### Business Separations—Downsizing Restructuring

*Sell-Offs (Divestitures).*   The sell-off is the most widely used strategy for separating out operations. Conceptually it is not complex—an exchange of a subunit (product line, division, title, subsidiary, etc.) for an agreed amount. The consideration (means of payment) can be cash or securities in the acquiring firm, or some combination thereof. The sell-off by itself does not reduce the assets of the firm; it only changes their composition. An operating asset is exchanged for cash or securities. If there is an associated special dividend as part of the proceeds are dispersed to stockholders, the firm can be reduced in size. The motivations for sell-offs vary from a need for cash so that the corporation may survive to having received offers so attractive that even prime assets such as cash cows are sold. It is widely anticipated that AOL Time Warner will sell-off its sports team as part of a downsizing restructuring in an attempt to improve the operating and financial performance of the company. Noncore assets where the company does not claim core competencies are prime candidates for sell-off.[29]

*Spin-Offs.*   Spin-offs are substantially more complex business separations than sell-offs. They involve separating out some operations from a firm, establishing them as a newly separate corporation, and distributing shares of ownership in that separated company as special dividends to stockholders of the parent corporation. The impact of spin-offs on the value of the divesting firm is substantial: The average percentage increase in stock price associated with spin-offs is approximately 7%.

Spin-offs have been used quite extensively by media firms. In some instances the use is entirely voluntary. For example, Columbia Pictures (under Sony ownership) spun-off Columbia Pictures Television from the rest of its entertainment operations. In others, the separating out of operations by spin-off follows antitrust action by the Justice Department or the Federal Trade Commission. The 1971 spin-off of Viacom by CBS is a prominent media example of the latter. It is widely anticipate that the AOL operations of AOL Time Warner will be spun off from the "old media" Time Warner operations and assets.

*Liquidations.*    As a voluntary restructuring strategy, the term *liquidation* does not necessarily imply financial distress. Firms might choose to liquidate for tax reasons, because of contests for control of the corporation such as tender offers, or because of some decline in the reputation of the organization that makes efficient transactions in the financial markets difficult. Simply closing down an unsuccessful unit is the extreme form of liquidation wherein the price received is zero (or even negative if there are significant shutdown costs). Voluntary liquidations can be partial or complete. In a partial liquidation, the process frequently involves the sell-off of a part of the firm, and paying a special dividend from proceeds. A *total liquidation* means that assets are sold piecemeal and liabilities are settled, the balance being distributed to stockholders, who are the residual claimants. Total liquidations are associated with major increases in the value of the liquidating firm's shares. On average, liquidating firms gain approximately 30% in value over the year ending with their liquidation announcement (see Hite et al., 1987). The reasons for voluntary liquidations wherein a firm "is worth more dead than alive" are varied. In the media sector, the increased value of radio and TV stations led to some voluntary liquidations. Reeves Telecom is an example of the voluntary liquidation by a media firm.

*Leverage Increasing Restructurings and Realignments.*    These restructuring strategies come in several forms. In essence, they involve the partial substitution of debt for equity in the financing and a realignment of operations. Often there are associated sell-offs and spin-offs of parts of the original operations. Such restructurings can occur without a change in management, and are often used as a preemptive measure by a firm facing a contest for its control (e.g., the threat of an unsolicited takeover offer). Alternatively, leverage-increasing restructurings can occur after a raider has taken control and attempts to increase the value of the firm. By many evaluations, CBS underwent a leverage-increasing restructuring in the mid-1980s when the Tisch Organization acquired a 25% interest in the firm.

Popularly, such transactions are often Leveraged Buyouts (LBOs) or Management Buyouts (MBOs). Essentially, these involve investors (or managers) acquiring control of a firm using large amounts of debt secured by the assets acquired. Often LBOs involve the whole firm and MBOs a division, but that alignment is not absolute. The distinction between a LBO and a MBO is not always clear because in most cases the services and financing of a buyout firm (such as Kolberg, Kravitz and Roberts [KKR], Thomas Lee, or Hicks Muse) will be employed.

This category of restructuring is often associated with the issue of large amounts of additional debt (sometimes including high-yield junk bonds). As a result, a debate has emerged regarding whether the later issued junk bond debt securities have a negative effect on the value of investment-grade bonds previously issued by the firm. Investment grade bonds are generally those with ratings in the "A" and "B" ranges. The major rating agencies are Moodys and Standard and Poors. When firms issue large quantities of junk bonds, the total risk of firm default is increased. Thus, although the junk bonds have a lower priority of claim than the earlier-issued debt, these outstanding investment grade bonds also become more risky. Increasingly, the evidence suggests that preexisting investment grade bonds do decrease in value in many transactions where there is a significant increase in the junk bonds issued by a firm.

### The Impact of Restructuring and Other Recent Developments on Media Economic Practices

The 1990s were characterized by a high level of restructuring. This was particularly the case in the media industries. But in the media, the focus was often on the creation of larger firms by combination in contrast to the downsizing restructuring that typified many other sectors. In the media sector there was a "merger mania," which was somewhat puzzling given the unimpressive track record of most very large, diversified firms. News of the most merger and combination competed with movie, TV, and Broadway reviews on newspaper entertainment pages.

It was reasoned that the media sector had unique features (particularly a changing regulatory environment) that ran counter to other industries and that "bigger and diversified is better." Potential for the delivery of synergies of production and distribution was considered to be higher for diversified media firms than that structure in other industries. And it is important to note that investors generally agree at the time of these combinations with that reasoning of managers. But of course the postscript is supportive of the hypothesis that, as in other industries, anticipation of synergies was not delivered in the form of enhanced operating efficiency and profits.

Usually, restructuring activity takes place when the previous organizational forms are perceived to be sub-optimal. For example, if a conglomerate has become too unwieldy as a result of bureaucratic considerations, then a breakup of the firm into smaller units may be efficient. In contrast, if separate firms are not able to complete with fully integrated firms, then mergers and combinations are suggested. As noted earlier, this latter perception prevailed within the media industries in the 1990s where combinations predominated in contrast to the downsizing restructuring that characterized many sectors.

The implications for the media sector are clear. With the profile of failure hanging over the behemoths created by the mergers of the 1990s, the likely scenario in the first decade of the new millennium will be downsizing restructuring. This will represent the undoing of dysfunctional organizations created during the era when a deal making focus on the part of top level managers predominated over the importance of day-to-day operations. Much of the deal making is already seen to have been a distraction from day-to-day operations and managers with a reputation for the appreciation of operational efficiency will likely get to manage the process of correcting the substandard media firms that were created.

## CONCLUSION

Many media firms are presently in a state of rapid change and some areas can be reasonably characterized as in turmoil. In such as state of flux, being able to understand the overall nature of media economics is uniquely important. This chapter has established the economic and corporate frameworks for media economics. The economic framework consists of the guidelines and constraints imposed by societal choices (political economy), the specific decision-making processes of consumers and firms (microeconomics), and the overall, aggregate attributes of the economy (macroeconomics). The corporate framework consists of the underpinnings of industrial organization, the various functional areas of the firm's operations, the demands of investors for acceptable returns and the impacts of globalization.

It is important for both understanding and managing firms in the media industries that the daily challenges are seen to take place within an established economic framework within which technological and regulatory change pose exacerbated challenges relative to many industries. Attempts to meet these challenges have over the past decade included many organizational changes via mergers and combinations. However, it is ever more clear that deal making is no substitute for the detailed knowledge and daily attention required for the successful operation of media properties. It is within this context that subsequent chapters focus on these details of particular sectors of the media industries. Overall success requires a combined appreciation of the overall framework from this chapter with the detailed operational knowledge and strategies developed in the following chapters.

## REFERENCES

Garneau, G. (1995, June). Another way to go online. *Editor & Publisher*, 24.

Grundfest, J. (1990). Subordination of American capital. *Journal of Financial Economics, 27*, 89–116.

Hite, G., Owers, J., & Rogers, R. (1987). The market for interfirm asset sales: Partial sell-offs and total liquidations. *Journal of Financial Economics, 18*, 229–252.

Picard, R. (1990). *Media economics*. Beverly Hills, CA: Sage.

Samuelson, P. (1976). *Economics* (10th ed). New York: McGraw-Hill.

## ENDNOTES

[1]Media industries can be classified a number of ways based on product (print, broadcast, film, recorded music, etc.), regulation, technology, and sequence in the production and distribution chain. Although systems of classification involve overlap, the most widely used categorization uses the Standardized Industrial Classification (SIC) Code. Many media industries fall into the 4800 and 2700 sections of the SIC Codes.

[2]The business operations and financial affairs of media firms refer to the complete set of activities encompassed in the production and distribution of media products and services. In all nations, business activities are undertaken within the overall structures and constraints set by society. The result is that media industries vary considerably from one country to another. The context for media firms is set by the political, social, and legal environment of the society within which the business is conducted.

The overall nature of the country's political organization is clearly a fundamental factor in the determination of the media industries and business practices of media firms. The political extremes are *communist-totalitarian* and *laissez-faire*, respectively. This volume concentrates on the media industries in the United States. The primary focus is on the political economy continuum often referred to by economists as the *mixed capitalist society*. This refers to an industrialized nation in which the property rights are primarily, although not exclusively, in the hands of private citizens, but where there are also regulatory and other constraints on permissible business conduct. Overall economic control is held by both public and private institutions. Yet most of the means of production are operated by private sector corporations, as distinct from government corporations owned by the government.

Examples of mixed capitalist economics include the United States, Canada, and the major Western European countries. Casual familiarity with these economies make it apparent that they have important structural differences. For example, in Western Europe the primary utilities (electric, gas, water, etc.) are typically provided by government corporations where there are direct controls over monopolistic-type, "exploitative" practices. In contrast, in the United States, these services are typically provided by private sector companies whose conduct is prescribed by regulations (e.g., public utility commissions or PUCOs) designed to protect consumers from unfair practices. The ownership of broadcast media also differs considerably between Western Europe and the United States.

Despite the differences encompassed by the expression mixed capitalist economy, its generality means that although the focus of this book is on media industries and firms in the United States, much of the material has applicability to other industrialized societies. This is particularly the case given recent trends. The recent deregulation, global integration, and privatization trends that are now influencing many Western (and other) economics will likely make the respective media industries more similar to the United States than previously.

Given the mixed-capitalist economic context, our consideration of the economic context for media firms can be partitioned into microeconomic and macroenconomic issues. This is perhaps the most important distinction in economics. Microeconomics focuses on the decision-making processes of individuals and firms, and the supply, demand, and price of particular goods and services. Macroeconomics refers to aggregates in the economy and how the economy works as a system. It is difficult to have substantial insights in economics unless there is familiarity with the different perspectives of macroeconomics and microeconomics.

[3]This is what surveys of consumer sentiment measure in an attempt to evaluate consumer's inclination to spend.

[4]Then importance of Disposable Income (DI) frequently influences government policy. For example, the proposal in 2003 to remove taxes on dividend income would have the effect of increasing DI, presumable leading to more spending and an improving economy.

[5]There are approximately 100 million "household units" in the U.S.

[6]At a technology trade show in 2000, many attendees asked "who is that?" with Bill Gates of Microsoft. The "mystery man" to many at the show was the long-term anchor of one of the major broadcast news programs!

[7]Definition of just what the "media industries" includes has become increasingly challenging and thus measures of growth and share relative to the total economy are somewhat imprecise.

[8]This was close to the previous record of 4.3 million set in 1961.

[9] Medical and life-style changes have had a dramatic impact on longevity. Life expectancy for those born in the U.S. in 1900 was approximately 45 years.

[10]By 2010 married couples may no longer constitute the majority of U.S. households.

[11]Early in the new millennium, Hispanics became the largest minority, having just surpassed Blacks in their traditional largest minority group standing. As of July 2001, of a total U.S. population of 285 million, 13% (37 million) were Hispanic and 12.7% (36 million) were Black.

[12]Experienced media managers know that although markets can have large concentrations of Hispanic population, they are often quite distinct and require different practices and strategies such as in advertising. The Cuban-dominated Miami market requires a different approach from the Mexican-profile in Los Angeles, and both are distinct from the Haitian and South American dominant profile in the New York City Metropolitan Statistical Area (MSA).

[13]For example, the initiative in 2003 to end the taxing of dividends is partly motivated by the goal of increasing investment.

[14]Given that the 1996 U.S. GDP was approximately $6 trillion and the federal governmental deficit was $120 billion, some interpret the small relative size to diminish the importance of the deficit.

[15]The policies employed by the U.S. Government in 2002 and 2003 are classic examples of these policies in practice.

[16]Curiously, there were increasing calls for restrictions on some content (leading to an expansion of the prohibition of indecent content), and some restrictions on media business practices (e.g., the Financial Interest and Syndication Rule) that were left intact. These apparent anomalies were clearly not philosophically in line with the Administration.

[17]However, as rates for basic cable and pay channels continued to increase, the public became more dissatisfied, and called for more regulation on the local, state, and federal level. Although no new cable legislation was approved in 1990, the FCC expanded local regulatory control to more systems.

[18]This is what is referred to as the *market capitalization* ("Market cap") of a firm. It is simply calculated as the price per share multiplied by the number of shares outstanding.

[19]The Balance of Payments has been a deficit of approximately $350 billion for the U.S. in recent years. Although large and something of a concern, it is only approximately 3.5% of the $10 trillion GDP.

[20]In recognition of challenges to the rationality paradigm (e.g., stock market and other bubbles) there has evolved a study of "behavioral" finance that aims to accommodate and explain such "irrationality."

[21]The price decline may be absolute (as in the case of some print magazine subscriptions and TVs) or relative (as in the rate for satellite versus cable TV).

[22]*Economic profits* are different from *accounting profits*. Economic profit is calculated after the cost of the stockholders' equity is subtracted and is what is used in the "value creation" metrics of recent times.

[23]In a more complex scenario, many observers consider that AOL Time Warner has experienced problems of this nature.

[24]Good examples of this principle at work are popular first-run movies and highly sought CDs.

[25]An interesting example is the large increase in taxes on cigarettes in New York City is 2002. Most of the incidence of the tax fell on the buyer. Of course, this has in turn led to more unofficial trade of cigarettes coming into NYC.

[26]This is the topic area of *Corporate Governance*. Given the notable failure of good governance in corporations such as Enron and WorldCom, principles of "good governance" are being established.

[27]This model specifies the risk/return relationship for a (any) particular asset "j" as follows:

Expected ROR = A risk free rate + a premium for risk.

$Ex(ROR_j) = R_f + [(R_m)-R_f)] \times Beta_j$

$R_j = R_f + [(R_m) - R_f)] \times B_j$

Where:

$R_f$ = the risk-free ROR, proxied by the T-Bill rate,

$R_m$ = the return on the overall stock market, proxied by the average return of the Standard and Poors 500 stocks, for example.

$Beta_j$ = The Covariance of returns of security "j" and the return on the market, standardized by the dividing the variance of the market return $(R_m)$

$$Beta_j = \frac{COV \ (R_m R_m)}{VAR \ (R_m)}$$

[28]Does maximizing stock price imply insensitivity to other parties with a legitimate interest in the affairs of the firm? In recent years, the notion that there are numerous parties interested in and affected by the conduct of any firm's business has been formalized in the concept of "stakeholders." There are several categories of stakeholders, shareholders being just one such party. Although appropriate and useful for a consideration of the role of firms overall, for the purposes of managerial decision making there is a need for an unambiguous goal. Maximizing the value of the firm to its stockholders reflects the legal structure of the limited liability corporation and provides management with an unambiguous goal.

Clearly this goal is contentious, but the logical implications of trying to simulta-neously maximize the worth of the firm to all its stakeholders generates inconsis-tencies and no viable framework for decision making. In addition, stockholders are typically the predominate stakeholders. When firms are not performing well, it is often cost cutting and other measures that are taken to protect the interests of stockholders, perhaps at cost to other parties (e.g., layoffs.)

[29]It has been shown that sell-offs result in increases in value to both divesting and ac-quiring firms. The findings of Hite et al. (1987) showed that in completed trans-actions, sellers gained 4.05% in equity value and acquirers approximately 1.39% in the week of the initial announcement. These seemingly small percentage mag-nitude should not be considered inconsequential—they can related securities (shares) with a value measured in billions of dollars. Indeed, they are significant both statistically and economically. The finding that acquires of divested units increased in value is also particularly noteworthy, given that the evidence on ac-quirers of whole firms in mergers and acquisitions suggests that typically acquir-ers do not substantially gain, and even experience small losses. Thus in whole-firm acquisitions, only the owners of target firms (i.e., those acquired) gain on a consistent basis when the immediate effect of the transaction of stock values is examined. The long-term impacts are more difficult to separate and measure. However, there is no strong evidence that acquirer firms (buyers) con-sistently gain from that activity.

The gains to both parties in sell-off divestitures and the formation of joint ven-tures, when contrasted with the evidence of whole-firm combinations, suggests that a key to mutually satisfactory business restructuring is the selectivity af-forded by divestitures and joint ventures.

# Chapter 2

# Economics and Media Regulation

ROBERT CORN-REVERE
*Hogan and Hartson*

ROD CARVETH
*Rochester Institute of Technology*

## INTRODUCTION

On February 1, 1996, after months of negotiations and political wrangling, Congress overwhelmingly passed the Telecommunications Act of 1996 (the Act). The Act was the first comprehensive rewrite of the Communications Act of 1934, and dramatically changed the ground rules for competition and regulation in virtually all sectors of the communications industry, from local and long-distance telephone services, to cable television, broadcasting, and equipment manufacturing.

For decades, communications policy—including ownership and service restrictions that maintained protected monopolies at both the state and federal levels—has been set largely by the Federal Communications Commission (FCC), state public utility commissions (PUCs), and the federal courts' enforcement of the 1984 antitrust consent decree that dismantled the Bell System. The ambiguity inherent in enforcing a 62-year statute, however, led to legal uncertainty and conflicting interpretations. With the 1996 Act, Congress adopted *competition* as the basic charter for all telecommunications markets.

The Act eliminated most cross-market entry barriers, relaxed concentration and merger rules, and placed new implementation obligations on the FCC and state regulators.[1] The Act overruled all state restrictions on competition on local and long-distance telephone service. The Bell Operating Companies ("Baby Bells") were freed to provide long-distance service outside their regions, and inside their regions once completing a series of steps to remove entry barriers for local telephone competition. New *universal ser-*

49

*vice* rules continued subsidization of telephone service for rural and low-income subscribers and assisted schools, libraries, and other public institutions in becoming connected to sophisticated telecommunications services, such as the Internet. The 1984 antitrust consent decrees were repealed, but their requirements for "equal access" ("1" + dialing) to all long-distance companies were maintained.

The Act relaxed the FCC's media concentration rules by allowing any single company or network to own TV stations that reach as many as 35% of the nation's television households (the previous limit was 25%). The FCC would be required to consider changing other limits on ownership in a single community. Networks would for the first time be allowed to own cable television systems, but no network could acquire another network. All nationwide limits on radio-station ownership were repealed, but local limits on concentration were maintained, albeit in a much relaxed form.

Television broadcasters were allowed *spectrum flexibility* to use additional frequencies for high-definition or other purposes, but would have to return any additional spectrum allocated by the FCC and possibly pay auction fees. In April 1997, the FCC announced rules governing the transition of broadcasters from analog to digital broadcasting, phasing in the transition in a manner such that major market stations would have to switch to digital channels earlier that small market stations.

The Act substantially relaxed rules governing cable television systems under the 1992 Cable Act, including rate deregulation. Ironically, the 1995 report on the competitiveness of the cable-TV industry concluded that although some progress had begun toward a competitive marketplace for the distribution of video programming, cable-television systems continue to enjoy market power in local markets. At the time of the Act, subscribership for cable operators was over 91% of total multichannel video programming distribution (MVPD) subscribership, dwarfing subscribership to direct broadcast satellite (DBS) multichannel multipoint distribution (MMDS) and satellite master antenna television (SMATV) systems (*Second Annual Report*, 1995).

## FCC Reaction to the Act

Reaction by the FCC to the Act was swift. The day President Bill Clinton signed the Act (February 8, 1996), the FCC granted several waivers to the Walt Disney Company to help facilitate its merger with Cap Cities/ABC. Within a month, the Commission implemented new rules on TV and radio station ownership, and by April had proposed to extend the license terms for television and radio to 8 years (the maximum allowable under the Act).

The Act is yet another example of how the legal and economic characteristics of media industries are inextricably related. With the advent of electronic communications technologies, governmental control moved to a system of regulation. The regulatory structure was designed to be flexible and adaptive to the changing shape of the industry. As economic power shifts among various media players, or as developing technologies alter the playing field, the governing agencies—most prominently, the FCC—react to maintain their views of the public interest. As a result, virtually all significant economic developments among the regulated media industries provoke some kind of regulatory response. As a corollary to this premise, regulations have profound implications for the economic well-being of media corporations.

## THE RISE OF FEDERAL REGULATION

Unlike newer communications technologies, broadcasting was born into an unregulated environment. Wireless communications had existed for almost a quarter of a century, but the first commercial broadcast did not occur until 1920. Consequently, existing law (The Wireless Ship Act of 1910 and the Radio Act of 1912) related principally to maritime uses of radio. With the November 2, 1920 transmission of election returns by station KDKA in Pittsburgh, commercial broadcasting began, and along with it, the justification for a whole new field of regulation.

Once initiated, commercial broadcasting grew quickly. By the beginning of 1922, the Department of Commerce had authorized 30 radio stations. That year, however, an additional 600 stations took to the air. In 1922, 1 in every 500 U.S. households was equipped with a radio receiver, but in 4 short years the number rose to 1 in every 6 households. The rapid proliferation of both transmitters and receivers led to a chaotic situation that promoted numerous calls for federal legislation. The growth of broadcasting (as well as the demand for regulation) accelerated in 1926, prompted in part by the decision in *United States v. Zenith Corporation* that the Secretary of Commerce lacked the authority to assign wavelengths or deny broadcast licenses.[2]

Congress responded by passing the Radio Act of 1927—the first attempt at establishing a comprehensive regulatory framework for radio, including broadcasting. The Act created the Federal Radio Commission (FRC) staffed with five commissioners charged with the general authority over radio broadcasting, regulating the medium in ways that would promote the public interest, convenience or necessity.

The public interest standard for broadcast regulation—a concept borrowed from the regulation of railroads—was not defined in the Radio Act. Rather, the FRC was mandated to perform various tasks, including classifying radio stations, describing the type of service to be provided, assigning frequencies, making rules to prevent interference, establishing the power and location of transmitters, and establishing coverage areas in a way that maximized the public good. Of course, this begged the essential question of what constitutes "the public good." The FRC took the position that the Supreme Court eventually would define the public interest on a case-by-case basis. Nevertheless, the Commission outlined the primary attributes of the public interest in its policy statements and licensing decisions.

The Radio Act was superseded by passage of the Communications Act of 1934. In addition to consolidating the government's regulation of radio, the new law created the FCC to succeed the FRC. The Communications Act simply recodified many of the essential features of the Radio Act, including the public interest standard. Other than a few general directives, as noted later, the Communications Act continued to leave the term *public interest* undefined.

Congress purposefully left the regulatory standard open, with the detailed filled in by the FCC over time. This had much to do with the fact that radio was a new and complicated technology. The FCC's broad powers were based on the assumption that "Congress could neither foresee nor easily comprehend ... the highly complex and rapidly expanding nature of communications technology" (*National Association of Regulatory Utility Commissioners v. FCC*, 1976). This approach has not lacked critics. As one court noted, "the [Communications] Act provides virtually no specifics as to the nature of those public obligations inherent in the pubic interest standard (*Office of Communication of the United Church of Christ v. FCC*, 1983). Some have taken the pragmatic view that the public interest means nothing than what a majority of commissioners say it means at any given point in time.

Nevertheless, shortly after the Communications Act was adopted, the Supreme Court ruled that the open-ended public interest approach was sufficiently precise to withstand constitutional scrutiny. In *FCC v. Pottsville Broadcasting Co.* (1940), the Court called the public interest standard "as concrete as the complicated factors for judgment in such a field of delegated authority permit," and labeled the approach "a supple instrument for the exercise of discretion."

Despite the lack of a categorical definition of the public interest, various provision of the 1934 Act operationally defined what Congress intended. For example, the 1934 Act directed the FCC to provide, to the extent possible, rapid and efficient communication service; adequate facilities at reasonable charges; provision for national defense and safety of lives and property; and a fair, efficient and equitable distribution of radio service to each of the states and communities. In 1983, Congress added to this list of objectives by adopting a new section establishing "the policy of the United States to encourage the provision of new technologies and services to the public." This new provision created a presumption favoring increased competition in the communications marketplaces.

The reliance on competition in the communications marketplace as a determinant of the pubic interest brought to the surface a notion that had always been implicit in the public interest standard: *Media economics help define the public good.* Although this is not quite the same as saying "what is good for NBC is good for the nation," one broadcaster summed up the industry by saying "there's been a lot of [talk] about money. You guys like to talk about the public interest. To us, it's the same thing." Or, as FCC Commissioner Sherrie Marshall explained to an audience at the 1990 National Association of Broadcasters Convention, there is often a "harmonic convergence" between the public interest and a given applicant's private interest.

Indeed, economic issues permeate virtually every category of FCC decision making. Under the 1934 Act, the Commission was responsible for allocating radio spectrum to various services, assigning licenses to competing parties, and otherwise managing the usage of the assigned frequencies. It is essential that the agency take into account economic factors when choosing which service should receive an allocation of increasingly scarce and valuable spectrum. Similarly, the marketplace phenomena can be important when deciding which applicant should receive a grant of a federal radio license. Moreover, regulatory choices, once made, are not necessarily permanent. Economic conditions often determine the shape of the pubic interest.

## ECONOMICS AND CHANGING REGULATIONS

The changing fortune of AM and FM radio provide a clear example of how market adjustments result in regulatory changes. Edwin Armstrong invented FM radio in the 1930s as a way of overcoming interference problems associated with AM service. FM (*frequency modulation*) is a means of encoding information on a carrier wave by varying the frequency. AM (*amplitude modulation*) encodes information by varying the strength of the carrier signal. AM is more susceptible to interference because outside sources of energy—atmospheric static, electric motors, or other devices—interact with the carrier wave to produce static. FM is not affected by such phenomena because the amplitude of the carrier remains constant and outside energy fluctuations do not affect the frequency. The net result of this technical difference is that FM made possible a system superior to the one that developed during the first decade of American broadcasting. AM broadcasting currently occupies 535-1705 kHz on the broadcast frequency spectrum and FM occupies 88-108 MHz.

After Armstrong secured patents for his FM system in 1933, he was invited to test his invention at RCA's Empire State Building facilities. Once he proved the superiority of his system, Armstrong believed that his friend David Sarnoff, head of RCA, would use the new technology to revolutionize the radio industry. Although initial test were more successful than even

Armstrong expected, RCA was slow at promoting the new system. In fact, Sarnoff opposed allocation of spectrum for FM broadcasting at FCC hearings in 1936. Instead, Sarnoff urged that the spectrum be reserved to test television.

The reasons underlying RCA's position were not difficult to understand. Promoting FM service would undermine the company's investment in AM facilities. Moreover, FM was in competition with television for spectrum allocation and RCA owned television patents. One historian has noted that "in almost every overt and covert action, it can be seen that RCA (and the majority of the AM industry) was trying to forestall something that would either cut down, or cut out, their operation" (Erickson, 1973).

The FCC finally allocated spectrum for commercial FM service in 1941. Four years later, however, the Commission moved FM service to another part of the frequency band. Justified as a means of avoiding interference caused by sunspots, the move was supported primarily by AM interests and adopted over the objections of the FCC's engineering staff. In a single order, all existing FM receivers were rendered obsolete. This action, along with several intervening regulatory measures, helped keep FM a second-class radio service for decades.

By 1964, FM radio was not in good financial shape. Many of the existing 1,300 FM stations were largely dependent on the revenues of more successful co-owned AM stations for their survival. As a result, the FCC initiated a rulemaking proceeding designed to promote FM as an independent service. This led to a rule prohibiting FM stations from duplicating more than 50% of the programming of co-owned AM stations in the same local area (*Report and Order*, 1964). The regulation was designed to serve two goals. First, it sought to strengthen FM service by forcing the creation of an independent programming service. Second, the Commission believed that a separate programming service would encourage consumers to buy and use FM receivers.

Ten years later, the FCC revisited the AM–FM duplication rules because the number of independent FM stations had increased, as had their revenues and the number of FM receivers. The economic advances of FM service led the Commission to strengthen the nonduplication prohibition. It limited the FM station of an AM/FM combination to not more than 25% duplication of either station in communities of 25,000 population or larger (*Report and Order*, 1976).

Further upheavals in the radio marketplaces led to even more profound changes. In 1986, the FCC found that "FM service is now a fully competitive and viable component of the radio industry" and that FM had captured more than 70% of the radio audience (Amendment, 1986, p. 1613). The number of FM stations had tripled between 1964 and 1986, far eclipsing the growth of AM service. Indeed, the FCC determined that "many heretofore profitable AM stations are now experiencing economic difficulties as a result of the shift of listeners to FM stations" (p. 1614). After examining the "structure and market conditions that have occurred in the radio industry in recent years" the Commission concluded that "the program duplication rule no longer appears necessary or desirable" (p. 1612). Consequently, it eliminated nonduplication rules because they were no longer necessary to foster independent FM service. The FCC also sought to help the now-ailing AM stations.

In 1991, the FCC suggested that it might reimpose the nonduplication rule as part of a package to save AM radio from economic demise. As part of a comprehensive set of changes, the Commission proposed weeding out marginal AM stations, in part by perhaps depriving stations of their ability to cut programming costs by simulcasting the FM signal of co-owned stations (Review of the Technical Assessment Criteria for the AM Broadcast Service, 1991). The FCC subsequently eliminated the duopoly rule in 1994, to allow for an owner to have more than one AM station per market, and raised national ownership caps. With this proposal, the FCC came full circle with regulations originally adopted in 1964—suggesting changes born entirely of the economic state of the industry.[3]

## THE CARROLL DOCTRINE AND RELATED POLICIES

Many times economic considerations force the FCC to choose between applicants for the same broadcast service. The classic statement of this approach was presented in *Carroll Broadcasting Co. v. FCC*, decided by the United States Court of Appeals for the District of Columbia in 1958. In that case, Carroll Broadcasting Company had opposed the grant of a radio station license in a community 12 miles from Carrollton, GA, the location of the Carroll station. The station licensee alleged that authorization of another station in such close proximity would impair its ability to serve the public adequately. Although the Supreme Court had established in *Federal Communications Commission v. Sanders Brothers Radio Station* (1940) that economic injury to an existing station was not grounds for denying a new application, Carroll argued its loss would be so significant as to deprive the public of service.

The Court of Appeals agreed, noting:

[W]hether a station makes $5,000, or $10,000, or $50,000 is a matter in which the public has no interest so long as service is not adversely affected; service may well be improved by competition. But, if the situation in a given area is such that available revenue will not support good service in more than one station, the public interest may well be in the licensing of one rather than two stations. To license two stations where there is revenue for only one may result in no good service at all. So economic injury to an existing station, while not in and of itself a matter or moment, becomes important on the facts when its spells diminution or destruction of service. At that point, the element of injury ceases to be a matter of purely private concern. (*Carroll Broadcasting v. FCC*, 1958)

This decision forced the FCC to adopt a procedure for assessing the economic harm from its new licensing decisions. Thus, under what became known as the Carroll doctrine, when an existing licensee offered proof of detrimental economic effect from a proposed new broadcasting station, the Commission was required to consider the issue, and, if sufficient evidence was presented, conduct a nearing and make findings on the issue. The petitioner in such cases had to provide sufficient statistical evidence "to enable the Commission to make an informed judgment as to the overall market revenue potential" (*WLVA, Inc. v. FCC*, 1972). The element of such a showing typically included information concerning the number of businesses in the area, the total volume of retail sales, other advertising media, and other data regarding the economics of broadcasting in the specific market.

As a direct result of the Carroll decision, the FCC was required to reconsider its decision regarding West Georgia Broadcasting Company—the potential competitor to Carroll Broadcasting. After examining the record and weighing the "speculative injury to the public interest," however, the FCC concluded that Carroll had not met its burden of proof on the economic injury issue and granted West Georgia's application.

Despite this inauspicious beginning, existing licensees routinely pleaded a *Carroll* issue when confronted with a new station applicant in its market. Although such tactics offered little chance of actually preventing competition, the required Commission review (and possible hearing) served to at least delay and drive up the cost of competition. Indeed, although the FCC applied the *Carroll* doctrine for a 30-year period, it never once denied a new license on the basis that a new station would result in a net loss of service.

In 1960, the Commission initiated a policy—the UHF television impact policy—protected UHF stations from economic loss associated with the licensing of new VHF television stations. This policy was enacted because VHF signals had a technical advantage over UHF signals (VHF signals were stronger and carried further). In contrast to the *Carroll* doctrine, the UHF impact policy protected UHF stations as a class, and not just individual stations, and, at least for a time, was applied rigorously by the FCC.

Market conditions prompted the FCC to reevaluate both policies in 1988 (Policies, 1988). The Commission found that changes in the media marketplace undermined whatever validity had ever existed for the economic theories that supported the *Carroll* doctrine and the UHF impact policy. The numbers of radio and TV stations had more than doubled, and newer communication technologies such as cable television had proliferated. Most importantly, studies indicated that the advertising market was continuing to expand, and that new stations tended to draw their advertisers from new sources rather than take business from existing ones. Given these findings, the Commission concluded that the *Carroll* doctrine should be eliminated. It thus held "that the underlying premise of the *Carroll* doctrine, the theory of ruinous competition, i.e., that increased competition in broadcasting can be destructive to the public interest, is not valid in the broadcast field" (*Policies*, 1988, p. 640). At the same time, because studies revealed that many UHF stations were now operating at a profit, the Commission also eliminated the UHF impact policy.[4]

## THE CONTINUING REGULATORY BATTLE
## BETWEEN BROADCASTING AND CABLE TELEVISION

The Commission's protection of existing services from prospective competitors has not been limited to those proposing to use the same transmission technology. Regulation also has been extended to new technologies in order to maintain a certain balance of power between competing media. This has been the history of broadcasting–cable-television relations. The Commission initially adopted rules to protect broadcasters from the new medium of cable. Later, it freed cable television from those restrictions in an effort to promote the new technology. Generally, the requirements changed over time as the relative fortunes of the various industries fluctuated.

Although the product of both broadcasting and cable is delivered through the same appliance—the television set—the different transmission media are subject to radically different regulatory regimes. Broadcasters transmit signals over the air subject to a federal license that imposes a number of public trustee conditions on the licensee. Cable, on the other hand, involves the transmission of electrical signals over coaxial cable or fiber-optic lines. Except for some auxiliary microwave authorizations, cable systems are not licenses by the federal government, but are regulated by local franchise agreements.

This difference is the key to the contentious regulatory relationship between the two industries. Government rules that are applied to one medium generally are not applied to the other. Yet, broadcasting and cable compete in the same marketplace for viewers. As a result, competition between broadcasting and cable has not been limited to the market, but has spilled over into the regulatory arena. Representatives of the regulated industries continuously implore the government to maintain a "level playing field." This is a shorthand way of calling on regulators to eliminate rules that, in one industry's view, unfairly favors its competition. More often, such rhetoric is employed in an attempt to manipulate the regulatory environment in ways that will have a positive effect on that industry's economic environment. As one lobbyist put it (half jokingly), "All I seek is a fair advantage." Over time, as the cable industry has grown, the regulatory "advantage" has shifted as if on a pendulum.

## Development of Cable Television

In some respects, cable television is not a new technology. It originated in the late 1940s—about the same time as the advent of commercial television. The first systems were installed in 1948 as a means of delivering quality television signals to viewers in locations where terrain prevented adequate over-the-air reception. Typically, such systems involved placing antenna on a mountaintop to receive television signals and transmitting them via cable to the homes below. At the time the system was aptly called *community antenna television*, or CATV. The first cable system was installed not as a stand-alone business; rather, it was built by an appliance store owner who wished to demonstrate good reception so that he could sell more television sets. Despite this prosaic origin, there were 70 cable systems providing service to 14,000 subscribers by 1950.

This earliest incarnation of cable caused broadcasters little concern. Quite to the contrary, broadcasters welcomed measures that would improve reception because it meant additional viewers (and more advertising revenue). This harmonious relationship ended, however, as cable systems expanded channel capacity and began to offer additional programming choices. In 1961, the cable operator serving San Diego began to import television signals from Los Angeles, which is more than 100 miles away. Although San Diego was already served by three VHF network affiliates, the cable system also provided four independent signals that otherwise would have been unavailable in the market. This competitive threat prompted broadcasters to seek FCC regulation of cable systems.

## Economic Analysis and Cable Regulation

Although the Commission previously eschewed direct regulation of cable systems, in 1962 it began to deny permission for carriage of broadcast signals that might adversely affect local television stations (*Carter Mountain Transmission Corp.*, 1962). The FCC subsequently adopted formal rules that banned the importation of distant signals into a top-100 market unless the cable operator could demonstrate that the transmission would not hurt UHF broadcasters in the affected market (*First Report and Order*, 1965). These rules were predicated on two assumptions. First, the Commission believed that importation of distant signals could fragment the audience for local stations, thus eroding their revenue bases, perhaps to the point of affecting their programming or driving them from the air. Second, the

Commission considered the retransmission of broadcast programming—
for which the cable systems paid nothing—to be an unfair advantage over
local broadcast stations. These conclusions were based on economic studies
submitted to the FCC by the *regulated* industries.

As time passed and technology developed, however, the validity of the
economic analyses became questionable. Moreover, the Commission's assumptions regarding industry evolution began to shift. For example, when
it first adopted distant signal and other protectionist rules, such as
"must-carry" obligations, the FCC viewed cable television as merely an ad-
junct of broadcasting. The rules were designed to ensure that cable did not
undermine the economic strength of television. But by 1975, the Commission began to seek ways "to assure the orderly development of this new
technology into the national communications structure" (*Report and Order*,
1975, p. 863).

This subtle, but significant, shift in emphasis hailed a change in how the
Commission assessed economic data presented to it. Moreover, the Commission became increasingly dissatisfied with its previous "intuitive
model" for predicting competitive effects of the development of cable television on broadcasting. Accordingly, in 1977 the Commission initiated a
Notice of Inquiry to reexamine the assumptions that an unregulated cable
industry would ravage existing broadcasters. This "broad inquiry into the
economics of the relationship between television broadcasters and cable
television" was premised on the concept that "[a] more complete understanding of the economics of the cable-broadcast interface [could] yield
many benefits." The Commission predicted that "[i]t may be show that certain of our rules are unnecessary; it is also possible that others should be
adopted, or that familiar rules should be applied to different situations"
(*Notice*, 1977, p. 14).

Notwithstanding its newly discovered interest in "the collection of economic data and analysis," the Commission did not await that outcome of its
economic inquiry before modifying its distant signal rules. Rather, it placed
the burden on broadcasters to prove that importation of a distant signal
would have an adverse economic effect and adopted a general policy that
presumed there would be little or no harmful impact (*Arlington Telecommunications Corp.*, 1977).

Two year later, the Commission released its Economic Inquiry Report,
which concluded that distant signal carriage rules should be eliminated.
The 350+ page report analyzed the supply and demand for cable television
and attempted to assess the impact of distant signals on local broadcast audiences. The FCC's analysis unabashedly embraced economic analysis as
the determinant of the public interest. Its principal criteria for defining the
*public interest* in its cable regulatory policies included the economic concepts of consumer welfare, distributional equity, and external or spillover

effects. Basing its findings on economic studies, the Commission stated its conclusions with a clarity and confidence "which is uncommon in matters of public policy" (*Inquiry*, 1979, p. 659).

On the strength of its conclusion that "few, if any, TV stations are likely to experience a reduction in real income" due to the growth of cable television, the Commission began to dismantle its web of regulations that previously protected broadcasters. In 1980, the Commission eliminated its syndicated exclusivity and network nonduplication rules, which had protected local broadcasters from duplication of both network and syndicated programming via distant signals (CATV, 1980). These rules differed from the general limits on signal importation in that they prohibited only duplication of programming for which the local broadcasters had obtained exclusive rights. The Commission concluded that deletion of the rules would not lead to a reduction in the availability of programming or otherwise diminish service to the pubic.

The same consideration ultimately led to the elimination of the FCC's "must-carry" rules. Like other measures designed to protect local broadcasters, the must-carry rules assumed that cable television could limit the ability of over-the-air television station to serve their intended audience. These rules addressed that concern by requiring cable systems to carry a specified number of local television signals. Cable operators challenged the rules on constitutional grounds, arguing that the government lacked a sufficient interest to support restrictions on the operators' editorial autonomy. Citing the Economic Inquiry Report, the United States Court of Appeals for the District of Columbia Circuit found that if the Commission "has repudiated the economic assumptions that underlie the must-carry rules, the suggestion that they serve an important governmental interest (or any interest at all) would be wholly unconvincing" (*Quincy Cable TV Inc. v. FCC*, 1985). The court concluded that the findings of the report, combined with the FCC's inability after 20 years to demonstrate a tangible economic threat to broadcasters, made "the continued deference to the Commission's concededly unsupported determinations plainly inappropriate" (p. 714). Consequently the court struck down the must-carry rules.

## Economic Adjustments and Reregulation

There is a fundamental difficulty with basing regulations on economic predictions—the predictions may be wrong. The 1979 Economic Inquiry Report, for example was predicated in the FCC's "estimates of what will happen to cable and to broadcasting on the basis of the best economic information at our disposal" (*Inquiry*, 1979, p. 659). The "best economic information" in 1979, however, was not very impressive at the threshold of the 1990s. In 1979, the Commission found that "all of the available information suggests that under foreseeable circumstances cable penetration is unlikely to exceed about 48% of the nation's television households" (p. 713). But 10 years later, the FCC found that cable penetration had grown from 37.3% of all television households (32 million homes) in 1985 to 56.4% (50.9 million homes) by mid-November 1989. By 1995, cable penetration rose to 65.2% (61.7 million homes).

Growth in all segments of the cable television industry was phenomenal through that decade. By 1990 there were approximately 9,010 cable systems in the United States—more than twice the number that existed in 1980. The average size of cable systems increased. In 1984, 57.4% of all cable subscribers were served by systems with channel capacity exceeding 30 channels. By 1989, the number had increased to 86.8% and to 96% in 1995. Cable systems with more than 53 channels accounted for the biggest growth during 1994, with a 9.9% increase in the number of such systems. Total cable revenues reached $9.94 billion (*Second Cable Report*, 1995).

Available programming also mushroomed. HBO became the first national cable network when, in 1975, it distributed uncut movies and sporting events to cable systems via satellite. By 1990, however, there were 104 cable-specific networks, including 39 regional network and 65 national networks. By 1995, the number of national programming services increased to 129, and by 2002, the number had more than doubled to 287 (NCTA, 2002). Between 1984 and 1989, investment in cable programming doubled—going from $1 billion to $2 billion per year.

These vast changes led Congress and the Commission to reconsider the regulatory regime for cable television. The FCC in 1988 reimposed syndicated exclusivity and network nonduplication rules (*Amendment*, 1988). The resurrection of rules that were interred in 1980 was based on the conclusion that the economic situation had fundamentally changed. The Commission concluded that "time has proved these predictions [about the growth of cable television] inaccurate" (p. 5304). The Commission found that cable had grown far faster than anticipated, thus presenting a serious competitive threat to over-the-air broadcasters. The FCC determined that "largely as a consequence of [measures deregulating the cable industry], the potential for duplicating broadcasters' programs, diverting broadcasters' audiences and advertising as a result of an unbalanced regulatory regime is far greater than we expected it to be when we rescinded our syndicated exclusivity rules" (p. 5305). Thus, the Commission reimposed the rules in order to help shift the economic balance of power between the two industries, and to insure the economic value of programs for local TV stations.

In December 1989, the FCC initiated another far-reaching inquiry to determine whether cable television had abused its market power because the industry was substantially deregulated by the Cable Communications Policy Act of 1984 (*Competition*, 1989). It was prompted, in part, by increasing consumer complaints about rising cable rates, poor service quality, and the dropping or repositioning of broadcast signals. Additional motivation for the inquiry came from allegations that vertically integrated cable operators were denying other video service providers access to programming services such as HBO, ESPN, and other cable networks.

The common denominator of the complaints was that the cable industry was alleged to be excessively concentrated, allowing it to impede competition by alternative video services. Consequently, the FCC sought to gather "hard evidence and empirical analyses" to determine the validity of the charges. Given the nature of the allegations at issue, it was predictable that the proceeding would focus almost entirely on the economics of the cable television industry.

Thus, it is not surprising that the Commission's conclusions were also cast in economic terms. The 1990 Cable Report concluded, for example, that "robust competition in the video marketplace has not yet fully evolved, but that the development of a fully competitive marketplace is possible (*Competition*, 1990, p. 9). The Commission found that cable operators possessed varying degrees of market power over the local distribution of video programming, but did not recommend imposing a wide array of new regulations. Instead, the Report proposed reliance on market forces to curb abuses, interceding only when a lack of competition can be explained by naturally occurring market forces. Further, the Report proposed that the government should encourage a more competitive marketplace for cable and other video services. Thus, the Commission's policy recommendations were the direct product of economic analysis.

Shortly after the FCC released its general cable inquiry, it issued a Notice of Proposed Rulemaking to reexamine the standard for allowing rate regulation of cable television systems (*Competition*, 1990). In 1985, as part of its implementation of the Cable Act, the Commission adopted a "three-signal standard" for determining whether cable systems were subject to "effective competition" and thus exempt from regulation of basic subscriber rates. Under this standard, a cable system was not subject to rate regulation if the community in which the system was located received three over-the-air broadcast signals. As with other aspects of cable regulation, growth of the industry and evolution of the marketing aspects of the business led the FCC to reevaluate its initial standard.

The Commission eventually adopted a new standard for measuring "effective competition" in June 1991. Again, the policy choice was a function of economic analysis. The Commission noted that since the three-signal test was adopted, the marketplace had rendered the standard obsolete. As the number of available cable channels increased, it took a great amount of over-the-air television signals to constitute a competitive alternative for viewers. Based on the comments filed by the various parties in the proceeding, the Commission found that six unduplicated over-the-air broadcast signals in a community would provide some type of market discipline for cable operators. Those communities with six broadcast channels were considered under the rules to be subject to "effective competition" and the cable operator exempt from rate regulation. Additionally, cable operators are exempt from rate controls in communities where there is a viable multichannel competitor to cable—such as in the form of a second cable system, direct broadcast satellite, microwave "wireless" cable system, or some other alternative (*Report and Order*, 1991).

Congress similarly took note of the changes in the media marketplace, passing over President George Bush's veto of the Cable Television and Competition Act of 1992. The new Act substantially reregulated cable television, imposing new standards for rate regulation, must-carry of broadcast signals, retransmission consent, cable programming access by competing technologies, customer service standards, and so on. Implementation of most provisions of the Act was vested with the FCC. Key economic concepts, such as when a cable system is subject to "effective competition" and what constitutes a "reasonable profit" were left to regulatory reevaluation.

The 1996 Telecommunications Act, in turn, repealed many of the major provisions of the 1992 Cable Act. On rate regulation, current FCC rules capping cable service rates were repealed on March 31, 1999, except for the "basic tier" that includes over-the-air channels and pubic and educational channels. Price caps were repealed for "small" cable operators (less than $25 million in revenues) immediately or for any cable system once it faced "effective competition" from local telephone companies offering "comparable" video services over telephone facilities.

The Act also repealed the FCC's "telco-cable cross-ownership" restrictions. Telephone companies were authorized to offer video services either by distributing programming as a cable television system or by establishing an "open video system" for transport of video programming on a common carrier basis. State and local regulation of telecommunications services provided by cable systems was prohibited.

One of the economic theories driving the Telecommunications Act of 1996 was that only companies of sufficient size would survive in the emerging global broadband marketplace. In other words, only companies with massive financial resources would be able to upgrade their infrastructures to provide high-capacity interactive services demanded by consumers and investors. In addition, cable companies would be competing in a developing international marketplace, sometimes against foreign competitors supported by subsidies from their governments.

Consequently, the large multiple systems operators (MSOs) sought new acquisition targets, which in turn drove up system prices. Many small, midsized and even large cable companies decided to cash in. For example, in 1999 one half of the top 10 cable MSOs were bought out. The largest purchase involved AT&T, which bought TCI for $48 billion in 1998. The next year, AT&T acquired MediaOne in a $60 billion takeover of MediaOne (which also netted the company a 25% stake in Time Warner Entertainment).[5] AT&T eventually merged with Comcast in November 2002.

The cable industry also moved to consolidating itself geographically, a process known as *clustering*. Cable companies began acquiring (either through purchase, or system swapping with other large MSOs) geographically adjacent systems to cluster them. Cox Communications, for example, has clusters in Arizona, Southern California, Florida and Texas. Such clustering allows the companies to take advantage of scale economies in both marketing as well as emerging technologies. As a result of clustering, the number of areas which had competing cable companies dwindled, so that the number of cable systems actually declined from a high of 11,200 in 1994 to less than 10,000 in 2002 (NCTA, 2002).

The end result of both FCC and Congressional action was a cable industry that in 2002 served 73,559,550 households (69.8% of all U.S. households), employed over 130,000 people, had a total annual revenue of over $48 billion, derived nearly $14.5 billion in advertising, and was delivering more services (e.g., the Internet) to more people than ever. On the other hand, from a competitive point of view, the top four MSOs serve over 47 million subscribers or about 64% of all subscribers. Although other video programming services, such as direct broadcast satellite, now capture about 18% of the video services market, it is hard to see where Congress and the FCC have defined *effective competition*. One thing is clear—as the marketplace changes, the Commission and Congress are forced to react and adapt to new conditions.

## CONCLUSION

More than 70 years of experience with regulation of communications industries has proven, if nothing else, that the *public interest* is an elusive concept. Given the 1934 Communications Act's lack of specificity as to the meaning of this essential term, it has been up to the FCC, and the Federal Radio Commission before it, to come up with a definition that takes into account practical realities. The most significant reality confronting this quest is the fact that broadcasting is a business and it generally can provide greater service to the public when business is good. Thus, economic issues historically have been part of the Commission's allocation and licensing policies.

Because of its dependence on economic factors, the pubic interest also has been a moving target. The changing fortunes in the broadcasting industry have prompted the FCC to adopt, and later rescind, the Carroll doctrine. Likewise, marketplace changes led the Commission to adopt, then rescind, and finally consider reimposing AM–FM simulcast restrictions. A similar cyclical pattern of regulatory upheaval describes the FCC's experience with cable television.

The FCC's task of divining its regulatory mission through economic analysis has become more complex in an age of rapidly changing technology. As new methods of delivering video programming to the public are thrown into the marketplace mix, the effect of FCC action in one area may cause a chain reaction that spawns effects elsewhere. The question is not whether the cable industry will prosper at the expense of broadcasters or vice versa. Rather, the Commission must consider what effects its regulations may have on both existing and potential new market entrants. For example, regulation of the rate that a cable operator may charge its subscriber could have an inhibiting effect on the development of cable program networks by reducing the amount of money available to pay for programming. Dampening the growth of programming sources in turn might hinder the growth of alternative video delivery systems, which depend on such programming to create a competitive business. Multifaceted analyses of this type are now required for virtually any important regulatory decision the Commission must make, from the development of high-definition television to the deployment of direct broadcast satellites.

The increasing importance of media and the financial strength of media industries guarantee that economic analysis will continue to be a vital component of regulatory policy. The questions still remains, however, as the number and complexity of necessary calculations increases, whether the tool will be sufficient to the task.

## FURTHER READING

Brock, G., & Rosston, G. (Eds.). (1996). *The Internet and telecommunications policy.* Mahwah, NJ: Lawrence Erlbaum Associates.

Carter, T., Franklin, M., & Wright, J. (1983). *The First Amendment and the fifth estate* (3rd ed.). Mineola, NY: Foundation Press.

Creech, K. (1996). *Electronic media law and regulation.* Newton, MA: Focal Press.

Pool, I. deS. (1983). *Technologies of freedom.* Cambridge, MA: Belknap.

## REFERENCES

*Amendment of Parts 73 and 76 of the Commission's Rules Relating to Program Exclusivity in the Cable and Broadcast Industries*, 3 FCC F2d. 5299 (1988), aff'd sub nom. *United Video v. FCC*, 890 F.2d 1173 (D.C. Cir. 1989).

*Amendment of Section 73.242 of the Commission's Rules and Regulations in Regard to AM-FM Program Duplication*, 59 Rad. Reg. (P & F) 2d 1613 (1986).

*Arlington Telecommunications Corp.*, 65 F.C.C. 2d 469 (1977), *recon.* 69 F.C.C. 2d 1923 (1978).

*Carroll Broadcasting Co. v. FCC*, 258 F.2d 440 (1958).

*Carter Mountain Transmission Corp.*, 32 F.C.C. 459 (1962). *Aff'd sub nom. Carter Mountain Transmission Corp. v. FCC*, 321 F.2d 359 (D.C. Cir.), *cert. denied*, 375, U.S. 951 (1963).

*CATV Syndicated Program Exclusivity Rules*, 79 F.C.C. 2d 663 (1980).

*Competition and Responsibility in Network Broadcasting, Docket No. 12782*, 23 F.C.C. 2d 382 (1970). *recon. denied*, 25 F.C.C. 2d 318 (1970)., *aff'd sub nom. Mt. Mansfield Television, Inc. v. FCC*, 442 F.2d 470 (2d Cir. 1971).

*Competition, Rate Deregulation and the Commission's Policies Relating to the Provision of Cable Television Service* (Notice of Inquiry), 5 FCC Rcd. 362 (1989).

Erickson, Don V. (1973). *Armstrong's Fight for FM Broadcasting: One Man vs. Big Business and Bureaucracy*. Tuscaloosa: University of Alabama Press.

*FCC v. Pottsville Broadcasting Co.*, 309 U.S. 134 (1940); 309 U.S. 470 (1940).

*FCC v. Sanders Brothers Radio Station*, 309 U.S. 470, 60 S.Ct. 693, 84 L.Ed. 869 (1940).

*First Report and Order Docket Nos. 14895 and 15233*, 38 FCC 683 (1965).

*Second Report and Order in Docket Nos. 14895, 15233 and 15971*, 2 FCC 2d 725 (1966).

*Inquiry Into the Economic Relationship Between Television Broadcasting and Cable Television*, 71 FCC 2d 632 (1979).

Kretchmer, S., & Carveth, R. (2001). Challenging boundaries for a boundless medium: information access, libraries, and freedom of expression in a democratic society. In T. R. Hensley (Ed.), *The Boundaries of Freedom of Expression and Order in a Democratic Society* (pp. 184–212). Kent, OH: Kent State University Press

*Mainstream Loudoun v. Board of Trustees of the Loudoun County Public Libraries*, case No. 97-2049, U.S. District Court, E.D. Virginia.

*National Association of Regulatory Utility Commissioners v. FCC*, 252 F.2d 630 n.37 (D.C. Cir. 1976).

*Notice of Inquiry, Docket No. 21284*, 65 FCC 2d 9 (1977).

National Cable Television Association (2002). *2002 Cable & Telecommunications Industry Overview (Mid-Year)*. Retrieved from http://www.ncta.com/pdf_files/Mid'02Overview.pdf

*Office of Communication of the United Church of Christ v. FCC*, No 81-1032, slip op. at 27 (D.C. Cir. May 10, 1983).

*Policies Regarding Detrimental Effects of Proposed New Broadcast Stations on Existing Stations*, 3 FCC Rcd. 638 (1988). *aff'd on reconsideration*, 4 FCC Rcd.2276 (1989).

*Quincy Cable TV, Inc. v. FCC*, 768 F.2d 1434, 1455 (D.C. Cir. 1985). *Cert. denied, sub nom. Office of Communication of the United Church of Christ v. FCC*, No. 81-1032, slip op. at 27 (D.C., Cir., May 10, 1983).

*Reno v. ACLU* (1997).

*Report and Order, Docket No. 15084*, 45 FCC 1515 (1964)

*Report and Order, Docket No. 20016*, 59 FCC 2d 147 (1976).

*Report and Order, Effective Competition*, 6 FCC Rcd. 4545, 69 RR2d 671 (1991).

*Review of the Technical Assessment Criteria for AM Broadcast Service*, MM Docket No. 87-267 (released Oct. 1991).

*Sable Communications of California, Inc. v. FCC*, 492 U.S. 115 (1989).

*Second Annual Report to Congress on Cable Competition*, Rep. No. DC 95-142 December 1995.

*Washington Utilities and Transportation Commission v. FCC*, 513 F.2d 1142 (9th Cir.), *cert. denied*, 423 U.S. 836 (1975).

*WLVA Inc. v. FCC* 1972 459 F.2d 1286 (1972).

## ENDNOTES

[1]The Act declares invalid all state rules that restrict entry or limit competition in telephone service, both local and long distance. It dismantles the AT&T and GTE antitrust consent decrees, including their controversial prohibitions on entry by the Bell Operating Companies (BOCs) into the interLATA telephone market. (LATAs, or Local Access and Transport Areas, are regional areas, similar to area codes, that divided the local and long-distance telephone markets under the AT&T consent decree.) Competitive safeguards, known as "separate affiliates" and a prohibition of cross-subsidization, are required to protect against anticompetitive behavior by local telephone companies.

The BOCs and GTE will be permitted to offer interLATA service once they have taken steps to remove entry barriers to competition for local exchange service, that is, local telephone service. The Act requires the BOCs to implement a series of reforms known as the "competitive checklist" in order to qualify for providing long-distance service outside their regions. It also requires all local exchange carriers (LECs) to interconnect with new entrants, unbundle their networks and allow resale by competitors, provide number portability so customers can keep their phone numbers when switching local providers, and other steps to promote an effectively competitive local exchange market. State PUCs are charged with a major responsibility in implementing local telephone competition.

[2]12 F.2d 614 (N.D. Ill. 1926). See also *Hoover v. Intercity Radio Corp.*, 286 F 1002 (D.C. Cir. 1923), *appeal dismissed*, 266 U.S. 636 (1924). Some have theorized that the government induced interference between broadcast stations as a pretext to justify regulation. See, for example, J. Emord, *Freedom, Technology and the First Amendment*, 153–157 (1991).

[3]It should be noted that AM radio benefited from two other events. The virtual elimination of ownership caps for radio with the 1996 Telecommunications Act strengthened the service by its stations being acquired in vast numbers by huge media corporations, such as Clear Channel Communications. Second, the audience demand for syndicated talk radio programs by personalities such as Rush Limbaugh and Dr. Laura Schlessinger made stations carrying such programs more competitive.

[4]Interestingly, the Commission retained a similar policy governing the licensing of common carriers (e.g., telephone companies; *Washington Utilities and Transportation Commission v. FCC*, 1975).

[5]By early 2001, however, AT&T sold a large number of its cable systems to Media-Com and Charter Communications in an effort to shrink its debt load.

Chapter **3**

# Structure and Change: A Communications Industry Overview

### GARY W. OZANICH
*University at Buffalo*

### MICHAEL O. WIRTH
*University of Denver*

The media industry has experienced an unprecedented level of structural change during the past decade. Due to financial transactions, primarily mergers and acquisitions, there is a higher degree of concentration of ownership, increased globalization, and increased conglomeration of the industry. This activity has been based on the perceived future prospects of this business sector; the perceived trend toward technological convergence; the perceived "synergies" of owning multiple distribution channels; a relaxation of regulatory policy; and the availability of capital, including historically highly valued stock prices, to finance the transactions.

These structural changes are significant to considerations of firm conduct and performance from both an economic and First Amendment point-of-view. They are also significant to questions of transnational conglomerate media ownership and the *globalization* of content. This chapter provides an overview of the structural changes that have occurred in the media industry and a discussion of their significance. Analysis of the apparent lack of success of some high profile megamergers including AOL-TimeWarner and the AT&T acquisition of cable giants TCI and MediaOne is also provided.

For the purposes of this analysis, the *media industry* is defined as those companies that either directly or indirectly own and operate broadcast stations or broadcast networks, program production and distribution facilities, cable television systems or networks, and newspaper, magazine, and book publishers. These firms are involved in content production services and/or content delivery services.

## THE ECONOMICS OF MEDIA MERGERS AND ACQUISITIONS

Due to First Amendment considerations, electromagnetic spectrum management, and common carrier regulation, communications companies have historically held a special place in public policy and have subsequently been subject to a unique degree of regulation. These policies have been critical in shaping the structure of the industry. However, within the sets of policies that define the structure of the marketplace, communication companies are not unique financial organizations. They are well suited for examination based on established theories and methodologies of economics and finance.

During the past decade an unprecedented combination of media companies and acquisitions by large media have resulted in six companies dominating the U.S. mass media and fewer than 10 dominating the global media market (Bagdikian, 2000). This merger and acquisition activity (M&A) has been driven by financial and strategic considerations. Media companies, similar to other enterprises are run by a management team under the oversight of a board of directors with the goal of maximizing the long run value of the shareholder's common stock.[1] M&A have become a key tool in trying to achieve this objective.

The technical distinction between a merger and acquisition can be complex. In the most basic sense in a merger transaction, two companies are combined into one company that assumes all assets and liabilities of both companies. In an acquisition, one company buys the common stock of another, thereby assuming ownership. In some cases, a company purchases all or a portion of a second company's operating assets instead of the common stock in a transaction referred to as an asset acquisition.

In the United States, the volume of merger and acquisition activity has varied greatly although the activity can be described as having occurred in *waves*. Macroeconomic factors have an obvious effect on M&A activity. Interest rates, inflation and their volatility are the most important variables in valuation models. They affect the return on capital as well as the ability to secure financing. Business cycle factors must also be considered in forecasts and are critical to valuation and deal structure (Reed & LaJoux, 1998).

The fundamental reason to undertake a merger or acquisition is one of economic gain: that two firms combined are worth more than the sum of each individual firm, or the classic argument of synergy, $1 + 1 > 2$. In finan-

---

[1]There is a significant literature debating whether long-term profit maximization is indeed the goal of corporations (see generally, Scherer & Ross, 1990).

cial terms, the net present value of the gain associated with the combination must exceed the cost of the transaction to the acquiring company.

Mergers and acquisitions are often categorized as horizontal, vertical, or conglomerate. In a horizontal merger a company acquires a second company in the same or similar business. An example of this are the acquisitions of radio stations by Clear Channel Communications, a company that already owns more than 1,200 radio stations. This concentration of radio station ownership results in economies of scale in operation resulting in greater efficiency and market power.

In a *vertical merger*, an acquiring company purchases a company, which provides input materials or purchases output material from it. This has been very common in the communications industry where there has been a perception of a software or programming shortage or "bottleneck." Examples of vertical mergers are the Disney (software and programming) acquisition of Cap Cities/ABC (distribution company) and the merger of Time Warner (cable and content) with America Online (Internet and online distribution).

A conglomerate is a company that owns a portfolio of businesses. Following the M&A activity of the past decades, virtually all large media companies are conglomerates in that they own a portfolio of companies (*Columbia Journalism Review*, 2002). In addition true conglomerates also own media properties, such as General Electric's ownership of NBC. The degree of synergism or scale economies between the portfolio companies own can be significant, but the key reasons for conglomeration are the cash flow of individual companies and the benefit of owning a diversified portfolio.

Prior to the successful completion of a merger or acquisition, the transaction is subject to regulatory approval. A combination or acquisition can be blocked by the Department of Justice (DOJ) or the Federal Trade Commission (FTC) under antitrust law. In some cases communication companies are subject to additional oversight from the Federal Communications Commission (FCC).

The implementation of a merger, or the integration of two companies is often a complicated process. This is where the theory of finance meets the reality of operations. Often the meshing of different operations and different corporate cultures produces diseconomies and unanticipated problems. However, if all goes according to plan, the combined companies become more valuable than the separate companies, and the shareholders of the acquiring company are rewarded with a higher stock price. If the combination does not go according to plan, the shareholders of the acquiring company will likely face a lower stock price. Two to three years after the transaction this was the case for two very high-profile media transactions: the AOL-TimeWarner merger and the AT&T acquisition of two of the three largest cable television operators, TCI and MediaOne (*The Economist*, 2002).

## Media Industry M&A Activity (1987–2002)

The data concerning communications industry transactions are difficult to delineate. Many transactions may be between privately held companies where there is no requirement of public disclosure. In addition, if nonpublic securities (i.e., Rule 144A Private Placements) are used to finance the transactions, no public documents or details will be filed with the SEC. Finally, the definition of media or communications industry varies greatly by data collector.

According to Thomson Financial, the media industry accounted for almost $1.1 trillion in M&A activity during the period from 1987 to 2002. Table 3.1 provides a summary of these transactions based on Census Bureau SIC Codes for the broadcast, cable television, newspaper, publishing, and the motion picture production and distribution industries.

Further, many of the communication industry transactions were "megadeals." These transactions were for assets carrying very high valuations. Table 3.2 provides a summary of the 10 largest M&A transactions in the media industry. Besides these megadeals there have been a large number of other media mergers and acquisitions from 1987 to 2002.

## MEDIA INDUSTRY M&A REGULATORY CONSIDERATIONS

Regulation plays a major role in determining the structure of the communications industry in the United States. It is necessary to understand the role of regulation before analyzing the specifics of merger and acquisition activity in the communications industry.

The communications industry is subject to unique regulation. This is due to three factors: (a) mass-media serve a special First Amendment role; (b) broadcasters are licensed to use a scarce resource, the electromagnetic spectrum, and cable operators are franchised to use a scarce resource, public rights of way; and (c) within at least some markets, newspapers have cost structures that preclude economic competition (i.e., they are natural monopolies).

The special First Amendment role served by the media has proved to be a powerful tool with respect to preventing government regulation of the print industry. However, broadcast entrepreneurs continue to enjoy less than full First Amendment rights due to continued adherence to the theory that broadcasters are public trustees who are granted a limited privilege to use a scarce public resource (the electromagnetic spectrum). The U.S. Supreme Court has yet to fully determine the extent to which cable operators enjoy First Amendment rights. However, the outcome of recent Supreme Court cases, such as *Turner Broadcasting System, Inc* (1997), suggests that cable operators' First Amendment rights will ultimately fall somewhere be-

**TABLE 3.1**

**Announced Media Mergers & Acquisitions 1987–2002**
**(Dollars in Millions)**

| Date | Cable/Broadcasting | Film Production & Distribution | Publishing | Total | Number of Deals |
|---|---|---|---|---|---|
| 1987 | 11,231.0 | 3,101.1 | 6,410.2 | 20,742.3 | 217 |
| 1988 | 6,774.6 | 3,432.1 | 9,852.0 | 20,058.7 | 271 |
| 1989 | 9,283.3 | 21,743.5 | 8,855.4 | 39,882.2 | 319 |
| 1990 | 3,961.6 | 10,643.9 | 2,174.3 | 16,779.8 | 247 |
| 1991 | 4,321.4 | 4,843.1 | 3,895.8 | 13,060.3 | 219 |
| 1992 | 2,235.7 | 593.3 | 1,573.4 | 4,402.4 | 201 |
| 1993 | 9,254.7 | 19,030.8 | 2,689.8 | 30,975.3 | 270 |
| 1994 | 21,108.4 | 10,025.9 | 3,244.1 | 34,378.4 | 317 |
| 1995 | 61,357.4 | 8,267.3 | 7,139.5 | 76,764.2 | 466 |
| 1996 | 26,396.8 | 2,758.5 | 7,962.2 | 37,117.5 | 384 |
| 1997 | 59,371.2 | 8,822.4 | 8,429.3 | 76,622.9 | 393 |
| 1998 | 91,824.6 | 4,629.4 | 15,295.6 | 111,749.6 | 418 |
| 1999 | 182,102.2 | 3,448.2 | 7,086.9 | 192,637.3 | 411 |
| 2000 | 64,087.1 | 183,615.0 | 31,331.2 | 279,033.3 | 351 |
| 2001 | 97,364.7 | 8,060.8 | 4,195.0 | 109,620.5 | 217 |
| 2002 | 12,929.9 | 3,912.8 | 1,507.4 | 18,350.1 | 124 |

*Source.* Thomson Financial.

73

# TABLE 3.2
## Largest Media M&A Transactions 1987–2002
### (Dollars in Millions)

| Date | Target Name | Target Business | Acquirer Name | Acquirer Short Business Description | RankValue of Deal ($mil) |
|---|---|---|---|---|---|
| 01/10/00 | Time Warner | Film/Publishing | America Online Inc | Internet Service Provider | 181,568.461 |
| 07/08/01 | AT&T Broadband | Cable TV | Comcast Corp | Cable TV | 72,041.150 |
| 06/24/98 | Tele-Communications Inc | Cable TV | AT&T Corp | Telecommunications | 69,896.491 |
| 04/22/99 | MediaOne Group Inc | Cable TV | AT&T Corp | Telecommunications | 51,873.866 |
| 09/07/99 | CBS Corp | Broadcasting | Viacom Inc | Cable TV | 40,882.163 |
| 10/04/99 | AMFM Inc | Broadcasting | Clear Channel | Broadcasting | 22,735.392 |
| 07/31/95 | Capital Cities/ABC Inc | Broadcasting | Walt Disney Co | Film/Parks | 18,280.392 |
| 03/04/89 | Warner Communications Inc | Film/Music | Time Inc | Publishing company | 15,113.400 |
| 08/15/00 | Infinity Broadcasting Corp | Broadcasting | Viacom Inc | Cable TV | 13,649.042 |
| 03/13/00 | Times Mirror Co | Publishing | Tribune Co | Publishing Company | 11,628.231 |

*Source.* Thomson Financial.

tween those possessed by the print media and those possessed by broadcasters. Use of such an intermediate First Amendment model will likely result in much of the current approach to regulating cable surviving constitutional scrutiny.

The criteria for gaining and keeping a broadcast license are of great significance to M&A activity in this area. As trustees of a scarce resource, the electromagnetic spectrum, broadcast station entrepreneurs are licensed to serve the public interest convenience, and necessity (47 U.S.C.A. Sec. 309(a)). As a result licensees are subject to periodic review (8 years for both television and radio licensees; 47 U.S.C.A. Sec. 307(c)(1)), and the FCC must approve any station transfer (47 U.S.C.A. Sec. 310(d)). Most station transfers are approved without incident. However, all parties in a transfer must comply with the FCC's rules and procedures in these areas to avoid unnecessary and costly delay. Another area of interest is cable regulation. Historically, most economists have believed that cable is a natural monopoly. As a result, very few of the nation's cable systems face direct competition from a multichannel wire-line competitor. However, regulators tried to create a more competitive multichannel video marketplace by passing the Telecommunications Act of 1996. In spite of the fact that the 1996 Act allows Local Exchange Carriers (i.e., telephone companies) to enter the cable business as either traditional cable operators, traditional common carriers or as open video systems, cable entrepreneurs currently face only a small amount of direct wireline multichannel competition from overbuilders. However, cable faces significant multichannel television competition from Direct Broadcast Satellite (DBS) providers DirecTV and EchoStar. In the long run, Congress' decision (in the 1996 Act) to move away from a monopoly regulatory approach and toward a competitive approach can be expected to have a significant impact on cable merger and acquisition activity. Ultimately, increased competition increases entrepreneurial risk. Thus, cable entrepreneurs can be expected to utilize varying merger and acquisition activities depending on their perception of the expected impact of competition on the long-term prospects of the cable marketplace.

In general, newspapers have not been subjected to the extensive regulatory schemes established for broadcasting and cable. As a result, the primary regulation of newspaper M&A activity occurs through traditional antitrust oversight. The one exception is the Newspaper Preservation Act (1970) under which the U.S. Department of Justice may allow two directly competing same market daily newspapers to form a joint operating agreement (JOA) for the purpose of combining their business operations while preserving their editorial independence. Because the premise of the policy is the Failing Firm Doctrine, the Justice Department must determine that one of the two newspapers would exit the market in the absence of a JOA in order to approve the merger as a permissible exception to the antitrust laws.

In addition to the general regulatory considerations discussed here, a number of FCC ownership rules have had a significant impact on the structure of the marketplace under which media M&A activity has occurred. Of most immediate concern is the FCC's regulation of television and radio station ownership. Such regulation takes three primary forms: limits on aggregate or national ownership (i.e., multiple ownership); limits in local markets (i.e., duopoly and crossmedia ownership); and limits on network interest in program ownership and distribution. It is the relaxation of these rules during the past several years that has led to a substantial increase in merger and acquisition activity and increased industry consolidation. In particular, the rescinding of the FCC's financial interest and syndication rules paved the way for many large transactions by allowing for vertical integration between television networks and program production and distribution interests. Likewise, Congress' liberalization of the Radio Duopoly Rules and its elimination of a cap on the number of radio stations an entrepreneur can own nationally led to an explosion of merger and acquisition activity in this segment.

Although the media (particularly broadcast and cable) are subject to national and local ownership constraints, limitations on crossmedia ownership, and some limitations on vertical integration, the foci of these constraints are on who the purchaser is, not on the nature of the transaction. Thus, the transfer of media properties, whether through an acquisition or merger, is not subject to any additional special considerations. An example of this was a review by the FCC of a request by Storer Communications to intercede during a hostile tender offer to the company's shareholders by an outside company. Storer management requested intercession based on financial disruption and the Public Interest Standard. In this case, the FCC acted to prevent Storer from insulating itself from the challenge and remained neutral during the proxy challenge (Storer Communications, 1985).

## FACTORS DRIVING THE MEDIA INDUSTRY STRUCTURE

In addition to the impact of the liberalization of various media ownership rules, the unprecedented merger and acquisition activities that have reshaped the structure of the media industry have been driven by strategic and financial factors. These factors are not mutually exclusive and most transactions occur as a result of both. The strategic factors are an attempt to gain synergies through leverage and economies of scale or to position the firm in a globalized media marketplace. The financial factors are tied to the stock market "bubble" during the late-1990s when the value of traditional and new media companies reached historic heights or are related to tax or accounting factors.

Strategy plays the greatest role in media mergers and acquisitions. The concept of *convergence* (i.e., the disappearance of technological differences among distribution networks so they begin to compete by delivering multiple applications over the same network to different platforms) has been well anticipated by media strategists. This anticipated convergence was the basis of the AT&T acquisition of TCI's and MediaOne's cable properties and the Time Warner merger with AOL. Because the time frame for convergence continues to be pushed back, and because there has been significant postmerger dissonance, AT&T decided to spin-off its cable subsidiary, and AOL Time Warner has decided to de-emphasize convergence as a strategy (Peers, 2003).

A second strategic reason for media concentration involves the attempt to *leverage content* such as programming over an increased number of distribution channels. This type of vertical integration not only provides the opportunity to amortize costs over increased channels and additional product release windows, but also provides a critical mass for the purpose of building brands such as with Disney products or Time Warner editorial content.

A related strategic consideration is the ability to crosspromote across media. Promoting a program or service on other media owned by a company can produce increased demand. Examples include the promotion of AOL service on Time Warner cable networks, of ESPN programs on various ABC networks, and of MTV via various Viacom owned video networks.

The *creation of barriers to new competition* is an additional reason for recent media merger and acquisition activity. By becoming more vertically integrated with respect to media content and distribution, large media companies make it more difficult for smaller content competitors and entrepreneurs to gain access to audience distribution. There is also a prevalent view that, similar to beachfront property, no new media properties are being created. This is due to the existence of numerous high barriers to media industry entry (Porter, 1984).

The final strategic factor is *globalization* of the media industry. Although viewed by some as a hegemonic threat of Western media, media companies have identified international markets as a prime source of future revenue growth (Baker, 2002). All major media conglomerates have international subsidiaries. Globalization is not limited to U.S.-based companies with foreign subsidiaries. European companies such as Bertelsmann and Vivendi Universal have a significant presence in the United States that was developed through mergers and acquisitions. The most successful foreign subsidiaries of media companies, such as Viacom's MTV, make extensive use of locally produced content.

*Financial factors* have also played a key role in the structure of the media industry. Figure 3.1 depicts the value of an index of media companies during the period of 1997 to 2002. The spike in valuation of media companies during the 1999–2000 "bubble" is apparent.

The valuation of media companies is important for two reasons. First, the company stock represents *currency* or an asset that can be used to pay

## Media Company Stock Index 1997-2002

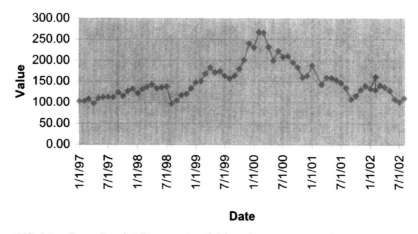

FIG. 3.1.    From *Prophet Finance*. Available online: www.prophet.net

for a target company in a merger or acquisition. Clearly, the high valuations of common stock made it an attractive currency for M&A activity.

A second factor is that with media valuations in parabolic ascent, companies were eager to make acquisitions before prices went higher. Management and boards of directors may have believed that they were buying cheap assets.

There are other financial reasons to undertake mergers and acquisitions. Tax issues are a consideration in every transaction. The economics of a merger can be partially premised on tax benefits such as sheltering earnings from taxation, the use of unused tax shields such as loss carry-forwards, and the deferral of taxes through capital gains compared to ordinary income taxes. Other factors can include the acquisition of technology, and the general redeployment of surplus funds for the purpose of corporate development. Critics have also cited merger accounting as a way to "smooth earnings" and reach the growth targets anticipated by investors (*Financial Times*, 2002).

## MEDIA M&A AND INDUSTRY STRUCTURE

The increased concentration of ownership resulting from the flurry of mergers and acquisitions during the past decade has dramatically changed the structure of the industry. This involves three relevant markets: local media, the U.S. national market, and the global market. There have been dramatic changes in each of these relevant markets.

## Local Ownership Concentration

The greatest change in the U.S. market resulted from the previously discussed relaxation of ownership rules that were part of the Telecommunications Act of 1996. Local radio and television stations have increasingly come under the same ownership. The result has been a dramatic increase in measurements of concentration.

In radio, depending on the market ranking, one owner can control between five and eight stations in the same service area with between three and five being either AM or FM, respectively. Based on FCC Reports for March 2001 in the largest 50 markets, the largest owner garnered 36% of all radio station revenues and the largest four owners 87% of all revenues. The largest four owners revenue share for March 1996 was about 75%. This concentration ratio increases in smaller markets so that in the largest 283 radio markets, the largest firm in each market accounted for an average of 45.8% of revenues and the largest four owners in each market accounted for 92.8% of revenues. As measured in terms of distinct owners present in each market, in March 2001, the average number of owners in each market was 10.3 as compared to 13.5 in March 1996 (*Review of Radio Industry*, 2001).

Relative to program diversity, the FCC found that the number of distinct radio formats in each market has been stable at about 10 during the 1996 to 2001 period. The data indicate that the number of formats has declined in the larger markets while they have increased in smaller markets (*Review of Radio Industry*, 2001).

Concentration of ownership is less critical in the television industry where rules are stricter than radio. As described earlier, in September 1999, the FCC introduced new duopoly rules relative to TV station ownership. (Local TV Ownership Rules, 1999). Among the rules is one that allows one owner to own two stations within one market as long as there are eight independent TV "voices" after the merger. According to a filing with the FCC, this allowed for mergers in approximately 70 markets, and mergers have taken place in approximately 50 of these markets (Reply Comments of Consumer Union et al., 2002). These mergers aside, due to the fact that owners are limited to one or two television stations per market, concentration ratios based on revenues in a local market are not meaningful.

Cross-media ownership is a second issue in local market concentration. In recent years, the focus of the debate has shifted from defining relative product markets to an analysis of the "independent voices" or independently owned media within a Designated Market Area (DMA; Local TV Ownership Rules, 1999).

In radio–television cross-ownership, within a DMA, one owner could hold one TV station (or two if allowed under the TV Duopoly Rules) and up to eight radio stations, depending on the number of independent voices remaining after the merger. The FCC is currently reviewing its regulations limiting broadcast and newspaper cross-ownership (In the Matter of Crossownership, September 20, 2001). Arguably, if not for these limitations on cross-media ownership, local media concentration would be far greater. Critics have charged that even with the FCC's focus on retaining "independent voices," most local markets are at best oligopolies and many smaller markets are monopolies (Bagdikian, 2002; Consumers Union et al., 2002).

## National Concentration

Whereas FCC policy has evolved to a focus on the number of "independent voices" present in a local market, aggregate or national ownership of media properties continues to be shaped by the FCC policy that caps national ownership of television stations to a reach of 35% of U.S. television households as well as by antitrust policy in general. In spite of these policies, the trend toward consolidation has accelerated in recent years.

Although somewhat restricted by public policy, the aggregate concentration of ownership within specific media industries has increased. According to the FCC, whereas the number of commercial radio stations has increased 7.1% since March 1996, the number of owners of radio stations has declined 25% (*Review of Radio Industry*, 2001).

Likewise, TV station ownership has bumped up against the limitations established by the FCC. A confounding factor is that broadcast station ownership is a strategic concern in order to "efficiently reach large audiences, and thus serve as the basis of the major networks" (Compaine & Gomery, 2002, p. 222). Thus, the largest five group owners have television properties that reach between 27% to 35% of the U.S. population.

For nonbroadcast media, national concentration is more pronounced than broadcasting. The cable television industry has become increasingly concentrated, with the six largest MSO's providing service to 60% of the cable subscribers in the United States (Kagan World Media, 2002; SG Cowen Securities Corp., 2002). While stabilizing, there will likely be a continued trend toward cable concentration including mergers with traditional telecommunications companies.

Chain ownership of newspapers has been well documented (Busterna, 1986; Compaine & Gomery, 2000). The Newspaper Association of America (2002) indicated that 20 newspaper companies account for about 70% of the circulation of daily newspapers.

The film industry and music industry are subject to an even greater level of concentration. The 10 largest film distribution companies, owned by six conglomerates, accounted for 92% of theatrical box office revenue in 2000. The music industry is also dominated by five companies that accounted for 90% of all revenues in 2000 (*Wall Street Journal*, 2001). The music industry is further complicated by the fact that there are few profitable artists. Of the 6,455 new CD releases in 2001 only 114 showed a profit (Ordonez, 2002). The contractual control of these profitable artists dictate the structure of the industry.

## Conglomeration

Clearly there is ample evidence of increased concentration within specific industries. More pronounced is the trend toward media conglomeration. The easy access to capital combined with the use of highly valued common stock to purchase media properties financed this trend toward conglomeration. Strategically driven by the concepts of synergy and convergence, investments in new media, and a desire to control the leveraging of content over the largest number of distribution channels, media conglomerates have been on an M&A binge during the past decade as evidenced by the data provided in Table 3.1.

The degree of conglomeration is determined by examining ownership structures. Depending on the analysis and threshold measures for domination, critics charge that the major media in the United States are owned by between 9 and 23 conglomerate companies (Bagdikian, 2002; *Columbia Journalism Review* 2002; The Project on Media Ownership, 2002).

## Globalization of Media Ownership

New distribution technologies, regulatory liberalization and the globalization of capital markets have allowed media conglomerates to expand transnationally. Of the major media conglomerates, two of them are non-U.S. companies, Bertelsmann (Germany), and Vivendi-Universal (France). The drive to expand transnationally is driven by the same factors that have driven expansion in the United States—a desire to leverage content products over as many distribution channels as possible, anticipation of convergence of distribution channels, a desire to develop new markets, and the financial attractiveness of the deals. Critics have charged that conglomerate domination of media ownership on a global basis is resulting in both a financial and cultural domination of Western companies (Baker, 2002; Schiller, 1999). However, it is significant to note that most of these companies rely upon locally produced content to some extent.

## MEDIA M&A STRATEGIES STUMBLE

As described, there are strategic and financial reasons for the structural changes that have occurred in the media industries. The torrid pace of mergers and acquisitions were anchored in future plans centered on convergence and a belief in synergistic benefits on both the revenue and cost side. The short run financial results of these activities, two to three years after the transactions and in the aftermath of the stock market bubble of the late 1990s, have been negative, as indicated by the price of securities, changes in management, disappointing financial results, and plans to break-up the merged companies (Orwall & Peers, 2002; Peers, 2002). Specific examples include top management changes at Vivendi-Universal and AOL Time Warner, the sale of AT&T Broadband, and the dramatically lower common-stock price experienced by virtually every media company.

There appear to be five major reasons for the disappointing results of recent media company megamergers. First, convergence, particularly between the Internet and traditional media, has been slow to develop. Second, management appears to have overestimated synergies between content and distribution channels. Third, companies appear to have overpaid for assets acquired and issued or assumed a great deal of debt in the transactions. Fourth, there are reports of cultural and organizational conflicts within the merged companies. Fifth, investors have shifted their focus from financial measures such as operating cash flow (EBITDA) to actual earnings. Such a shift has had a negative impact on the valuation and/or creditworthiness of media companies.

This does not mean the situation will not turn around. The potential remains for an increased trend toward technological convergence and the ability to leverage content over multiple delivery channels leading to improved earnings. Further, as companies sort-out the strategic fit between operating assets, performance should also be improved, particularly as under-performing assets are divested. Ultimately, the media industry has an inherent element of organic growth that should be reflected in the performance of these media conglomerates. Only time will tell whether changes in the media industry's market structure resulting from the M&A boom will be justified by positive long run financial performance.

## DOES STRUCTURAL CHANGE MATTER?

As indicated in this chapter, a number of factors have driven structural changes in the media industries. Do these changes matter? New technologies, including the Internet, have dramatically increased the number of media channels or "voices" available to individuals around the world. Paralleling the increase in the number of channels available has been an increase in the conglomeration of media ownership.

Arguably, if the managers of media companies are attempting to profit maximize or revenue maximize, they are pursuing content that maximizes general or target audiences. To that extent performance should theoretically be independent of ownership, while profits benefit from scale economies and other synergies. Thus, an argument can be made that ownership issues are moot because the audience is the ultimate arbiter of content and that the empowerment of the user would potentially increase under the increased interactivity and choices resulting from future bandwidth expansion associated with technological convergence. Currently, the expanding number of narrowcast channels available to consumers is a significant enhancement to the marketplace of ideas regardless of industrial structure.

A confounding factor is that evidence is mounting that the trend toward conglomeration has peaked and that the next trend may be spin-offs resulting in deconglomeration. This would be based on a belief that the securities market would value a company's parts individually more than they value the company as a conglomerate. If the value of the common stock prices of media conglomerates are to be used as a guide, there is evidence that some media M&A activity was strategically and financially misguided.

Finally, as discussed earlier, media companies are subject to the same antitrust review and economic performance requirements as other businesses. Thus, the burden appears to be on the critics of conglomeration to prove substantive harm that goes beyond innuendo.

## FURTHER READING

Bagdikian, B. H. (2000). *The media monopoly* (6th ed.). Boston: Beacon Hill.
Baker, C. (2002). *Media, markets, and democracy.* New York: Cambridge Press.
Compaine, B., & Gomery, D. (2000). *Who owns the media? Competition and concentration in the mass media industry* (3rd ed.). Mahwah, NJ: Lawrence Erlbaum Associates.
Porter, M. F. (1984). *Competitive strategy: techniques for analyzing industries and competitors.* New York: Free Press.

## REFERENCES

Bagdikian, B. H. (2000). *The media monopoly* (6th ed.). Boston: Beacon Hill.
Baker C. (2002). *Media, markets, and democracy.* New York: Cambridge Press.
Busterna, J. (1988). Trends in Daily Newspaper Ownership. *Journalism Quarterly, 65,* 831–838.
Columbia Journalism Review. (2002). *Who owns what?* Retrieved from www.cjr.org.
Compaine, B., & Gomery, D. (2000). *Who owns the media? Competition and concentration in the mass media industry* (3rd ed.). Mahwah, NJ: Lawrence Erlbaum Associates.
The Economist. (2002, May 25). *Special report: Media conglomerates tangled webs,* 67–69.
FCC. (2001, September). *Review of radio industry.*
FCC Report and Order. (1999, August 5). *In the Matter of Review of the Commission's Regulations Governing Television Broadcasting, MM Docket No. 91-22.*

Financial Times. (2002). *Capitalism in Crisis.* Retrieved from www.ft.com

Hollywood Reporter. (2001, August). *Independent producers and distributors special issue, 1.*

*In the matter of cross-ownership of broadcast stations and newspapers, newspaper/radio cross-ownership waiver policy; MM Docket No. 01-235 and 96-197,* FCC 01-262.

Kagan Word Media, May 16, 2002. As cited in *Chief executive resigns position as Adelphia expands inquiry. New York Times National Edition,* p. C-1.

*Local Television Ownership Rules MM Docket No. 91-221 and 87-8.* (FCC, 1999).

Newspaper Preservation Act. (1970) 15 U.S.C.A. Sec. 1801 et. seq.

Ordonez, J. (2002, February 26). *Pop singer failing a chord despite millions spent by MCA. Wall Street Journal,* p. A-1.

Orwall, B., & Peers, M. (2002, May 10). *The message of media mergers: So far they haven't been successful. Wall Street Journal,* p. C-1.

Peers, M. (2002, May 5). In shift AOL to de-emphasize convergence. *Wall Street Journal,* p A-1.

Peers, M. (2003, January 14). Reality time: Facing crisis media giants scrounge for fresh strategies. *Wall Street Journal,* p. C-1.

Porter, M. F. (1984). *Competitive strategy: Techniques for analyzing industries and competitors.* New York: Free Press.

Project on Media Ownership. (2002). Retrieved from www.bettertv.org

Reed, S. F., & LaJoux, A. R. (1998). *The art of M&A: A merger and acquisition handbook.* New York: McGraw-Hill.

*Reply Comments of Consumer Union, Consumer Federation of America, Media Access Project, Center for Digital Democracy, and the Civil Rights Forum.* (2002, February 15). MM Docket No. 01-235 and MM Docket No. 96-197 (p. 33).

*Review of the radio industry.* (2001, September). FCC, Mass Media Bureau. Retrieved from www.fcc.gov/mb/crsptpg.html

Scherer, F. M., & Ross, D. (1990). *Industrial market structure and economic performance* (3rd ed.). Boston: Houghton Mifflin.

Schiller, D. (1999). *Digital capitalism: Networking the global market system.* Cambridge: MIT Press.

SG Cowen Securities Corporation. (2002, March 25). *AOL Time Warner Inc.* New York: Analyst Report.

Storer Communications Inc. (1985). *Shareholders proxy statement.* Washington, DC: Securities and Exchange Commission.

*Turner Broadcasting, Inc. v. FCC,* 520 U.S. 180 (1997).

Wall Street Journal. (2001, September 6). *Time Warner, EMI face the music in Brussels,* p. A-18.

# Chapter 4

# The Economics of International Media

**C. ANN HOLLIFIELD**
*University of Georgia*

In the last two decades of the 20th century, the rapid expansion of media companies into global markets significantly reshaped the industry's economic landscape. Particularly dramatic was the globalization of the electronic media—telephone, radio, television, and cable. Prior to the 1980s, those media sectors were largely domestic industries that, in many countries, were dominated by public service broadcast networks.

The seemingly sudden globalization of the media industry resulted from a series of technological, political, and economic changes in the 1980s. The development of satellite and cable technologies created new demand for programming and made worldwide distribution of programming faster and more economically feasible. The shift in developed countries from industrial to information- and service-based economies led to changes in global trade regimes that made foreign expansion easier for media companies. Finally, the collapse of the Eastern Bloc and the development of many Asian nations' economies investments increased global consumer demand for media products and opened new markets. The result was a dramatic increase in foreign direct investment (FDI) by media companies. By 2002, 100% of the top 10 media groups and at least 64% of the top 25 media groups had some form of overseas operations or investment (Higgins, McClellan, & Kerschbaumer, 2001).

Among the largest media corporations, the extent of international expansion was breathtaking. By the end of the 1990s, Australian-based News Corp.'s media products reached nearly 75% of the world's population (News Corp., 1998) or 500 million people in 70 countries every 24 hours (News Corp., 1999). Similarly, in 2001, an estimated 1.2 billion people used at least one Disney product (Walt Disney Co., 2001), AOL Time Warner's CNN subsidiary alone reached more than 1 billion people in 212 countries (AOL Time Warner, 2002), and Discovery Communications reported more than 700 million subscribers to its various cable channels in more than 150 countries (Hoover's Online, 2002).

The globalization of the media industry was an immensely important development that concerned critics, policymakers, and mass-communication scholars. Global expansion has fundamentally changed both the economics of the media industry and the management of media companies. It has redefined the market for media products and, therefore, has changed the selection and production processes that determine what media products and messages reach the public. Finally, the dominance of transnational media corporations in the global market raises questions about the effects of foreign ownership and media production on media performance, the ability of the media to serve the public interest, and the long-term effects of media on society.

There are a number of ways to approach the study of international media economics, including the economic motivations and environmental factors that encourage global media expansion and international trade in media products. This chapter examines both topics.

## ECONOMIC AND ENVIRONMENTAL FACTORS BEHIND MEDIA GLOBALIZATION

The globalization of the media industry was not a 20th-century phenomenon. Throughout history there has been a vibrant international trade in media products, and foreign ownership of media companies such as book publishers has not been uncommon. But if the media's global expansion was not unprecedented, its pace and extent undeniably increased during the last two decades of the 20th century.

The trend was set into motion by a series of complex technological, economic, and political forces that interacted with one another to reshape media economics. Underlying the process were the fundamental economic characteristics of information and entertainment products, which create specific incentives for producers to distribute to the largest possible number of consumers. However, despite the long-standing economic advantages of global distribution, until the 1980s international expansion was difficult for media corporations to achieve, particularly for those in the electronic media. In order to understand the issues and implications of media globalization, it is necessary to understand the forces behind the globalization trend.

### The Economic Characteristics of Information

The economic characteristics of information and entertainment products are a key factor driving media companies to expand globally. Priest (1994) identified 12 different economic characteristics of information, and a number of them make it highly advantageous for media companies to move into foreign markets.

First, information and entertainment products are *public goods*, meaning they can be consumed by one user without diminishing the quantity of the product available to others. Consequently, any number of people can watch a program or film over an indefinite period of time—days, weeks, or even years—without forcing the producer to incur additional production costs. Thus, the product can be resold endlessly, and, once the program's initial production costs are covered, the revenue generated from additional sales is largely profit. That means media corporations reap tremendous financial returns from achieving the widest possible distribution of their products.

Second, information products also have a high production-to-reproduction cost ratio. They are expensive to produce but relatively inexpensive to reproduce for mass distribution. In recent years, digital technologies have further lowered reproduction costs, making global distribution easier and more profitable.

Third, media production is characterized by high levels of uncertainty and risk. The full value of any information or entertainment product cannot be assessed until after the producer has paid almost the full cost of creating it. There are only limited opportunities to test market specific media products (e.g., a film, book, or CD), and it can be done only in the late stages of production after most development costs have been incurred. This increases the financial risk in every act of new production and means producers must sell each product to the largest possible number of consumers in order to recover the development costs of both successful and unsuccessful productions.

Adding to the already high-production risks is the fact that media products' low-reproduction costs make them susceptible to theft, known as *piracy*. Because consumers generally buy information and entertainment products only once—they don't buy multiple copies of the same book, CD, or film—producers lose their one opportunity to sell to a specific customer, if the customer buys a pirated version. This gives media companies an incentive to consolidate in order to offset the costs of piracy through economies of scale and scope (Priest, 1994). Global expansion is, of course, a form of industry consolidation.

Fourth, information products, in particular, are highly instrumental, meaning their value to society is much greater than their market value and can never fully be measured. Economists describe the current global economy as an "information economy" where information has become a key input—and in some cases, *the* key input into other economic processes. In the closing decades of the 20th century, innovation became the engine driving the economies of the developed world. Innovations, however, build upon other innovations and, thus, the ability to rapidly access information about emerging ideas is critical to the innovation process. As governments and economists recognized this, the global demand for information products such as books, technical magazines, and scientific journals grew rapidly.

Information and entertainment products also have economic characteristics that hinder their value in global markets, and which, therefore, increase the challenges of global media distribution. The relevance of a specific media product varies widely from consumer to consumer, a characteristic that increases production risks. The relevancy issue is even more problematic in cross-national environments because media products, whether entertainment or information, are language and culture-based.

At the very least, media products sold into global markets are subject to a cultural discount in pricing (Doyle, 2002; Hoskins, McFadyen, & Finn, 1997). That discount varies depending on the degree of the cultural relevancy. Humor, for example, generally does not travel well. Consequently, the prices a media company can charge in foreign markets for situation comedies are usually low compared to what it can get for films and, in some cases, dramas.

For example, in 2001, U.S.-produced sitcoms were selling for $1,600 per one-half hour to Thailand and an average of $2,250 across Scandinavia, but $25,000 per one-half hour to the United Kingdom where language and culture are more closely aligned with the United States (U.S. Program Price Guide, 2001). In contrast, the same year an hour of U.S.-produced drama was selling for $1,400 in Thailand—a slightly lower per-minute price than for sitcoms—but $7,000 in Scandinavia and $150,000 in the United Kingdom. However, even the relevancy of dramas and documentaries varies according to the cultural distance between the country of origin and the country of import. Such differences make it difficult to predict how successful any given media product will be in the international market.

But these economic characteristics are fundamental to the nature of information and entertainment products. As such, they always have been an element of media economics and do not, in themselves, explain why media companies began aggressively moving into international markets in the last decades of the 20th century. The timing of the most recent period of global media expansion was caused by a series of simultaneous changes in the global political economy and communication technologies.

## Changes in the Global Political Economy

In the 1970s and 1980s, the global political economy underwent a major transformation. New communication technologies allowed parent companies to quickly exchange information with foreign-based subsidiaries, making it easier to coordinate far-flung operations and move products globally. Consequently, industrial production began shifting from high-cost developed nations to less-developed countries where labor and materials costs were lower. The United States and other developed nations found their economies being transformed from an industrial to an information base, with growth increasingly driven by innovation and service industries such as financial services, health care, and media.

For the United States, it was a period of significant economic transition. Even as America's industrial jobs were lost to foreign competition, U.S. policymakers recognized an opportunity. The United States was arguably *the* dominant player in the global information sector, including computer and telecommunications equipment and services and copyright industries such as films, books, music, and television. The film industry, for example, has been credited with being the only U.S. industry with a surplus balance of trade with every country in the world (Valenti, 2002), and the nation's copyright industries have long provided a critical offset to the U.S.'s hemorrhaging trade balance. By the mid-1980s, U.S. policymakers were recognizing the importance of the information and communication sectors to the overall health of the broader economy (Hollifield & Samarajiva, 1994; U.S. House of Representatives, 1981).

As a result, in the 1980s and 1990s, Congress, the Courts, and the Federal Communication Commission (FCC) moved to deregulate telecommunications and media industries in order to support their growth. Internationally, U.S. policymakers fought to ensure that the media, service, and information-sector industries were included in international trade agreements such as the Uruguay round of the General Agreement on Trade and Tariffs (GATT), the North American Free Trade Agreement (NAFTA), and later, the Trade-Related Aspects of Intellectual Property Rights (TRIPS), and World Trade Organization treaties (WTO). These trade agreements sought to force nations to open their markets to free trade in media products, something many countries were reluctant to do on both economic and cultural grounds.

U.S. negotiators had only limited success with their trade agenda. The various international treaties included media but generally permitted nations to exclude selected service sectors from market access and "Most Favored Nation" (MFN) trade rules, whereas less-developed nations were allowed to delay enforcing international copyright laws. Many countries, including Canada and the European Union nations, continue to stipulate the minimum amount of domestically produced programming that broadcasters have to carry (Doyle, 2002; Hoskins et al., 1997). For example, Europe's "Television Without Frontiers" directive requires that at least 50% of all content transmitted by European broadcasters be of European origin (Doyle, 2002).

There were other changes in the economic and political landscapes that also affected media globalization. Strong consumer economies emerged in a number of Asian and Latin American countries such as Argentina, Venezuela, Chile, Korea, Singapore, Taiwan, India, and China. With economic development came more demand for media products, creating opportunities for foreign direct investment, international joint ventures, and content exports.

Similarly, the collapse of the Eastern Bloc in 1989 opened new investment opportunities in Central and Eastern Europe. After the fall of the Berlin Wall, Western media incursions into Eastern Europe were so rapid that by 1994, up to 80% of the capital investment in Hungarian media came from the West (Gross, 2002; Sukosd, 1992). For some media corporations, Eastern Europe was their first attempt at foreign direct investment and laid the groundwork for future global expansion.

### The Effect of New Communication Technologies

At the same time that the global political economy was undergoing such dramatic change, new communication technologies emerged that encouraged a worldwide trend toward privatization and deregulation of communication industries. These trends reduced or eliminated many of the barriers to entry that had prevented media companies from investing overseas.

The 1983 breakup of the AT&T monopoly and subsequent deregulation of the telecommunications industry in the United States drastically reduced the price of telecommunications services and brought a flood of new communication technologies onto the U.S. market. By the late-1980s, other nations started deregulating telecommunications industries in order to gain the same advantages.

In the process, many countries opened their telecommunications industries to foreign investment. This trend often trickled over into the media sector at least in part because the emergence of digital technologies rapidly erased the technological barriers between telecommunications and media industries. Consequently, many nations, including the United States, eased some restrictions on foreign ownership of electronic media.

Even as nations restructured global telecommunications regimes, new technologies changed the face of the media business. Prior to the 1980s, the scarcity of spectrum meant that most nations had only two or three television broadcast channels and, in many countries, those operated as public service networks. However, the development of cable and satellite technologies made it inexpensive to deliver large numbers of television channels. This had two effects: The new channels spawned private commercial television industries in many countries for the first time and created a surge in worldwide demand for programming.

For example, in 1971, five countries in Western Europe had only one television channel, only two European nations had more than two channels

(*Screen Digest*, 2001c), and there was no such thing as a 24-hour channel. In contrast, by the late-1990s, at least 700 channels were available on satellites that reached Europe, many of them on the air 24/7 (European Audiovisual Observatory, 1997).[1] In 1999, Western European and Scandinavian networks acquired more than 80,590 hours of programming, much of it imported. Total programming sales in Eastern and Western Europe from all sources reached $3.7 billion, up 13.8% from 5 years before (*Screen Digest*, 2000, April 1).

The effect of all of these changes was to make it easier for media and telecommunications companies to expand internationally through both foreign direct investment and global exports. As a result, in the 1990s a new wave of media consolidation began, with much of the merger and acquisition activity occurring across national borders.

### The Changing Media as a Factor in Globalization

New communication technologies encouraged media globalization in another way: They fragmented domestic media markets by increasing competition for the audience's attention. In television, for example, cable, VCRs, direct-satellite broadcasting, the remote control, and the World Wide Web all helped significantly erode the broadcast networks' audience share. Film producers faced new competition from video rentals, cable premium channels, and pay-per-view services. For radio broadcasters, CD technology eroded the audience for broadcast music, and by the end of the 1990s satellite radio and online music swapping were posing new threats. Book and magazine publishers faced the possibility of Internet-delivered competition, while losing share to the explosion of electronic media, which competed for readers' time.

The increased competition for audiences led to declines in market share for media producers in most sectors. In the U.S. television market, the average number of hours Americans spent watching TV rose through the 1990s, but the average ratings for the major television networks dropped 50% during the last two decades of the 20th century. At the same time, the percentage of households tuned into the networks at any given time dropped from one half to one third (Adams & Eastman, 2001).

For radio, the numbers were arguably even worse. U.S. Census data showed that the average number of hours that American spent listening to radio fell 3% between 1993 and 1998 and were projected to continue falling until at least 2003 (U.S. Census Bureau, 1994, 2000). Newspapers faced similar declines. Between 1964 and 1997, average readership of newspapers on a weekly basis fell from 79.9% to 54.9% of the U.S. population (Newspaper Association of America, 1999), whereas the average number of hours each reader spent with the newspaper dropped almost 19% between 1994 and 1998 (U.S. Census Bureau, 1994, 2000).

U.S. media corporations were not alone in facing audience fragmentation. Producers in Europe and other regions also saw significant declines in audience share because of emerging media competition. Additionally, increased cultural diversity in national populations throughout the developed world further fragmented audiences. A global wave of immigration from less-developed to developed nations made mass audiences much less of a mass, increasing the percentage of the domestic audience for whom cultural relevancy *was* an issue. Simultaneously, in many countries such as the United States, minority populations gained significant economic power, attracting advertisers and encouraging the creation of targeted media such as Black Entertainment Television (BET). The loss of audience share in domestic markets from these combined factors provided yet another incentive for media companies to seek opportunities overseas.

## Changing Capital Markets

The shift in the global political economy and the media industry's competitive environment coincided with another important change: the standards by which capital markets and investors evaluated publicly held corporations.

In the 1980s and 1990s, a variety of factors including government deregulation and industry mergers created impressive growth in corporate profits and stock prices across most industries. But the higher stock prices were based, in part, on the expectation that profit growth would continue. In the media sector, however, industry consolidation resulted in heavy debt loads. Because investors did not adjust their profit expectations to account for the debt-service costs companies took on as they consolidated, executives faced pressure to find new revenue sources so profits could be maintained even as interest costs grew.

During the same period, corporate governance changed in key ways. Many companies started making stock options a major part of executive compensation. That meant top executives were personally affected by the financial performance of the companies they directed. Consequently, media executives had strong incentives to seek steady revenue and profit growth, even as their domestic markets were eroding. Overseas expansion was one strategy for meeting investors' expectations for growth in the face of increased competition, declining market share, and rising costs.

In summary, although the economic characteristics of information have always provided an incentive for media producers to seek the widest possible distribution of their products, it was not until the last two decades of the 20th century that a combination of changes in technology and the global political economy encouraged nations to deregulate and privatize their media industries. The process of deregulation and privatization made media cor-

porations' rapid global expansion possible, even as intensified competition, audience fragmentation, and changes in capital markets made it in
increasingly desirable.

## INTERNATIONAL TRADE IN MEDIA PRODUCTS

### Film & Television

Historically, the United States has dominated the television and film exports. For example, in 2000, 73.7% of European theater ticket sales were for
films from the United States (*Screen Digest*, 2001a), whereas 80.6% of the
films released in Australia in 2001 were American (*Screen Digest*, 2002b).
Similarly, in 1999 71% of the fiction programming imported by European
television channels originated in the United States, up from 69.8% in 1994
(European Audiovisual Observatory, 2001). By some estimates, the United
States accounted for 75% of all television programming exports worldwide
through the decade (Hoskins & McFadyen, 1991; Johns, 1999).

As film production and marketing costs have risen, the global market
has become much more important for producers. Only an average of 2 out
of 10 U.S. films are able to recover their investment costs through domestic
ticket sales (Valenti, 2002), making receipts from overseas markets crucial.
Similarly, the use of deficit financing for television production, the fragmentation of the U.S. audience, and the end of the Financial and Syndication rules in 1995 have made it increasingly difficult for television
producers to meet rising production costs. Foreign distribution of programming helps offset some of the negative effects of the changing television market structure and generates revenues that can be used for future
projects (Fry, 2001; Turow, 1992).

Global distribution also offers producers other benefits. Wider distribution creates more opportunities to sell merchandise and secondary products linked to TV and film productions, an increasingly important source of
revenue. Being in multiple markets around the world also can help stabilize
corporate revenues. An economic decline in one region of the world may be
offset by growth in another (Lico, 2001).

As a result of these benefits, the appeal of proposed film projects to overseas audiences has become an important consideration for studios. In 2000,
$2.2 billion of the revenues for the six major Hollywood studios came from
outside North America: $1.2 billion from Europe, $668 million from Asia
and Australia, and $328 million from Latin America (*Screen Digest*, 2001b).
That represents about 28.5% or just less than one third of the $7.7 billion in
total revenue generated by the film industry that year (Schaffler, 2001). Similarly, U.S. studios now produce television series directly for overseas markets, without offering them for domestic syndication.

The United States dominates the international film and television industries for a number of reasons. U.S. producers gain cost advantages through the economies of scale provided by the size of the American market. That also makes the issue of cultural discount less important, because U.S. producers can expect to recoup most of their production costs in their home market where the cultural discount does not apply (Hoskins et al., 1997).

The comparative quality of American media productions also confers an advantage. The size and affluence of the U.S. market make it possible for U.S. producers to undertake high-budget projects that would be riskier for producers in smaller markets, who would be more dependent on culturally discounted overseas markets to recoup the costs of top talent, expensive locations and innovative special effects.

U.S. studios also draw upon the world's largest pool of media talent and technical expertise. The creation of *knowledge communities*, which form when a critical mass of experts in a given field locate in the same geographic area, allows professionals to engage in a constant exchange of information, ideas, and knowledge. Media knowledge communities formed around film and radio production in Southern California and New York early in the 20th century and later expanded to include television. They were further enhanced in the 1960s and 1970s by computer hardware and software expert groups that developed along the West Coast and in New England, within easy reach of the media hubs of Southern California and New York. At least partly as a result of this convergence of expert communities, U.S. film and television producers unveiled a constant stream of major innovations in film and television production techniques during the last two decades of the 20th century.

Although the United States dominates television and film exports, it is by no means the only player. European films picked up more than 61.5 million admissions out of the North American market in 2001 (*Screen Digest*, 2002a). Moreover, three of the six major U.S. film studios are actually owned by foreign conglomerates, which also hold some of the United States' leading television production studios. Japan-based Sony Corporation owns Sony Pictures; Australia-based News Corporation owns the Twentieth Century-Fox studio; and the French water-utility and media corporation Vivendi owns Universal Studios (Compaine & Gomery, 2000).

The United States also is not the only factor in the international television distribution market. In 1999, Western European nations broadcast an average of 1,983 hours of programming imported from other European countries, primarily Germany, the United Kingdom, Spain, France, and Italy (Origin of European Fiction, 2001). European nations with strong economies, established broadcast industries, and high-consumer demand for films tended to import less U.S.-produced fictional programming (Dupagne & Waterman, 1998; Jayakar & Waterman, 2000). Research showed that imported programs increasingly were used as filler in non-primetime hours or secondary channels even in countries with high-import levels. Primetime hours and leading channels tended to be programmed with domestic content (De Bens & de Smaele, 2001; Fry, 2001), which gave producers the largest audiences for expensive original programming and increased the likelihood that the programs eventually would generate revenues from syndication and merchandising.

On the other side of the transaction, the U.S. television market has remained largely resistant to imported programming. Public Television and some cable networks use British dramas and comedies, but U.S. audiences generally are perceived as unwilling to accept dubbing or subtitles, so relatively few non-English language programs or films make it into the U.S.'s English-language electronic media market. Despite that, producers overseas remain interested in the American market because of its size, affluence, and potential for programming-related merchandise sales (Fry, 2001).

One growth area in U.S. programming imports in the 1990s was the non-English language media. The expansion of the U.S.'s Spanish-language population spurred the development of Spanish-language media, including at least three television networks and numerous local radio and television stations. Univision, the United States' largest Spanish-language network, was watched by an estimated 3.5 million people each day in 2002 (Rutenberg, 2002), while number 2, Telemundo, attracted another 1 million viewers. Much of the programming on Spanish-language networks and stations was imported from Latin America and Europe. Similarly, in areas of the country with large immigrant populations, cable channels that air imported programming in other languages were common.

In general, however, audiences around the world prefer locally produced content (Straubhaar, 1991). Consequently, a strong international market has emerged in *format sales,* the sale or licensing of a successful program concept that is then reproduced in some form overseas using local talent, thus eliminating the cultural discount. *All in the Family, Three's Company, America's Funniest Home Videos,* and *Who Wants to Be a Millionaire* are just a few of the hit programs in the United States that originated in other countries (Fry, 2001; Lico, 2001). Similarly, American programs such as *Sesame Street* and *Charlie's Angels* have been sold as formats to other countries (Lico, 2001).

Another trend that reflects the issue of local preference is the increase in international coproductions. The number of cross-border coproductions climbed 68% between 1990 and 1996 in European Union countries alone (*M2 Presswire,* 1998), claiming 9.4% of the European market for fiction programming in 1999, up from 4.9% in 1994 (European Audiovisual Observatory, 2001). International coproductions serve a number of purposes: They bring a multicultural perspective to the creative process and help reduce the problem of cultural relevance. They also help producers avoid import quotas by allowing the content to be classified as domestic, and they provide new sources of capital, mitigating financial risks.

Because of the growing value of both programming and related merchandise, television programmers around the world began in the late 1990s to develop global brands. BBC, CNN, Time Warner, Disney, Viacom, News Corp., Discovery Communications, and even NBC launched global roll-outs and marketing campaigns for their channels. Although a relatively recent trend in the industry, the development of global programming brands almost certainly will be one of the industry's key strategies in the foreseeable future.

## Magazines

The international market for print media is more varied than that for television and film content. The book and magazine industries have long histories of both transnational ownership and foreign trade. The newspaper industry, however, remains primarily a domestic industry, with comparatively low levels of foreign ownership and little demand for imported product. Nevertheless, the United Nations Educational Scientific and Cultural Organization (UNESCO) estimated that in 1995, international trade in printed materials including books, pamphlets, newspapers, and periodicals was more than (U.S.) $14.3 billion.

The magazine industry, in particular, is characterized by transnational ownership and global distribution. The content of consumer magazines tends to focus on topics of broad interest and appeal, so it faces fewer problems with cultural relevancy and cultural discount. Additionally, advertisers are increasingly interested in reaching worldwide audiences, providing a major incentive for magazine publishers to expand their markets (Doyle, 2002). The globalization of the economy also has increased the global demand for business and trade publications, as businesses try to monitor the business environment and competitors in their far-flung markets. Similarly, the development of the knowledge economy has greatly increased international demand for scientific, professional, and academic journals. Finally, in most nations, magazines are not subjected to the same level of scrutiny and regulation as the television and film industries, making it easier for publishers to both export to, and invest in, foreign markets.

Although the United States dominates electronic media industries, there is more balanced international competition in the magazine publishing industry. European publishers have a large share of the international market and have made significant inroads into the U.S. market. Reed-Elsevier, the largest foreign-owned publisher in the United States based on revenues, published 76 titles in the United States in 1997, most of them in the area of business and trade. Bertlesmann, Germany's largest publisher, ranked as the fifth largest magazine publisher in the United States in 1997, based on total circulation per issue, distributing such titles as *Family Circle, McCall's, Inc.,* and *Parents.* The French company Hachette-Filipacci was the foreign-based magazine publisher with the most consumer titles in the United States that year, including *Woman's Day* (Compaine & Gomery, 2000).

But U.S. publishers also have a strong presence overseas. Hearst publishes 107 magazines in 28 languages in more than 100 countries (Hearst Corp., 2002). AOL-Time Warner publishes approximately 140 magazine titles, many of which are distributed overseas, and in 2001 the company acquired IPC, the United Kingdom's leading magazine publisher with 80 titles (AOL Time Warner, 2002).

Language and cultural differences do, of course, affect the ability of magazine publishers to operate internationally. Content must be translated and adaptations must be made to stories, pictures, recipes, and project designs to account for local views, tastes, conditions, and the availability of supplies. But such adaptations are usually fairly easy to manage with a local staff. Less easy to deal with are issues of literacy and affluence, which are both strongly related to demand for magazines by readers and advertisers.

## The Newspaper Industry

In contrast with the magazine sector, the newspaper industry has remained largely local in nature. However, in the past 25 years, the level of transnational ownership of newspapers has increased. For example, News Corp., an Australian company, has newspaper holdings in the United Kingdom, New Zealand, Fiji, Papua New Guinea, and the United States, in addition to Australia (News Corp., 2002). Bertlesmann's subsidiary, Gruner & Jahr, owns newspapers in Yugoslavia, Romania, and Slovakia (Bertlesmann, 2002), and indeed, many Western companies, including Germany's Axel Springer Verlag have invested in Central European newspapers.

But despite such examples, transnational ownership of newspapers remains relatively limited compared to other media sectors. Newspapers are still primarily a local product, with little demand for them outside of their home markets and even less in the international arena. Only a few highly specialized newspapers such as the *Wall Street Journal, USA Today, International Herald Tribune,* and England's *Financial Times* circulate widely in markets outside of their home nations. Research has shown that although many newspapers now are putting their content online—meaning that technically, at least, they are reaching a global audience—relatively few users of online newspapers are from outside the papers' local circulation areas and online newspaper content remains largely targeted to the interests of local readers (Chyi & Sylvie, 2001).

Worldwide, UNESCO estimated that the combined international trade in newspapers and periodical journals of all types topped (U.S.) $4.6 billion in 1995 (UNESCO, 1999).[2]

## The Book Publishing Industry

The book industry also is a truly global industry. A number of the largest publishers that sell into the U.S. market are foreign corporations, including Bertlesmann, which holds the Random House, Bantam, Doubleday, and Dell imprints; News Corp., which is the parent company of HarperCollins; Pearson, a company based in the United Kingdom that owns Penguin, Addison-Wesley, Putnam and Viking; and Thomson, a Canadian-based company (Compaine & Gomery, 2000; Greco, chap. 6, this volume).

Exports are an important source of revenue for U.S. publishers, generating about $1.7 billion or 7% of the revenues generated by the book publishing sector in the United States in 2000 (see Greco, chap. 6, this volume).

The book publishing industry is similar to the film and television production industries in being dependent on hits or blockbusters. This means publishers must try to reach the largest possible audience with successful titles because the majority of books do not generate a profit, and successful titles must cover their own production costs and the losses generated by failures. Consequently, publishers seek global distribution. However, the amount of text in books makes translation expensive and time-consuming and not cost-effective for most titles. As with all cultural products, books also suffer from issues of cultural relevancy as they cross borders, another factor in calculating the economics of international distribution.

For foreign publishers, on the other hand, the United States is an attractive market because of its size, affluence, and literacy rate. The magnitude of the market generates economies of scale, and the United States places no restrictions on foreign direct investment or imports of books. Revenues from U.S. book sales represented 35% of Bertelsmann's book sales worldwide in the late 1990s, and about 50% of Pearson's operating profit (Compaine & Gomery, 2000).

In the global market, book publishing is a major export industry. UNESCO estimated that international trade in books and pamphlets topped (U.S.) $9.7 billion in 1995, with the United States serving as the world's largest importer of books at (U.S.) $1.4 billion (UNESCO, 1999). However, UNESCO data showed that only about 25 nations reported a positive trade balance in books for even 1 year in the 3-year period of 1995 and 1997, and far fewer reported positive balances in books for 5 or more years between 1991 and 1997.

## The Radio Industry

The radio industry remains an essentially local medium, although there are indications that may change in the next decade. The primary content of the radio industry—music—sometimes has global appeal, but the greatest demand in the music sector is for local artists. Additionally, most nations limit the amount of foreign ownership allowed in broadcast operations. Consequently, foreign direct investment in radio remains relatively limited.

Despite these factors, global expansion is beginning in the radio industry. Some countries have eased restrictions on foreign investment, and media corporations are taking advantage of the new opportunities. Clear Channel, the largest owner of radio stations in the United States, had investments in 250 stations in foreign markets by 2002, including Mexico, Australia, New Zealand, and Europe (Clear Channel, 2002). Walt Disney Co. launched Radio Disney in Argentina and was expecting to expand it across Latin America and into Europe and Asia (Walt Disney Co., 2001).

Equally importantly, new technological developments that affect the cost structures in radio may encourage global expansion. Low-cost satellite transmission has led many companies in the radio sector to cut costs by moving to automated programming. The use of voice tracking and other prepackaged programming reduces radio's local focus. Similarly, subscription satellite radio channels are not designed to be local media (see Albarran, chap. 10, this volume). These developments may help create an international market for some types of prepackaged radio programming.

## The Recorded Music Industry

Other media sectors are far more international. The music industry is truly global in scope in terms of both ownership and distribution. The industry is dominated by five major corporations—Warner (AOL Time Warner), Universal (Seagrams/Vivendi), EMI, BMG (Bertlesmann), and Sony, which between them are estimated to control between 80% and 90% of the worldwide revenues generated by the industry (Compaine & Gomery, 2000; Hull, 2000). Of the "Big 5" in the music industry, only one company, Warner, is a U.S.-based corporation.

In all, global sales in the music recording industry were estimated at (U.S.) $33.7 billion in 2001 (International Federation of the Phonographics Industry [IFPI], 2002). A handful of the largest markets including the United States, Japan, and the United Kingdom account for the majority of sales (IFPI, 2002).

The economics of the recorded music industry are based on economies of scale, making global sales desirable. However, the sale of music encounters significant relevancy issues—both in terms of cultural relevancy and relevancy to the individual consumer. One of the primary strategies of the "Big Five" is to affiliate with small companies and independent producers around the world (Burnett, 1992). This allows the "majors" to identify local artists who have the potential to develop a global fan base, as well as to tap revenues generated by those who may not have worldwide appeal but are successful locally (AOL Time Warner, 2002).

As a result, some of the industry's most significant growth has been in the area of local music. In 2000, recordings by local artists rose to 68% of all music sales worldwide, up from 58% in 1991. In 2001, 7 out of every 10 records or CDs sold worldwide featured local artists, with growth in sales occurring across all regions of the world except the Middle East and Africa (IFPI, 2002).

## The New Media Industry

The new media sector also cannot be ignored as a factor in the globalization of media. The emergence of the Internet and World Wide Web as public-access media in the 1990s made international distribution possible for virtually all media producers. However, with more than 2 billion Web sites around the world, competition for Web audiences is intense and only a few media sectors, such as the newsletter industry, have developed viable business models for distributing content over the Web. Although media content uploaded to the Web is, by definition, available to global audiences, most of it continues to be produced primarily for the local or regional audience. In media sectors such as radio and newspapers, the primary revenue stream comes from local advertisers, and the economic value of global online distribution is questionable.

One area in which the new media industry and the Internet have had significant impact is in content piracy. The high initial production costs for media, coupled with low reproduction and distribution costs make media products prime targets for theft. Digital media technologies make reproduction even easier and less expensive. The recorded music industry, for example, saw global music sales fall 9.2% in value and 11.2% in units for the first 6 months of 2002 from the previous year, which also had seen significant worldwide sales declines (IFPI, 2002). Research in countries most affected by falling sales indicated downloading music from the Internet was a major factor, with respondents to surveys saying they were burning their own CDs rather than buying commercial product. Similarly, the film industry estimated that piracy costs U.S. film producers more than $3 billion annually, although estimates vary (Valenti, 2002).

In the context of global media economics, then, digital technologies present a conundrum. They lower production and distribution costs for some types of media products and make it easier for media companies to capture marketing synergies. However, few effective models for actually selling content over the Internet have emerged, even as digital technologies have facilitated both the theft and the international distribution of pirated media products.

## THE SOCIAL IMPLICATIONS OF INTERNATIONAL MEDIA

The rapid expansion of media corporations into global markets over the past 25 years has generated many concerns among critics and observers. The media's importance lies in the critical roles they play in government and civil society, their long-term effects on culture and society and, in the era of the knowledge economy, their role as an engine of economic development.

One of the primary concerns about media globalization is that it may allow a handful of corporations to control much of the news and information available to people around the world. Critics fear that global media consolidation will reduce the quality, diversity, and independence of the content audiences receive. For example, with fewer competitors, there would be less likelihood that a story damaging to the parent company's interests would make its way to the public. This becomes increasingly important as media companies consolidate into corporate conglomerates with major holdings in nonmedia industries. NBC, for example, is owned by General Electric, a major U.S. defense contractor. Media corporations' market power and their worldwide dominance of information creation and distribution also potentially could give them tremendous influence with governments.

Critics of global media also fear the loss of local media. Media consolidation has encouraged companies to capture economies of scale by programming on the national and international level. U.S. film studios, for example, consider a project's global appeal before greenlighting it. U.S. television station groups negotiate syndicated programming deals for all their markets, paying more attention to the savings gained through multiple-market buys than to the programming needs of specific local audiences. Television and radio duopolies in local markets have encouraged the elimination of some local news operations.

Another issue is the homogenization of culture. Research has demonstrated that media have long-term effects on society, influencing such things as values, language, and behavior. As media companies generate content for global audiences, there is concern that cultures will become increasingly homogenized and indigenous cultural values will be lost. Particularly vulnerable to the cultural influences of global media would be members of ethnic or language groups that are comparatively small in size. Because of the economics of media production, such groups would be more likely to import the majority of the media content that reaches them as opposed to producing media for themselves.

The potential economic implications of media globalization are equally important. The media industry is, itself, a major economic force in developed countries. It generates jobs, taxes, and export revenues. Global media companies command tremendous market power and have the potential to undermine local media industries as they move into smaller foreign markets. Major media enterprises are accused of "dumping" content into foreign markets in an effort to drive out domestic competitors through price wars. Less developed countries fear the destruction of their domestic commercial content industries, which would make them more dependent on

foreign producers for media. Such a situation would have both economic
and cultural implications.

The knowledge economy is another critical factor in the debate. In a
world economy driven by innovation, rapid access to information is a necessary condition for full participation. Media corporations, however, are interested only in those markets where consumers are sufficiently affluent to
pay for content. Consequently, there have been few efforts by the major
world media corporations to invest in Africa and other economically struggling regions. There also is at least some evidence that efforts to tighten the
enforcement of international copyright laws in developing nations are related to reductions in local production of education and scientific materials
(Hollifield, Vlad, & Becker, 2003). Critics charge that media corporations'
market-driven investment and copyright enforcement strategies harden
the gap between the world's information rich and information poor, making it increasingly difficult for struggling nations to progress economically.

Not all of the implications of global media are negative. Just as access to
information is necessary for economic participation, so is it necessary for
the operation of democratic political systems. Technologies such as satellites, faxes and the Internet have made it harder for authoritarian governments to control information, helping to empower individuals and groups
in many nations.

Global media also are credited with helping to spread values such as
equality for women and minorities, freedom of speech and democracy, and
tolerance for diversity (Demers, 1999). They are seen by some as an integra-
tive force, helping to bring world communities together, providing more
information about the world than small, local media companies can afford
to produce, and countering the often nationalistic messages of local media.

Even in developed countries, technological developments, the changing
political economy, and the global spread of media have meant that the
range and variety of information now available to people is exponentially
greater than it was 25 years ago. Consequently, even as some critics fear the
potential for global control of information by a handful of major corporations, others counter that the same technological and political forces that facilitated worldwide media expansion also have made more content
available to audiences from more sources than at any time in world history.

## CONCLUSION

Globalization has been one of the most important trends in the media industry in the past 25 years. Driven by economic, technical, and political factors, it has transformed the industry's structure and economics and is
increasingly influential in shaping content and production decisions. But
without major shifts in national and international information and commu-

nication policies worldwide since the 1970s, the industry's global expansion would not have been possible at the levels currently seen, no matter how economically advantageous it might have been for media corporations. Consequently, policy remains a powerful tool to be used in the future to balance conflicts of interest between media corporations and the countries and regions in which they operate.

Finally, although there has been a great deal of discussion worldwide about the globalization of the media industry and its social and economic implications, there has been relatively little empirical research on the topic. Most studies of media globalization have focused on macroeconomic and policy issues. There has been relatively little research on the actual firm-level behaviors and decisions of media companies as they operate in foreign markets and the effects of those behaviors on the countries in which they occur (Hollifield, 2001). Much remains to be learned about the economics, management and effects of media companies as they move into a truly global business environment.

## FURTHER READING

Compaine, B. M., & Gomery, D. (2000). *Who owns the media? Competition and concentration in the mass media industry.* Mahwah, NJ: Lawrence Erlbaum Associates.
Demers, D. (1999). *Global media: Menace or messiah?* Cresskill, NJ: Hampton Press.
Doyle, G. (2002). *Understanding media economics.* London: Sage.
Gershon, R. A. (1997). *The transnational media corporation: Global messages and free market competition.* Mahwah, NJ: Lawrence Erlbaum Associates.
Hoskins, C., McFadyen, S., & Finn, A. (1997). *Global television and film: An introduction to the economics of the business.* Oxford: Oxford University Press.

## REFERENCES

Adams, W. J., & Eastman, S. T. (2002). Prime-time network entertainment programming. In S. T. Eastman & D. A. Ferguson (Eds.), *Broadcast/Cable/Web Programming: Strategies and Practices* (pp. 111–150). Belmont, CA: Wadsworth.
*AOL Time Warner.* (2002). Retrieved from http://www.aoltimewarner.com/corporate_information/index.adp
Bertlesmann. (2002). *Gruner + Jahr facts and figures.* Retrieved from http://www.bertelsmann.com/divisions/gruner_jahr/facts/facts.cfm
Burnett, R. (1992). The implications of ownership changes on concentration and diversity in the phonogram industry. *Communication Research, 19*(8), 749–769.
Chyi, H. I., & Sylvie, G. (2001). The medium is global, the content is not: The role of geography in online newspaper markets. *Journal of Media Economics, 14*(4), 231–248.
Clear Channel. (2002). Clear Channel International reaches 65 countries. Retrieved from http://www.clearchannel.com/International/
Compaine, B. M., & Gomery, D. (2000). *Who owns the media? Competition and concentration in the mass media industry.* Mahwah, NJ: Lawrence Erlbaum Associates.

De Bens, E., & de Smaele, H. (2001). The inflow of American television fiction on European broadcasting channels revisited. *European Journal of Communication, 16*(1), 51–76.
Demers, D. (1999). *Global media: Menace or messiah?* Cresskill, NJ: Hampton Press.
Doyle, G. (2002). *Understanding media economics.* London: Sage.
Dupagne, M., & Waterman, D. (1998). Determinants of U.S. television fiction imports in Western Europe. *Journal of Broadcasting & Electronic Media, 42*(2), 208–220.
European Audiovisual Observatory. (1997). *Statistical yearbook.* Strasbourg: Council of Europe.
European Audiovisual Observatory. (2001). *Statistical yearbook.* Strasbourg: Council of Europe.
Fry, A. (2001). Europe and programming: A global perspective. *TV Trends, 3*(4), 6–9.
Gross, P. (2002). Entangled evolutions: Media and democratization in Eastern Europe. Washington, DC: Woodrow Wilson Press & Johns Hopkins University Press.
Hearst Corp. (2002). *The Hearst Corporation.* Retrieved from http://www.hearstcorp.com/
Higgins, J. M., McClellan, S., & Kerschbaumer, K. (2001, August 27). Top 25 media companies. *Broadcasting & Cable,* 17.
Hollifield, C. A. (2001). Crossing borders: Media management research in a global media environment. *Journal of Media Economics, 14*(3), 133–146.
Hollifield, A., & Samarajiva, R. (1994). Changing discourses in U.S. international information-communication policy: From free flow to competitive advantage? *Gazette, 54,* 121–143.
Hollifield, C. A., Vlad, T., & Becker, L. B. (2003). The effects of international copyright law on national economic development. In L. B. Becker & T. Vlad (Eds.), *Copyright and consequences: United States and Eastern European perspectives* (pp. 163–202). New York: Hampton Press.
*Hoover's Online.* (2002). Discovery Communications, Inc. Retrieved from www.hoovers.com/co/capsure/1/0,2163,43731,00.html
Hoskins, C., & McFadyen, S. (1991). The U.S. competitive advantage in the global television market: Is it sustainable in the new broadcasting environment? *Canadian Journal of Communication, 16*(2). [Electronic version]. Retrieved from http://www.wlu.ca/~wwwpress/jrls/cjc/BackIssues/16.2/hoskins.html
Hoskins, C., McFadyen, S., & Finn, A. (1997). *Global television and film: An introduction to the economics of the business.* Oxford: Oxford University Press.
Hull, G. P. (2000). The structure of the recorded music industry. In A. N. Greco (Ed.), *The media and entertainment industries* (pp. 76–98). Boston: Allyn & Bacon.
International Federation of Phonographics Industry (IFPI). (2002). Global sales of recorded music down 9.2% in first half of 2002. Retrieved from http://www.ifpi.org/
Jayakar, K. P., & Waterman, D. (2000). The economics of American movie exports: An empirical analysis. *Journal of Media Economics, 13*(3), 153–169.
Johns, B. (1999). *Globalism cannot be a one-sided affair.* Speech before the Asia-Pacific Broadcasting Union General Assembly: World Trade in Audiovisual Services. Retrieved from http://www.abc.net.au/corp/pubs/s527202.htm
Lico, G. (2001). North American content: The move across the pond and beyond. *TV Trends, 3*(4), 2–5.
M2 Presswire. (1998, March 3). *Eurostat: Movies make an EU comeback.* Dow Jones Interactive Publications Library. Retrieved from http://nrstgls.djnr.com/cgi-bin/DJInteractive?cgi=WEB_FLAT_PAGE&page=wrapper/index&NRAUTOLOG=01Qa9EsCbxmT3PZ1fldaXYSwEA&NRLBRedirect=nrstgls&entry_point=1

News Corp. (1998). Annual report. Retrieved from http://www.newscorp.com/report98/cer.html

News Corp. (1999). Annual report. Retrieved from http://www.newscorp.com/report99/

News Corp. (2002). *Company news: Newspapers.* Retrieved from http://www.newscorp.com/index2.html

Newspaper Association of America. (1999). *Daily newspaper readership trends.* Retrieved from www.naa.org/marketscope/databank/tdnpr.htm

Origin of European fiction imported by Western European TV channels (2001). (# of hours broadcast). *TV Trends, 3*(4), 6.

Priest, W. C. (1994). *An information framework for the planning and design of "information highways."* Retrieved from http://www.eff.org/Groups/CITS/Reports/cits_nii_framework_ota.report

Rutenberg, J. (2002, April 11). U.S. approves NBC purchase of Telemundo. *New York Times,* C7.

Schaffler, R. (2001, September 1). Tough call: Can film studios survive without blockbusters? *CNNfn: Market Coverage—Morning.* Dow Jones Interactive Publications Library. Retrieved from http://nrstgls.djnr.com/cgi-bin/DJInteractive?cgi=WEB_FLAT_PAGE&page=wrapper/index&NRAUTOLOG=01Qa9EsCbxmT3PZ1fldaXYSwEA&NRLBRedirect=nrstgls&entry_point=1

*Screen Digest.* (2000, April 1). European TV programme market buoyant: Content owners gain from new channel launches. Dow Jones Interactive Publications Library. Retrieved from http://nrstgls.djnr.com/cgi-bin/DJInteractive?cgi=WEB_FLAT_PAGE&page=wrapper/index&NRAUTOLOG=01Qa9EsCbxmT3PZ1fldaXYSwEA&NRLBRedirect=nrstgls&entry_point=1

*Screen Digest.* (2001a, May 1). Databox. Dow Jones Interactive Publications Library. Retrieved from http://nrstgls.djnr.com/cgi-bin/DJInteractive?cgi=WEB_FLAT_PAGE&page=wrapper/index&NRAUTOLOG=01Qa9EsCbxmT3PZ1fldaXYSwEA&NRLBRedirect=nrstgls&entry_point=1

*Screen Digest.* (2001b, August 1). Databox. Dow Jones Interactive Publications Library. Retrieved from http://nrstgls.djnr.com/cgi-bin/DJInteractive?cgi=WEB_FLAT_PAGE&page=wrapper/index&NRAUTOLOG=01Qa9EsCbxmT3PZ1fldaXYSwEA&NRLBRedirect=nrstgls&entry_point=1

*Screen Digest.* (2001c, November 1). Generation of change: Thirty years of *Screen Digest.* Dow Jones Interactive Publications Library. Retrieved from http://nrstgls.djnr.com/cgi-WEB_FLAT_PAGE&page=wrapper/index&NRAUTOLOG=01Qa9EsCbxmT3PZ1fldaXYSwEA&NRLBRedirect=nrstgls&entry_point=1

*Screen Digest.* (2002a, May 1). Databox. Dow Jones Interactive Publications Library. Retrieved from http://nrstgls.djnr.com/cgi-bin/DJInteractive?cgi=WEB_FLAT_PAGE&page=wrapper/index&NRAUTOLOG=01Qa9EsCbxmT3PZ1fldaXYSwEA&NRLBRedirect=nrstgls&entry_point=1

*Screen Digest.* (2002b, August 1). Databox. Dow Jones Interactive Publications Library. Retrieved from http://nrstgls.djnr.com/cgi-bin/DJInteractive?cgi=WEB_FLAT_PAGE&page=wrapper/index&NRAUTOLOG=01Qa9EsCbxmT3PZ1fldaXYSwEA&NRLBRedirect=nrstgls&entry_point=1

Straubhaar, J. (1991). Beyond media imperialism: Asymmetrical interdependence and cultural proximity. *Critical Studies in Mass Communication, 8*(4), 1–11.

Sukosd, M. (1992, October). *No title.* Paper presented to the Battelle-Mershon conference on technology and democracy, Columbus, OH.

Turow, J. (1992). The organizational underpinnings of contemporary media conglomerates. *Communication Research, 19*(8), 682–704.

UNESCO. (1999). *Statistical yearbook*. Paris: United Nations Educational, Scientific and Cultural Organization Publishing.

U.S. Census Bureau. (1994). *Statistical abstract of the United States* (114th ed.). Washington, DC: U.S. Government Printing Office.

U.S. Census Bureau, (2000). *Statistical abstract of the United States* (120th ed.). Washington, DC: U.S. Government Printing Office.

U.S. House of Representatives. (1981). *Telecommunications and information products and services in international trade: Hearings before the subcommittee on telecommunications, consumer protection, and finance* (Subcommitee on Telecommunications, Consumer Protection and Finance). Washington, DC: Government Printing Office.

U.S. program price guide. (2001). *Variety, 384*(7), 70. [Electronic version]. Retrieved from http://proquest.umi.com/pqdweb?TS=1033931145&Did=000000083163238&Sid=1&Mtd=1&RQT=309&Dtp=1&Fmt=5&TN=2&Uno=3

Valenti, J. (2002, April 23). A clear present and future danger: The potential undoing of America's greatest export trade prize. Statement by Jack Valenti, chairman and CEO, Motion Picture Association, to the House Appropriations Committee, Subcommitee on Commerce, Justice, State, the Judiciary, and Related Agencies. Retrieved from http://www.mpaa.org.jack/2002/2002_04_23b.htm

Walt Disney Co. (2001). Annual Report. Retrieved from http://disney.go.com/corporate/investors/financials/annual/2001/index.html

World Trade Organization (WTO). (2002). Agreement on Trade-Related Aspects of Intellectual Property Rights. Retrieved from http://www.wto.org/wto/english/tratop_e/trips_e/t_agm2_e.htm

## ENDNOTES

[1]The European Audiovisual Observatory (1997) noted that by the late 1990s, the complexity of the structure of the European television market made it difficult to determine exactly how many channels were being delivered to European homes.

[2]Based on self-report data from nations. Many nations do not report such data to UNESCO and fewer reported it in years subsequent to 1995, making the data for 1995 the most complete available.

# II

---

# Industries
# and Practices

# Chapter 5

# The Economics
# of the Daily
# Newspaper Industry

**ROBERT G. PICARD**
*Jönköping University, Sweden*

The newspaper industry is the second oldest mass media industry in the United States, surpassed slightly by the book industry, and is now more than three centuries old. During its history, the newspaper industry has evolved to play important social and economic roles and now accounts for approximately $50 billion in sales annually.

The mission of newspaper enterprises includes both commercial and social facets. Like most other media, newspapers play important roles as facilitators of commerce, promoting consumption by creating consumer wants for products through advertising, and serving the financial interests of newspaper owners as part of the competitive economic system. Newspapers, however, play a greater role as facilitators of social and political expression than other media. As a result, newspaper firms tend to emphasize conveyance of information and ideas about contemporary events and issues to a greater degree than other media that are more entertainment oriented. The mission of newspapers affects the structure of the industry and economic decisions made by managers.

The newspaper industry is the most profitable of all media industries and one of the most profitable of all manufacturing industries in the country. In order to produce its product, the newspaper industry combines technology (the capability for production), information gathering and packaging services, and financial support from advertisers and readers to produce a perishable product that is usable by literate audiences and whose usefulness to most consumers diminishes within a day. A variety of unique economic characteristics distinguish newspapers from other media.

As the new millennium began the country had 1,480 daily newspapers and 917 papers published on Sunday. Most newspapers are small- and medium-sized enterprises and the average newspaper's circulation is relatively small. The average daily newspaper has a circulation of only 37,684 and the average Sunday paper has a circulation of 64,799. More than 85% of the nation's newspapers have circulations below 50,000 daily and only 3% have circulations above 250,000 daily. The industry employs 445,000 persons, about 3.2% of all employment in the United States (*Facts About Newspapers*, 2001).

The nation's daily newspapers are almost equally split between morning and evening publications, but morning newspapers account for five times as much circulation because the afternoon papers tend to be located in small towns.

## MARKET STRUCTURE

The newspaper industry in the United States is characterized by monopoly and its attendant market power, with 98% of newspapers existing as the only daily paper published within their markets. In the few cities where local competition exists, it nearly always occurs between differentiated newspapers such as a broadsheet and a tabloid intended for different audiences or between papers that target substantially different geographic markets than their competitors (Picard & Brody, 1997).

The markets for most papers are the retail trading zones in which they exist. A national market is relevant for papers that circulate throughout the country and have the majority of their circulation outside the city of main publication. The national newspaper market in the U.S. includes papers such as the *Wall Street Journal*, *USA Today*, and *Christian Science Monitor*. This national list is usually supplemented with the *New York Times*, which gains only about one quarter of its circulation in the national market but is included because of its standing as the national newspaper of record.

A tidal wave of afternoon newspaper deaths taking place between World War II and the year 2000, in which about 25% of all afternoon papers closed, led many observers to incorrectly assume that afternoon papers were becoming economically inviable and relics of the past. The deaths, however, were primarily among secondary newspapers and more attributable to advertisers' preferences for the largest paper in a town than the publication time (Benjaminson, 1984; Picard, Winter, McCombs, & Lacy, 1988).

In recent decades, advertisers have increasingly come to view newspapers as means of reaching mass audiences, rather than as means of reaching segmented audiences that were once available when multiple papers existed. Today, advertisers use other media—particularly radio, magazines, and cablecasts—to segment audiences and rely on newspapers, a print medium, for reaching mass audiences. In large local markets, some newspapers have begun to segment portions of their markets in geographic terms by providing cost-saving zoned editions that appeal most to local retail stores that serve customers only in a small portion of the entire newspaper's market and to classified advertisers interested only in reaching nearby readers.

The general reliance on newspapers as a mass medium by national and large advertisers has created a systemic economic problem that makes it nearly impossible for competing papers to survive in the same market. When more than one paper exists in a market, the secondary paper is disadvantaged because a disproportionate amount of advertising is given to the leading paper, regardless of how closely the second paper approximates its circulation (Picard, 1988; Udell, 1978).

This "circulation elasticity of demand" (Corden, 1953, p. 182) creates an impetus toward failure known as the "circulation spiral." The paper with the largest circulation in a market has financial and economic advantages that enable it to increase advertising and circulation sales by attracting customers from the smaller paper. As the leading paper attracts more circulation, it attracts more advertising, which in turn attracts more circulation, trapping the secondary paper in a circulation spiral that ultimately leads to its demise (Engwall, 1981; Furhoff, 1973; Gustafsson, 1978).

Although several hundred daily newspapers died in the second half of the 20th century, they produced an aggregate loss of only about 16% of the total number of U.S. daily newspapers. Dying metropolitan papers were generally replaced with newspapers established in suburban communities that were created by migration out of major cities and toward the south and southwestern parts of the county. Although it is popular to attribute the large number of closures to large metropolitan markets, the majority of newspaper deaths occurred because of the shakeout of secondary and joint monopoly papers in small and mid-sized markets (Picard & Brody, 1997).

### Current State of Consolidation

Although there is consolidation in the newspaper industry and the majority of newspapers are owned by newspaper and media groups (Bagdikian, 1993), the levels of consolidation are relatively low by comparison to levels of consolidation found in other media or in newspaper industries in other nations.

*Community Newspaper Holdings* is the largest owner of daily newspapers in the United States. Together the top four firms in the newspaper industry own a total of only 19.9% of U.S. daily newspapers and the top eight companies own only 27.5% (see Table 5.1).

Raw ownership numbers, however, do not provide a full view of the scope of that ownership, so circulation figures provide a better consolidation indicator. In terms of circulation consolidation, Gannett Co. controls the largest circulation in the country and together the top four newspaper

companies control 31.8% of the market (Table 5.2) and the top eight firms
control 46.5%. In concentration terms, this situation is moderate.

### TABLE 5.1
**Top 10 Newspaper Companies by Number of Dailies Owned**

| Rank | Company | # of Dailies | % of Total Dailies |
|------|---------|--------------|--------------------|
| 1 | Community Newspaper Holdings | 115 | 7.8 |
| 2 | Gannett Co. | 99 | 6.7 |
| 3 | Media News Group | 46 | 3.1 |
| 4 | Knight Ridder | 34 | 2.3 |
| 5 | Morris Communications | 30 | 2.0 |
| 6 | Freedom Newspapers | 29 | 2.0 |
| 7 | Advance Publications | 27 | 1.8 |
| — | Lee Enterprises | 27 | 1.8 |
| 9 | Media General | 25 | 1.7 |
| 10 | E. W. Scripps Co. | 22 | 1.5 |

*Source.* *Facts About Newspapers* (2001).

### TABLE 5.2
**Top 10 Newspaper Companies by Circulation**

| Rank | Company | Circulation | % of Total Circulation |
|------|---------|-------------|------------------------|
| 1 | Gannett Co. | 7,287,914 | 13.1 |
| 2 | Knight Ridder | 3,867,512 | 6.9 |
| 3 | Tribune Co. | 3,650,429 | 6.5 |
| 4 | Advance Publications | 2,903,225 | 5.2 |
| 5 | New York Times Co. | 2,402,797 | 4.3 |
| 6 | Dow Jones & Co. | 2,356,616 | 4.2 |
| 7 | Media News Group | 1,772,554 | 3.2 |
| 8 | Hearst Corp. | 1,670,970 | 3.0 |
| 9 | E.W. Scripps Co. | 1,521,356 | 2.7 |
| 10 | McClatchy Co. | 1,347,779 | 2.4 |

*Source.* *Facts About Newspapers* (2001).

## FINANCIAL ISSUES OF THE NEWSPAPER INDUSTRY

The business model of daily newspapers is based on selling two products (Corden, 1953; Reddaway, 1963). First it sells the newspaper product to readers and then it sells access to that audience to advertisers through advertising space (Picard, 1989).

Circulation sales have an effect on advertising sales because the desirability of a paper to advertisers normally increases as circulation rises and decreases as circulation decreases. Thus price increases as circulation rises, but the cost per person declines until the advertisers pay a premium price for the nation's largest papers, as illustrated in Fig. 5.1.

Today, about two thirds of the content of the average newspaper is advertising and a good portion of the non-news editorial matter, such as articles in food and lifestyle sections, are devoted to promoting sales and use of products available from advertisers.

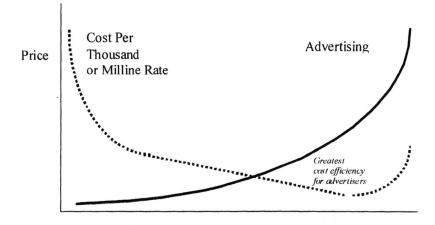

Circulation

FIG. 5.1. Relationships between advertising price and newspaper circulation. *Source.* R. G. Picard (1998), A note of the relationships between circulation size and newspaper advertising rates. *Journal of Media Economics,* *11*(2), 47–55.

## REVENUE STREAMS
## AND POTENTIAL NEW REVENUE STREAMS

The two primary revenue streams for newspapers are circulation and advertising. During the second half of the 20th century papers became increasingly dependent upon advertising (see Fig. 5.2). In 2000 advertising provided 81% of the total income of daily newspapers.

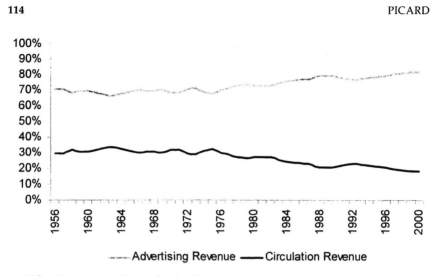

FIG. 5.2.    Income shares for the U.S. newspaper industry 1950–2000.

Circulation grew from approximately 53 million copies daily in 1950 to 62.3 million in 1990, an 18.9% increase, but declined 3.2 million (about 5%) from 1990 to 2000, primarily due to the loss of evening editions of morning papers (*Facts About Newspapers*, 2001). These numbers are problematic because changes in circulation did not keep up with changes in population, and the circulation of newspapers declined from 353 per 1,000 population in 1950 to 202 per 1,000 in 2000.

Demand for newspaper advertising space has been more consistent than demand for advertising space and time in other media. Today newspapers receive about 20% of all dollars spent for advertising, the largest amount devoted to any one medium.

Three major categories of advertising are published in newspapers: national advertising from large companies with business outlets or products distributed throughout the country; retail advertising (sometimes called display advertising) from local businesses making retail sales for goods and services; and classified advertising, small ads by businesses and individuals that are divided into categories by the type of goods or services offered or sought.

## Profitability

The newspaper industry is one of the most profitable industries in the nation, as well as one of the most profitable among communications industries. In 2001, for example, major public companies had operating profits averaging about 15% and net profits averaging about 12%.

The major newspaper companies are now among the larger corporations in the nation. In 2001 the Tribune Co., for example, had assets totaling $14.5 billion, Gannett Co. surpassed $13 billion, Knight Ridder had assets of $4.2 billion, the New York Times Co. had assets of $3.5 billion, and Dow Jones & Co. had assets totaling $1.3 billion. Although not the size of firms such as General Motors, General Electric, IBM, and Exxon, the major newspaper companies rank in the top 150 in terms of assets, in the range of companies such as Colgate-Palmolive, General Mills, Kimberly-Clark, and Ralston-Purina.

## Expense Picture

Newspaper costs can be broadly distinguished by the costs of gathering and preparing the product and the costs of printing and disseminating the paper. Newspapers have relatively high *first-copy* costs, that is, the cost for procuring and packaging the information and preparing it for printing. In this view, only one copy of a newspaper is really produced and the costs are relatively high for that copy. In the second part of the process, newspapers face costs for reproducing the product (printing) and distribution. These costs decline as economies of scale develop when the number of copies produced increases (Rosse & Dertouzous, 1979).

When considering newspaper budgets, it becomes clear that the largest contributors to newspapers' expenses are production and reproduction costs associated with the printing aspects of the business (see Table 5.3). Even excluding overhead costs, expenses for "back shop" activities account for 30% to 35% of a newspaper's operating expenses, and about one half of that cost is attributable to newsprint costs alone. Administration (absorbing overhead costs), circulation, and editorial costs contribute about 10% each to operating expenses.

## Labor

Despite the increasing reliance on mechanical and electronic equipment, labor is still a primary cost in the newspaper industry, requiring about 40% of operating revenue to pay for labor costs. Nearly one half a million persons are employed in the newspaper industry nationwide and 48% of employees are now women (Fig. 5.3). About one half of the employees are involved in prepress labor. Production and maintenance activities account for about 48% of the nation's newspaper workforce. Editorial and administration (including executives) activities each account for about 15% of the total, circulation activities for about 12%, and advertising and promotion for about 10%.

In many large newspapers and geographical areas in which organized labor has historically been strong, newspapers and employees engage in

## TABLE 5.3

### Revenues and Expenses as Approximate Average Percentages of Operating Budgets

| | |
|---|---|
| *Operating Revenues* | |
| Advertising | 65%–80% |
| Local/retail | 55%–60% |
| Classified | 20%–35% |
| National | 10%–15% |
| | |
| Circulation | 20%–35% |
| | |
| *Operating Expenses* | |
| Editorial | 7%–10% |
| Advertising | 5%–6% |
| Circulation | 9%–10% |
| Promotion | 1%–2% |
| Mechanical | 13%–15% |
| Newsprint | 15%–30% |
| Administration | 8%–12% |
| Building and land | 1%–3% |
| | |
| *Operating Margin* | |
| Before taxes & interest | 15%–20% |

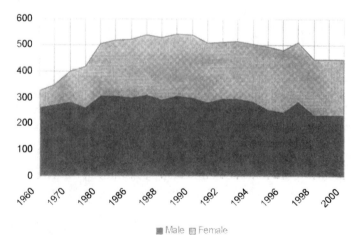

■ Male ▨ Female

FIG. 5.3.   Newspaper industry employment (in thousands).

collective bargaining. Primary labor unions involved in the newspaper industry include the Communication Workers of America (which includes the former International Typographical Union and the Newspaper Guild), the Graphic Communication Union, and the Brotherhood of Teamsters. In the smaller papers and in regions of the country in which right-to-work laws prevail or antiunion sentiments are strong—such as the southeastern states—unions represent employees in few newspapers. Unions representing composing and printing employees and vehicle drivers have had the most success in gaining members and agreements because of their specialized knowledge and historic strength nationwide. Nevertheless, unions play only a small role in the newspaper industry as a whole, but are an important economic factor in the largest newspapers.

Although unions have had a minor effect on the newspaper industry as a whole, the increasing power of large newspaper companies created by public ownership has led unions to establish cooperative efforts to increase their representation of newspaper employees, particularly those working for newspaper groups, in the 1990s. As a result, large newspaper corporations are becoming more active in establishing and pursuing antiunion activities. These actions precipitated lengthy labor disputes at the *New York Daily News* in 1990 and 1991 and the *Detroit Free Press* and *Detroit News* in 1995 and 1996.

## Sales

Income produced through sales of newspaper circulation and advertising is continuing to grow despite the fact that the newspaper industry is mature and many newer media and communication devices are challenging newspapers' positions as information and advertising providers.

Income from newspaper circulation rose from $1.3 billion in 1956 to $10.7 billion in 2000 (Fig. 5.4). When adjusted for inflation, however, it is clear that income has been stable in real terms for about a decade, after declining from a height in 1987.

Advertising expenditures in newspapers grew from $2.1 billion in 1950 to approximately $48.7 billion in 2000 (Fig. 5.5). When adjusted for inflation, the figures indicate that in real terms newspapers get 2.5 times more advertising revenue today than they did at mid-century.

## Products

Many newspapers offer a portfolio of print products, including total market coverage papers and real estate and auto guides. Efforts to develop revenue from developing online editorial and advertising sites are being made and today about 90% of U.S. papers have online operations, but very few papers

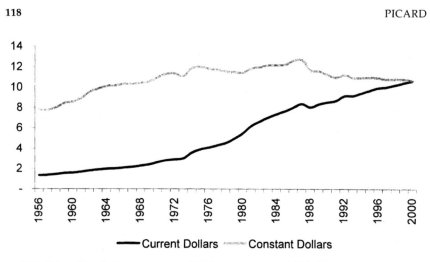

FIG. 5.4.   Circulation revenue of U.S. newspapers, 1956–2000
($ billion, constant dollars at 2000 index).

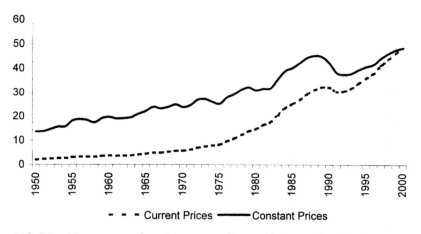

FIG. 5.5.   Newspaper advertising expenditures (daily and Sunday),
1950–2000 (current and constant prices, $ billion).

have found ways to make these operations profitable. Despite the financial
difficulties online newspaper sites tend to be the most visited local sites and
are used more often than online sites operated by television stations.

The growth of mobile telephony is leading some newspapers to develop
headline and notification services using short messaging systems (SMS)
and to develop mobile Internet products.

With the growth of these additional operations, newspaper managers
are seeking ways to effectively integrate and coordinate cross-media activi-

ties, including operations with radio and television stations that may be owned by the same firm or through joint ventures with those owned by other companies.

## Distribution

The costs of getting printed copies of newspapers to readers now accounts for about 10% of most newspapers' expenses (see Table 5.3). Although the costs of transportation and labor are high, newspapers rarely meet these costs directly but enter into subcontracts with distributors bearing the majority of the costs.

The most common delivery system is that of independent distributors, which is used by more than three fourths of all daily newspapers. Independent distributors purchase papers at wholesale prices and sell at retail prices. Their distribution territories are typically small, and the average newspaper has one carrier for each 100 subscribers. Adult independent distributors typically serve routes ranging from 200 to 600 customers, and youth carriers usually have routes ranging from 20 to 100 customers (Thorn, 1987). About 15% of all papers use contract distributors, that is, agents paid a set fee for delivering papers, and about 10% use employees who receive hourly wages or salaries

The costs of distribution are particularly problematic for newspapers because costs rise as the distances to customers increase and distribution densities decrease. Distance and density issues can combine to create situations in which newspapers may have potential customers who want to receive the paper but the papers cannot serve them without incurring a loss (Picard, 2002).

This occurs because it takes more time and effort to reach customers, and the costs for transportation vehicles, operating costs, personnel, etc. rise as distance from the production to the delivery point increases.

## IMPACT OF NEW TECHNOLOGIES

Significant changes in printing and production technology in the past three decades have altered the structure and functions of newspaper organizations. The developments of offset printing, phototypesetting, and prepress production by news and advertising personnel using computer-based equipment have altered the industry significantly.

The primary effect of the new technologies was a reduction in the number of personnel needed to produce a paper. Technology has allowed advertising and editorial departments to take the place of typesetters, allowed national and international news and feature agencies to provide material in forms that no longer require typesetting, reduced the activity necessary for laying out pages, and simplified the printing process. These changes in technology have made it possible for contemporary newspapers to reduce personnel by one third to one half, depending on their sizes and the technology employed.

A second effect of the new technologies has been increased speed in preparing and printing the newspaper. This has been used by managers to make the content of the newspapers "fresher" because it has allowed them to shorten deadline time so that breaking news and information can be placed in a paper closer to the time the paper is distributed, thus increasing the paper's ability to compete with broadcast media in coverage of breaking news stories.

The impact of new technologies on newspaper costs has been explored and indicates that economies of scale are not created equally across all sizes of newspapers (Dertouzous & Thorpe, 1982). The introduction of offset printing and phototypesetting equipment apparently reduces first-copy costs and minimum efficient scale, particularly for papers in the 10,000 to 100,000 circulation range, but the efficiencies are not equally enjoyed by papers below and above that size (Norton & Norton, 1986). The higher cost of the new technologies makes some older systems more efficient for smaller papers. Larger papers often do not enjoy the same rate of cost savings because the new technologies must be specifically adapted for their requirements. Because there are fewer large papers that need the adaptations, the cost of the adapted versions is much higher.

Industry observers do not expect huge technological advances during the next decade but look forward to the increasing development of new applications for electronic technology in composition and printing departments. Technological advances expected to be widely accepted include: conversion of plate departments (which transfers layouts onto metal plates for printing) to electronic darkrooms with computer-to-plate composition capabilities; acquisition of equipment for electronic integration and control of multiple press units and functions; computerized control of color printing; and automated folding, inserting, sorting, and labeling of newspaper bundles for carriers and mailed copies.

A result of the increasing reliance on advanced technology has been a rapid increase in equipment costs. Since the 1960s the costs for composition and printing equipment have increased dramatically and today require extensive capital investments and financial planning. The types of equipment expected to enter newspaper plants in the first decades of the 21st century are not expected to result in as significant labor costs as the introduction of offset printing and phototypesetting. Although some reduction in composition, printing, and mailing personnel will occur, a good portion of those salary savings will be redirected to technicians needed to operate and service the new machinery. In the long run, however, savings from reduced costs for employee benefits, reduced costs for supplies, reduced waste of newsprint, and increased desirability of newspaper advertising because of higher quality color printing are expected to result in favorable returns on investments in technology.

The integration of information and communication technologies throughout newspapers increases the opportunities for convergence with other media activities. Today, however, convergence and cross-media activities are primarily limited to moving news, archives, and some advertising onto the Internet, but financial benefits have been elusive.

## GLOBALIZATION

The newspaper industry is not significantly affected by globalization and remains primarily a domestic industry, both in the United States and abroad. The primary reasons for the lack of globalization are that newspapers' primary product (content) is local and localized by nature and that linguistic limitations limit the exportability of newspapers.

In terms of ownership, few American newspaper firms are globalizing their operations for strategic reasons and lack of company structures and capabilities to support international activities. A notable exception has been Dow Jones & Co., which has aggressively pursued globalization through the establishment of regional editions, such as *Wall Street Journal Europe* and *Wall Street Journal Asia*. The Gannett Co. makes *USA Today* available in some parts of the world through satellite printing and distribution agreements and the New York Times Co. owns the Paris-based *International Herald-Tribune*. A number of large U.S. newspapers offer their editorial content to foreign newspapers through syndication services.

## COPYRIGHT ISSUES

Although copyright is an important factor for content produced by American newspapers, it is not a significant issue because copyright legislation currently provides broad protection. U.S. law incorporates the *work-for-hire* principle, which provides newspapers the full rights to content produced by staff so this material is owned by the paper and can be used in archival and multimedia activities.

During the 1990s many newspapers began inserting clauses into contracts for rights acquired from freelancers and stringers to provide broad ownership rights. In some cases negotiations over these secondary rights took place between unions representing employees and newspapers to obtain additional compensation for secondary uses (Picard & Brody, 1997).

### Policy Issues

No comprehensive economic policy toward the industry has ever been established in the United States, but a patchwork of policies applies, including a few policies established directly for newspapers. For the most part, government policies are oriented toward the maintenance of private enterprise and competition, but critics are increasingly charging that the policies have acted to prevent rather than encourage competition and that reconsideration of the policies is necessary (Owen, 1975; Picard 1982).

Federal, state, and local governments have traditionally provided a variety of special economic supports to the industry, including exemptions from newspaper and advertising sales taxes and excise taxes on telecommunications equipment used for information gathering. In addition, a variety of fiscal advantages, including regulatory relief from wage and hour laws, have provided special support (Picard, 1982).

The single most notable economic policies established by the federal government specifically for newspapers have been postal rate advantages and the antitrust exemptions for joint operating newspapers under the Newspaper Preservation Act (Busterna & Picard, 1993; Kielbowitz, 1989; Picard et al., 1988). Newspapers in York, Pennsylvania, Las Vegas, Nevada, and Detroit, Michigan, have been the most recent to use the provisions of the Newspaper Preservation Act. Today 12 cities served by formerly competing newspapers now in joint operating agreements (*Editor & Publisher International Yearbook*, 2001; *Facts About Newspapers*, 2001).

Newspapers enjoy the general tax exemptions and incentives available to other businesses and, with the exception of 24 papers operating with joint operating agreements, are subject to the same antitrust law and enforcement as other industries.

The result of application of general tax policies to newspapers has been an increase in chain ownership, because inheritors of independent papers have been forced to sell the papers to chains in order to pay estate taxes that are based on fair market prices. In addition, newspaper groups and conglomerates use pretax funds to acquire additional papers and the acquisitions can be depreciated over time, two factors that provide them significant tax advantages (Dertouzous & Thorpe, 1982).

Antitrust laws are rarely invoked by government to halt concentration in the industry and are now primarily used by newspapers and other media against each other in disputes over marketing and pricing practices (Busterna, 1988, 1989).

Because of Federal Communications Commission regulations, ownership of television stations and newspapers in the same market by the same owner is prohibited but significant efforts are now underway to remove that prohibition.

## CONCLUSIONS

The future of the newspaper industry in the United States is unclear because of declining readership, illiteracy, and technological changes, but there is no reason to believe the functions of newspapers will no longer be required or that newspaper companies do not have the ability to adapt and survive.

Newspaper companies are concerned because it appears that the decline in readership of newspapers among the population as a whole will continue. Many persons, especially young people, appear uninterested in the current content of newspapers and make greater use of other media. Persons of all ages who cannot read, or do not read well, can be expected to increasingly use broadcast and cable services for their news, information, and advertising needs.

Nevertheless, a great number of people can still be expected to want information of the type found in newspapers and there will continue to be a need for firms to gather and convey such information. Some futurists predict, however, that the newspaper itself will disappear because of changes in production and distribution. They argue that the printing aspects of the industry will disappear and the electronic product currently being produced by the news and advertising portions of newspaper companies will be transposed into an electronic newspaper delivered via cable or computer.

Traditionalists disagree, arguing that the portability of newspapers and the nonportability of video monitors will halt or delay such electronic distribution. To date, audience acceptance of electronic distribution of material traditionally found in newspapers has been low. Cable and other video-based experiments suggest a current unwillingness of newspaper consumers to give up newspapers for those services.

In the short term, the prospects for the newspaper industry remain good. Habitual use and steady demand for the information product, as well its continuing attractiveness to advertisers, indicate that it should remain a profitable industry well into the 21st century.

In the long term, the financial prospects of the newspaper industry are favorable even if technological and lifestyle changes lead consumers to accept electronic video-based distribution and the printing portion of the industry disappears. Under such a scenario, newspaper companies would replace their high-cost composition, printing, and distribution departments with a lower cost department that facilitates distribution or access through existing telecommunication or cable services, while continuing to use their prepress activities to provide the news and information for the new media product.

## FURTHER READING

Bagdikian, B. (1993). *The media monopoly* (4th ed.) Boston: Beacon Press.
Owen, B. M. (1975). *Economics and the first amendment: Media structure and the first amendment.* Cambridge, MA: Ballinger.
Picard, R. G. (2002). *The economics and financing of media companies.* New York: Fordham University Press, 2002.

Picard, R. G., & Brody, J. (1997). *The newspaper publishing industry*. Boston: Allyn & Bacon.

# REFERENCES

Bagdikian, B. (1993). *The media monopoly* (4th ed.) Boston: Beacon Press.

Benjaminson, P. (1984). *Death in the afternoon: America's newspaper giants struggle for survival*. Kansas City, KS: Andrews, McMeel & Parker.

Busterna, J. C. (1988). Antitrust in the 1980s: An analysis of 45 newspaper actions. *Newspaper Research Journal, 9*, 25–36.

Busterna, J. C. (1989, March). Daily newspaper chains and the antitrust laws. *Journalism Monographs*, No. 110.

Busterna, J. C., & Picard, R. G. (1993). *Joint operating agreements: The Newspaper Preservation Act and its application*. Norwood, NJ: Ablex.

Corden, W. M. (1953). The Maximisation of profit by a newspaper. *Review of Economic Studies, 20*, 181–190.

Dertouzous, J. N., & Thorpe, K. E. (1982). *Newspaper groups: economies of scale, tax laws, and merger incentives*. Santa Monica, CA: Rand Corp.

*Editor & Publisher international yearbook*. New York: Editor & Publisher.

Engwall, L. (1981). Newspaper competition: A case for theories of oligopoly. *Scandinavian Economic History Review, 29*, 145–154.

*Facts about newspapers*. (annual). Reston, VA: Newspaper Association of America.

Field, R. (1978). Circulation price inelasticity in the daily newspaper industry. Unpublished thesis, University of Oklahoma.

Furhoff, L. (1973). Some reflections on newspaper concentration. *Scandinavian Economic History Review, 21*, 1–27.

Gustafsson, K. E. (1978). The circulation spiral and the principle of household coverage. *Scandinavian Economic History Review, 28*, 1–14.

Kielbowicz, R. B. (1989). *News in the mail: The press, post office, and public information. 1700–1860s*. Westport, CT: Greenwood Press.

Norton, S. W., & Norton, Jr., W. (1986). Economies of scale and new technology of daily newspapers: A survivor analysis. *Quarterly Review of Economics and Business, 26*, 66–83.

Owen, B. M. (1975). *Economics and the first amendment: Media structure and the first amendment*. Cambridge, MA: Ballinger.

Picard, R. G. (1982). State intervention in U.S. press economics. *Gazette, 30*, 3–11.

Picard, R. G. (1988). Pricing behavior of newspapers. In R. G. Picard et al. (Eds.), *Press concentration and monopoly: New perspectives on newspaper ownership and operation* (pp. 55–69). Norwood, NJ: Ablex.

Picard, R. G. (1989). *Media economics: Concepts and issues*. Newbury Park, CA: Sage.

Picard, R. G. (1998) A note of the relationships between circulation size and newspaper advertising rates, *Journal of Media Economics, 11*(2), 47–55.

Picard, R. G. (2002). *The economics and financing of media companies*. New York: Fordham University Press.

Picard, R. G., & Brody, J. (1997). *The newspaper publishing industry*. Boston: Allyn & Bacon.

Picard, R. G., Winter, J. P., McCombs, M., & Lacy, S. (Eds.). (1988). *Press concentration and monopoly: New perspectives on newspaper ownership and operation*. Norwood, NJ: Ablex.

Reddaway, W. B. (1963) The economics of newspapers. *The Economic Journal, 73*, 201–218.

Rosse, J. N., & Dertouzous, J. N. (1979). The evolution of one newspaper cities. In Federal Trade Commission, *Proceedings of the symposium on media concentration* (Vol. 2, pp. 429–471). Washington, DC: U.S. Government Printing Office.

Thorn, W. J., with Pfeil, M. P. (1987). *Newspaper circulation: Marketing the news.* White Plains, NY: Longman.

Udell, J. G. (1978). *The economics of the American newspaper.* New York: Hastings House.

# Chapter 6

# The Economics of Books and Magazines

ALBERT N. GRECO
*Fordham University*

## INTRODUCTION

Books and magazines play a pivotal role in the intellectual, cultural, and economic life of the United States (Daly, Henry, & Ryder, 1997; Greco, 1997a). However, between 1995 and 2001, there was a dramatic, unsettling shift in consumer book (i.e., adult, juvenile, mass-market paperback, religious, book clubs, and mail-order books) and consumer magazine (i.e., *U.S. News and World Report, Time, Ms.*, etc.) usage and expenditure patterns of Americans, and the prognosis for 2002 through 2005 is equally disconcerting because Americans are spending less time perusing consumer books and consumer magazines. The impact of this trend on American culture and democracy has yet to be fully explored by social scientists.

Consumer book usage (i.e., hours per person per year) declined 11.88% between 1995 (101 hours) and 2001 (89 hours), and Veronis Suhler projects an additional drop of 4.55% between 2002 (89 hours) and 2006 (84 hours; Veronis Suhler, 2001a). Overall, consumer books will experience a total decline of 16.83% between 1995 and 2005.

Consumer magazines, on the other hand, sustained a 6.19% deterioration in hours between 1995 (113 hours) and 2001 (106 hours) with an additional 3.85% falling off between 2002 (104 hours) and 2005 (100 hours); Veronis Suhler (2001a) estimates a total weakening of 11.5% in the consumer magazine sector between 1995 and 2005.

Data on media expenditures is equally alarming. Between 1995 ($70.94) and 2001 ($78.90), annual increases in consumer book allocations limped along, lagging behind the Consumer Price Index (CPI) in 4 of these 6 years. Magazine expenditures were even more dreadful (1995: $38.30; 2001: $40.02), outpacing the CPI only once (1996). Projections generated by Veronis Suhler

(2001a) and the U.S. Congressional Budget Office (CBO; 2002) for 2002 through 2005 indicate more disconcerting trends; consumer book expenditures should surpass the CPI only twice; magazines will fall short of the CPI in 3 of these 4 years (U.S. Department of Commerce, 2001). These events are even more shocking because media usage increased 6.3% in the United States between 1995 (3,306 hours) and 2001 (3,519), and media expenditures surged a staggering 45.7% between 1995 ($465.49) and 2001 ($678.06).

Despite these startling statistics, the book and magazine industries in the United States generated significant revenues, published important works, and contributed to the cultural life of this nation. All of the available econometric datasets indicate that, in spite of downward usage and expenditure trends, these two formats will retain their positions of preeminence through 2010.

## THE BOOK PUBLISHING INDUSTRY
## IN THE UNITED STATES MARKET STRUCTURE

### Number of Firms

There is intense competition in the U.S. book industry. In 1997 the U.S. Department of Commerce tracked more than 2,684 establishments employing 89,898 individuals with an annual payroll in excess of $3.6 billion (U.S. Department of Commerce, 1997; Commerce will not release another Census until 2004). By 2002, the R. R. Bowker Company monitored more than 53,000 book companies (Bogart, 2002). The disparity in these tallies is due to Commerce's definition of a *book publisher*: it must have one paid employee; pay federal taxes; and its primary business must be book publishing. Bowker relies on the total number of publisher ISBN numbers. *ISBN* is a unique bar code assigned to a specific book publisher; Bowker is the sole provider of all ISBN codes in the United States. Bowker also reported that U.S. publishers released approximately 120,000 new titles in 1999 and again in 2000. By 2001, the total exceeded 135,000. These tallies for 1999 through 2001 exclude books imported into the U.S. In addition, Bowker revealed that there were approximately 3.5 million titles in print in 2002.

Barriers to entry into book publishing are rather minimal. Almost all editorial and production operations can be subcontracted out (to minimize overhead expenditures). The First Amendment provides ample protection for this industry, and foreign individuals can purchase and operate book houses. The real entry barrier problem centers on the distribution function, and convincing buyers at the largest book chains or other retail establishment to carry a title is a formidable task. However, anyone with enough capital can launch a book company with a great deal of ease.

Clearly, competition in the U.S. marketplace for authors, books, and sales is intense, especially in light of the number of publishers, books, bookstores, other retail outlets selling books (e.g., discount stores, terminals, supermarkets, convenience stores, price clubs, etc.), expanded revenue streams from sub rights (i.e., motion pictures, magazines), foreign rights, and the export market. Compounding this situation is the need of publishers to meet the financial objectives of their corporate owners.

## Book Categories and Net Publishers' Revenues

The book industry is divided into distinct categories (Greco, 1997a, 1997b). In 2001, total net publishers' revenues (i.e., gross sales minus returns) hovered near the $23.7 billion mark on sales of 2.4 billion cloth and paperback units (Book Industry Study Group, 2002). The *trade* category (i.e., adult and juvenile books) accounted for $6.4 billion (a 26.8% share of the entire market) with almost 846 million units sold. Professional books (i.e., nontextbooks books written for professionals, including attorneys, bankers, etc.) were second with $4.7 billion (20% share; 168 million units). Elhi (i.e., elementary and high school textbooks) placed third with $4.2 billion (a 17.6% share; 349 million units). University press tallies hovered near the $443 million mark, down from previous years (Greco, 2001a, 2001b). The Book Industry Study Group, Inc. (BISG) expects net publishers' revenues to top $28 billion by 2006 on sales of 2.5 billion units. Table 6.1 outlines these trends.

## Consolidation

Since the 1960s, there have been a number of mergers and acquisitions (Greco, 1989, 1996). In the 1980s Bertelsmann (a German media company) purchased Bantam Books, and a few years later it acquired Doubleday. In 1998, it added Random House (changing the name of the newly consolidated company to Random House). By 2002, Random House was the largest trade book publisher in the U.S. Subtext (a major book industry research company) estimated Random House had total U.S. trade revenues of $1.7 billion in 2000 (Oda & Sansilo, 2002b). Penguin Putnam (owned by the United Kingdom's Pearson PLC) resulted from a series of mergers involving, G.P. Putnam, Viking Press, and the famed Penguin house, and Subtext indicated Penguin Putnam was the second largest publisher in the United States with $820 million in revenues. HarperCollins, owned by the Australian based News Corp., was created with the merger of Harper & Row and the United Kingdom's Collins; it is the third largest book publisher in this nation with about $800 million in revenues (Oda & Sansilo, 2002b).

Some individuals, in a series of impassioned books and essays, raised concerns about an alleged "media monopoly" in the book industry, espe-

## TABLE 6.1

### Publishers' Net Dollar Revenues
### ($ Million; All Numbers Rounded Off)

| Category | 2001 | 2002 | 2003 | 2004 | 2005 | 2006 |
|---|---|---|---|---|---|---|
| Trade (Total) | 6369.9 | 6382.9 | 6404.5 | 6693.3 | 6889.9 | 7059.2 |
| Adult Trade | 4,553.7 | 4,630.7 | 4,712.6 | 4,871.9 | 5,022.0 | 5,145.6 |
| Juvenile Trade | 1,816.2 | 1,752.2 | 1,693.9 | 1,821.4 | 1,866.9 | 1,913.6 |
| Mass Market Paperbacks | 1,546.6 | 1,585.8 | 1,632.7 | 1,679.9 | 1,727.4 | 1,775.4 |
| Book Clubs | 1,334.5 | 1,361.2 | 1,385.7 | 1,406.5 | 1,427.5 | 1,449.0 |
| Mail Order | 353.9 | 333.8 | 269.8 | 233.6 | 173.8 | 125.9 |
| Religious | 1,305.1 | 1,343.2 | 1,376.3 | 1,411.2 | 1,446.5 | 1,482.6 |
| Professional | 4,739.1 | 4,855.2 | 5,006.5 | 5,160.7 | 5,317.6 | 5,477.9 |
| University Press | 443.0 | 454.2 | 468.2 | 482.4 | 496.8 | 511.4 |
| Elhi Textbooks | 4,183.6 | 4,459.7 | 4,786.6 | 5,137.5 | 5,513.8 | 5,918.1 |
| College Textbooks | 3,468.9 | 3,633.4 | 3,799.4 | 3,949.3 | 4,087.9 | 4,219.2 |
| Totals | **23,744.6** | 24,409.4 | **25,131.7** | 26,154.4 | **27,080.2** | 28,018.7 |

Note.   From *Book Industry Trends* (2002).

cially because so many of the top firms are owned by large, global media corporations (Bagdikian, 2000; Greco, 2000). Although the First Amendment protects freedom of the press, a series of major federal laws (e.g., the Sherman Act of 1890, the Clayton Act of 1914, etc.), stipulated any merger or acquisition involving parties with revenues beyond a certain minimum dollar threshold must submit documents to the Department of Justice (DOJ) for review by DOJ or the Federal Trade Commission (FTC) prior to the formal merger. DOJ and the FTC rely on a series of standard mathematical formulas, including the Herfindahl-Hirschman Index (HHI) along with other appropriate review mechanisms, to ascertain if there is a violation of the antitrust laws (Greco, 1999). All of the mergers listed here, involving U.S. and foreign firms, passed federal scrutiny because no substantive empirical evidence was presented to DOJ or the FTC in the last 40 years that a "media monopoly" exists in the U.S. book industry; and DOJ and FTC have not opposed any mergers or acquisition in the book publishing industry during those years. Table 6.2 lists the ten largest trade publishers as of 2002.

TABLE 6.2

**The 10 Largest Trade Book Publishers: 2000 ($ Million)**

| Rank | Publishers | Trade Revenues | Percentage Share of U.S. Trade Market |
|------|-----------|---------------|---------------------------------------|
| 1 | Random House | 1,685 | 25.8% |
| 2 | Penguin Putnam | 820 | 12.5% |
| 3 | HarperCollins | 800 | 12.1% |
| 4 | Simon & Schuster | 596 | 8.8% |
| 5 | Scholastic | 325 | 5.0% |
| 6 | Warner/Little Brown | 300 | 4.2% |
| 7 | St. Martin's/Holt/Fararr Strauss | 280 | 4.3% |
| 8 | Hungry Minds | 230 | 3.1% |
| 9 | Thomas Nelson | 202 | 3.1% |
| 10 | Houghton Mifflin | 103 | 1.5% |

*Note.* From *Subtext Perspective on Publishing 2001–2002: Numbers, Issues & Trends.*

## FINANCES

### Business Model

How do book companies make a profit? What business models do they employ? What expenses do publishers incur?

Most books are discounted (generally between 42% and 48% off the suggested retail price) by publishers to bookstores, distributors, jobbers, and so forth. A publisher makes money if the book's net sales are high enough to recoup expenses. To ascertain costs and possible profits, editors prepare a *profit and loss* (P & L) analysis for every book under consideration for publication. Table 6.3 is a typical P & L analysis.

If we assume an initial print run of 100,000 copies for an adult trade hardcover book (perhaps a history of the Second World War by a prominent historian), about 2,000 copies are usually set aside for internal use by editors, free copies for the author, etcetera, for gross sales of 98,000 copies. Books have a high return rate, and hardcover titles average about 35% in 2002. This means 34,300 copies of this book will be returned to be publisher for a full refund. Whereas all hardcover books are returned, a different policy exists for paperbacks. The cover of a paperback book is stripped off and returned to the publisher; the bookseller will destroy the actual book, or least they are supposed to be destroyed (Greco, 1992). This book has net sales of 63,700 copies (a sell-through rate of 65%). With a suggested retail price of $24.95 and a 47%

## TABLE 6.3
### Profit and Loss (P&L) Analysis

*Assumptions:*

| | |
|---|---|
| Print Quantity: | 100,000 |
| Number of Free Copies: | 2,000 |
| Gross Sales: | 98,000 |
| Returns: | 34,300 (35% return rate) |
| Net Sales: | 63,700 (65% sell through rate) |
| Suggested Retail Price: | $24.95 |
| Average Discount: | 47% |
| Publishers' Net Income | $13.22 |

*Royalty Terms:*

| | |
|---|---|
| • 10% | First 5,000 units at Suggested retail Price ($24.95) |
| • 12.5% | 5,001–10,000 units at Suggested retail Price ($24.95) |
| • 15% | +10,001 units at Suggested retail Price ($24.95) |

*Sub and Foreign Rights:*

| | |
|---|---|
| • Reprints | |
| Gross | $50,000 |
| Author's Share | $30,000 (60%) |
| • Book Club | $5,000 |
| Author's Share | $2,500 (50%) |
| • Foreign Rights | $8,000 |
| Author's Share | $6,000 (75%) |
| • Misc. | 0 |
| • Totals | $63,000 |
| Author's Share | $38,500 (61.11%) |
| Publisher's Share | $24,500 (38.89%) |
| Unit PPB: | $1.10 (Paper, Printing, & Binding) |
| Plant | $10,000 (Editorial, Proofreading, etc.) |
| Royalty Advance: | $0 (Advance Against Future Royalty Earnings) |
| Direct Marketing: | $100,000 |

*Profit & Loss Analysis*

| | |
|---|---|
| • Gross Sales | $1,295,560 (98,000 units at $13.22@) |
| • Returns | $453,446 (34,300 units at $13.22@) |
| • Net Sales | $ 842,114.00 (100%) |
| • Plant | $10,000 |

| | |
|---|---|
| • PPB | $110,000 (100,000 units at $1.10@) |
| • Royalty | $229,041 |
| • Total Cost: | $349,041 |
| Gross Margin "A": | $493,073 |
| Other Publishing Income: | $24,500 |
| Inventory Write-Off: | $37,300 |
| Royalty Write-Off: | 0 |
| Gross Margin "B": | $480,273 |
| Direct Marketing: | $100,000 |
| Overhead (30%): | $252,634.20 (30% of Net Sales) |
| Net Profit: | $127,638.80 |

discount rate, $13.22 per copy was paid to the publisher. Manufacturing costs were sizable; printing, paper, and binding (PPB) averaged $1.10 per printed copy; and plant costs (i.e., editorial expenses, etc.) reached $10,000. Direct-mail expenses topped $100,000 (generally a publisher will spend $1 for every unit printed). The author received no advance.

Gross sales were $1,295,560 (98,000 copies at $13.22 each), returns reached $453,446 (34,300 copies at $13.22 each), and net sales (gross minus returns) were $842,114.

PPB and plant cost the publisher $120,000, and the royalty reached $229,041. The author was not paid an advance, which means that the author's royalty was triggered with the sale of the first copy of the book. Based on the sliding royalty scale described in Table 6.3, the royalty for the first 5,000 books was $12,475 (10% of $124,750 in receipts), $15,593.75 for the next 5,000 units ($124,750 at 12.5 percent), and $200,972.25 for all units above 10,000 ($1,339,815 at 15%).

All of this generated total costs of $349,041 (net sales minus these three expenses) for a Gross Margin "A" of $493,073. The estimated "other publishing income" (sub rights) of $24,500 and the inventory write off of $37,300 (34,300 returned copies at $1.10 PPB) generated a Gross Margin "B" of $480,273 (gross margin plus other publishing income minus the inventory write off). However, $100,000 (the direct marketing costs) was deducted from Gross Margin "B" along with $252,634.20, the company's standard 30% charge to cover overhead cost (i.e., 30% of net sales).

So this "typical" book had a net profit of $127,638.80 (15.16% of net sales). Other potential revenue streams for this book could include: film rights; audio book and e-book sales; etcetera. However, these revenues were excluded from this sample P & L statement to simplify matters.

The financial success of this book is not "typical" for consumer book publishing, which is a hit-driven business. The majority of all new hardbound books do not generate profits, and neither do most paperbacks. In reality, most profits are from the sale of "backlist" book (i.e., titles more than 9 months old). Also, about 20% of the top authors (e.g., John Grisham or May Higgins Clark) generate about 80% of the revenues for many consumer book publishers (the classic "80-20" rule).

## Consumer Book Industry Financial Data

A review of the statistics in Table 6.4 reveals consumer book publishing is cyclical, dependent clearly on classic supply and demand issues. Demand sagged in 1998 because of consumer indifference to new title output. Although total revenues were up (because of increases in both suggested retail prices of books) from 1997, operating income sagged sharply (–45.84%) as did operating cash flow (–23.67).

By 1999, the industry was on the upswing with a plethora of attractive authors and books, and modest gains were posted in revenues (+2.92%); operating income rebounded (+49.54%) and operating cash flow (+17.75%). Similar patterns were evident operating income margins, operating cash flow margins, operating income ROA, operating cash flow ROA,

### TABLE 6.4
### Consumer Book Industry Financial Data ($ Million)

|                                          | 1997     | 1998   | 1999   | 2000   | 2001   |
|------------------------------------------|----------|--------|--------|--------|--------|
| Revenues                                 | $3099.2  | 3951.9 | 4067.4 | 4196.8 | 4552.2 |
| Operating Income                         | $340.1   | 185.9  | 278.0  | 471.0  | 483.2  |
| Operating Cash Flow                      | $536.5   | 409.5  | 482.2  | 695.3  | 815.3  |
| Assets                                   | $3099.6  | 3086.1 | 3433.6 | 3646.1 | 3722.1 |
| Operating Income Margins                 | 11.0%    | 4.7%   | 6.8%   | 11.2%  | 10.6%  |
| Operating Cash Flow Margins              | 17.3%    | 10.4%  | 11.9%  | 16.6%  | 17.9%  |
| Operating Income Return on Assets        | N/A      | 6.0%   | 8.5%   | 13.3%  | 13.1%  |
| Operating Cash Flow Return on Assets     | N/A      | 13.2%  | 14.8%  | 19.6%  | 22.1%  |
| Asset Turnover                           | N/A      | 1.28   | 1.25   | 1.19   | 1.24   |

*Note.* From *Veronis Suhler Stevenson Communications Industry Report 2002.* Reprinted with permission.

and asset turnover (times/year). The industry continued its recovery in 2000 and 2001, with positive gains in all of the major financial categories.

Yet nagging fears surfaced. If steep declines were followed by pointed surges, how can effective medium and long-range planning occur? These financial concerns will preoccupy book industry executives in the first decade of the 21st century as they craft effective strategic plans to minimize cyclical swings in revenues and operating income in order to maintain some semblance of fiscal stability.

## PRINTED BOOKS AND THE IMPACT OF NEW TECHNOLOGY

Printed books have been published since the days of Gutenberg. However, the emergence of sophisticated computer systems and networks compelled publishers to reevaluate the preeminence (and cost) of printed books. Theoretically, the electronic distribution of book content allows a publisher to keep a book in print "forever," expand the market for this book, and reduce significantly most (but not all) publication costs. As of 2002, the electronic distribution of content (via e-books, computer networks, PDAs, etc.) failed to entice consumers, although some librarians purchased e-books for their patrons to minimize the impact of the "one book, one use at a time" model. However, many industry analysts believe consumer acceptance of electronically distributed books will not occur before 2010 (and possibly not before 2020) because: (a) e-book readers are too small and too expensive; (b) reading long texts on a computer screen is not very appealing; (c) the printed book is cheap, portable, and remarkably easy to use (no batteries; no access to electricity); and (d) by 2002 many large publishers privately de-emphasized the e-book channel of distribution. In essence, publishers said, "show me the money and profits" from e-book sales; and in 2002, there were not any.

## GLOBALIZATION

Book publishing is a global industry, and many of the top U.S. publishers are foreign owned. BISG estimated that in 2001 about $1.7 billion (7% of all net publisher revenues) were generated through the export of books; it is anticipated that foreign sales will reach slightly more than $2 billion in 2006. In 2002, the major export destination of U.S. books included: Canada; the United Kingdom; Australia; Hong Kong; Mexico; the Netherlands; Taiwan; and the Philippines. Most large publishers have international operations, sending sales representatives to Asia, Europe, Africa, the Middle East, and Latin America to sell English language books. In addition, the sale of foreign rights (i.e., selling the right to publish a book in a foreign language) is an important revenue stream. All of these sales are dependent on a number of complex social and economic issues, especially the strength of the U.S. dollar.

## COPYRIGHT ISSUES

Article 1 Section 8 of the U.S. Constitution, as well as a number of international copyright conventions, provide copyright protection for books. However, the availability of inexpensive copying machines and computer scanners revolutionized the pirating business, costing book publishers $636.4 million in 2001 in lost sales (Siwek, 2002). Although a number of national and international book trade associations fight pirating, especially with the strong support of the United States and many foreign governments, pirating remains a blight on the landscape, especially in certain emerging markets.

## SUMMATION

Television is glamorous, newspapers are influential, and magazines are exciting to read. Books, on the other hand, are the permanent record of our history, our achievements, and our ideas. Books are the primary conduits of ideas in the world. Some of them are passed down from one generation to another because they matter. Our civilization has been influenced in a substantive way by the works of Homer, Aristotle, and Plato, the key religious works, the ideas of Franklin and Jefferson, the wisdom of Lincoln and King, and the social concerns of Morison Weisel.

Books are portable, they are easy to use, and they are everywhere; people read them at the beach, on the train, and sometimes even for a class; and the installed base of people who can read grows annually. Some dictators tried burning books and banishing authors. Yet books prevailed because they are ubiquitous and inexpensive. Books educate, entertain, and inform readers in every country in the world, characteristics that make them an immensely powerful and influential medium.

## THE MAGAZINE PUBLISHING INDUSTRY IN THE U.S.

Magazines are "glitzy," filled with pages of cleaver advertising campaigns and fantastic four-color photographs (Byron, 1984; Clurman, 1992; Gill, 1975; Kitch, 2001; Kover, 1995; Posgrova, 1995). Yet magazine publishing in the United States is a hotly competitive $30 billion industry with about 6,300 companies and +137,000 employees publishing approximately 17,694 magazines (also called *titles*; the precise number of magazines in the United States is unknown) fighting it out for scarce revenues (U.S. Department of Commerce, Bureau of the Census, 2001). In this industry, a faulty business model will lead ultimately to an untimely death, and the landscape is littered with thousands of titles that died (e.g., *Look, Talk, The Saturday Evening Post, Brill's Content, Inside*).

In the United States magazines are also called *serials*; and there are three types of magazines:

1. "consumer" or general interest titles (e.g., *Newsweek*; *O—The Oprah Magazine*) or the increasingly popular "niche" oriented books (e.g., *American Baby*; *Working Mother*);
2. trade magazines (also called *business-to-business* or *b-to-b*) category, publishing "must have, need to know" information a professional requires to perform his or her job (Greco, 1988, 1991). Books in the *b-to-b* category include *The ABA Journal, Variety, PC Magazine,* and *W*. Although these titles lack some of the *panache* associated with, perhaps, *The New Yorker*, b-to-b titles are immensely important books, diligently read and followed by millions of individuals each week; and
3. *scholarly journals*, titles produced for academics and scholars. Some of the more prominent journals include The *Journal of American History*, the *Journal of Scholarly Publishing*, and the *Journal of Media Economics*. Since scholarly journals are so specialized, they will be excluded from this chapter.

### New Magazine Launches

First Amendment protection allows anyone to publish a magazine, and, aside from some difficulties related to distribution, all anyone needs to launch a title is enough capital to hire (or subcontract) editorial and protection functions. In 1985, 231 new magazines were launched in the United States, and the annual total increased at a rapid rate, reaching 557 in 1990; 838 in 1995; 1,065 in 1998; and 874 in 2000. Overall, 11,045 new titles were launched between 1985 and 2000 (annually averaging 690 new titles), flooding the channels of distribution and ratcheting up pressure for scarce advertising dollars (Veronis Suhler, 2001a, 2002).

Although it may seem a bit odd, in 2002, a year marked by profound problems in the advertising sector, a significant number of new titles were launched, including *9 Magazine* (for Porsche enthusiasts), *Elite Traveler* (luxury travel), *Grace* (for women size 12 and above), *Rev* (off-road motorcycling), and *Women's Health & Fitness* (wellness and relationships). Hope springs eternal in the magazine business, even though the odds of launching and sustaining a new magazine beyond the 3-year mark are almost insurmountable.

### Circulation Issues

The laws of supply and demand cannot be rescinded (Becker, 1998); and the combination of existing and established titles with this staggering outpouring of new titles ultimately affected consumer magazine circulation (also known as *circ*) by the end of the 1990s. Many of these newly launched magazines initially offered heavily discounted subscription rates. When the trial periods ended in 1997 and 1998, many individuals decided not to renew; by 2000 the economy began to sour and some advertising began to dry up; and in 2001 the harsh combination of a recession, the impact of the September 11th terrorist attack on the United States, and a debilitating drop in advertising expenditures took a toll on the entire magazine industry.

Total consumer magazine circulation stood at 292.2 million copies in 1996. During the next 2 years, the industry posted modest increases of 0.9% (294.8 million) in 1997, 0.4% (295.9 million) in 1998, and 0.6% in 1999. The market declined sharply in 2000 (–1.2%; 294.1 million) and 2001 (–0.6%; 292.3 million). The prognosis 2002 through 2005 is unsettling: 2002, –0.7%, 290.4 million; 2003, –0.6%, 288.7 million; 2004, –0.5%, 287.4 million; and 2005, –0.3%, 286.5 million. Overall, circulation posted a compound annual growth rate (CAGR) of 0.1% between 1996 and 2000. The projections is for a –0.5% CAGR for 2000 through 2005.

The total number of magazines purchased per adult stood at 1.49 copies in 1996. By 2000, this total fell to 1.44 copies, and industry analysts believe continued deterioration in the marketplace will result in a 1.34 total in 2005. Clearly, concerns about the economy in 2002 (and in all likelihood through 2003), stiff competition from cable and satellite television, the emergence of the DVD as the platform of choice (about 40% of all U.S. households will have DVD players sometime in 2003), and the inevitable "sticker shock" associated with steep increases in the price of magazines at newsstands influenced consumers to readjust their purchases and subscriptions of consumer magazines. Cutbacks in corporate profits triggered declines in company subscriptions and advertising campaigns for many trade magazines.

Compounding this problem were two other substantive trends. First, there was an increase in the average cost for a single copy at newsstands, growing from $2.13 in 1996 to $2.76 in 2000. The CAGR edged up 6.7% between 1996 and 2000. Second, consolidation in the wholesaler distribution network made it far more difficult to get magazines placed at newsstands, convenience stores, supermarkets, etcetera.

A declining circulation base meant that a magazine's guaranteed circ was not achieved, forcing publishers to provide space for free or at reduced rates. Many consumer magazines addressed these declines by purchasing subscription lists from defunct books. The goal was to boost circulation and hide a declining readership base. Although this practice appealed to publishers, the newly acquired readers had no loyalty to their new magazine; and many advertisers complained about this practice in 2001 and 2002.

## Magazine Industry Consolidation

This industry was also affected by the growing consolidation in the global mass-media industry. Many industry analysts insisted that economies of scale could be achieved if large media (and magazine) companies were created to take advantage of the bulk buying of paper and negotiate better terms with commercial printers and distributors. The end result was the formation of some exceptionally large, influential magazine operations, many of which were owned by foreign corporations. AOL Time Warner was the largest owner of magazines in the United States with revenues hovering near the $4 billion mark in 2000. The Hearst Corp. was a distant second ($1.9 billion); Advance Publications ($1.6 billion), International Data Group ($977 million), and the British-Dutch conglomerate Reed-Elsevier ($956 million) rounded out the top five. Some of the other major foreign corporate owners included Hachette Fillipacchi Magazines ($627 million, France, 10th); Gruner & Jahr ($573 million, owned by Germany's Bertelsmann AG company; 11th), and VNU ($466 million, another Dutch corporation, 12th).

## FINANCES AND REVENUES

In 1990, there were 14,049 consumer and trade magazines in the United States. By 2001 that tally reached 17,694, up 25.9%. Yet this statistic is misleading. Magazine publishing sustained declines in the late 1990s, and the total number of books dropped from a high of 18,606 in 1998 to 17,694 in 2001, off 4.9% in only three years.

### Revenue Streams

Consumer and trade magazines generally have a number of revenue streams: (1) paid circulation; (2) newsstand circulation; (3) advertisements (classified and display); (4) mailing-list rentals; (5) reprints; (6) book spin-offs of articles; (7) *advertorial* sections (i.e., an advertisement with the look and feel of regular editorial material in the magazine); (8) special issues; (9) trade shows (especially in the b-to-b segment; (10) exports; and (11) franchising the magazine to foreign publishers (who might translate the U.S. editorial content and insert their own ads).

A number of b-to-b titles rely on a *controlled* (i.e., nonpaid) circulation strategy, insisting their readers *qualify* (e.g., fill out a card indicating income, job title, etc.) to receive the title; these magazines dependent solely on advertising revenues. A small number of "Sunday newspaper" magazines (e.g., *Parade, USA Weekend*, etc.) are provided free of charge to purchasers of a newspaper; these magazines rely on advertising and fees paid by the paper to the magazine.

### Advertising

The advertising-editorial (ad-edit) ratio is an important barometer of a consumer magazine's economic health (Ha & Litman, 1997). In the early-to mid-1990s, the percentage of editorial pages were higher than ad pages: 1991, an ad-edit ratio of 48.6% (ads)–51.4% (edit); 1994, 48.1%–51.9%; 1998, 48.3%–51.7%. By 2001, consumer titles had a 45.1%–54.9%, indicative of a flattening of advertising revenues in 2001 (off 8.2% from 2000) and a crushing decline in advertising pages in 2001 (dropping 17.2% from 2000). Major advertisers curtailed ad budgets in 2001, with the technology sector leading the way (–28.8%). Other sectors that reduced their ad placements included automotive (–2.5%), media and advertising (–15.7%), the finance, insurance, and real-estate area (–16.6%), and retail (–16.45). Other advertisers posted rather modest increases in ad budgets, including apparel and accessories and transportation, hotels, and resorts. Table 6.5 describes these trends.

Fourteen of the top fifteen magazines (based on total gross dollar revenues) rely on three revenues streams: paid circulation, newsstand circulation, and ads. The exact ratio between these streams varies (Summer, 2001; Vakratsas & Ambler, 1999). For example, *People* depends heavily on advertisers (62.1%) rather than paid (18.8%) or newsstand dollars (19.2%). *TV Guide* is split almost eventually between advertising (42.1%) and paid subscribers (44.6%). *Business Week* counts on advertising for almost 91% of its total revenues. Overall, the majority of all consumer and trade magazines

TABLE 6.5

**Magazine Advertising Revenues and Advertising Pages for Measured Magazines: 1990–2001 ($ Billions)**

| Year | Advertising Revenues | Percent Change From Previous Year | Advertising Pages | Percent Change From Previous Year |
|------|------|------|------|------|
| 1990 | $ 6.753 | — | 171,689 | — |
| 1991 | 6.538 | –3.18% | 156,650 | –8.76% |
| 1992 | 7.141 | 9.22% | 163,513 | 4.38% |
| 1993 | 7.625 | 6.78% | 176,973 | 8.23% |
| 1994 | 8.504 | 11.53% | 180,589 | 2.04% |
| 1995 | 10.114 | 18.93% | 208,378 | 15.39% |
| 1996 | 11.179 | 10.53% | 213,781 | 2.59% |
| 1997 | 12.754 | 14.09% | 231,371 | 8.23% |
| 1998 | 13.813 | 8.30% | 242,383 | 4.76% |
| 1999 | 15.508 | 12.27% | 255,146 | 5.27% |
| 2000 | 17.655 | 13.84% | 286,932 | 12.35% |
| 2001 | 16.213 | –8.22% | 237,612 | –17.19% |

depend primarily on advertising revenues; and the impact of the ad revenue declines in 2001 and 2002 impacted severely on almost magazines in
the United States. Only two titles in the top 15 magazines posted a positive
increase in 2001 over 2000 in advertising pages: *Power & Motor Yacht*
(+6.5%); and *Transworld Skateboarding* (+17.5%). Six titles were up on the ad
dollar column, although four were in the single digit range: *Modern Bride*
(+2.4%), *Vogue* (+1.7%), *In Style* (+2.9%), and *New York* (+1.6%). Table 6.6
outlines these trends.

**Business Model**

Magazines sell advertisers access to readers, and the very successful magazines provide advertisers with direct access to desirable demographics
(women 18–49; men 25–39, etc.; Batra & Ray, 1986; Englis & Solomon, 1995;
Hall, 2002; McCracken, 1993; Ohman, 1996). Ad rates are based on the cost
per thousand of readers (CPM), and publishers guarantee advertisers a
base readership.

An analysis of *Business Week* (a consumer not a trade magazine) highlights its advertising strategy. This title offers an exceptionally strong demographic base to advertisers in terms of its readership's age, educational,
occupational, and income levels. It guarantees advertisers a North American subscriber base of 950,000, and it delivers on a weekly basis about
971,756 subscribers (95.02% are paid subscribers, effectively negating the
vagaries of weekly newsstand sales). *Business Week* offers advertisers national, regional, and metro-area editions as well as special ad sections, guaranteeing (and exceeding) rate bases every edition. In 2002 the standard
one-page advertising space rates for black and white ($64,100), black and
one color ($83,700), and 4-color ($94,800) advertisements are rather high,
but discounts are available for multiple insertions. *Business Week* also publishes international editions (Asia and the South Pacific, China, Europe,
Latin America, the Middle East, and Africa). Other magazines completing
in this same niche must offer attractive rates and demographics as well as
effective editorial content that rivals or exceeds what *Business Week* offers,
not an easy task.

Clearly, most of the major magazines (including *Time, Jet, Latina, Forbes*,
etc.) developed similar strategies regarding national, regional, or international editions, Internet based sites, and global connections, especially as
markets converge and transportation hubs increase in efficiency.

**Financial Issues**

*The major financial indices (1997–2001, the last year data was available)*
and the events of 2001 and 2002 indicate a conundrum (Veronis Suhler,

## TABLE 6.6
### Top 15 Magazines: Advertising Pages and Advertising Revenues: 2000–2001 ($ Million)

| Magazine | Advertising Pages | | | Advertising Dollars | | |
|---|---|---|---|---|---|---|
| | 2001 | 2000 | Percent Change | 2001 | 2000 | Percent Change |
| Fortune | 4011.5 | 6258.5 | -35.9% | 333808417 | 476848553 | -30.0% |
| Bride's | 3853.5 | 4245.5 | -9.23% | 127565478 | 128437896 | -0.68% |
| Business Week | 3785.6 | 6005.7 | -37.0% | 394302612 | 573262687 | -31.2% |
| Forbes | 3735.4 | 6083.5 | -38.6% | 305823809 | 434344335 | -29.6% |
| People | 3612.2 | 4228.1 | -14.6% | 656222102 | 723914428 | -9.4% |
| Modern Bride | 3188.4 | 3334.4 | -4.4% | 107272419 | 104822284 | 2.4% |
| Vogue | 3156.2 | 3308.7 | -4.6% | 201693314 | 198254506 | 1.7% |
| In Style | 2961.6 | 3216.5 | -7.9% | 238437517 | 231820743 | 2.9% |
| TV Guide | 2765.2 | 3194.8 | -13.5% | 388879915 | 450406442 | -13.7% |
| New York | 2764.2 | 2844.3 | -2.8% | 67627599 | 66571615 | 1.6% |
| Power & MotorYacht | 2609.5 | 2450.1 | 6.5% | 27725627 | 24563932 | 12.9% |
| The Economist | 2585.3 | 3250.8 | -20.5% | 61276035 | 69413551 | -11.7% |
| Transworld Skateboarding | 2545.2 | 2166.0 | 17.5% | 21251821 | 16543106 | 28.5% |
| PC Magazine | 2493.7 | 3315.5 | -24.8% | 185950333 | 222005942 | -16.2% |
| Time | 2398.8 | 3008.6 | -20.3% | 557622780 | 662773814 | -15.9% |

Copyright © 2002 Magazine Publishers Association. All numbers were rounded off and may not add up to 100%. Reprinted with permission.

2001a, 2001b, 2002). This business posted gains in all of the major categories between 1997 and 1999: revenues +2.31%, operating income +21.63%, operating cash flow +20%, and assets +10.14%. Revenues continued to increase in both 2000 and 2001, but, as the data revealed in Table 6.5, concerns materialized regarding ad pages and revenues. Ultimately, business conditions unraveled. Operation income sank horribly in 2000, off 94.52%. By 2001, conditions worsened and negative dollar totals were recorded. Similar patters emerged in operating cash flow in 2000 (–15.97%) and 2001 (–10.86%), and these declines were mirrored in unsettling tallies in operating income margins, operating cash flow margins, operating income return on assets, operating cash flow return on assets, and asset turnover. Table 6.7 outlines these dismal results.

The prognosis for the rest of this decade is disconcerting. This industry slipped, and it will take a number of years before magazines rebound to their pre-2000 levels, a situation that prompted some Wall Street investment bankers to eschew backing too many magazine mergers and acquisitions in these uncertain market conditions.

## THE IMPACT OF NEW TECHNOLOGY

The electronic distribution of magazines via the Internet captured a great deal of attention in the 1990s (Leong, Huang, & Stanners, 1998; Yoon & Kim, 2001).

### TABLE 6.7
### Consumer Magazine Industry Financial Data ($ Millions)

|  | 1997 | 1998 | 1999 | 2000 | 2001 |
|---|---|---|---|---|---|
| Revenues | $6952.1 | $7311.4 | $7112.8 | $7244.7 | $7460.4 |
| Operating Income | 841.9 | 938.0 | 1024.0 | 56.1 | –204.9 |
| Operating Cash Flow | 1031.8 | 1127.0 | 1238.2 | 1040.4 | 927.4 |
| Assets | 4515.7 | 4852.6 | 4973.6 | 27404.3 | 31357.0 |
| Operating Income Margins | 12.1% | 12.8% | 14.4% | 0.8% | –2.7% |
| Operating Cash Flow Margins | 14.8% | 15.4% | 17.4% | 14.4% | 12.4% |
| Operating Income Return on Assets | N/A | 20.2% | 21.0% | 0.3% | –0.7% |
| Operating Cash Flow Return on Assets | N/A | 24.1% | 25.3% | 6.4% | 3.2% |
| Asset Turnover | N/A | 1.56 | 1.45 | 0.45 | 0.25 |

*Note.* From *Veronis Suhler Stevenson Communications Industry Report* 2002. Reprinted with permission.

Some industry consultants suggested all magazines must have a web presence in order to compete in this new-media environment. Other analysts insisted that a Web-based magazine could act as an effective subscription and marketing tool for a magazine. Still others believed that the print and electronic version of the magazine must be integrated, allowing advertisers to buy simultaneously both print and electronic ads (Bezjian-Avery, Calder, & Iacobucci, 1998). The overall logic of these suggestions was rather compelling. Electronic magazines could break new stories, update existing articles, and provide readers with links to useful sites (Gallagher, Parsons, & Foster, 2001). The Internet held great promise for editors and readers alike. For example, *The Economist* developed an effective Web site and an e-mail system alerting readers, and potential readers, about new articles. They crafted special Web sites, linked directly via their e-mails, to special editorial-advertising supplements (e.g., "The Future of the MBA"). This magazine realized that convergence allowed them to maximize their reach and strengthen the bottom line.

However, a few problems surfaced in the transformation of print magazines into electronic "zines." Despite the hype, and the rapid penetration of computers into households, universities, libraries, and offices, Internet-based magazines generated advertising revenues that were at best modest; and very few Internet magazine sites operate in the black. Of the dozens of on-line magazines in the AOL Time Warner stable, only two are in the black, and one just escaped from the red in early 2002. Don Logan, president and CEO of Time, Inc., stated, "its been historically difficult to buy across media; we are not set up to sell that way, and agencies are not set up to buy that way" (Hatfield, 2001).

So if new technology ventures are unsuccessful financially, why continue them? Magazine publishers essentially are trying to position their magazines for the future. So when consumers decide to start paying for an Internet based title, and even the experts cannot predict with any certainty when this will happen, their magazine will be there, an expensive (and, so far, an exceptionally unprofitable) endeavor.

## COPYRIGHT ISSUES

The copier and digital revolution opened many new doors for editors and readers. Unfortunately, one drawback was a sharp increase in copyright infringement. Although the magazine industry worked closely with counterparts in the newspaper, book, and film industries, very little progress has been made, and is likely to be made, in curbing this pernicious undermining of copyright protection.

## SOCIAL ISSUES AND CONCLUDING THOUGHTS

Magazines continue to meet their basic mission: to educate, inform, and entertain readers. A plethora of titles, sophisticated printing and distribution systems, and talented writers entice readers, even casual ones, to view magazines as pivotal formats in an ever changing, evolving media landscape. Magazines are ubiquitous, essentially inexpensive (especially in light of low annual subscription rates), and portable, characteristics that will allow them to remain an important contributor to society, public debates, and the marketplace of ideas well into the 21st century.

People just seem to love magazines, their feel, their use of type, and enchanting color. Yet magazines are an important component of American society. Their history is filled with sterling examples of exposing deplorable conditions in various segments of American society, from the harsh inequality of segregation to terrible working conditions in factories. Magazines have an ability to present pivotal information in long essays, something newspapers rarely can do. They are timely, hitting the street on a weekly basis, something books cannot match. But best of all, magazines are just enjoyable to read, a fact readily evident to anyone waiting for an airplane in the early days of the 21st century.

## FURTHER READING

Daly, C., Henry, P., & Ryder, E. (1997). *The magazine publishing industry.* Boston: Allyn & Bacon.

Greco, A. N. (1997). *The book publishing industry.* Boston: Allyn & Bacon.

Heidendry, J. (1993). *Theirs was the kingdom: Lila and DeWitt Wallace and the story of Reader's Digest.* New York: Norton.

Picard, R. (2002). *The economics and financing of media companies.* New York: Fordham University Press.

Tebbel, J., & Zuckerman, M. (1991). *The magazine in America: 1741–1990.* New York: Oxford University Press.

## REFERENCES

Bagdikian, B. (2000). *The media monopoly.* Boston: Beacon Press.

Batra, R., & Ray, M. L. (1986). Affective processes mediating acceptance of advertising. *Journal of Consumer Research, 13*(2), 234–249.

Becker, B. W. (1998). Values in advertising research: A methodological caveat. *Journal of Advertising Research, 38*(4), 57–60.

Bezjian-Avery, A., Calder, B., & Iacobucci, D. (1998). New media interactive advertising vs. traditional advertising. *Journal of Advertising Research, 38*(4), 23–32.

Bogart, D. (Ed.). (2002). *The Bowker annual: Library and book trade almanac, 47th edition.* New Providence, NJ: R. R. Bowker).

Book Industry Study Group, Inc. (2002). *Book industry trends 2002.* New York: Author.

Byron, C. (1984). *The fanciest dive.* New York: Norton.

Clurman, R. (1992). *To the end of time.* New York: Simon & Schuster.

Daly, C., Henry, P., & Ryder, E. (1997). *The magazine publishing industry.* Boston: Allyn & Bacon.

Englis, B. G., & Solomon, M. R. (1995). To be or not to be: Lifestyle imagery, reference groups, and the clustering of America. *Journal of Advertising, 24*(1), 13–22.

Gallagher, K., Parsons, J., & Foster, K. D. (2001). A tale of two studies: Advertising effectiveness and content evaluation in print and on the web. *Journal of Advertising Research, 41*(4), 71–81.

Gill, B. (1975). *Here at the New Yorker.* New York: Random House.

Greco, A. N. (1988). *Business journalism: Management notes and cases.* New York: New York University Press.

Greco, A. N. (1989, Fall). Mergers and acquisitions in publishing, 1984–1988: Some public policy issues. *Book Research Quarterly, 5,* 25–44.

Greco, A. N. (1991). *Advertising management and the business publishing industry.* New York: New York University Press.

Greco, A. N. (1992, Fall). U.S. book returns, 1984–1989. *Publishing Research Quarterly, 8,* 46–61.

Greco, A. N. (1996, Fall). Shaping the future: Mergers, acquisitions, and the U.S. publishing, communication, and mass media industries, 1990–1995. *Publishing Research Quarterly, 12,* 5–15.

Greco, A. N. (1997a). *The book publishing industry.* Boston: Allyn & Bacon.

Greco, A. N. (1997b, Spring). The market for consumer books in the U.S.: 1985–1995. *Publishing Research Quarterly, 13,* 3–40.

Greco, A. N. (1998, Fall). Domestic consumer expenditures for consumer books: 1984–1994. *Publishing Research Quarterly, 14,* 12–28.

Greco, A. N. (1999, Fall). The impact of horizontal mergers and acquisitions on corporate concentration in the U.S. book industry: 1989–1994. The *Journal of Media Economics, 12*(3), 165–180.

Greco, A. N. (2000, November). Market concentration in the U.S. consumer book industry: 1995–1996. The *Journal of Cultural Economics, 24*(4), 321–336.

Greco, A. N. (2001a, January). The general reader market for university press books in the United States, 1990–2000, with projections for the years 2000 through 2004. *The Journal of Scholarly Publishing, 32*(2), *61–86.*

Greco, A. N. (2001b, April). The market for university press books in the United States: 1985–1999. *Learned Publishing, 14*(2), 97–105.

Ha, L., & Litman, B. R. (1997). Does advertising clutter have diminishing and negative returns? *Journal of Advertising, 26*(1), 31–42.

Hall, B. F. (2002). A new model for measuring advertising effectiveness. *Journal of Advertising Research, 42*(2), 23–31.

Hatfield, S. (2001, May). The new task for publishers: Making the web pay. *Ad Age Global,* 23.

Kitch, C. (2001). *The girl on the magazine cover: The origins of visual stereotypes in American mass media.* Chapel Hill, NC: University of North Carolina Press.

Kover, A. J. (1995). Copywriters' implicit theories of communication: An exploration. *Journal of Consumer Research, 23*(4), 596–611.

Leong, E. K. F., Huang, X., & Stanners, P. (1998). Comparing the effectiveness of the web site with traditional media. *Journal of Advertising Research, 38*(5), 44–51.

McCracken, E. (1993). *Decoding women's magazines.* New York: St. Martin's.

Oda, S., & Sansilo, G. (2002a, May). Fiction output projected to reach all-time high in 2001. Subtext: The book business in perspective. *Subtext, 1*(1), 3.

Oda, S., & Sansilo, G. (2002b). *The Subtext 2001–2002 perspective on book publishing: Numbers, issues & trends.* Darien, CT: Subtext.

Ohman, R. (1996). *Selling culture: Magazines, markets, and class at the turn of the century.* New York: Verso.

Picard, R. (2002). *The economics and financing of media companies.* New York: Fordham University Press.

Posgrova, C. (1995). *It wasn't pretty, folks, but didn't we have fun? Esquire in the sixties.* New York: Norton.

Siwek, Stephen E. (2002). *Copyright industries in the U.S. economy: The 2002 report.* Retrieved from http://www.iipa.com

Summer, D. (2001). Who pays for magazines? Advertisers or consumers? *Journal of Advertising Research, 41*(6), 61–67.

U.S. Congressional Budget Office (2002, March). *CBO's current economic projections.* Retrieved from http://www.cbo.gov

U.S. Department of Commerce, Bureau of the Census (1997). *1997 Economic census: Manufacturing industry series book publishing.* Washington, DC: G.P.O.

U.S. Department of Commerce, Bureau of the Census. (2001). *The statistical abstract of the United States, 2001.* Washington, DC: G.P.O.

Vakratsas, D., & Ambler, T. (1999). How advertising works: What do we really know? *Journal of Marketing, 63*(1), 26–43.

Veronis Suhler (2001a). *Veronis Suhler communications industry forecast.* New York: Veronis Suhler.

Veronis Suhler (2001b). *Veronis Suhler communications industry report.* New York: Veronis Suhler.

Veronis Suhler Stevenson (2002). *Veronis Suhler Stevenson communications industry forecast.* New York: Veronis Suhler.

Yoon, S., & Kim, J. (2001). Is the Internet more effective than traditional media? Factors affecting the choice of media. *Journal of Advertising Research, 41*(6), 53–60.

# Chapter 7

# The Broadcast Television Networks

**DOUGLAS A. FERGUSON**
*College of Charleston*

Television is a business. Most consumers view their television set as a source of diversion, information, and entertainment. The average viewer probably does not think much about the cost of programs or commercials. As a cultural force, television is a teacher, a companion, a babysitter, a means to procrastinate, and a steady stream of amusement. But to the people who create the content, television is a business. Business is concerned with money and television needs an abundant supply of money. Understanding television economics is essential to an understanding of broadcast television.

Television networks have two primary customers: the audience and the advertisers. In addition, each network relies on affiliated broadcast stations to distribute the network programming. Each economic stakeholder (audience, advertiser, broadcaster) approaches the same system of broadcast television economics in different ways. Viewers want information and entertainment, advertisers want viewers for their commercials, and broadcasters want viewers in sufficient number to generate a profit. The common consideration among all of these entities, however, is how they use resources to generate profit by maximizing revenue and minimizing expenses.

According to Higgins (2002), the four largest broadcast television networks share the top 6 slots with cable networks QVC and ESPN (Table 7.1). Only 10 years before, the broadcast industry had accounted for most of the revenue associated with television programming. But for the past decade, cable television (see chap. 8, this volume) has been the leading sector. As this book went to press, Veronis Suhler Stevenson's annual *Communications Industry Forecast* was calling for only a 4.1% rise in broadcast TV expenditures to $42.9 billion and an annual compounded growth rate of only 3.8% to 2006, when it should reach nearly $50 billion (in *Electronic Media*, 2002, August 5). Cable and satellite TV spending, on the other hand, was predicted to fare better, rising 9.5% to $76.9 billion in 2002 and growing at an annual compounded rate of 7% to $106.3 billion by 2006. Broadcast television no longer enjoys the supremacy it did between the late 1940s and the early 1990s.

Nevertheless, this chapter focuses on broadcast television economics and specifically examines the economic activity of the broadcast television

TABLE 7.1

**Top 25 Television Networks**

| Rank | Network | Revenue* |
|:---:|:---:|:---:|
| 1 | NBC | $4,110 |
| 2 | QVC | $3,770 |
| 3 | CBS | $3,590 |
| 4 | ABC | $2,890 |
| 5 | ESPN | $2,120 |
| 6 | Fox | $2,100 |
| 7 | HBO | $2,050 |
| 8 | HSN | $1,790 |
| 9 | TNT | $1,210 |
| 10 | Nick | $1,090 |
| 11 | Showtime | $989 |
| 12 | USA | $940 |
| 13 | MTV | $847 |
| 14 | CNN | $823 |
| 15 | Disney | $810 |
| 16 | TBS | $799 |
| 17 | Lifetime | $790 |
| 18 | Discovery | $620 |
| 19 | The WB | $589 |
| 20 | Starz! | $580 |
| 21 | A&E | $550 |
| 22 | CNBC | $539 |
| 23 | Cinemax | $522 |
| 24 | Fox News | $490 |
| 25 | Univision | $480 |

*Estimated 2002 revenue in millions
Higgins (2002)

networks. Despite the networks' failure to capitalize on either cable TV in the 1980s (Auletta, 1991) or the Internet in the 1990s (Motavalli, 2002), many observers expect these spectrum mastodons to be around for some time to come for reasons to be made clear in the following.

## MARKET STRUCTURE

Broadcast network television is, and always has been, an oligopoly. The cost of nationwide interconnection and the limited supply of affiliate stations within market areas (each called *Designated Market Area*, or DMA, by A. C. Nielsen) have served as limiting factors to competition. In the 1950s, each DMA could reasonably support four networks: ABC , CBS, Dumont, and NBC. Just as competition for domestic automobiles led to three dominant players (Chrysler, Ford, and General Motors) by the late-1950s, the number of broadcast networks dwindled to the "Big 3": ABC, CBS, and NBC. The old Dumont stations formed the Metromedia independent stations that later comprised the large-market affiliates for the Fox network in the 1980s. By the 1990s, Fox began to rival the Big 3. Today the Big 4 have been joined by three additional part-time broadcast networks: the WB, UPN, and Pax TV.

### Current State of Consolidation

The history of network ownership is best documented elsewhere (Auletta, 1991), but the Big 3 have had few owners. At present, ABC is owned by Disney, CBS and UPN by Viacom, Fox by News Corporation, NBC by General Electric (GE), Pax TV co-owned by Paxson Communications (68%) and NBC (32%), and the WB by AOL-Time Warner. Each entity is a huge entertainment conglomerate, with all but NBC having an allied TV and motion picture production studio: ABC (Disney, Touchstone, Buena Vista, Miramax), CBS (Paramount), Fox (Twentieth Century Fox), and the WB (Warner Brothers).

Viacom/CBS also controls King World and a host of such cable channels as BET, MTV, VH1, Nickelodeon, Showtime, TNN, CMT, and TV Land. NBC owns the MSNBC and Bravo cable channels along with the Telemundo network for Spanish-language programs and a 32% interest in Pax TV. Fox has the fx channel and Fox News, whereas ABC uses its ABC Family cable channel to *repurpose* programs across separate platforms.

### Economies of Scale and Scope

During the past decade, the increase in competition in the television market has driven both broadcast networks and station groups to seek ever-greater economies of scale and scope to offset challenges to their revenue. Scale and scope are part of a larger system of resource allocation, based on perceived value. To some extent, information and entertainment on television are a social good beyond any economic value. Certain televised events like moon landings and Olympic contests have a value to viewers and society beyond the price paid for the service. Nevertheless, television remains a business, and economic decisions are necessary for the allocation of scarce resources. For broadcast network television, allocation decisions are made in several markets.

First, there is a competition for audience and programs among sources of television broadcasting, usually among the networks and stations but also with nonbroadcast forms of programming. This macrolevel involves an industry that seeks an optimal system of resource allocation to benefit the greatest number of producers and consumers. Broadcast networks compete with premium services such as cable television by offering major events through support from advertisers (e.g., Super Bowl) and by declining to carry lesser events (e.g., soccer). On the other hand, some events with high revenue potential (e.g., title boxing matches) are supplied by pay-per-view channels.

The second market concerns the internal efficiency of the television station or program producer, both of whom are interested in holding down the cost of making a television show. Large companies take advantage of economies of scale (full-time utilization of expensive studios) and economies of scope (the producer and the distributor comprise the same organization). The networks can afford to commission very expensive programs, where individual stations (or ad hoc consortia of stations) cannot. The four largest networks combined spend $18 billion per year for their vast array of programming. Over the decades, the system has evolved from advertiser-controlled programs in the 1950s, to network-controlled programs in the 1960s, to studio-controlled programs in the heavily regulated 1970s and 1980s, and finally returning to network-controlled shows in the deregulated 1990s. Starting with the Fox network in 1987, association with Hollywood studios became primarily a matter of ownership.

Networks also widened their scope by aligning with or acquiring additional cable channels and broadcast networks. As mentioned before, repurposing was made possible and eventually adopted by some networks (e.g., ABC in 2002) as an overarching strategy. ABC and CNN began serious discussion about merging their news operations in 2002. Networks also attempted to establish a foothold on the World Wide Web.

In the third market, the consumers (viewers) of broadcast products look for their own cost-benefit goals. The television audience seeks the channels to satisfy its needs and wants at a reasonable cost. In the case of advertiser-supported broadcasting, the consumer pays very few direct costs but does pay the opportunity cost of leisure time allocation. This latter cost—lost time for other activities, like sleeping or studying—is sometimes trivial to the individual because it is not usually measured like money.

Finally, the fourth market is where stations and other programmers sell the attention of audiences toward programs. The buyer is the advertiser who wants access to those audiences. Noncommercial television broadcasters do not compete in this market, although they compete with other receivers of public funding.

The structure of choices in television broadcasting is under two pressures (Collins, Garnham, & Locksley, 1988). One is the competition of distribution technologies, including cable television, direct-to-home satellites, home video (DVDs), and digital interactive television. The other is the pressure to broaden their market base to pay for the increased cost of competing with others.

This final point cannot be overemphasized. In the recent past, television broadcasters comprised a small oligopoly of stations for each market, fed by an oligopoly of national broadcast networks. The competition was fierce but self-contained. Stations benefitted from a predictably certain zero-sum game among a small number of players. If NBC had the best shows on Thursday, another network was the winner of the three-way race on a different night. As other sources of video entertainment have appeared, however, the television broadcasters have continually needed to attract more revenue to pay for more desirable products—at the same time that their audience has been segmented into less-valuable pieces in an advertiser-supported scheme. The advertiser who bought a commercial in the last-place program was assured a goodly portion of the potential viewers when only three choices competed. Today, an advertiser in the first-place program may only reach a fifth of the viewers because of competition from cable networks.

### Vertical–Horizontal Integration

Most media businesses influence up to three areas: production, distribution, and exhibition. As distributors, networks have long exerted vertical control over exhibition and production, especially in the distant past, but less so later on owing to the government's "financial interest" regulations that kept the networks at bay. Today, however, networks have once again become increasingly vertical.

Where 10 years ago the network's owned-and-operated (O & O) affiliated stations reached 25% of TV homes, today these stations carry the Big 4 to 35% of households, which was the limit set by the 1996 Telecommunications Act. In some cases they may reach up to 39% via special dispensation that may come to be judged the rule rather than the exception if Federal courts have their way. For example, NBC has 13 O & O stations and CBS has 17. The influence over exhibition is heightened by long-term affiliation contracts with nonowned affiliates, which are compensated for access to their commercial audiences.

The vertical influence over production also has grown. Where 10 years ago the networks produced less than 15% of their prime-time programs, nearly all studio production today is controlled or owned by networks. Government deregulation came in response to the vertical control exerted by the cable networks and a small group of multiple system operators (MSOs), which are collectively the prime competitors to broadcast networks.

Despite the strength of the vertical chain, barriers to entry have not proven as insurmountable as once thought. The deregulation of ownership and the suggestion of duopolies has led to a climate where broadcast network competitors have appeared: the WB, UPN, and Pax TV.

As the networks have themselves acquired and allied with cable television networks, the presence of horizontal integration has surfaced in the recent past. Repurposed programming has slowly proliferated (e.g., NBC's *Conan O'Brien Show* on Comedy Central). By October 2002, ABC had made plans to be more even more horizontal, repurposing several of its prime-time shows onto its ABC Family Channel, which it had acquired from Fox.

***Barriers to Entry.*** For many years, economies of scale and a shortage of VHF signals barred broadcast competitors from entering into competition with the Big 3 networks. By the 1980s, however, improved UHF signals and 68% cable television penetration helped Fox slowly roll out a fourth network.

On another front, the Hollywood studios foresaw the eventual deregulation of the financial interest rules and began in earnest to create fifth and sixth networks to leverage control over their production prowess. As long as the broadcast networks were gatekeepers, the studios had to be content with whatever was bought, usually under the risk of *deficit financing* by the networks, whose license fees seldom covered the front-end cost of production. Today, the level of competition at the production and exhibition levels has shrunk, whereas the number of viable players has slightly risen. In all, the number of competitors, broadcast and nonbroadcast, deprives the advertisers of it mass audience—replaced by a fragmented landscape of video alternatives.

## FINANCES

### Basic Business Model

Advertising revenue is the fuel that drives the economics of broadcast television. The sale of local, regional and national spot advertising announcements (commercials) accounts for nearly all of a broadcast station's income.

The remainder, typically only 10% of total revenue, comes from any network compensation that flows from the network to the affiliate. *Independents* (broadcast television stations without a network affiliation) derive no additional income through compensation, but the number of true independents has diminished greatly with the arrival in the mid-1990s of newer broadcast networks.

*Compensation*, as the name suggests, is revenue that compensates an affiliate for the lost opportunity to sell advertising during network time periods. For example, an independent television station may broadcast a 2-hour movie and sell between 20 to 30 minutes of advertising. A network-affiliated station (*affiliate*) may simultaneously carry a similar film from a network but only receive three or four interior *station breaks* in which perhaps 5 minutes of "local" advertising can be sold. Most of the advertising revenue flows to the network, so the affiliates must be compensated.

On the surface, it appears that the hypothetical independent has greater revenue potential because of increased inventory of time. In reality, the network can usually exploit its own scope and scale to provide more expensive programs that attract a far larger audience, which then delivers more value to the local station breaks. Broadcast stations are eager to affiliate with powerful networks that can provide programming that meets the wants and needs of a huge audience. In almost all cases, stations that are affiliated with networks have higher total revenue than independent stations in the same market. This fact helps explain why former independent stations have often become part-time affiliates of networks, even if the networks are fledgling (e.g., UPN, the WB, Pax TV).

The source of advertising revenue is influenced by cyclical events. For example, political advertising increases dramatically during Presidential election years, such as 2000 when a record $606 million was tracked by the Television Bureau of Advertising (2002). Another source of advertising revenue in 2000 came from the Olympics, which generated $1.27 billion, although most of this sum would have been spent in some other promotional venue (Downey, 2002).

Advertising also depends on particular manufacturing sectors. When the automobile industry is robust, its advertising budgets for television broadcasting are substantial. As a general rule, however, television advertising is very healthy even during recessionary times. Advertisers seem more willing to fight harder to protect their share of the market during tough times, thus spending a larger share of their money on television commercials than during prosperous times.

## Dual Market

Broadcast economics appear unusual because the seller has two different customers operating in two different markets with two different products.

The first customer is the consumer who watches the television programming (the first product). In the United States, the viewer pays nothing for this service beyond the intangible opportunity cost of not doing something else instead of viewing. Some direct costs are involved for the consumer (the TV receiver, the electricity to operate it, and often the cable service to enhance the signal), but the supplier realizes no direct revenues from the mass audience.

The second customer is the advertiser who is interested in the huge audience for the programs produced or purchased by the network, or in some cases, the individual stations. The networks and their affiliated stations sell time in the form of commercial announcements, which are the second product. The revenues from advertising more than cover the cost of programming for the station or network, assuming a situation where profit is possible. As profitable as broadcast television can be, some stations and networks lose money because their expenses are too high or their revenues are too low or both.

Owen and Wildman (1998) stressed the importance of understanding that commercial broadcasters produce audiences, not programming:

> The first and most serious mistake that an analyst of the television industry can make is to assume that advertising-supported television broadcasters are in business to broadcast programs. They are not. Broadcasters are in the business of producing audiences. These audiences, or means of access to them, are sold to advertisers. The product of a television station is measured in dimensions of people and time. The price of the product is quoted in dollars per thousand viewers per unit of commercial time, typically 20 or 30 seconds. (p. 3)

### Revenue Streams and Potential New Revenue Streams

The cost of advertising is based on actual audience size, which is measured by Nielsen Media Research. Potential audience size is influenced by the size of the market area in which the station broadcasts, and, to some extent, by the station's ability to affiliate with a popular network. The unit of comparison is cost-per-thousand (CPM). Programs that attract large audiences are usually more cost-effective (unless the advertiser seeks a small, highly targeted audience), despite the higher cost of advertising. The average CPM for a commercial in a network primetime program is about $15, whereas a commercial in daytime is only $4 (Higgins & Romano, 2002).

According to information from *Advertising Age*, the price for a 30-second commercial ranges from $12,871 in *UPN Friday Movie* to $455,700 for an identical spot in *Friends* on NBC's Thursday lineup (Table 7.2). Prices are higher in the early evening when audiences are larger and lower on those nights when people are less likely to be at home, such as Friday and Saturday.

# TABLE 7.2

## Average 30-Second Commercial Prices

| | | | | | | |
|---|---|---|---|---|---|---|
| 24 | FOX | $184,550 | Dateline NBC | NBC | $106,817 |
| 20/20 | ABC | $72,118 | Dawson's Creek | WB | $69,657 |
| 30 Seconds To Fame | FOX | $50,125 | Dinotopia | ABC | $60,038 |
| 48 Hours | CBS | $37,840 | Do Over | WB | $33,430 |
| 60 Minutes | CBS | $90,000 | Drew Carey | ABC | $84,377 |
| 60 Minutes II | CBS | $68,322 | Ed | NBC | $99,733 |
| 7th Heaven | WB | $83,752 | Enterprise | UPN | $71,383 |
| 8 Simple Rules | ABC | $144,438 | ER | NBC | $438,514 |
| ABC Big Picture Show | ABC | $63,069 | Everwood | WB | $72,204 |
| According to Jim | ABC | $137,750 | Everybody Loves Raymond | CBS | $301,640 |
| Alias | ABC | $144,890 | Family Affair | WB | $27,537 |
| American Dreams | NBC | $108,288 | Fastlane | FOX | $133,271 |
| America's Funniest Home Videos | ABC | $63,460 | Fear Factor | NBC | $100,833 |
| America's Most Wanted | FOX | $61,780 | Firefly | FOX | $81,000 |
| | | | Frasier | NBC | $252,067 |
| Angel | WB | $55,609 | Friends | NBC | $455,700 |
| Becker | CBS | $107,115 | Futurama | FOX | $90,100 |
| Bernie Mac | FOX | $166,375 | George Lopez Show | ABC | $136,594 |
| Birds of Prey | WB | $57,420 | Gilmore Girls | WB | $82,287 |
| Boomtown | NBC | $114,729 | Gilmore Girls: Beginnings | WB | $51,295 |
| Boston Public | FOX | $146,887 | Girlfriends | UPN | $39,300 |
| Bram and Alice | CBS | $87,133 | Girls Club | FOX | $178,400 |
| Buffy the Vampire Slayer | UPN | $59,032 | Good Morning Miami | NBC | $279,813 |
| Cedric the Entertainer | FOX | $117,213 | Greetings From Tucson | WB | $46,865 |
| Charmed | WB | $48,672 | Grounded for Life | FOX | $136,215 |
| Cops | FOX | $55,917 | Hack | CBS | $49,320 |
| Cops 2 | FOX | $61,892 | Half & Half | UPN | $38,006 |
| Crossing Jordan | NBC | $122,960 | Haunted | US | $28,400 |
| CSI: Crime Scene Investigation | CBS | $280,043 | Hidden Hills | NBC | $172,854 |
| CSI: Miami | CBS | $164,870 | In-Laws | NBC | $96,500 |
| *Dateline* | NBC | $63,950 | JAG | CBS | $97,355 |
| Dateline NBC | NBC | $79,608 | | | |

*(continued)*

TABLE 7.2    (*continued*)

| | | | | | | |
|---|---|---|---|---|---|---|
| Jamie Kennedy Experiment | WB | $35,964 | | Scrubs | NBC | $294,667 |
| John Doe | FOX | $102,350 | | Septuplets | FOX | $85,500 |
| Judging Amy | CBS | $118,857 | | Simpsons | FOX | $248,300 |
| Just Shoot Me | NBC | $115,575 | | Smallville | WB | $111,439 |
| King of Queens | CBS | $168,425 | | Still Standing | CBS | $186,100 |
| King of the Hill | FOX | $212,500 | | Survivor | CBS | $418,750 |
| Law & Order | NBC | $266,220 | | That '70s Show | FOX | $164,950 |
| Law & Order: SVU | NBC | $114,320 | | That Was Then | ABC | $65,369 |
| Law and Order: Criminal Intent | NBC | $124,889 | | The Agency | CBS | $55,228 |
| | | | | The Amazing Race | CBS | $96,112 |
| Less Than Perfect | ABC | $141,679 | | The Bachelor II | ABC | $136,334 |
| Life With Bonnie | ABC | $121,222 | | The District | CBS | $64,580 |
| Malcolm in the Middle | FOX | $196,725 | | The Grubbs | FOX | $13,817 |
| | | | | The Guardian | CBS | $82,239 |
| MDs | ABC | $102,019 | | The Parkers | UPN | $39,267 |
| Meet The Marks | FOX | $64,750 | | The Practice | ABC | $180,106 |
| Monday Night Football | ABC | $29,800 | | The Twilight Zone | UPN | $28,613 |
| | | | | The West Wing | NBC | $282,248 |
| My Wife | ABC | $156,257 | | Third Watch | NBC | $126,270 |
| NBC Saturday Night Movie | NBC | $61,892 | | Touched By An Angel | CBS | $42,342 |
| NYPD Blue | ABC | $157,249 | | UPN Friday Night Movie | UPN | $12,871 |
| Off Centre | WB | $40,379 | | | | |
| Oliver Beene | FOX | $122,780 | | What I Like About You | WB | $49,766 |
| One on One | UPN | $40,456 | | Whose Line Is It Anyway? | ABC | $64,594 |
| Presidio Med | CBS | $61,457 | | | | |
| Primetime Thursday | ABC | $82,199 | | Will & Grace | NBC | $376,617 |
| | | | | Without A Trace | CBS | $115,298 |
| Providence | NBC | $96,160 | | Wonderful World of Disney | ABC | $107,127 |
| Push, Nevada | ABC | $95,812 | | | | |
| Reba | WB | $48,856 | | WWE Smackdown! | UPN | $30,500 |
| Robbery Homicide Division | CBS | $43,620 | | Yes, Dear | CBS | $165,801 |
| Sabrina The Teenage Witch | WB | $45,112 | | | | |

Note.   From *Advertising Age*, October 2, 2002.

Another scheme used by buyers and sellers of television advertising time is by *rating point*. A rating point is a percentage of the potential audience tuned to a particular program. The cost of a commercial is calculated on the basis of the accumulated percentage points, a system known as *cost per point* (CPP). Advertisers buy *gross rating points* (GRPs) to reach their target audience. For example, a local news program on the number-one station may deliver 25% of the viewers in a particular market. If an advertiser buys eight commercials on that station for $1000 apiece, the purchase achieves 200 GRPs (8 × 25) at a $40 CPP ($8000 ÷ 200).

The purchase, then, is for access to the audience for a program. The value of the program to the viewer is unaffected by the number of viewers, but the value of the commercial to the advertiser is directly tied to audience size. However, television networks do not necessarily seek out the largest possible audiences for two reasons (Owen & Wildman, 1992). First, advertisers are interested in particular audiences, based on demographic characteristics. Second, the cost of a program that would reach the maximum audience in a competitive situation might exceed the profit potential. Broadcasters can only spend enough to maintain overall profitability. However, in some cases, like the grocer who loses a few pennies on some items (loss-leaders) to get people into the store, television networks will lose money on some programs, especially major sporting events.

In a very practical sense, a broadcast television network must carefully manage the price of commercials. It makes no sense to quickly sell a network's inventory at a given price. Transient business often comes in at the last minute in search of last-chance purchases of air time. If the network is sold out, this premium-priced business is lost. For example, a business that needs to run a sale on merchandise that is unexpectedly overstock will need to run many commercial messages in a wide variety of time slots over a short period of time. If a network is sold out, the advertiser sometimes is upset and refuses to come back again in the future when time is available. On the other hand, if commercials are priced too high, the advertising time may remain unsold. Typically, networks aim for an 85% sellout rate so that they can accommodate last-minute buys.

The present system is threatened by video-on-demand technology, and some observers foresee a decline of spot advertising support, with *product placement* and *sponsorship* taking up the slack. If digital video recorders (DVRs) like TiVo discourage viewers from allowing commercial interruptions, some products will integrate into the narrative or appear as virtual signs in live events. Just as other aspects of broadcasting come full circle, the return of sponsored segments and branded programs make present-day shows look like something out of the 1950s.

Networks are also experimenting with other revenue streams, such as direct sales of merchandise related to popular programs (e.g., the *Survivor* bandana or *All My Children* jewelry). Interactive advertising and video-on-demand (VOD) offer other opportunities for revenue. Networks have created fan Web sites for their programs, occasionally selling subscriptions to streaming Internet videos unavailable via broadcast (e.g., live camera views from the *Big Brother* house).

## Financial Indicators

In 1991 Auletta wrote that the networks had "lost their way," but NBC managed to remain profitable because of its prime-time dominance. By the end of 1996, NBC posted its fifth straight year of 20% operating-profit margin increases (McClellan, 1996). More recently, but before the advertising downturn in the wake of September 11, all of the Big 4 networks returned to profitability (McClellan, 2001).

Traditional economic indicators show the relative strengths and weaknesses among the major networks (Table 7.3).

## Expense Picture

The cost of a broadcast program cannot be scaled down to the price paid by the viewer, but it must be consistent with advertiser demand. The overall structure of the channel and its offerings is key. In the case of a full-service network-affiliated television station, some programs are produced cheaply because the potential audience size is affected by the time of day. Those advertisers who cannot afford to spend huge sums to reach mass audiences are sometimes attracted to late-night programs for which there is a smaller audience, and therefore lower advertising rates. It would not make economic sense to produce expensive programs for these time periods.

### TABLE 7.3
**2001 Annual Report Data (in millions of dollars, pro forma)**

|                 | Broadcast Revenue[a] | Operating Income |
|-----------------|---------------------|------------------|
| ABC/Disney      | 5,713               | 728              |
| CBS/UPN         | 7,248               | 402              |
| Fox [6/30/02]   | 3,950               | 315              |
| NBC             | 5,769               | 1,602*           |
| WB [AOL]        | 7,050**             | 618***           |

*Note.* From corporate annual reports. [a]Includes O&O affiliates; *operating profit; **includes cable channels; ***intersegment revenue.

A built-in cost-inflation dynamic for broadcast programs results from competition, peer-group rivalry among broadcasters, and an ideology of creativity (Collins et al., 1988). The term *Baumols disease* is attached to the rapid inflation of television program costs over time, where the price of commercials cannot keep pace with the cost of programming (Collins et al., 1988). The simple truth is that networks try to outspend one another in order to procure the most attractive programming at the same time that audience expectations escalate.

The result of the continuous growth in program costs is that the broadcasting industries grow larger and more consolidated, even though broadcast television networks have proliferated in recent years. As with the automotive industries, among others, the broadcasting industries expand their activities to lower level or higher level distribution activities, a form of vertical integration. To some extent, new technologies such as cable television and competition from new television networks can shake up the economic near-monopoly of program providers and distributors, but the upward pressures on costs are not abated because audience demand for more choice and better shows continues to rise.

The consolidation of media industries can be compared to similar conditions in the retail world. Some huge chain stores have become *category killers*. Local hardware stores struggle against Home Depot, and regional electronics stores lose out to superstores like Circuit City and Best Buy. Similarly, cable TV undermines some categories of shows on broadcast networks by offering a single channel dedicated entirely to one category of programming: news on CNN, sports on ESPN, and so on. With vertical integration within the broadcasting industry, however, the networks can own pieces of the category killers. For example, Disney/ABC owns ESPN and seeks a strategic alliance with CNN.

The high cost of programming is not the only major expense for the networks, however. The changeover from analog NTSC-standard signals to digital ATSC-standard signals has been a huge cost over the past several years, because the FCC has mandated that all stations (including network O & O affiliates) convert to a HDTV format that is incompatible with conventional television sets.

## Clients

The primary revenue for broadcast networks is the sale of advertising to national clients. In the late 1990s, the networks benefitted greatly from a new category of clients: the dot-com companies, which were flush with "venture capital" money that ran up the stock market values until the bubble burst in 2000. While the ride lasted, the networks profited from a steady stream of new media clients.

The chief competition, of course, comes from the cable channels that fragment the viewing audience into niche markets. Although the reach, frequency and selectivity of the broadcast television networks has remained constant, the overall efficiency of a national campaign has shrunk. Advertising agencies have continued to clamor for marketing presence on the major networks, however, because of the superior qualities of television as a sales vehicle.

## PRODUCTS

Of all media, television is certainly the most dynamic. According to finderbinder.com, TV's strong point is high impact, combining sight, sound, and motion. It can be attention-getting and memorable. TV comes as close as any medium can to face-to-face communication. The personal message delivered by an authority or celebrity spokesperson can be very convincing. Advertisers can demonstrate their product or service on the TV screen, and show their organization in detail and full color. TV offers audience selectivity by programming. It offers scheduling flexibility in different programs and day parts, and the opportunity to stress reach or frequency. TV is relatively low in cost, considering the price paid for an advertisement on the basis of gross impressions.

The downside is that viewers' loyalty is to individual television programs, not stations or networks. People watch TV to be entertained, and, when many commercials are competing for the viewer's attention and memory, it is not an easy battle to win. It takes a good-sized budget to make an efficient TV buy. Production and talent tend to have sizable price tags, too. Advertisers run the risk of the most popular shows being sold out. With the growth of cable, satellite and home video, TV viewership is becoming more and more fragmented.

### Product Lines

Television programming fits a variety of program types, or genres. According to Mermigas (2001), news programming is expensive to produce. Annual news budgets average $500 million per network and the competition is fierce to be first with the most accurate and compelling coverage. Fortunately, the excess capacity of news divisions can be marshaled to construct 1-hour infotainment news programs such as 60 Minutes, Dateline NBC, and 20/20. These programs are less expensive to produce than series entertainment and have the potential to attract very large audiences.

In the pure entertainment realm, the primetime lineup for the television networks is the most expensive to produce, even after some networks began reining in their expenses (Martin, 2002). For example, NBC paid more than $6 million dollars for two telecasts of each half-hour original episode of *Friends* in the 2002–2003 season. Kelsey Grammer, star of *Frasier*, receives $1.7 million per episode. Thanks to *deficit financing*, however, the networks do not bear the entire expense for each episode and the *back-end* revenue, often substantial, comes when rerun episodes are *syndicated* to local stations or such broad appeal cable channels as USA Channel or TNT. Despite the extreme cases, the typical half-hour sitcom costs about $900,000 per episode to produce, with the network paying $500,000 to $600,000 per show for first year broadcast rights. A new drama costs approximately $1.5 million per episode, of which the network pays two thirds (McClellan, 1998).

Sports programming is even more expensive than primetime and is far from profitable. Fox lost $20 million on the 2002 Super Bowl, for example, even though it charged $2 million per 30-second commercial in the telecast. The entire NFL package for Fox was estimated to cost $2 billion for a single season, as part of a 1999 deal that saw Fox and other networks pay $17.8 billion for rights to air National Football League games for 8 years. On the other hand, professional football in 1992 helped solidify Fox' parity with the Big 3 networks and led to affiliation switches in such major markets as Denver and Detroit after CBS was outbid for the NFC Conference.

The least expensive network programs, and often the most profitable, are live news/talk shows like *The Today Show* or *Good Morning, America*, which attract large audiences during low-competition dayparts at a reasonable production cost. As evidence of this profit center, NBC's Katie Couric was able to negotiate a $60 million 4-year contract.

***Emerging Products.***    Reality shows (e.g., *Survivor, Fear Factor, The Bachelor*) have emerged in recent years as an alternative to expensive series. These shows are much less than one-half the cost of regular programming, and they hold the potential to match or exceed the audience size of their more costly counterparts.

Magazine-format news programs in primetime also have continued to be an inexpensive alternative to scripted narrative programming, as mentioned earlier. Game shows, led by *Who Wants to be a Millionaire*, had a brief resurgence in the late-1990s, but then all but disappeared, replaced by reality shows.

## Emerging Product Strategies

According to Eastman and Ferguson (2002), one key programming strategy is *conservation of resources*, which has traditionally meant running each episode twice a year or reusing program segments edited in new ways. As *mentioned previously*, the latest version of this idea is *repurposing*, whereby the network shares a program with another channel. As networks make strategic alliances or acquire competing networks and channels, repurposing becomes more commonplace.

Broadcast networks continue to make "seamless" transitions between their programs to discourage viewers' tuning out to check other channels. Networks also try to make it more difficult to skip over commercials, but may ultimately lose the battle when viewers adopt DVRs to watch what they want, when they want. ReplayTV, for example, has a DVR that automatically skips commercials.

## Production Issues

In the so-called Golden Age of television, the Big-3 networks—especially CBS, which was known as the Tiffany Network—consistently set the benchmarks for high-quality programs and were regularly rewarded with critical acclaim or such prestigious awards as the Emmy or Peabody. In the past decade, however, such premium cable channels as HBO and Showtime have developed programs (e.g., *The Sopranos*) that moved the spotlight away from the traditional broadcast networks.

Networks have responded to competitive pressures by lowering their standards to match the expectations of multichannel subscribers. Such programs as *Fear Factor* and *Dog Eat Dog* rival the content excesses of MTV's *Jackass*, for example.

## Distribution Issues

The combined penetration of cable and satellite delivery of a multichannel environment had reached 80% of U.S. households by 2002. The elaborate system of network compensation to affiliates might seem unnecessary if the government put on the auction block all spectrum set aside for television, after subsidizing a 10-channel "lifeline" service to the 20% who actually rely on over-the-air signals. Over 95% of homes are already passed by cable or fiber, and the remaining households are in the footprint of satellite services that currently plan to offer local channels. No one has seriously proposed this scheme because the networks themselves derive a good deal of their operating profits from their O & O stations.

In the near term, broadcasters will need their over-the-air signals. This is especially true with the roll-out of HDTV signals that do not qualify as must-carry stations. Still, it seems odd that network signals are distributed via satellite and then broadcast by stations that are only seen by a tiny subset of viewers, leaving the typical household to get its signals over a wire or through different portions of the spectrum, the same ether that delivers the signals to affiliates in the first place.

Withers (2002) pointed out that changes in the way television is distributed have been so great that any special status accorded broadcasting in policy has disappeared: "The key effect of new spectrum management technology and improvement in alternative delivery technologies, including cheap, high quality satellite and cable delivery, is that the traditional spectrum limits that underpinned past economics and policy are changed" (p. 10).

## IMPACT OF NEW TECHNOLOGY

Beyond the arena of distribution, the convergence of video sources has an impact on the value of network broadcasters' content. Video-on-demand is experimenting with FOD (free-on-demand), repurposed "free" programs to attract users to the more expensive pay movies and events. For example, Comcast rolled out VOD and FOD in Philadelphia in 2002, offering new movie releases for $3.95, with full rewind, fast forward, and pause capabilities over a 48-hour window and free episodes of signature cable programs.

If programs could be put on centralized video servers or transmitted to set-top boxes (STBs) equipped with TiVo-like hard drives, then networks and their elaborate, competitive program schedules might be obsolete. Viewers would watch what they want, when they want, with greater control over how they negotiate commercial advertising. Automobile manufacturers are already testing short-form entertainment segments that feature their products.

The Internet, of course, and the World Wide Web have had the greatest impact on broadcast television networks. The number of viewers who watch TV and surf the web at the same time in the same room has grown dramatically in the short lifespan of the World Wide Web. Networks have struggled with how to stay ahead of the technology curve, sometimes making foolhardy investments. For example, NBC and ABC both believed that having an AOL-style web portal (through which web users would seek content and be exposed to advertising) would keep each network competitive with new services doing the same, so they created their own portals: www.go.com and www.snap.com, respectively. What the adventurous networks did not fully understand was that the usual content/distribution system did not translate well to the Web: It was the experience, or context, that drew users to the Internet, not the content (Motavalli, 2002). Content was less relevant and apparently impervious to branding, as traditional news dissemination, for example, was upstaged by the likes of www.drudgereport.com and others.

Laurel (2000) portrayed video production and distribution as fundamentally altered by the Internet because barriers to entry are less expensive:

Think about the inherent benefits of streaming media versus today's television. The FCC does not regulate streaming media, de-facto global standards are already in place, and there is a growing body of content. The

major networks are no longer the gatekeepers of distribution. And anyone who can get their content to an Internet hosting service has global distribution from day 1, without the complex international distribution
agreements currently required in television.

New technology is also lowering the barriers to production. Today's digital video technology and inexpensive PC-based video production solu-
tions make it possible to assemble a workable web video production
system for around $3,000.

Such views, in hindsight, were an exaggeration of the immediate benefits of video streaming, as the collapse of numerous dot-com ventures
proved within a year of Laurel's opinion. But the idea itself will likely get
another chance to be made manifest as the World Wide Web matures.

The clearest example of actual financial impact was the acquisition of
Time-Warner (which included the WB broadcast television network) by
AOL, the online portal, and Internet service provider (ISP). A young, up-
start company has thus swallowed up an older entertainment-based industry. In another case, CBS was acquired in the 1990s by Viacom, which had
grown from a syndication distributor (spawned by CBS itself in the 1970s)
into a multichannel giant and cable television competitor by the 1980s.

**Impact of New Technologies on Distribution Systems**

Castells (2000) predicted that the mass audience itself, not the broadcast
network, is the true "dinosaur" in the media environment. Technologies
like DVDs and DVRs and streaming videos on the Internet have removed
the middleman from the distribution equation: Such *disintermediation* questions the need for broadcast networks at all.

In the next decade, the rollout of HDTV conversion and the attendant
concerns of content and distribution will likely consume the attention of
media users. After that transition settles, however, networks may become
anachronistic in an interactive environment, where the lean-back, passive
experience is slowly replaced by a lean-forward, active media consumption
metaphor.

## GLOBALIZATION

For decades, the major television networks ignored the overseas markets
except for purposes of exportation. Cultural differences have not kept
public television from importing series, but the commercial channels prefer domestic production, or at least domestic versions of ideas originating
elsewhere (e.g., *All in the Family* originated in England, recent reality
shows produced by such companies as Endemol first gained popularity in
Europe).

Nevertheless, the global market for television programs is comparable to theatrical movies (see chap. 4, this volume). Situation comedies like *Seinfeld* do not play well in Europe because humor is regionally subjective, whereas action-adventure and serialized dramas often become major hits.

Ownership, however, is a different matter entirely. Although only Fox is foreign owned (The News Corporation is Australia-based), some of the production studios from which the networks still buy many of their programs are not U.S. controlled: Columbia-TriStar Television is owned by Sony (Japan) and Universal Studios is owned by Vivendi (France). NBC is the only network not aligned with a studio, which makes it a possible acquisition for Sony or Universal.

## Future Trends

Global media conglomerates are unwieldy, regardless of the owner's nationality. In recent years, the Europeans have had as many difficulties building empires as the Americans. And for every Rupert Murdoch, there is a Kirch, whose German media empire crumbled in 2002.

The UK's ITV network has struggled of late and France's Vivendi is choking on the pieces of its Universal Studios empire. The gold rush to mine the anticipated synergy of convergence has left many companies scrambling to show a profit—be they AOL or Vivendi.

## COPYRIGHT ISSUES

Copyright is a difficult area for broadcast networks and their co-owned production studios, largely because of the transition from analog to digital media. Although it was eventually shut down, Napster forever changed the nature of digital copyright as music lovers "share" their content through multinational consortia (e.g., KaZaa) and, as a result, copyright holders lose billions. Broadcast networks and other video copyright holders worry that what happened to music also will happen to video.

A case in point is ReplayTV. This maker of digital video recorders (DVRs) released a new model in 2001 that encouraged its users to share recorded materials with their friends. A lawsuit against ReplayTV by the major Hollywood producers and a countersuit against the studios by the Electronic Freedom Foundation were pending ReplayTV's bankruptcy as this chapter was written. It is safe to say that the issues speak louder than the eventual outcome, and the implications for protecting the economic assets of video creators are immense.

The mass-media conglomerates also have difficulty protecting their intellectual property, as the companies and their core identities grow older than the usual limits of copyright. Disney (ABC) lobbies Congress every few years to extend the number of years that it can keep Mickey Mouse from passing into the public domain. The courts are expected to decide this one, too.

## SOCIAL ISSUES

### Impact on Public Interest and Society

As a national resource, value of the electromagnetic spectrum has far-reaching impact for the public and society. Although the spectrum itself has absolutely no intrinsic value until corporations spend billions, at their own risk, to improve the resource, the public owns the airwaves. Scarcity was the basis for government-controlled spectrum allocation, although today's digital compression technologies have created more extra space than was ever imagined in the 1930s.

Nevertheless, broadcasters must balance their economic goals against their legal commitments. The federal government regulates stations, which promise to serve in the "public interest, convenience, and necessity." The station is the focal point of regulation. Although the network often provides the programming, the individual affiliate is responsible to the Federal Communications Commission for the station's performance of promises made to serve the public. Special interest and pressure groups also can influence the programming policies of broadcasters. Even in a more relaxed regulatory climate where the threat of license revocation is negligible, "stations must consider their relationships with local government and community leaders and with advertisers" (Owen & Wildman, 1992, p. 151).

The most important stations, the ones with the largest reach, are owned by the networks, of course. Thus, networks have an economic stake in protecting the freedom of stations to provide news and sell political advertising. The economic importance of government regulation is evident by the lengths to which broadcasters attempt to influence legislators. Lobbying organizations like the National Association of Broadcasters exert powerful influence on Congress and the FCC. However, audiences for broadcast television also make their complaints about program content known to government regulators.

Although regulations are a concern, the public behavior of many television broadcasters is heavily influenced by economic interest: It is good business to offend the least number of viewers. With the growth of pay cable channels, however, broadcasters are in a bind. Some of their national audience, often those most desired by advertisers, is attracted to program content that is too adult-oriented for broadcasters. Viewers, for example, want motion pictures on television to be more like the films they see a theaters. The result has been a slow erosion of standards over the years. For example, of the original seven dirty words one could never say on broadcast television (as popularized by comedian George Carlin), only four remain. Advertisers serve as willing accomplices to this lowering of standards as long as their products are not targeted by pressure groups.

Not only is program content under constant scrutiny, some categories of broadcast advertising are severely restricted by government regulation or industry self-regulation. Legal products like cigarettes (prohibited by government regulation) and distilled spirits (discouraged via self-regulation) are not advertised on broadcast television in the United States, although some stations in Texas began flaunting broadcasting industry guidelines in 1996. Individual states occasionally restrict advertising of services by professionals like lawyers and doctors.

One interesting dynamic between government and television broadcasting involves political advertising. Broadcasters view elections as money-making opportunities. Legislators, on the other hand, exploit requirements for "equal time" to minimize the cost of advertising under the guise of fairness. For example, candidates with less money than their competitors can sometimes demand television exposure at no or low cost. Other forms of advertising (e.g., print and outdoor) that compete with broadcasters are not subjected to regulations, but stations must sell political time at the lowest unit cost.

Other issues, primarily linked to newer digital forms of content and distribution, have surfaced in recent years. The Consumer Federation of America (2002) identified this short list: consumer privacy, multicasting as "direct mail on steroids," digital divide, and program diversity.

Privacy concerns result when DVRs collect aggregated data about precise viewing behavior and can transmit it back to the manufacturer (who sells advertising that appears on menu listings). The potential misuse of borrowed spectrum set aside for HDTV for the purposes of multicasting, giving each station the means to transmit a half-dozen signals from one channel, is seen as marketing gone wild. The relative lack of access to the World Wide Web by underprivileged publics is the essence of "digital divide" issues.

Public interest groups also worry that ethnic diversity is absent on commercial television. Interestingly, the groups that track media behavior apply pressure to the broadcast networks rather than the cable networks, despite the latter's primetime dominance as of the 2001–2002 season. According to Discovery Communications, the four-network broadcast share is 45%, but basic cable networks' share is 46% (Myers, 2002).

## THE FUTURE

Networks are not dinosaurs. The need for someone to aggregate news and entertainment will not go away because the business model may shift. Even if the networks' current advertising-support model somehow changes to a paid-subscription model—which some people believe may happen because of DVRs, which make commercial messages less intrusive and thereby ineffective or devalued—the broadcast conglomerates that exist today will not vanish. Future television viewers will enjoy controlling their own video environments, but they will probably welcome the attempt by a programming service to put on a big show for them, regardless of how the signal is distributed or compensated. The functions of media products are enduring and the need to study the economic impact shall continue forever.

## FURTHER READING

Albarran, A. B. (1996). *Media economics: Understanding markets, industries and concepts*. Ames, IA: Iowa State University Press.
Doyle, G. (2002). *Understanding media economics*. Newbury Park, CA: Sage.
Ferguson, D. A. (1998). The economics of broadcast television. In J. R. Walker & D. A. Ferguson (Eds.), *The broadcast television industry* (pp. 42–63). Boston: Allyn & Bacon.
Lieurouw, L., & Livingstone, S. (2002). *Handbook of new media*. London: Sage.
Owen, B. M., Beebe, J. H., & Manning, Jr., W. G. (1974). *Television economics*. Lexington, MA: Lexington Books.
Picard, R. G. (1989). *Media economics: Concepts and issues*. Newbury Park, CA: Sage.

## REFERENCES

Auletta, K. (1991). *Three blind mice: How the networks lost their way*. New York: Random House.
Castells, M. (2000). The culture of real virtuality: The integration of electronic communication, the end of the mass audience, and the rise of interactive networks. In *The rise of the network society* (pp. 355–406). London: Blackwell Publishers.
Collins, R., Garnham, N., & Locksley, G. (1988). *The economics of television: The UK case*. Newbury Park, CA: Sage.
Consumer Federation of America. (2002). *Notice of inquiry: Comments of the Consumer Federation of America*. Retrieved from http://www.bettertv.org/99360cfa.html
Downey, K. (2002, February 14). Olympics a modest ad $ boon for NBC. *Media Life*. Retrieved from http://209.61.190.23/news2002/feb02/feb11/4_thurs/news1thursday.html
Eastman, S. T., & Ferguson, D. A. (2002). *Broadcast/cable/web programming: Strategies and practices*. Belmont, CA: Wadsworth.
Higgins, J. M. (2002, December 2). Biggest still holding their own. *Broadcasting & Cable*. Retrieved from www.broadcastingcable.com
Higgins, J., & Romano, A. (2002, February 4). Cheaper by the thousand. *Broadcasting & Cable* Retrieved from www.broadcastingcable.com
Laurel, J. (2000, June). *The future of television in a streaming world*. Retrieved from http://www.spectare.com/technology/tvfuture.html

Martin, E. (2002, January 10). NBC gets tough on costs and content. *Jack Myers Report*. Retrieved from http://www.myers.com/pdf/01-10-02.pdf

McClellan, S. (1996, December 16). NBC posts $1 billion in earnings. *Broadcasting & Cable*, 64.

McClellan, S. (1998, June 8). Can the Big 4 still make big bucks? *Broadcasting & Cable*, 24–30.

McClellan, S. (2001, May 28). Big four in the black. *Broadcasting & Cable*, 36.

Mermigas, D. (2001, October 22). Programming costs about to be squeezed. *Electronic Media*. Retrieved from http://www.craini2i.com/em/archive.mv?count=3&story=em84221697869872500

Motavalli, J. (2002). *Bamboozled at the revolution: How big media lost billions in the battle for the Internet*. New York: Viking Press.

Myers, J. (2002, May 14). Cable nets lay out upfront strategies. *Jack Myers Report*. Retrieved from http://www.jackmyers.com

Owen, B. M., & Wildman, S. S. (1998). *Video economics*. Cambridge, MA: Harvard University Press.

Television Bureau of Advertising. (2002). Ad revenue track: Political advertising. Retrieved from http://www.tvb.org/rcentral/adrevenuetrack/politics/politics.html

Withers, G. (2002, April). *Economics and regulation of broadcasting*, Discussion Paper No. 93. Retrieved from http://www.anu.edu.au/pubpol/Discussion%20Papers/No93Withers.pdf

# Chapter 8

# The Economics
# of the Cable Industry

**BENJAMIN J. BATES**
*University of Tennessee*

**TODD CHAMBERS**
*Texas Tech University*

The cable industry is entering its third incarnation. It began in the late 1940s and 1950s as a means to extend local broadcast television signals, a community antenna system, if you will, that used wires to bring television where the broadcast signal didn't reach. Beginning in the 1960s, some cable systems started importing distant signals, bringing more television to communities. This transition boomed in the 1970s when satellites became cheap enough to distribute networks nationally, encouraging the development of alternative cable networks. Within a decade, cable transformed itself into what some called *television of abundance*, a multichannel video programming provider in more or less direct competition with traditional over-the-air broadcasters. The third transition began in the 1990s, with the rise of digital and fiber optic networks, which improved system capacity and encouraged interactivity, paving the way for a range of new services in addition to the traditional multichannel video programming. The 1990s also saw policy shifts that began to open cable markets to direct competition, pushing cable operators to look for new sources of revenue. As a result, cable is beginning to transform into a broadband interactive telecommunications network, offering a variety of services to consumers.

Throughout all this, the essence of cable has remained fairly consistent: It is a wired multichannel television distribution system, a mechanism to deliver a number of television signals to homes and offices for a fee. Its nature as a multichannel wired system distinguished itself from traditional over-the-air broadcast television. Its network development as a broadband *mass-communication* system also differentiated itself from the traditional narrowband switched wired networks of the telephone industry. Over the years, technology, policy, and market economics have defined its particular nature, and as those factors developed and shifted, the cable industry has had to redefine both itself and its market. Certainly, the markets and business of cable have also changed, if not the basic economics.

In this chapter, the evolution of the cable industry is discussed, outlining how technological advances have impacted on costs and values, changing cable services, markets, and business operations. Also discussed is the general economics of cable, shifting markets, and industry trends.

## THE EVOLUTION OF CABLE

### Cable as CATV

The cable industry in the U.S. largely began as Community Antenna Television Service (CATV). Cable began around 1950, emerging in areas where early television reception was problematic. Using upgraded reception facilities, recently developed wideband amplifiers, and coaxial cables, CATV systems basically offered a wired retransmission of existing local or nearby signals. Entrepreneurs saw an opportunity in communities along the fringe of broadcast signals: build a network throughout the community and offer services for a fee. The cable industry was born, its product a stronger, clearer television signal.

*The Market & Economics.* Even in fairly small communities, building the network infrastructure required considerable initial investment: You needed some means to acquire and bring in the signal, a central facility to process and strengthen the signal, and the wired network to distribute it. You also needed permission to use municipal rights-of-way for the cable network, which led to community franchising. However, once you had built the network, operating costs were fairly low, and new customers could be added without significant added costs (as long as they were within the area covered by the network). Operating costs were mostly generated by the few personnel required, electricity and repairing equipment. Installations were usually charged separately. Revenues came from offering access to the signals delivered by the cable system. Low demand values and the high cost of alternatives prompted an emphasis on a basic subscription model. Customers paid a fee, usually weekly or monthly, for access to the channels distributed by the CATV system operator. If the cable operator could attract sufficient revenues to cover operating costs and pay down investment, they were successful.

*Impact & Structure.* In this form, CATV initially supported the development of terrestrial broadcast television, extending local station reach in those, generally small, communities not adequately served by terrestrial television signals. Local stations welcomed CATV's ability to extend their signal area. Cable as CATV tended to be located in small and rural communities, their networks built and extended piecemeal as demand and finances warranted. The fact that the product hardly differed from what was available free from local over-the-air television broadcasters kept demand low in those areas with adequate signals, limiting cable's capacity to grow into larger markets. In addition, the low demand for channel capacity kept equipment and infrastructure needs fairly low. In general, the scale and scope of most CATV systems were below the point where significant economies developed. Thus, CATV market structure tended toward small, single-system, local owners.

## Cable as Competition, as "Television of Abundance"

Once the technology had established its ability to transmit multiple television signals, a variety of entrepreneurs started investigating whether cable could be more than a retransmitter of local television. The rapid adoption of television and cable seemed to indicate a demand for programming that was not always being met by over-the-air broadcasters. As early as the mid-1950s, a few entrepreneurs started looking into the idea of pay television as a distribution system for programming (primarily movies and sports) that was not available on local stations. In some smaller broadcast markets where there may have been only one or two local stations, people wanted access to the missing network programming or even the programming they'd heard was available on the independent TV stations in the largest markets. This prompted a reconsideration of what was cable's product: Was it merely local broadcast television signals, or was it a wider range of television programming? The answer seemed clear: If people were willing to pay for local TV, they should be willing to pay more for even more television programming. As a multichannel service provider, cable had the unique ability to offer more television as its product.

The early attempts at pay-TV type systems were strongly opposed by both the television and motion picture industries, which fostered regulations limiting their ability to offer competitive programming. Those systems were also hampered by the early economics of cable—existing systems were in low-population areas, and acquiring and transmitting programming to multiple systems was quite expensive. The transition from CATV to cable began in earnest in the 1960s, when some cable systems started importing more distant signals in response to growing consumer interest in having access to a full range of television signals. Cable systems imported the signals from nearby network affiliates and independent stations. They paid little, if anything, for the signals themselves, and the emerging microwave technology offered a cheaper distribution system for higher bandwidth signals. With the additional programming options providing incentives for consumers in good reception areas to subscribe, cable began to spread into larger markets. It was still limited, however, by the limited range and value of the alternative programming it could offer consumers.

In the early 1970s, satellite technology had progressed to the point where it became economically viable for even small television networks to distribute their programming nationally. Small-scale programmers saw the opportunity to take their signals national, allowing them to take advantage of the economies of scale offered by networking and the greater potential for advertiser support that a national reach would provide. Adoption of the new channels was also encouraged by the fact that many of these new networks offered to pay cable systems to get them to carry their signals in order to achieve the national distribution that their advertisers demanded. Cable networks were born and started to fulfill the promise of cable being able to offer "television of abundance." With more channels and more choice, cable's product began to differentiate itself from regular broadcast TV signals.

*The Market & Economics.*    The additional channels helped to increase demand for service and to justify cable expansion into new markets, particularly those already adequately served by over-the-air broadcast television stations. The real success were the premium channels that offered access to programs (primarily movies and some special sporting events) that were not yet available to broadcast networks and stations, and the genre channels that offered the sports fan or news junkie 24- hour access to their favorite types of content instead of broadcasters' more limited offerings. Cable increasingly offered not just TV; it offered options not available from traditional over-the-air broadcasting, providing choice and control to consumers. Consumers found that they valued this choice and control, and demand for cable jumped even as subscription rates increased.

The shift in product definition had some significant implications for the cable market and industry. Expanding the product helped to expand market viability. The larger scale and higher population density in the larger markets let cable systems realize some of the fundamental economies of scale and offered increased profit potential. There always had been the basic network economies of scale in cable infrastructure with the high fixed costs of building a comprehensive wired network and the relatively lower variable costs of operation. With construction costs often running at $20,000 a mile (or more), the more homes per mile and the higher the proportion of subscribers, the lower the average costs. On the other hand, the rapid rise in the number of cable networks, and the quickly apparent consumer demand for more choice, meant that many cable systems had to reinvest and upgrade their distribution networks and equipment.

There were other scale economies as well. With the larger scale possible in the bigger markets, investment economies were available: Larger firms could attract better financing, and MSOs (multiple system operators) could even self-finance from operating profits of other systems. In addition, larger systems and MSOs could use their size to gain a degree of purchasing power (both for equipment and programming), and some operating economies became more apparent.

In this incarnation, cable's scale was larger—it was moving into larger urban and suburban markets—with higher capital requirements for building and upgrading infrastructure, yet it was able to take advantage of scale economies and was able to offer higher value, higher demand, and significantly higher profit services. Offsetting these economies somewhat were the added costs involved with the new product. Systems needed regular upgrades to add channel capacity. Programming costs began to increase, as did promotion and marketing and customer service requirements.

The higher demand characteristics of cable as "more TV" allowed systems to increase revenues by both increasing penetration levels and increasing prices. This shift also brought new revenue streams to cable. Premium service networks, like HBO, were offered to subscribers at a separate, higher price. Other cable-only networks not only offered to pay for carriage, initially, they offered the opportunity for local cable systems to sell and insert local advertising. Shopping channels offered revenue-sharing opportunities. Over time, as some cable networks became more popular, drawing an ever-increasing share of the viewing audience, they were able to insist on cable systems paying them for carriage. That popularity, though, also increased the value of local advertising opportunities for cable systems, and as technology for ad insertion became more economical, systems found local advertising sales a profitable new revenue stream.

Larger systems could also benefit more from cable advertising, both in terms of their larger audiences having greater value and in their ability to cover the added costs of the insertion and tracking systems necessary to transmit local advertising over those channels. As the value of local advertising increased, systems also found emerging economies of scale and scope through system aggregation, through combining adjacent local systems. This prompted a wave of MSO "rationalization" in the late-1990s, as larger MSOs traded systems to concentrate activities in geographic clusters to take advantage of both advertising and general operating economies of scale and scope.

*Impact and Structure.*    Cable also began to pose more of a threat to local television, whose programming now had to compete with the imported program choices for a fragmenting audience. Broadcasters began pressuring the FCC to do something about cable. The problem was that the FCC

had the legal authority to regulate all forms of radio (broadcasting), and telephony, but cable was a new medium. Being a wired system, it did not use
the airwaves. Neither did it fit the definition of telephony as a switched
common carrier system. The FCC tried a variety of rationales to regulate cable throughout the 1960s and 1970s, sometimes supported and sometimes
overturned by the courts. These attempts created a degree of uncertainty
during this period and imposed some additional costs, thus tending to slow
the expansion of cable somewhat.

The trend toward cable as additional television programming took off
in the 1970s with the development of cable programming networks. Technical advances and changes in regulations made satellite distribution of
network programming economically viable. That opened up programming markets, prompting a rapid expansion in the number of signals
available to cable systems, and thus to subscribers. Cable rapidly expanded throughout the 1970s and 1980s, reaching into larger markets and
suburban areas. The number of cable systems grew from roughly 2,500 in
1970 to more than 9,000 by the end of the 1980s, and cable penetration almost tripled between 1980 and 1990 from 22.6% to 59% (National Cable
Television Association, 2002b).

Growth was aided by the passage of the 1984 Cable Act. The first explicitly cable federal legislation, the 1984 Cable Act finally provided the FCC
with the direct legislative authority to regulate cable, nationalizing what
had previously been primarily local regulation of cable systems. Cable
systems needed access to utility rights-of-way in order to build their networks, and thus had to make arrangements with local governments. They
were also interested in protecting those investments by obtaining local
service monopolies, and thus found themselves accepting local franchise
conditions, which evolved into local regulations. If there was competition
for the local monopoly, bidding firms would compete by offering more
services or granting greater regulatory authority. The licensing and regulatory conditions could vary widely across communities, however, and
the monopoly grants being limited in term-subjected cable systems to local demands at renewals. Although not a big problem for many smaller
systems, larger firms operating in multiple communities (multiple system
operators [MSOs]) found the variation in regulatory structures and the
uncertainties of license renewal a bit more problematic. As more and more
local systems were acquired by MSOs, pressure to rationalize regulation
increased, and the 1984 Act was passed following negotiations between
the cable and broadcast TV industries.

Ostensibly nationalizing regulation, the 1984 Act was, in essence, more
deregulatory. While explicitly shifting regulatory authority from states and
local bodies to the FCC, both Congress and the FCC were in a deregulatory
phase. National standards were set low, as was the threshold for permitting

price regulation. The Act specified that basic service prices could only be regulated in the absence of competition. Competition was defined as the availability of several broadcast stations serving the community, a condition that over 90% of cable systems met. Thus, most cable systems found themselves effectively freed from most price regulation.

As might be expected, cable consumers found themselves facing several rounds of price increases, fueled by both the relaxing of local price regulation and the rapid expansion in the number of programming channels offered. The large consumer response raised concerns in Congress, and prompted the 1992 Cable Act. By redefining the conditions of competitiveness, the 1992 Act brought most cable systems back under price regulation and set conditions for significant price rollbacks in many systems. The redefinition also illustrated the changing perception of cable's basic nature: The 1984 Act deemed competitiveness in terms of available local broadcast signals, whereas the 1992 Act specified competition in terms of a competitive multichannel service provider available in the community.

New technologies also contributed to the growth in consumer demand and the rise of alternative revenue streams. Cable had experimented with interactivity in the 1980s, but the tree and branch architecture of networks made truly interactive systems problematic and expensive. However, increased intelligence in set-top boxes permitted a high degree of addressability in the system, providing a form of interactivity that fostered new services such as pay-per-view and expanded premium service options.

This higher demand (which has held fairly steady at about two thirds of homes passed for most of the last decade) pushed cable expansion to the point where cable was available to about 97% of U.S. homes with television sets. This era of higher demand and profitability also prompted the entry of larger firms, and an increase in consolidation as those firms sought to take advantage of various economies of scale and scope. This era saw the rise of the large MSO and an increase in mergers and acquisitions in the cable industry. The high-demonstrated demand for cable programming also encouraged the development of alternative multichannel video systems (SMATV, MMDS, and home satellite systems).

In the meantime, the telecommunications industry was booming. Demand for video programming was rapidly growing, but that was nothing compared to the growth forecasts for other telecommunications sectors. Telephony was ubiquitous, and the rise of cellular and faxes multiplied both supply and demand to the point where the United States was running out of phone numbers. Add to that the rise in computer communications and data transmissions and you have a rapidly growing demand for communication networks and services. In this emerging digital communications market, cable found itself positioned with the largest pipe, if only it could solve the interactivity problem.

## Cable as Broadband

The rise of digital communications and fiber optics initiated cable's third incarnation as a broadband telecommunications network. Fiber optics became economically competitive with coaxial cable in the early 1990s, and systems began upgrading their infrastructure. Fiber was cheap and had a higher signal capacity, which meant it could carry more channels, and was installed in bundles, which meant separate fibers could be used to send signals in different directions. As installed fiber networks came closer and closer to homes, a truly interactive cable system became economically viable. The development of digital packet-switched communications allowed virtually any kind of communication signal (video, voice, data) to be sent over the same network, not only toppling the old boundaries between telecommunications services, but offering the promise of bringing interactivity to traditionally broadcast services. As cable upgraded capacity, they also added a greater degree of interactivity and became poised to enter new markets, particularly in data communications, telephony, and the emerging interactive television services.

The breakdown in old service boundaries was an integral presumption underlying the 1996 Telecommunications Act. The 1996 Act presumed that competition would emerge between and within telecommunications industries, if only regulatory boundaries were removed in support of the already evident destruction of technical and market boundaries brought about by technological advances. The 1996 Act removed both cable and telephony's local monopoly status and encouraged those industries to compete directly with one another. The Act specified cable price regulation would disappear in 1999, arguably under the assumption that the newer definition of effective competition would be satisfied.

In a general sense, Congress was correct. The new definition of competition required that there exist at least one competing multichannel video service provider, that reached at least 50% of the local community and was subscribed to by at least 10% of the homes in the cable service area. In the 1990s, opportunities for several new forms of multichannel services developed and began to compete with local cable systems (see Table 8.1). Home satellite reception (as HSD) had been around, primarily in rural areas, since the 1980s, yet remained a fairly expensive alternative, achieving only 1% to 2% penetration. Satellite Master Antenna TV (SMATV) systems had also been around for decades, but those systems were restricted to single buildings or small complexes, as they lacked the access to utility rights-of-way. Thus, they could never achieve the necessary market penetration levels. The FCC had repurposed several broadcast services to open up the potential for wireless cable systems (as MMDS), but these were not widely successful. Telephone companies had planned and tested videodialtone

**TABLE 8.1**

**Cable and Competing Technologies**

| Technology | Dec. 1996 | June 1998 | June 2000 |
|---|---|---|---|
| TV Households | 97,000,000 | 98,000,000 | 100,801,720 |
| Multichannel Video | 72,370,950 | 76,634,200 | 84,423,717 |
| Cable Subs | 63,500,000 | 65,400,000 | 67,700,000 |
| MMDS | 1,180,000 | 1,000,000 | 700,000 |
| SMATV | 1,126,000 | 940,000 | 1,500,000 |
| HSD (satellite) | 2,277,760 | 2,028,200 | 1,476,717 |
| DBS | 4,285,000 | 7,200,000 | 12,987,000 |
| Open Video System | 2,190 | 66,000 | 60,000 |

*Note.* From National Cable Television Association, Federal Communications Commission.

services (a variety of video on demand), but these had not proven to be economically viable under existing technology. Still, the potential for a new open video standard (OVS) emerging from telephony was being developed and tested.

What *had* become a viable competitor was DBS (direct broadcast services). Using digital compression technology and higher powered satellites, DBS offered the potential of hundreds of channels accessible from a small, inexpensive, fixed dish. Their service area was national, clearly satisfying the service-area penetration requirements. And the DBS services were successful in attracting customers. By the end of 1996, roughly 5% of U.S. households were DBS subscribers, and by 1998, it was roughly 10%. By December 2001, DBS accounted for 18.6% of the U.S. multichannel market (over 17 million homes; National Cable Television Association, 2002b). Although DBS penetration may not be consistent across markets, it clearly has developed into a significant competitor for cable.

Developments in fiber optics and digital communications have created new broadband and multichannel video distribution options as the low cost of fiber networks and the increasing demand for cable and other telecommunications services are encouraging broadband overbuilds. Through DSL, local phone companies and other telecommunication network providers can offer limited multichannel service (OVS), once the necessary network upgrades are completed. In some markets, new firms are seeking to provide a mix of cable, data, and telephone services.

Continuing increases in audience demand for cable programming, coupled with growing interest in cable modems have created an attractive economic atmosphere for the cable industry. Despite a slowing economy, industry analysts continue to project growth for cable television in terms of advertising revenues, subscriptions, and advanced digital services, predicting that cable will become the largest segment of the communications industry by 2005 (Mermigas, 2001).

## CABLE SYSTEM ECONOMICS

For all the talk about the cable industry and conglomeration, cable remains an essentially local operation. From a local market structure perspective, cable television can be conceptualized as a system of local cable operators, each providing their subscribers access to a mix of video programming provided by a variety of local (public access channels, local governments, local cable advertising, local broadcast television stations), regional (regional cable networks), national (national cable networks), and international (international cable networks) programmers. There are almost 10,000 local cable systems in the United States, serving roughly 69 million cable subscribers (National Cable Television Association, 2002b). As an industry, cable offers some distinctive economic structures and insights.

### Market Structure

Most markets fostered a natural monopoly for local cable operators through lengthy exclusive franchise agreements. Although the 1996 Telecommunications Act prevented these local franchises from being exclusive (i.e., giving cable a legal monopoly), the significant costs of overbuilding the network has limited the amount of direct competitors. Thus, there are only a few areas with directly competing cable systems. However, as noted earlier, a variety of other multichannel video programming services have entered the market, bringing an increasing degree of competition into the TV marketplace. Further, as cable used fiber to become more interactive, telephone and data networks are using fiber to become broadband providers, hoping to enter the market with their own mix of telephone, data, and multichannel video services. As cable penetration is near maximum and as market boundaries continue to break down, local cable markets are likely to become increasingly competitive. This suggests that cable systems will need to develop new businesses and revenue streams and are likely to continue to seek economies through increased conglomeration and concentration.

### Revenues

The business model of cable television revolves around the subscriber. Cable systems package sets of channels in a variety of subscription *tiers*, from basic cable and premium cable channels to pay-per-view channels. Cable operators generate 80% of income through subscriptions to these various tiers of services (Federal Communications Commission, 2002a), with the oldest and largest source of revenue coming from basic subscription fees. After basic, the next tier of service is *expanded basic,* which includes all networks not included in the basic service and not included in the per-channel service (Parsons & Frieden, 1998). That's followed by the premium cable network services, which are dominated by movie channels such as HBO, Showtime and Starz!. Subscribers pay an additional monthly fee to gain access to these networks. The final type of service is the per-channel or pay-per-view service. Access to these services is based on a viewing session by viewing session basis. Sporting events, movies, and other types of events are provided for a one-time, flat-fee basis.

Pay-TV channels are charged separately, with the network normally splitting the basic monthly charge with the local cable system. Other emerging cable networks pay local cable systems to carry their channels. These payments run from a few cents per subscriber per month to as high as a few dollars, providing additional revenue to the local cable operator. With shopping channels, cable systems receive a percentage of the sales coming from people in their service areas. Regulations mandating leased channel access also have provided a new, if not widely used, revenue source.

Other revenue (see Table 8.2) comes from equipment rental, installation charges, and, increasingly, new services based on emerging technologies (Federal Communications Commission, 2002a). Local advertising sales also have become an important source of revenue for cable systems. At first, growth in local advertising was slow; systems had to acquire the equipment and staff to sell and insert the local ads, and cable network ratings were low. However, as cable network viewership increased, so did demand for local advertising spots. Over time, commercial insert equipment also became cheaper and more reliable. Local advertising is now a significant and growing part of most cable systems' revenue streams.

## Expenses

The cost of doing business in the cable industry revolves around expenses related to acquiring, distributing, and marketing programming and services. In local markets, the cable system operates with the same types of expenses as other media outlets with one major exception, the costs associated with the network distribution system. Although the normal operating expenses mirror those of other media, cable tends to have significantly higher infrastructure investment in order to provide their product to consumers. Cable systems also face local franchise fees (typically 3% of gross subscriber revenues) and a variety of other state and federally mandated fees (typically 2% of gross).

TABLE 8.2

**Cable Revenue Sources ($ in millions)**

| Type of Service | 1996 | 1998 | 2000 (est.) |
|---|---|---|---|
| Basic Tiers | $18,395 | $21,830 | $24,445 |
| Pay Tiers | $4,955 | $5,084 | $5,177 |
| Local Advertising | $1,662 | $1,850 | $3,128 |
| Pay-per-View | $647 | $627 | $1,522 |
| Home Shopping | $145 | $187 | $202 |
| Advanced Services (inc. cable modem) | $91 | $452 | $4,238 |
| Equipment & Installation | $2,055 | $2,631 | $3,029 |
| Total Revenue | $27,950 | $32,661 | $41,741 |
| Operating Cash Flow | $11,972 | $14,602 | $17,160 |
| Average Basic Subscriptions | 62.8 million HH | 65.4 million HH | 67.7 million HH |
| Revenue per sub | 445 | 499 | 617 |

*Note.* From National Cable Television Association, Federal Communications Commission.

Cable requires a significant investment in infrastructure before it can offer its service to consumers. At the basic level, a local cable system faces the capital costs of antennas for both satellite and broadcast reception, the headend (signal processing center), and the components (cable and fiber, signal processors and amplifiers) of the distribution network. In addition, cable systems must pay a pole attachment fee to telephone and utility companies. Cable systems also have to invest in customer premises equipment (the familiar cable boxes). For cable systems offering a wider variety of services such as high-speed Internet access, telephony, and data services, there is a need to purchase and maintain telephone switchers and other types of equipment such as servers.

Since the passage of the Telecommunications Act of 1996, the cable industry has spent billions upgrading cable plants, systems, and infrastructure to handle the demand for broadband applications such as digital television, high-speed Internet access, and cable telephony. Cable industry investment has averaged around $15 billion a year over the past 4 years (National Cable Television Association, 2002b). This investment must be paid for and, hopefully, recouped over a period of years. From a normal operating budget perspective, these capital expenditures have a current expense component: the associated need to install, maintain, and repair the wires and equipment. One of the largest segments (30%) of the local cable system's operating budget is the payroll for cable installers and repair personnel (U.S. Department of Labor, 2001). As more cable systems roll out new services, the number of fixed and operating expenses related to the technical acquisition and distribution of cable programming will continue to increase.

Another large expense category for a cable system is the cost of program acquisition. Per subscriber, program expenses including licensing fees, copyright fees and network services are on the increase. New networks usually pay around $7 to $10 per subscriber to get carriage on cable systems (Grillo, 2001). The average monthly subscriber fee for basic channels ranges from 50¢ to $1. Some sports networks are demanding monthly subscriber fees of up to $2 per subscriber (Berkowitz, 2002). Program costs range from about $100,000 per hour for an independently produced show to $250,000 per hour for a special event (Petrozello, 1998). These variable programming and production costs currently account for almost 36% of cable's operating expenses (U.S. Census Bureau, 1999). Cable operators spent almost $9 billion for programming in 2000 (Federal Communications Commission, 2002b).

Outside of program acquisition and distribution expenses, the largest operating expense for local cable systems involves administration and marketing. Because cable television uses a subscription model, customer service and billing departments account for almost 35% of the payroll budget (U.S. Department of Labor, 2001). The consolidation of the cable industry is creating opportunities for companies like Cox Communications to create regional cable service providers by purchasing smaller systems. At the regional level, the cable provider can consolidate customer service and telemarketing centers to create efficiencies across several markets. The next largest payroll category for the local cable system is in the area of marketing the cable system and its core video products and other services to advertisers, subscribers, and businesses.

As an advertising medium, cable television continues to increase its local, regional, and national advertising revenues. The increase in the number of viewers to cable television programming has been associated with an increased demand for advertiser access to the audience. While providing additional revenues, it also increases the size and cost of the sales and marketing departments. The cost of soliciting new clients and maintaining old clients involves competitive salary and benefits packages as well as investments in employee training programs. The growth in the number of pay-television choices, high-speed Internet access, and digital cable television has created marketing needs, along with associated costs, for cable systems as they add new services and "bundles" of programming.

There has always been a fairly high degree of turnover, or *churn*, in cable, particularly in the higher service tiers. In the marketing battle with DBS providers and other competing uses, local cable systems must continually invest in advertising and marketing campaigns to prevent subscriber turnover (churn). In addition, the deployment of the fiber optic distribution network for cable systems has provided opportunities to market high-speed data services to local and regional businesses, as well as the more traditional residential customer. All this has added to marketing and promotions costs.

Many cable systems face another quite significant expense, one that has recently eroded most of the profit margins in the large MSOs. Many cable firms carry a substantial debt load, partly as a result of the need to invest in system upgrades. For many MSOs, though, the largest portion of the debt load is a result of mergers and acquisition activities over the past 20 years. System purchases and the costs of infrastructure upgrades have piled up huge debts, which cable is finding harder to pay off in today's more competitive environment. For many MSOs, debt service is currently wiping out most or all of the systems average 40% operating profit margin (Federal Communications Commission, 2001).

## Industry Structure

As noted earlier, cable emerged and developed locally. In the early days, what few economies of scale and scope that existed were contained in cable's status as a natural, local, monopoly. Local licensing also meant local regulation, which tended to offer little in benefits for greater system aggregation.

The growing emphasis on imported and additional programming redefined cable's product into something economically viable in larger markets, where the economies of scale and scope really began to kick in. These economies combined with the growing demand for cable's redefined product, leading to higher profits and a greater interest in acquisitions and the rise to prominence of MSOs. The MSOs' growing coverage and scope gave them negotiating power with cable networks, and many even helped to finance new networks in order to generate additional programming resources. Further, many smaller systems, faced with the prospects of having to invest in significant system upgrades to reach the higher channel capacities the new product demanded, took advantage of the high demand and prices for systems by selling out. The 1980s and 1990s were marked by significant merger and acquisition activity, and the rise in conglomeration and concentration by MSOs.

Ownership of these systems is dominated by Multiple System Operators or MSOs. According to the FCC, the top 10 MSOs serve 87% of all cable subscribers (Federal Communications Commission, 2001). At the national level, a few large companies such as AT&T Broadband, AOL Time Warner, Cox Communications, and Comcast control the majority of cable subscribers. Based on information from the National Cable Television Association (NCTA), the top 25 MSOs serve 63,855,900 subscribers. Prior to the merger of Comcast and AT&T's cable unit, the top five MSOs accounted for almost 50 million of the nation's 69 million cable subscribers (see Table 8.3).

Although MSOs have dominated the cable industry for years, it is important to review the economic importance of this structure. MSOs exercise market power through relationships with subscribers and program distributors. A recent study of cable prices by the FCC found that MSOs have monthly subscriber rates that are 23% higher than non-MSOs (Federal Communications Commission, 2002a). In 2000, cable operators spent almost $9 billion producing and acquiring programming (Federal Communications Commission, 2002b). Of this $9 billion, 71% went to license fees, 24% went to license fees for premium programming, and the remaining went to copyright fees and production of original programming.

Since 1996, there have been two massive mergers in cable television that changed the industry. First, in February 1999, the Federal Communications Commission approved the merger of AT&T and TCI, at the time the nation's largest cable television operator (Federal Communications Commission, 1999). The FCC justified its decision based on the idea that the merged company would provide certain procompetitive benefits to consumers such as local telephone service alternatives (Federal Communications Commission, 1999). This merger catapulted the nation's leading long-distance telephone provider into the leading role as a cable television operator. Later, however, AT&T spun off its cable and Internet operations before merging the cable portion with Comcast.

Less than a year after the AT&T/TCI announcement, the Internet Service Provider (ISP) America Online announced its $350 billion stock merger

TABLE 8.3

**Largest MSOs by Number of Subscribers (Sept. 2002)**

| Rank | MSO | Subscribers |
|------|-----|-------------|
| 1 | Comcast Corp. | 21,625,800 |
| 2 | Time Warner Cable | 10,862,000 |
| 3 | Charter Communications | 6,697,900 |
| 4 | Cox Communications | 6,263,400 |
| 5 | Adelphia | 5,775,000 |

Source. National Cable Television Association (2002b).
Note. The AT&T Broadband and Comcast merger has been approved by the FCC.

with Time Warner. The merger of the largest ISP with the second largest cable television MSO created AOL Time Warner, a multiplatform media company with 26 million AOL subscribers, 12.6 million Time Warner cable subscribers, residential high-speed Internet lines, video programming networks such as CNN and HBO (among others), a movie studio, magazines, music labels, a broadcast television network, and other interests including sports franchises (Federal Communications Commission, 2001). The FCC approved the AOL-Time Warner merger because of the potential economic benefits to consumers in terms of deployment of broadband technologies and the development of advanced services for those technologies (Federal Communications Commission, 2001). The AOL-Time Warner merger highlighted the evolutionary shift from cable television as a local provider of video content to a local access point to a variety of broadband telecommunications services.

In order to understand this shift from basic cable television provider to a sophisticated provider of bundled telecommunications services, it is important to examine the basic premise of cable—paying for access to content via a cable. Cable television is not broadcast television. Although cable operators use satellite distribution as a form of signal capture, cable television, by definition, requires an actual wire or cable to deliver its programming. That system, in a digital age, can also be used to deliver a range of communication services and products. In an increasingly competitive environment, future growth and profitability is likely to depend on the ability to identify and deliver the services consumers want and are willing to pay for. Thus, many of the larger MSOs sought partners who they thought could provide those services.

MSOs have had a long affiliation with cable programming networks (see Table 8.4). MSOs sought out and sponsored networks as a means of providing additional programming for their systems, and networks sought affiliation with MSOs as a means of gaining access to their systems. Of the 20 most widely distributed cable networks, only C-SPAN has no MSO or broadcast network ownership (and 95% of its funding comes from cable systems). As of December 31, 2001, there were 287 national cable television networks (National Cable Television Association, 2002b). On a system-by-system basis, there was an average of 59 channels available on analog cable systems in the United States (Federal Communications Commission, 2002a). About 80% of systems offer digital services, with hundreds of channels available. Digital video had approximately 15 million subscribers in 2001, with predicted growth reaching 48 million homes in 2005 (National Cable Television Association, 2002b).

### Rate Regulation

Throughout its history, the FCC has been charged with both regulating and deregulating the demand side of the industry—basic cable television rates.

## TABLE 8.4
### MSOs and Number of Cable TV Networks

| MSO | Number of Networks | Prominent Franchise(s) |
|-----|--------------------|------------------------|
| AT&T | 49 (17%) | Encore, Starz!, SciFi, Telemundo, TLC, USA |
| AOL Time Warner | 39 (13%) | CNN, HBO, Cartoon Network, TBS, TNT |
| Cablevision | 10 (3%) | Bravo, AMC |
| Comcast | 17 (6%) | E!, QVC |
| Cox | 24 (8%) | Viewers Choice, Discovery Channel |

Source. Federal Communications Commission, *8th Annual Video Competition Report* (2002).

Starting with the Cable Communications Policy Act of 1984, basic cable rates were deregulated. After years of consumer complaints and Congressional hearings, basic cable rates were reregulated with the passage of the Cable Television Consumer Protection and Competition Act of 1992. In a recent study measuring the impact of the 1992 Cable Act on household demand for welfare, Crawford (2000) concluded that the there were no welfare benefits to households as a result of rate regulation. In other words, despite the Congressionally mandated rate regulation, cable subscribers did not realize the benefit.

By the time the 1996 Telecommunications Act passed, Congress had linked rate deregulation in 1999 with the desire to open advanced telecommunications and information technology service markets to competition (Federal Communications Commission, 2000). In addition, the 1996 Act granted small cable operators—those serving less than 1% of the United States and without connection to companies with less than $250 million in revenue—an exemption from rate regulation.

Since 1999, certain groups of consumers have complained about the increases in basic cable rates (McConnell, 2001). In its *8th Annual Video Competition Report*, the FCC (2002b) reported that cable rates increased at a rate higher than inflation. The FCC noted that the average basic cable rate was $33.75 per month—a 7% increase from the previous year (Federal Communications Commission, 2002a). Cable companies have argued that the rate increases also are due to technology upgrades and new cable services such as digital cable, high-speed Internet access, and local telephone service. They argue that there was not much of an increase based on a per-channel basis. In other words, consumers are "getting more for their money."

## THE FUTURE OF CABLE

The cable industry is seeing a number of new opportunities, and new challenges, emerging. One of the major growth areas for the cable industry has been the consumer interest in cable modems for high-speed Internet access. According to the FCC (2002b), a cable modem "allows cable subscribers to access high-speed data services, interactive television, including the Internet, Internet Protocol ("IP") telephony, video conferencing and telecommuting" (pp. 78–79). Cable modems provide subscribers with continuous access and download rates 50 to 100 times higher than a traditional dial-up modems (Howe, 2002). Although cable modems provide the benefits of high-speed access to the Internet, one of the criticisms of the technology is that a subscriber shares bandwidth with others on the network and, thus, the effective rate tends to be slower. From a competition perspective, the telephone companies might be able to strategically market their dedicated high-speed DSL services against cable modems.

The Telecommunications Act of 1996 also allowed the cable industry to venture into telephony and other telecommunications services. Overall, cable companies have invested $50 billion in technological upgrades to provide for new services like cable telephony, and MSOs like Cox Communications, Time Warner Cable, and AT&T have initiated local telephone service in dozens of markets. In fact, Cox Communications had become the nation's 12th largest telephone company by March 2001 (National Cable Television Association, 2001). From an economic perspective, a cable company interested in providing local telephone service must have the financial resources to invest in upgrading to a truly interactive network, a substantial investment. On the other hand, the telephone and telecommunications market is substantially larger than the cable market.

## CONCLUSION

Despite the technological advances in infrastructure and services, the economic pressures of operating a multiplatform telecommunications provider have highlighted some of the challenges facing the cable industry. As a result of the dot-com bust, investors have cast new scrutiny on new media industries. The legal problems faced by Adelphia Communications Corporation amplified the calls for accountability in accounting practices of publicly-traded companies.[1] Another challenge facing the cable industry is the

---

[1]On July 24, 2002, the Securities and Exchange Commission filed fraud charges against Adelphia Communications, the sixth largest cable television operator in the United States. According to the lawsuit, Adelphia, under the direction of its founder, his sons and other executives, violated antifraud, periodic reporting, record keeping and internal controls provisions of federal securities laws (United States Security and Exchange Commission, 2002). Prior to the lawsuit, Adelphia was delisted from the NASDAQ Stock Exchange in 2002 and its stock price dropped from around $31 at the beginning of the year to less than $1 at the time of its delisting (Adelphia defaults, 2002).

globalization of content and distribution markets. Companies such as AOL Time Warner, SBC Communications, News Corp., and General Electric have invested millions of dollars in the development of programming and infrastructure across the globe. Copyright and issues related to American cultural imperialism have created unique challenges for producers and distributors in the cable television industry.

The investment in programming and technology, however, has positioned cable well in terms of the future. In redefining its product once again (to broadband), cable has opened new markets and created the opportunity for substantial growth, even in the face of increased competition. Although infrastructure needs have eaten into profits in recent years, and increased competition is likely to eat further into cable's historically high cash flows, most systems are putting themselves in the position to take advantage of new products and services as they develop. They are building a flexible digital network for the future.

In conclusion, the cable television industry continues to develop as a sophisticated telecommunications provider. As an industry, cable television has exchanged its role as a single-platform, broadcast television relay for its status as a multiplatform, advanced telecommunications provider. From basic cable channels to high-speed Internet access, the cable industry has strategically positioned itself for competition in local, national, and global markets.

## FURTHER READINGS

*Cable TV Facts.* (Annual). New York: Cabletelevision Advertising Bureau
Federal Communications Commission. www.fcc.gov
Kagan, Paul & Associates. (Annual). *Cable TV buyer broker.* Carmel: Author.
National Cable Television Association. www.ncta.com
*Report on Television/Nielson.* (Annual). New York: A. C. Nielson.

## REFERENCES

Adelphia defaults on bank agreements. (2002, May 31). *USA Today Online.* [Electronic version]. Retrieved June 26, 2002 from http://www.usatoday.com/money/telecom/2002-05-31-adelphia.htm
Berkowitz, H. (2002, May 8). Cable execs air views on YES, Cablevision. Newsday.com. [On-line]. Retrieved September 22, 2002 from http://www.newsday.com/entertainment/tv/nybzyes082698317may08.story?coll=ny-television-print
Crawford, G. (2000). The impact of the 1992 Cable Act on household demand for welfare. *The Rand Journal of Economics, 31*(3), 422–449.
Federal Communications Commission. (1999, February 17). Citing pro-competitive benefits to consumers, commission approves AT&T-TCI merger. *News Release,* Report CS-99-2.
Federal Communications Commission. (2000, June). *Fact Sheet: Cable Television.* Retrieved June 26, 2002 from http://www.fcc.gov/mb/facts/csgen.html

Federal Communications Commission. (2001). *Fact Sheet: FCC's conditioned approval of AOL Time Warner merger.* Retrieved June 24, 2002 from http://www.fcc.gov/Bureaus/Cable/Public_Notices/2001/fcc01011_fact.doc

Federal Communications Commission. (2002a, April 4). *Report on Cable Industry Prices.* MM-Docket 92-266. Retrieved June 24, 2002 from http://hraunfoss.fcc.gov/edocs_public/attachmatch/FCC-02-107A1.pdf

Federal Communications Commission. (2002b, January 14). *8th Annual Video Competition Report.* Retrieved from http://hraunfoss.fcc.gov/edocs_public/attachmatch/FCC-01-389A1.pdf

Grillo, J. (2001, May 28). What's up with originals? *Broadcasting & Cable, 131*(23), 18–22.

Howe, P. (2002, May 29). AT&T Broadband to hike rates for cable modem owners. *The Boston Globe*, C-1. [Electronic version]. Retrieved May 14, 2002 from Lexis-Nexis Academic Universe.

Mermigas, D. (2001, August 6). Next 5 years belong to pay TV, Veronis reports. *Electronic Media, 20*(32), 13, 20.

National Cable Television Association. (2001). *Cable Telephony: Offering Consumers Competitive Choice.* [Electronic version]. Retrieved May 2002 from http://www.ncta.com/pdf_files/Telephony_ReportComplete.pdf

National Cable Television Association. (2002a). *The Transition to Digital Television.* White Paper. Retrieved June 27, 2002 from http://www.ncta.com/pdf_files/WhitePap4-2002.pdf

National Cable Television Association. (2002b). *Industry Overview.* [On-line]. Retrieved June 27, 2002 from http://www.ncta.com/industry_overview/indStat.cfm?indOverviewID=2

Parsons, P., & Frieden, R. (1998). *The cable and satellite television industries.* Boston: Allyn & Bacon.

Petrozzello, D. (1998, October 26). Only on cable. *Broadcasting & Cable, 128*(44), 42–44.

United States Department of Labor. (2001). *Cable and Other Pay Television Services.* [On-line]. Retrieved June 28, 2002 from http://www.bls.gov/oco/cg/pdf/cgs017.pdf

United States Census Bureau. (1999). *1998 Annual Survey of Communication Services.* [On-line]. Retrieved June 28, 2002 from http://www.census.gov/svsd/www/ascs.html

United States Securities & Exchange Commission. (2002). *SEC Charges Adelphia and Rigas Family with Massive Financial Fraud.* News Release. [Electronic version]. Retrieved August 1, 2002 from http://www.sec.gov/news/press/2002-110.htm

# Chapter 9

# The Economics
# of Hollywood:
# Money and Media

## DOUGLAS GOMERY
### *University of Maryland*

Anytime one sees a movie blockbuster—from George Lucas' expected regular mega-creations to the unexpected small hit such as *The Full Monty*—one implicitly understands the continuing economic power of the Hollywood major studios. George Lucas alone can not distribute his films; he needs a Twentieth Century Fox. His only other choices, the sole corporations that cover the world, are Disney, Paramount, Sony, Universal, and Warner Bros. Whether in a movie theater, a reshowing on cable, satellite, or broadcast television, or viewing on home video or DVD, the "Big Six" oligopoly— Hollywood—defines a movie hit.

As the 21st century begins, the Hollywood film industry remained a closed oligopoly of the Big Six—(in alphabetical order) Disney (owned by The Walt Disney Corporation), Paramount Pictures (owned by Viacom), Sony Pictures (owned by Sony), Twentieth Century Fox (owned by News Corporation), Universal Pictures (owned by Vivendi), and Warner Bros. (owned by AOL/Time Warner). All competed to produce and release the top hits, but all cooperated to make sure the game remained only among each other. Who was on top which year varied, but only the Big Six premiered possible blockbuster hits in multiplex theaters during the 1990s— and surely will well into the future. (Compaine & Gomery, 2000).

With all the new sources of revenues, Hollywood's Big Six has kept growing despite all the ways one can see a film. Indeed, there long have been doomsayers predicting that Hollywood films in theaters will disappear, yet as seen in Fig. 9.1 the box office take in theaters continues to grow. Table 9.1 shows that even the absolute number of fans to pay now close to $10 increased through the 1990s. Hollywood is booming (www.mpaa.org).

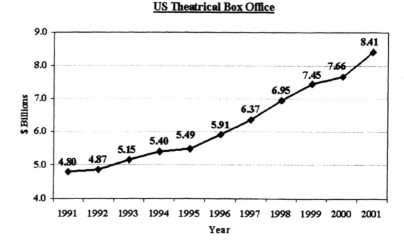

FIG. 9.1.   U.S. gross box office reached an all-time high of $8.4 billion—a
9.8% increase over last year.

## TABLE 9.1
### U.S. Theatrical Admissions

| Year | Admissions (mil) | Yearly Change | 2001 Versus |
|------|------------------|---------------|-------------|
| 2001 | 1,487.3 | 4.7% | — |
| 2000 | 1,420.8 | –3.0% | 4.7% |
| 1999 | 1,465.2 | –1.0% | 1.5% |
| 1998 | 1,480.7 | 6.7% | 0.4% |
| 1997 | 1,387.7 | 3.7% | 7.2% |
| 1996 | 1,338.6 | 6.0% | 11.1% |
| 1995 | 1,262.6 | –2.3% | 17.8% |
| 1994 | 1,291.7 | 3.8% | 15.1% |
| 1993 | 1,244.0 | 6.0% | 19.6% |
| 1992 | 1,173.2 | 2.9% | 26.8% |
| 1991 | 1,140.6 | –4.0% | 30.4% |

*Note.*   Total admissions have increased by 5% since last year and reflect a 30% increase
(+346 million) since the beginning of the decade.

Source.   1989 to present, based on NATO average ticket price.

Why does Hollywood prosper? Here is classic price discrimination—releasing a film so as to maximize the revenues from each separate "window." Basically, this means that the Big Six release films in the following

order: theaters, home video and DVD, pay-per-view, pay cable, and finally, broadcast and basic cable television. Each window in this sequence is an exclusive. A new window opens only when all value of the previous window had been captured. Customers know that if they wait, the cost they pay at that window would be lower than the prior one. Home video and DVD also allowed the customer to view the film whenever she or he desire. If one waits long enough, she or he could purchase a blank tape and copy it from free over-the-air broadcast television. No wonder by the close of the 20th century, while theatrical premieres drew the most publicity, most of the monies paid came from home video purchase or rental.

But with all this additional money pouring into the system, still only six major studios gathered the bulk of it. Whatever the venue—theatrical, cable TV, or home video—the focus of the production and distribution of most of the films most people saw as the 20th century ended continued to be Hollywood in general, six major studios in particular. In a profile of a former powerful Hollywood agent, Michael Ovitz, Lynn Hirschberg (1999) of *The New York Times* put it best: "Hollywood is a small community—there are only six big movie studios, four big TV networks, and three big talent agencies. [The people who own and run these organizations] talk to one another every day. They confide, they feud., they forgive, they do business together, they vacation together."

Audiences of film fans in the United States seemed to love the system. The past 25 years surely ranked as a "Golden Age" of interest in movie watching—benefitting the Big Six studios. The majors typically take in well in excess from their divisions that handle movies. High revenues—surging into the billions if one properly counted all the multiple sources of revenues—and the costs of producing that precious first negative also grew. In the late-1990s, the average motion picture cost neared $60 million and inflated to more than $80 million—if one properly added in marketing and publicity costs, primarily television advertising.

Because of this long-term inevitable profitability, the Big Six studios retained a growing appetite for hot new talents. By the late-1990s newcomers Gwyneth Paltrow and Ben Affleck, as well as proven box-office winners like Jim Carrey and Tom Cruise, could command $20 million a picture. Here is where the role of the agent came in; they negotiated on behalf of their clients with the Big Six. An agent's job was to try to maximize salary and participation in profits. The star system had ever been thus, certainly since it was developed as a cornerstone of the Hollywood film industry by Charlie Chaplin and Mary Pickford more than 75 years earlier. Agents came in during the 1950s as manipulating tax laws offered advantages to freelancing by actors and actresses no longer under sole contract to one studio (Rose, 1995).

Yet with new stars, the basic structure of the industry has changed little. These six Hollywood operations—Warner Bros., Paramount, Twentieth Century Fox, Sony, Disney, and Universal—still define the world's motion picture dominant makers and distributors. Although many fans look back to the 1930s and 1940s as the Golden Age of the movie business, in fact the end of the 20th century was the era when the Big Six in Hollywood achieved its greatest power and profitability. Pretenders, as analyzed later, try to enter, but none have succeeded, although the DreamWorks SKG experiment continues. Dozens have tried and failed; so the odds against DreamWorks SKG are long indeed. Through the 1980s and 1990s, MGM virtually had dropped out, unable to match the power of the Big Six (Albarran & Dimmick, 1996).

By the beginning of the 21st century each of the Big Six studios effected a different business strategy, reflecting the personality of the studio chief as well as the financial condition and strategic objectives of the parent company.

- Disney is part of the vast Walt Disney Corporation. One of the world's largest media companies, led by CEO Michael Eisner for early two decades, Disney is best understood as a well-oiled machine, fashioning films in an almost paramilitary manner, but succeeding less as the 1990s ended. Whether under the brand of mainstream Hollywood Pictures, Touchstone Pictures, or specialized "independent" fare from division Miramax, during the 1990s Disney led the way as a major Hollywood power. Eisner tried to continue his amazing streak of making Disney's profits grow quarter after quarter.
- Paramount, a division if the Viacom Corporation, reflected an overall policy pursuing less risky films as deemed by CEO and owner Sumner Redstone. Unlike Disney—where no one shareholder controlled the company, even Michael Eisner—Sumner Redstone did effectively control National Amusements, Inc. He was a classic executive owner who did not like to take risks, even purchasing dominant home-video renter, Blockbuster, to guarantee access to that important market segment.
- Sony, one of the largest electronics manufactures in the world, was still seeking to make consistently profitable its grand experiment of marrying a movie studio and an electronics maker. That experiment has not worked. Through the 1990s it seemed despite Sony's vast success as an innovator and seller of Walkmen and Trinitron TV sets, it was unable to make the movie synergy work. Yet by hiring new executives, the Sony movie making and distribution subsidiary remained profitable.
- Twentieth Century Fox, like Paramount, in the end, is under the control of one man, Rupert Murdoch. It is the core part of Murdoch's international media empire, News Corporation, and because Murdoch alone, like Sumner Redstone, controlled enough stock, he was both owner and CEO. The difference is, Murdoch was and is a greater risk taker. No better example can be highlighted than his massive bet on *Titanic*, the greatest financial success in Hollywood history.

- Universal, owned since 2000 by France's Vivendi, evidenced a certain skittishness as new management constantly tinkered to invent a new diversified media conglomerate. Lew Wasserman controlled the company and offered stability through the 1960s, 1970s, and 1980s. Then he sold to Matsushita, which in turn sold to Seagrams, which in turn sold to Vivendi. As 2002 progresses, Vivendi is having its problems, and no one is sure what the state of the studio will be 5 years down the pike.

- Warner Bros. was a studio seemingly caught in the greatest case of media synergy ever attempted as its 2000 merger with AOL floundered. Warner Bros., part of the Time Warner media colossus, was part of a 1990s experiment that commenced with the Time plus Warner merger in 1990. That worked. As the world's largest media company, Warner has had a long, profitable record, but as the 1990s ended, like Universal, its short-term prospects were uncertain. Then in 2000 came the merger of all mergers—with AOL. The Internet would unite with the movies, but as of the middle of 2002, this experiment has proven an utter failure.

## THE BIG 6 HOLLYWOOD OLIGOPOLY OPERATES

Corporate strategies came and went, but the Hollywood oligopoly remained. During the 1990s and into the 21st century, this six-member oligopoly retained tight and firm control. The movie business oligopoly in Hollywood was one of the tightest in the media business. Two scholars who looked at the position in 1994 and concluded that "an examination of concentration ratios indicates that high levels of concentration exist in most of the [media] industry segments" were surely correct for motion pictures, and so this industry deserves our close our attention.

We can see most easily oligopoly power in the activities of the Big Six's trade association—the Motion Picture Association of America (MPAA)—where the six deal with common concerns from rating films to smoothing the way for international distribution to protecting their valuable copyrights around the world. While critics of the film industry usually focus only on the MPAA's ratings system, its long time head, Jack Valenti, earns his 1 million dollar a year salary by helping the Big Six oligopolists expand revenues from around the world. Indeed Valenti more often can be found abroad, far from his home office at 16th and "I" Street in Washington, D.C., two blocks from the White House. One poll ranked the MPAA the 18th most powerful lobby in Washington, D.C. as 1997 ended. Although Valenti's total association budget ($60 million per annum it is estimated) would make and market but a single modest blockbuster, the Big Six know it is money well spent—protecting their turf and expanding their markets (www.mpaa.org).

Yet with all the monies generated from a film over the course of its ever continuous life, we rarely know what is the true cost of a film. As part of the

1999 open trial of former Disney executive Jeffrey Katzenberg verses his former boss Michael Eisner, an internal Disney company memo was revealed showing 10 ways that a Disney accountant hid cost data so as not to reveal the data necessary to pay Katzenberg any more than was necessary under Katzenberg's percentage of the profits deal. An agent may negotiate a good deal, but the Big Six were all skilled at making sure that they paid out as little as possible. The Big Six publicize these cost figures that prove that the vast majority of feature films lose money when the actual data would reveal just the opposite conclusion: Few ever lose money in the long run (Grover, 1999).

The Big Six use their cost data to argue for cost cutting and producer restraint. They argue they simply can not afford to pay what the star or her or his agent seeks. Indeed, during the 1990s the Big Six seemed to be doing a good job of keeping agents and their star clients demands in check; it was the costs of special effects that seemed to be out of control as the 20th century ended. In that the third key expensive variable—presold stories—also remained in check, we anticipate that early in the 21st century there will be a scandal in that cost factor with some screenwriter demanding and getting 3 or 4 million dollars for one script, and executives then going on the record as "outraged!"

The trend as the 21st century began was as it had always been—to collude. The studios joined together to cooperate, even to the point of coproducing expensive feature films as with Twentieth Century Fox and Paramount's cofinancing of *Titanic* as the key example. In the end the game is profit maximization. Because these are the only six players in town, the worries are not about losing money in the long run, but maximizing profits. So the studios spend enormous efforts to craft hits in their theatrical runs so that the revenues will be as high as possible, all the while trying to keep costs as low as possible. Such has been the case since Universal's Lew Wasserman pioneered the blockbuster strategy with the June, 1975 release of *Jaws*.

Year after year they controlled between 80% and 90% of the expanding movie business in the United States and a bit less in the rest of the world. Every few years a couple of bold pretenders—during the 1980s Orion Pictures and New World—emerged to challenge the Big Six, but none ever survived after creating only a modest hit or two. No challenger has survived in the long haul, although as the 1990s were ending DreamWorks SKG was mounting a serious challenge. In the real Hollywood industry, the dozens of independent producers have no choice but to distribute their films through one of the six major studios if they wish to maximize their return on investment and if they want the largest possible audience to see their work.

The Big Six majors' power continues to derive, as it has since the 1920s, from their unique ability to distribute films around the world. At considerable expense, all six maintain offices in more than a dozen cities in North

America (and up to 50 overseas), where their representatives are in constant contact with the heads of the dominant theater chains. A studio's "hit parade" record at the box office is what impels theater owners (a conservative lot with most of their assets invested in real estate) to consistently rent its products. Most movies that most people think of in the United States are funneled through Hollywood's Big Six. Thus as much as the history of the Hollywood film industry has changed, it has remained the same.

Modern Hollywood commenced in the mid-1970s as the industry fashioned the blockbuster strategy to turn television into a friend, not a foe. Through the final quarter of the 20th century, the oligopoly learned to generate billions of dollars in profits from creations that may start with a feature film but then go on to touch all forms of mass media, from radio advertising to music sound tracks, from novelization of film stories to magazines discussing the latest cinematic trends, from presentation of television to entertainment sites galore on the World Wide Web. Each movie aspired theatrically to become a smash hit because if it does then it turns into a product line, designed to fill all entertainment needs and desires from toys to theme park rides, from T-shirts to campaigns to sell more McDonalds hamburgers. An endless array of licensed tie-ins generate additional millions to the studio of origin (Wyatt,1994).

The cycle of a Hollywood feature film from one of the Big Six is quite regular and rests the power in distribution of the Big Six. To create a feature film that will be seen around the world it must be "green lighted" or picked up by one of the Big Six. So *production* is the initial phase. Some production companies work directly as units of the Big Six, but more often than not the producer is an affiliated independent company, formed by a star, director, or producer through her or his agent. Most feature films, after a script has been fashioned, start shooting on location, often with considerable help and subsidy by a local government that has wooed the production to theoretically boost the local economy. After some weeks of location shooting, production then finishes up in a Hollywood studio. As a consequence, all the states and many of the cities during the 1990s ran bureaus to lure film-making companies to their locales to spend monies on local talent, lodging, and food. Some states and cities have even financed small studio developments to tempt film makers. Hotel taxes for film crews staying more than 30 days are waived, and the police regularly rope off whole sections of cities so location filming can take place.

*Distribution* never gets much attention, but insiders recognize its far greater importance. Although Hollywood publicity focuses on the production of films—its stars, stories and special effects—distribution has always been a key to corporate longevity. Indeed, worldwide distribution has long been the very basis of Hollywood's power. No other national film industry has been ever been so far reaching. More than any other mass-media business—closely followed by music—the film industry of Hollywood proved the vast and important advantages of globalizing, with its consider power from economies of scale, long before the term *global media* was ever invented (Gomery, 1992).

Globally, only in the rare nation does Hollywood not capture more than one half the business. Hollywood's regular production of hit films provides a strong incentive for foreign theater, pay TV, home video, and DVD companies to consistently deal with the six majors rather than take a flyer with a true independent. In recent years this has led to joint deals with foreign companies to build theaters in Britain, Australia, Germany, Spain, and France, and to run cable TV networks all over the world. Through all these new technologies of presentation, the Hollywood Big Six have stood at the center of profit maximizing strategies, much to the chagrin of policy makers who seek to protect their native culture industries.

During the 1990s the global theatrical market expanded significantly. The Hollywood oligopoly had long been global, but a new push came in the 1990s. Once the monies had been committed to the promotion of a film blockbuster event, it made sense to amortize that cost across the whole planet. And these blockbusters flow around the world. The major Hollywood companies pioneered the selling of their products around the world, beginning in the days after World War I. By the mid-1990s the Big Six were taking in an estimated $5 billion in rentals worldwide—the monies they kept after sharing box office take with exhibitors. Yet foreign revenues are coming more often in the form of payments for pay TV and rentals and sales for home video. There was also a trend to upgrade cinemas abroad, modeling them after the mega-plexes being built in the United States. With the emancipation of state control television broadcasting and the wiring of cable and the spread of satellite services, the vehicles for distribution became more and more in place in the 1990s. Homes in Europe, for example, acquired VCRs in almost the same numbers as in the United States. Rupert Murdoch knew this as he came to Hollywood from abroad.

*Presentation*—too often misleadingly referred to as simply theatrical exhibition—starts with the process of release on premiere weekends of the 150 or so potential blockbusters Hollywood distributes. The aforementioned millions of dollars spent on TV advertising focuses the public's attention on the next hoped-for blockbuster. A strong first weekend, the theory goes, will lead to positive "word of mouth," and then increasing revenues on down the line—Pay TV and home video principally. Indeed, it was the aftermarket—the streams of income from pay TV, home video, and DVD—that gave the Big Six one of their most sizable advantages. They alone could milk a hit through years of revenues after the initial major cost. Competitors would have to wait and hope.

A series of windows of presentation became formalized in the 1990s. For Hollywood studios' most notable product, feature films, the process still began in theaters and then went "downstream" to the former "ancillary" markets of pay TV, home video, and DVD. There are rare exceptions. A handful of films each year fail in U.S. theaters, but are able to garner significant box-office returns in video. However, such cases are the exceptions. In the vast majority of cases, the theater remains the "voting booth" where the return on the $60 million investment for the average theatrical feature is determined. A theatrical blockbuster guarantees millions of additional dollars from the home video, DVD, and pay-TV arenas. That is why the major Hollywood companies work so hard to craft a hit in the theaters because once they have a proven commodity there, the rest of the way is usually much smoother.

Interestingly, the continuing importance of theaters became more obvious during the 1990s. Consider that at the beginning of the 1980s, a number of serious pundits, including Arthur D. Little, Inc., the multinational consulting firm, studied the film industry and predicted that there probably would be no need for movie theaters by 1990. Everybody could (and would) stay home and view Hollywood's best through pay TV, home video, and DVD. Instead, going out to the movies has remained a viable leisure time activity. Few predicted that during the 1990s more screens would be added, creating more than 30,000 available theatrical screens in the United States, setting an industry record each time a new multi-screen complex opened. As seen in Table 9.2, theatrical release in the 1990s required more and more theater screens so Hollywood could take full advantage of the economies of scale from television advertising to fashion a hit that would pay for itself through successive windows of presentation. Because the cost of marketing a feature film can often exceed $30 million, if it is spread over more theaters, marketing costs per theater per film can remain relatively low. The economies of scale of television advertising of theatrical features provides the foundation of the multiplex, and the creation of blockbusters.

One of the key innovations of the final quarter of the 20th century in the film business is overnight data generation. It is important to know when and if a blockbuster is being voted in. By the late-1990s, A. C. Nielsen's Entertainment Data, Inc., founded as the blockbuster era commenced, was functioning as an integral part of the motion picture distribution and exhibition community. Entertainment Data innovated the collection and dissemination of box-office data by creating a centralized computer reporting service. By 1997, Entertainment Data was collecting data from approximately 32,000 screens—indoor and drive-in—based in the United States, Canada, the United Kingdom, Germany, Spain, and France. Its products and services not only included daily box-office reports, but also instant analysis of trends. Its

## TABLE 9.2
### Total Number of U.S. Screens

| Year | Total Screens | 2001 Versus | Indoor Screens | 2001 Versus | Drive-In Screens | 2001 Versus |
|------|--------------|-------------|----------------|-------------|------------------|-------------|
| 2001 | 36,764 | — | 36,110 | — | 654 | — |
| 2000 | 37,396 | −1.7% | 36,679 | −1.6% | 717 | −8.8% |
| 1999 | 37,185 | −1.1% | 36,448 | −0.9% | 737 | −11.3% |
| 1998 | 34,186 | 7.5% | 33,440 | 8.0% | 746 | −12.3% |
| 1997 | 31,640 | 16.2% | 30,825 | 17.1% | 815 | −19.8% |
| 1996 | 29,690 | 23.8% | 28,864 | 25.1% | 826 | −20.8% |
| 1995 | 27,805 | 32.2% | 26,958 | 33.9% | 847 | −22.8% |
| 1990 | 23,689 | 55.2% | 22,774 | 58.6% | 915 | −28.5% |
| 1985 | 21,147 | 73.8% | 18.327 | 97.0% | 2,820 | −76.8% |
| 1980 | 17,590 | 109.0% | 14,029 | 157.4% | 3,561 | −81.6% |

Source.  MPAA.

weekend box-office results defined success and failure every Monday morning, as well as influenced future multimillion-dollar marketing campaigns.
Its reports ranged from estimates of the size of the annual box-office take in
Peoria, Illinois to the average opening weekend gross for R-rated action pictures released during the summer. Big Six executives poured over this data
and analysis, without needing to go out to the field from their offices in Los
Angeles and New York (www.entdata.com).

If there is a secret, as noted earlier, it is that the Big Six have expanded the
markets that generate monies to pay off these costs. The Hollywood movie industry produces theatrical films that first show up in 30,000 multiplexes in the
United States and thousands more around the world. Here is where the publicity is generated as to which film is a hit and which one is a bust. But the mon-
eys really come later—when the film appears on pay TV, is sold or rented for
home video, and later shown on basic cable TV and on broadcast TV.

Indeed, home video and DVD have changed everything. Indeed the
home video matured as a market outside the United States during the 1990s
but still lagged rental fever in the United States. But billions of dollars
flowed through the video window. Then, as the 21st century started, came
DVD and the window of home viewing—through sales or rental—expanded. Surely in the future, there will be more new technologies to watch
one's favorite films.

In the end, these forces have led the Big Six to integrate horizontally and
vertically. Horizontally all—year after year—the Big Six have generated

considerable profits from a wide spectrum of mass-media enterprises, including theme parks (Vivendi and Disney in particular), recorded music (Vivendi, Sony, and Time Warner), and all forms of television production and presentation. Each helped the movie division. Movies inspired theme-park rides, film scores and songs supplied hits for the music divisions, and television supplied presold stars and stories. And make no mistake about it, the major Hollywood companies will continue to be the big winners with this horizontal diversification. Consider that Disney, Paramount, Warners, Vivendi's Universal, Sony, and Twentieth Century Fox— all of the Big Six—"instantly" became the defining producers in home video at the end of the 20th century, and in DVD as the 21st century opened (Compaine & Gomery, 2000).

Vertically, during the 1980s and 1990s the Big Six built up considerable power by spending millions to acquire interests in movie theater chains, cable television systems, over-the-air television stations, TV networks, and home-video operations such as Viacom's Blockbuster Video. All figured that controlling the markets "downstream" was vital for the long-term survival and prosperity of any dominating Hollywood operation. The Big Six wanted to be there, as full participants, when the customer handed over her or his dollars.

They all had long been in the business of producing prime-time television. While NBC and CBS struggled in the 1990s to throw off the days of the financial interest and syndication restrictions and produce their own shows the new model in late-1990s Hollywood was to own a network. Disney had ABC, Twentieth Century Fox had the Fox network, Time Warner had the WB, and Viacom had CBS and UPN.

Two economic motivations lead the chief executive officers of the major Hollywood companies to spend millions to secure vertical control. First, vertical integration enables a company to take full advantage of reductions in costs associated with only having to sell to another part of the same company. Thus, Sony can take a Sony movie and book it into one of its many Loews multiplexes. Time Warner can offer a Warner Bros. movie directly to subsidiary HBO, and show it to the millions of households that subscribe to a Time Warner cable system, and then tender sales through Warner's video arm. This can be coordinated without a fleet of salespeople to drum up business. The positive effects of vertical integration can be debated, but they do exist and do help create barriers to entry to the Big Six (Blackstone & Bowman, 1999).

More importantly, however, is the issue of market control. A vertically integrated company need not worry about being shut out of one of those key ancillary markets. Indeed, one of the majors would rather work with a known rival than see a new competitor arise. So, despite all their alleged struggle in the merger talks of 1989, Paramount and Time Warner continued to always jointly own and operate a vast theater circuit that gave both a strong, dependable position in key cities (principally Los Angeles), guaranteeing that their movies would receive the best possible opening in their jointly owned chain. Indeed today's "theatrical window," despite all the talk of the impact of cable television and home video, remains the most important venue to create the blockbusters that can be exploited in other media. However, the vertical stream extends far past traditional theaters and video outlets. In 1995 Disney stunned the world by purchasing ABC/Capital Cities. There were many reasons for this acquisition, but the most significant was that Disney gained control over access to a major over-the-air TV network as well as to cable TV outlets. Vertical integration has extended to all forms of movie presentation, principally pay TV, home video, and DVD.

All these advantages added up to a huge and almost predictable flow of revenues. Whatever additional new television technologies appear in the future, the business of the Hollywood major studios will continue to seek top dollar charges for seeing the film as early as possible, whereas less fervent fans can wait and see it for a few cents on basic cable TV or "free" broadcast television. Starting with a theatrical showing, then home video, pay cable, cable television, network television, local over-the-air television, and any other possible venues that come along in the forthcoming years, the object of this price discrimination will continue to be to get as much revenue from a product as the various markets will permit.

Thus, the Hollywood film industry—as it is often labeled—must be viewed as more than just the film business. Although their film divisions may focus on the creation of feature films with highly hyped theatrical premieres, the vast accumulation of profits really comes from presentation on television. During the final quarter of the 20th century Hollywood became far more than a film business and embraced and used television to considerable advantage, and also provided spill-over profits for nearly every division of media conglomerate. Yet television never threatened the oligopoly power of the Big Six. They have remained and will remain.

All theatrical films start their life on a screen in a multiplex. These multiplexes are organized as chains to take advantage of the economies of scale of operation, and important to negotiate discounts on items sold at their concession stands. The theater chains can keep all the monies from selling popcorn and the like, but share the box office revenues with which ever of the Big Six that was distributing the film. Although the Big Six control nearly all of production and distribution, they do not even come close to owning every movie screen in every multiplex in the United States. Indeed there exist only two chains affiliated with the Big Six—Sony and Universal's Loews Cineplex chain, and Viacom's National Amusements chain.

The majority of the ownership of the theatrical side of the movie business was not with vertically integrated Hollywood affiliated companies.

During the 1990s outsiders took over this portion of the business. For example, in early 1998 two of the United States' leading investment companies—Hicks, Muse, Tate & Furst, Inc., and Kohlberg Kravis Roberts & Company—poured vast sums into Tennessee-based Regal Cinemas Companies to fashion a chain that summed to 5,347 screens in 727 locations in 35 states. But this proved too much expansion, and Regal went into bankruptcy in 2001.

## THE HOLLYWOOD OLIGOPOLY AND THE FUTURE

The motion picture seen in a theater, on pay TV, or as home video will continue to play a vibrant part of media economics. Realistically, as we end the 20th century, nothing looms on the horizon that will threaten the oligopolistic power of the major studios. The Big Six major Hollywood studios will continue to enjoy the fruits of their formidable economic power. Their influence will keep reaching throughout the world, more powerfully than any other mass medium. The Hollywood oligopoly has learned to thrive in the age of advanced technologies, based on skilled use of media economics. This oligopoly will continue to operate with its safe and predictable formulae. The Big Six Hollywood will continue to compete over small differences rather than important considerations of expression. Sequels had a built in recognition factor, a simplicity of appeal that make the job of profit maximization much easier than trying to locate a new film after another new film after another new film. The homogenization of content and style—within well-accepted limits and properly called the classic Hollywood style—derives from the oligopoly of the Big Six, and the Big Six will continue their power and this style well into the 21st century.

As to what might disrupt the vast power of the Big Six critics point first to technological innovation. By the close of the 20th century, nearly every facet of the movie industry has been pushed with transformation possibilities in recent decades—from production (computerized dinosaurs and other special effects) to distribution (the collection and analysis of box office data) and presentation ( a host of alternatives to home video). But even with all the possibilities of digital wizardry and computer video replacing chemical celluloid, the motion picture reels as the 20th century ended were still made through a chemical film process and then projected onto screens using technology that fundamentally has changed little.

As to the federal government breaking up the Big Six by way of antitrust action, that possibility also seems unlikely. Deregulation continues as the basic government policy, and with all the outlets for movies, the industry claims no power in presentation exists. They also point to the fact that anyone with enough resources can make a film. What they avoid speaking of is the global power of distribution. And as long as that remains in place, the

Hollywood Big Six will continue to dominate and define the movie industry as we know it in the 21st century (Orwell & Peers, 2002).

## FURTHER READING

Compaine, B., & Gomery, D. (2000). *Who owns the media?* (3rd ed.). Mahwah, NJ: Lawrence Erlbaum Associates.
Gomery, D. (1992). *Shared pleasures.* Madison: University of Wisconsin Press.

## REFERENCES

Albarran, A. B., & Dimmick, J. (1996). Concentration and economics of multiformity in the communication industries. *The Journal of Media Economics, 9*(4), 41–50.
Blackstone, E. A., & Bowman, G. W. (1999). Vertical integration in the motion picture industry, *Journal of Communication, 49*(1), 123–140.
Compaine, B., & Gomery, D. (2000). *Who owns the media?* (3rd ed.). Mahwah, NJ: Lawrence Erlbaum Associates.
Gomery, D. (1992) *Shared pleasures.* Madison: University of Wisconsin Press.
Grover, R. (1999, May 17). This Mickey Mouse case should disappear. *Business Week,* 48.
Hirschberg, L. (1999, May 9). Michael Ovitz is on the line. *The New York Times Magazine,* 49.
Orwell, B., & Peers, M. (2002, May 10). The message of media mergers: So, far, they haven't been hits. *The Wall Street Journal,* A1, A5.
Rose, F. (1995). *The Agency.* New York: Harper Business.
Wyatt, J. (1994). *High concept: Movies and marketing in Hollywood.* Austin: University of Texas Press.

# Chapter 10

# The Economics of the Contemporary Radio Industry

ALAN B. ALBARRAN
*The University of North Texas*

This chapter examines the economic aspects of the contemporary radio broadcasting industry. As the oldest form of electronic media, the radio industry has experienced significant changes since its humble beginnings in the early 20th century. Radio did not become a commercially viable medium until advertising was introduced in 1922. Radio became the dominant source of entertainment and information in a pretelevision world, but after the 1940s and the advent of television, radio began a metamorphosis as a medium that continues to the present era.

The contemporary radio industry operates on two bands of the electronic spectrum, AM and FM. FM is superior in that an FM channel provides a better quality signal due to the size of each FM channel, and it broadcasts in stereo. AM signals are of lower quality, where the medium has flourished in recent years with a number of ``news, talk, and sports-related formats. Digital radio transmission is now possible via subscription with the debut of digital audio radio services (DARS) in 2002.

The radio marketplace is fiercely competitive, as radio competes for audiences and advertising revenues in local and national markets with television, newspapers, books, magazines, and the Internet. This chapter focuses on several topics, including the structure of the radio industry, finances, products and product lines, the impact of new technologies, radio's efforts to globalize its operations, and the social issues associated with the contemporary radio industry.

## RADIO INDUSTRY MARKET STRUCTURE

The contemporary radio industry in the United States has experienced massive structural change since the passage of the 1996 Telecommunications Act that removed national ownership restrictions (Albarran & Pitts, 2001). From 1996 to 1999, with the national economy soaring, interest rates near record lows, and financing capital readily available, a sellers market dominated the radio industry. By 2002, the radio industry was transformed into an industry dominated by two leading companies: Clear Channel Communications and Infinity Broadcasting, the latter being a division of the conglomerate Viacom. These two companies together own nearly 1,400 radio stations, slightly more than one tenth of all commercial stations in operation in the United States.

Radio consolidation abated somewhat since 2000, as the U.S. economy suffered a downturn fueled by the collapse of the dot-com industry and reductions in corporate earnings. Although there are still some mergers and acquisitions taking place, the level of activity has dwindled since the maddening rush of the late-1990s.

Prior to 1996, the radio industry resembled a monopolistic competitive market structure. This was due primarily to national ownership limits previously capped at 40 stations (20 AM and 20 FM).[1] There were numerous companies that owned the maximum number of stations, and regulatory limits meant the companies could not grow any larger in terms of their radio holdings. Historically, radio ownership regulations developed around the concept of scarcity, the principle that more people would want to broadcast than available frequencies allowed.

By the mid-1990s, many radio broadcasters and group owners had lobbied Congress for years for relaxation of ownership limits, claiming that there was a multitude of information and entertainment sources available for consumers (especially via television and cable), and that scarcity was no longer an issue. Policymakers eventually agreed, as the 1996 Act allowed unlimited ownership at the national level, while maintaining limits in local markets using a tiered approach depending on the number of signals available to the audience.

In the largest markets (those with 45 or more signals) owners are limited to a maximum of 8 stations, with no more than 5 in one class (AM or FM). In markets with 30 to 44 stations, the limit is 7 stations with no more than 4 in one class. In markets with stations that total 15 to 29, the limit is 6 stations with no more than 4 in the same class, whereas in markets with 14 or fewer stations the limit is 5 stations with no more than 3 in the same class provided the company does not exceed 50% of the stations in the market.

Allowing a single company to own as many as eight stations in a market meant managing and operating radio stations would be radically different. Theoretically, one General Manager could run eight different stations, along with a single set of departments providing the various support functions (e.g., engineering, accounting, human resources, etc.). Personnel, any companies' greatest expense, could be drastically reduced resulting in greater budgetary efficiencies. Likewise, greater economies of scale would be realized in the marketing and selling of advertising, as account executives would be enabled to sell for an entire group of stations. Combined with similar efforts going on in other markets, economies of scope were much more achievable for radio companies after the 1996 Act.

The growing realization that the business of radio would change led to a key dilemma for many radio group owners: Either get bigger, or sell out. Small companies owning only one to two stations in a market would have great difficulty competing against larger clusters for advertising revenues. Hence, many companies chose to collect profits by selling their holdings when stations were selling at inflated prices. In fact, today's Clear Channel Communications and Infinity Broadcasting are the amalgamation of some 75 separate companies prior to 1996. According to one industry source, in 1995 the top 50 radio groups owned 8.6% of all radio stations; by 2000 they owned 27.5% of all stations (Fratrick, 2001).

The overall impact of radio industry consolidation means in many local markets the radio industry has moved away from a monopolistic competition market structure toward more of an oligopoly. Further relaxation of local ownership caps could move the entire industry toward an oligopoly, although regulators (in the form of the Department of Justice's Antitrust Division) have been concerned about allowing one to two companies to dominate local advertising revenue in the market.[2] In several instances, the DOJ halted merger approval until the impact on the local market could be carefully studied.

The restructuring of the radio industry also consolidated the financial earning power of the top companies. In 2001, the top 10 radio groups accounted for approximately 50% of all radio industry revenues, even though they owned only 17% of all stations (Fratrick, 2001). Of course, most of these revenues are generated in the top markets. The top 10 radio groups, as of July 2002, are listed in Table 10.1.

## RADIO INDUSTRY FINANCES

Radio industry finances are rather simplistic in that the primary revenue source for radio stations comes from the sale of local advertising. In the larger markets some revenues are derived from the sale of regional and national spot advertising. Another category of advertising is network advertising—time sold by radio networks and programs in national syndication (e.g., Rush Limbaugh, Dr. Laura, Howard Stern). Table 10.2 illustrates trends in the radio advertising for selected years of analysis.

The data in Table 10.2 indicate the importance of the local advertising market for radio. Historically, the radio industry derives approximately 75% to 80% of total revenues from the sale of local advertising. Radio is also

TABLE 10.1

**Top 10 Radio Groups, Ranked by 2001 Revenue**

| Group | Number Stations Owned | Revenues (Millions) |
|---|---|---|
| Clear Channel Communications | 1,200 | $3,527 |
| Infinity Radio (Viacom) | 183 | $2,355 |
| Cox Radio | 79 | $452 |
| ABC Radio (Disney) | 54 | $436 |
| Entercom | 96 | $423 |
| Citadel Communications | 205 | $349 |
| Radio One | 62 | $301 |
| Emmis Communications | 23 | $295 |
| Hispanic Broadcating Corporation | 49 | $254 |
| Susquehanna Radio Corporation | 33 | $235 |

*Note.* Adapted from Fratrick (2001).

TABLE 10.2

**Radio Advertising Revenues (In Millions of Dollars)**

| Year | Local | Spot | Network | Total |
|---|---|---|---|---|
| 1980 | $ 2,643 | $ 740 | $ 158 | $ 3,541 |
| 1985 | 4,915 | 1,319 | 329 | 6,563 |
| 1990 | 6,780 | 1,626 | 433 | 8,839 |
| 1995 | 9,120 | 1,920 | 430 | 11,470 |
| 1996 | 9,850 | 2,090 | 470 | 12,410 |
| 1997 | 10,740 | 2,410 | 650 | 13,800 |
| 1998 | 11,920 | 2,770 | 740 | 15,430 |
| 1999 | 13,590 | 3,210 | 880 | 17,680 |
| 2000 | 15,232 | 3,596 | 1,029 | 19,857 |
| 2001 | 14,552 | 2,898 | 919 | 18,369 |

*Note.* Adapted from *Radio revenue.* Available online at www.rab.com.

very sensitive to macro and microeconomic conditions. For example, advertising flourished from 1995 to 2000 reflecting a strong and vibrant economy, but fell dramatically in 2001 with an economic downturn coupled with the terrorist attacks on September 11, 2001, that further hampered business activity.

The radio industry wants to transform the Internet into a new source of revenues, but no successful business model has been developed to date. Further, potential copyright fees for playing music online (discussed later in this chapter) has tempered enthusiasm for the Internet, with many stations no longer streaming live content on the Web but instead using their Web sites for promotion, marketing, and research purposes.

One new revenue stream that has emerged in recent years is the rise of nontraditional revenue (NTR), primarily found in the larger markets. NTR can come in many forms, but the primary manifestations have been via sponsorships, contests, live remotes, and other solicitations from area businesses. For example, a station may hold a dance or other public event in the community, and invite businesses to serve as cosponsors by paying a fee. Such events can potentially draw crowds in to the thousands, offering many opportunities for crosspromotion and marketing with other business partners. Although NTR is not a revenue category that compares equally with advertising, it can generate extra revenues and promotion for local radio stations.

In terms of expenses, personnel represent the greatest expense category for radio stations in terms of salaries and benefits.[3] Other cost centers include sales and marketing, programming, and general and administrative expenses. As mentioned earlier, consolidation has actually improved the economics of the radio industry by eliminating excess staff and creating greater efficiencies. The result is that profit margins for radio stations are very strong, ranging from a low of 40% in smaller markets to as much as 60% in medium and larger markets (Albarran, 2002).

One controversial technique that has emerged to control expenses is voice tracking (see Mathews, 2002). This technique is actually very simple to enact with the available technology in the industry. Voice tracking works as follows: A popular radio personality simply records the voice tracks for an entire air shift for another "sister" station a group owns (typically in another market). The tracks are stored electronically on a server, and networked to another station where an entire 4- to 6-hour shift can be assembled and stored on a computer hard drive in a manner of minutes. The end result is the station receiving the voice tracks can eliminate an air personality, saving thousands of dollars in salary and benefits.

There are of course drawbacks to voice tracking. The "tracked" personality is never able to make any appearances outside his or her local market, and it certainly limits the spontaneity and creativity that has always attracted radio audiences. Voice tracking is also seen as a denigration of the historic public service responsibilities of the radio industry. The techniques and technology are so good many audience members cannot distinguish when a shift is being voice tracked. It is difficult to predict if voice tracking will become a national phenomenon, or a short-lived experiment. Voice tracking is one of the newer programming innovations that give radio managers an opportunity to improve revenues.

## RADIO PRODUCTS AND PRODUCT LINES

The radio industry functions like many other media industries in that it operates in a dual product market, offering its content to listeners, and in turn sells access to those listeners to advertisers seeking targeted demographic groups (Albarran, 2002). This dual product market functions at both the local and national levels. At the local level, stations provide entertainment and information to audiences and advertisers, whereas at the national level, radio networks and syndication provides programming that seeks the same mix of listeners and advertisers. The most popular radio formats include country, rock, classic rock, contemporary hit radio, news and talk, and urban and hip hop. Format tastes and preferences vary by region across the United States. Cost structures also vary in the selection of a radio format. Generally speaking, news, news and talk, and all-sports formats are more costly to operate and maintain than stations opting to program a music format because they require more personnel, equipment, and resources.

Applying basic principles of supply and demand to the radio industry, supply can be thought of in several different ways. First is the physical supply of radio stations available to audiences and advertisers. The number of radio stations available in a market are a combination of many factors, including population, regulation, and economics. Larger markets that serve large populations usually have the most stations, whereas smaller markets often contain a limited number of stations audiences can access. In the United States, except in the most remote areas, most audience members have access to several radio stations on both the AM and FM bands.

The majority of radio stations in medium and large markets operate continuously, 24 hours a day, 7 days a week, 365 days a year. This continuous operation promotes loyalty and stability among radio listeners. The audience knows their favorite stations will always be on the air. Radio's ubiquitous nature provides an unending supply of time available to audiences and advertisers, whenever access is desired.

Finally, stations target different demographic groups, forming another way to think about the supply of radio. Radio's ability to reach different formats makes it particularly attractive to advertisers who seek particular audience profiles. For example, women 18 to 49 tend to listen to formats like soft rock and country whereas men 35 to 49 usually listen to rock, classic rock, country, or sports talk. There are stations that target ethnic audiences (e.g., Spanish language, rhythm and blues, hip hop), and others that appeal to older audiences (news and talk, beautiful music). The ability to reach defined audience groups—along with the ability to reach commuters—makes radio a particularly attractive medium for advertisers. Coupled with advertising in television and print, radio adds a very cost-efficient means to capture additional audiences.

Demand relationships in radio take three different forms. First is the demand by consumers for the various stations and the content they offer to listeners. Second is the demand by advertisers. Third is the demand for the radio stations by owners and potential owners.

Consumer demand for radio is perhaps best illustrated by statistics compiled by the Radio Advertising Bureau that show the strength and pervasiveness of radio as a medium (see www.rab.com). Approximately 99% of all households own at least one radio receiver. In fact, the average U.S. household has an average of 5.6 radios. In a typical week, radio reaches 95% of all Americans age 12 and up, and the average American listens to the radio for 3 hours each weekday and 5 hours each weekend.

Advertisers find radio particularly useful as a medium to reach target audiences. Larger and national advertisers utilize radio in conjunction with television, newspaper, direct mail, and other forms of advertising to deliver targeted demographic groups. Radio allows advertisers the opportunity to reach commuters going to work and school, a unique capability offered by the medium. Finally, radio advertising is often less expensive than other forms of advertising, especially television and newspapers. With its ability to reach so much of the population, radio represents an efficient advertising medium when used in a mix of media advertising vehicles.

Since the passage of the 1996 Telecommunications Act, demand for radio stations mushroomed as consolidation lead to the formation of radio clusters in many larger and medium markets. In 1995, the average price of an AM station was just under $500,000, whereas an FM station averaged $2.1 million. Five years later, the average prices for AM and FM stations surged to $3.0 million and $8.5 million respectively (Albarran, 2002). The pace of radio station transactions slowed in 2001 and 2002 due to a sluggish economy, the aftermath of September 11, 2001, and increasing consolidation (many groups had reached their desired goals of local ownership). Future relaxation of ownership limits at the local level would no doubt result in another wave of ownership changes. However, the FCC continues to show no indications of modifying radio ownership limits.

## IMPACT OF NEW TECHNOLOGY

Throughout its history, the radio industry has continually been impacted by the introduction of new technologies. The advent of television in the 1950s created a massive structural shift in radio programming, as stations moved from a block type of scheduling similar to today's television environment, to one dominated by different types of music and talk formats. When FM began to grow in the 1960s, the better music quality led to music formats abandoning the AM dial for the higher quality FM bandwidth.

Satellite delivered programming was introduced in the 1970s, creating changes in how the radio industry received their audio network feeds. Prior to satellite transmission, network feeds were provided over long-distance telephone lines, and in some cases, via microwave transmission. Satellites eventually led to the birth of satellite-delivered radio formats, enabling stations to have the sound of a professional staff but without the need for full-time announcing and production personnel.

At the beginning of the 21st century, the radio industry is again feeling the impact of new communication technology. This impact has been manifested in two areas: digital audio radio services (DARS) and radio services delivered via the Internet.

## DARS

Although the FCC in the mid-1990s originally authorized the DARS service, successful industry lobbying kept the services at a conceptual level until 2001. In mid-2002 two services were operating in the United States: XM Radio and Sirius. Both services offer a package of 100+ digital radio channels to subscribers for a monthly fee ranging from $9.95 to $12.95 per month. The subscriber must also purchase a receiver for his or her automobile in order to receive the signals.

The DARS providers offer virtually every type of programming. There is a wide array of music formats, plus talk, sports, news, and ethnic-oriented channels. Both services offer a block of channels that are commercial-free. By mid-2002, both services were floundering, and well below corporate expectations for paid subscribers (Radio services, 2002). If subscribership does not improve, one could expect the two services to merge into one entity in order to try and survive. DARS has the financial backing of the major automobile manufacturers and several major radio companies, such as Clear Channel. But the primary challenge for DARS is the consumer's willingness to pay for a service (radio) that has always been available for free.

### The Internet

The Internet's challenge to the radio industry is multifaceted, and takes many forms. As radio stations began to embrace the Internet, they quickly realized that by streaming their broadcasts via their Web site (*web casting*), they could potentially be heard by listeners anywhere around the globe with a network connection. But the bubble soon burst with this innovation over issues related to economics and intellectual property.

The recording industry, stung by the creation of Napster and other peer-to-peer music exchange services, raised the issue of royalty payments for Internet broadcasting. The Recording Industry of American (RIAA), the powerful industry trade organization supported by all the major and minor record labels, claimed that the royalties paid by radio companies only applied to distribution on AM and FM. The Internet represented another form of distribution with the RIAA believing stations should pay separately for the right to broadcast via the Internet.

This controversy led to a huge battle over royalty payments, left primarily to the recommendation of the Copyright Arbitration Royalty Panel (CARP). CARP was developed as part of the Digital Millennium Copyright Act (DMCA) in 1998 to set compulsory license fees for nonsubscription digital audio transmissions, which encompass web casting and the distribution of audio files over the Internet. The CARP proceedings actually began in November 1998, and continued through many different hearings and legal challenges until a final report and order was issued on July 8, 2002 (Determination, 2002).

Many different stakeholders had interest in the CARP decision-making process. The stakeholders included the various web casters (including Internet-only radio stations and other web-based services), the FCC-licensed radio stations, the recording industry, and trade unions like the American Federation of Television and Radio Artists and the American Federation of Musicians. The end result was the development of a multilayered fee-structure[4] effective on September 1, 2002, requiring web casters, broadcasters, and other entities to pay royalty fees to transmit copyrighted music over the Internet (Determination, 2002).

CARP has a much greater impact on Internet-only radio stations (there are several thousand Internet-only stations operating around the world), noncommercial stations, and personal radio services (see next paragraph) that lack the financial resources to pay these fees. College radio stations not affiliated with National Public Radio were particularly hard-hit, with many stations forced to cancel Internet broadcasting (Carnevale, 2002).

The Internet also allows users to set up their own "personal" radio services via the Internet. Although not as popular as regular web casting, personal radio presents yet another distraction from regular radio listening. Using a personal radio service, users enter information regarding the types of music and other features they want to listen to on a user profile (Bulkeley, 1999). By adding a zip code, local weather information also can be obtained on some sites. Personal radio services can be found with just about any good Internet search engine. One popular site is www.groovesite.com

The combined Internet radio audiences are minimal compared to the audiences delivered by traditional radio stations. But radio managers are concerned that Internet radio applications and DARS do provide alternatives to

local radio listening. If these fledging services are able to attract enough listeners, advertisers could eventually follow, leading to a slow migration of
both audiences and ad dollars to these new technologies. The only way radio
can combat these innovations is by emphasizing its local qualities, and providing listeners with the entertainment and information they desire.

## GLOBALIZATION

Radio is of course a global phenomenon, with many regions of the world
dependent on radio as the primary source of news and information. Outside the United States, radio broadcasting encompasses AM, FM, and
shortwave transmission. Shortwave radio has declined in recent years with
the advent of the Internet but is still very popular in third world and other
developing nations.

Clear Channel Communications, the largest radio owner in the United
States, owns and operates over 250 radio stations in Mexico, Australia,
New Zealand, and Europe with other international partners (see http://
www.clearchannel.com/International/). Clear Channel is also interested
in moving into ownership of British radio stations, pending new deregulatory reforms in the United Kingdom that will allow media ownership by
outside companies (see Cassey, 2002; Free TV 2002; Guess who's coming to
dinner, 2002).

While Clear Channel is the most aggressive U.S. radio owner pursuing
globalization, other companies have yet to follow suit, apparently wanting
to concentrate within domestic borders.[5] One area where more globalization is likely is in Spanish-language radio broadcasting. The Spanish-
speaking audience is a huge market, covering most of Latin America (except Brazil), Mexico, and Spain. In the United States, several companies are
targeting the Spanish-language market, including Hispanic Radio Broadcasters (expected to merge with Univision), Spanish Broadcasting System
Inc., Radio Utica, and Entravision Communications.

It is unlikely that any foreign radio companies will move into the U.S.
market due to regulatory restrictions that prevent majority foreign ownership of broadcasting stations. Coupled with the heavy consolidation of U.S.
stations and regulatory restrictions, encroachment on the U.S. domestic radio market seems out of reach.

## RADIO AND SOCIAL ISSUES

Throughout its history the radio industry has had an evolving relationship
with audiences and society in general. During radio's nascent years of development, the new medium captured the attention and imagination of the
public by bringing information and entertainment into the home. Radio be-

came an important source of news during World War II, and the primary form of evening entertainment in a pretelevision world.

As television emerged in the late-1940s to early-1950s, the radio industry was forced to change, as its principal entertainers and advertisers moved away from the medium. Pundits predicted the demise of radio. Instead, the industry responded by emphasizing music formats, and moving away from being a national medium to becoming more of a local medium. Radio stations embraced the communities they served and built new relationships with audiences as rock and roll and other format innovations were introduced. Radio networks refocused their mission, providing news reports and various types of feature programs to affiliates instead of 30- and 60-minute programs.

The medium continued to evolve with the growth of FM in the 1960s and 1970s, and expansion of formats and programming. When MTV (Music Television) debuted in 1981, there were concerns that music videos would lead to the end of radio. Likewise, AM radio was given little hope to survive during the 1980s, only to experience a renaissance with the surging popularity of talk radio in the 1990s. Despite these concerns, radio audiences continued to grow, as well as the amount of individual time spent with the medium.

So where is radio in the young 21st century? Radio remains an important medium for audiences, with its ability to provide local audiences with news, weather, and traffic information, as well as entertainment in the form of music and personalities. Many individuals wake up with radio, and spend time listening to the radio while commuting to work or school. Radio is also a source of companionship, or background material while performing other tasks.

But radio also competes for attention in a very crowded media landscape, where individuals have many options for entertainment and information from other types of radio services (DARS, Internet), television, and other media forms. Consolidation has enabled radio to embrace economies of scale and financially stabilized the industry, but it has not guaranteed success in delivering audiences. In order to attract and maintain audiences, radio must continue to embrace localism and provide the information and entertainment local audiences need and want—otherwise there is nothing to separate a local radio station from any other type of audio service that simply delivers music.

Successful radio stations in the 21st century will use their promotion and marketing efforts to uniquely brand their stations, and engage the communities they serve with a variety of programs and events. Sponsorships, civic activities, and community involvement will strengthen the audience–station relationship, and promote loyalty and return listening. In turn, advertisers will continue to support the medium, knowing it has the ability to generate desired audiences for their messages.

Stations that fail to embrace the communities they serve, and instead simply focus on selling advertising and increasing the bottom line will, in the opinion of this author, suffer in the long run. This is why innovations like voice tracking can actually end up harming radio over time. A station using voice tracking with a friendly professional voice that offers no local ties will be no different than a service delivered by satellite or via the Internet.

## CONCLUSION

The economics of the contemporary radio industry in the United States changed dramatically with the passage of the 1996 Telecommunications Act, allowing owners to own an unlimited number of radio stations nationally—while enacting limits at the local level. The 1996 Act enabled radio owners to fully engage in economies of scale and scope, generating strong profit margins and efficient management practices.

Although the shift in regulatory policy led to a restructuring of the major radio groups, as an industry, radio remains a medium very dependent on its ability to sell local advertising in the communities it serves. The ability of station groups to market themselves as clusters in local markets, and thus sell advertising on a range of stations, gave the industry a much stronger competitive position to compete with local television stations and newspaper operations.

Still radio faces a number of competitive challenges that can undermine its economic potential in local markets. The ability to capture a larger share of local advertising dollars remains a huge task. Digital audio radio services like XM Radio and Sirius, and Internet web casting via Internet-only radio stations and other stations around the world streaming content can all theoretically draw listeners away from local radio stations.

In order for radio to meet these significant challenges, stations must market and promote themselves with strong branding, good programming, and involvement in the local communities in which they are licensed. Localism has been a mainstay of radio for decades, and stations must retain their unique position as an important source of local information to the audiences they serve. Research is also critically important to the overall economic picture of contemporary radio. In a heavily competitive and fragmented media landscape, research can help management pinpoint strategies and techniques needed to build and maintain audiences.

As the oldest form of electronic media in operation, the radio industry has shown time and again its ability to transform itself in new directions. At the beginning of the 21st century, radio has moved into a new phase characterized by consolidation and a heavier emphasis on the medium as a business than at any time in its previous history. Yet, the fundamentals of the industry remain the same, to provide entertainment and information to the local markets they serve and to sell access to those same audiences to advertisers seeking to promote their goods and services.

## FURTHER READING

Albarran, A. B. (2002). *Management of electronic media* (2nd ed.). Belmont, CA: Wadsworth.
Albarran, A. B., & Pitts, G. G. (2001). *The radio broadcasting industry.* Boston: Allyn & Bacon.
Compaine, B., & Gomery, D. (2001). *Who owns the media?* (3rd ed.). Mahwah, NJ: Lawrence Erlbaum Associates.
McFarlane, D. (1990). *Contemporary radio programming strategies.* Mahwah, NJ: Lawrence Erlbaum Associates.
Sterling, C. S., & Kittross, J. M. (2002). *Stay tuned: A history of American broadcasting.* Mahwah, NJ: Lawrence Erlbaum Associates.

## REFERENCES

http://www.clearchannel.com/International/
Albarran, A. B. (2002). *Media economics: Understanding markets, industries and concepts* (2nd ed.). Ames: Iowa State Press.
Albarran, A. B., & Pitts, G. G. (2001). *The radio broadcasting industry.* Boston: Allyn & Bacon.
Bulkeley, W. M. (1999, September 9). Start-up wants web surfers to play tunes. *Wall Street Journal,* B8.
Carnevale, D. (2002, August 16). Radio silence. Fees force college stations to stop webcasting. *The Chronicle of Higher Education,* A33–A34.
Cassey, J. (2002, July 5). *Now Clear Channel wants to rule Britain's airwaves.* Retrieved from http://media.guardian.co.uk/broadcast/story/0,7493,749674,00.html
Determination of reasonable rates and terms for the digital performance of sound recordings and ephemeral recordings; final rule. (July 8, 2002). Federal Register. Retrieved from http://www.copyright.gov/carp/webcast_regs.html#background
Fratrick, M. R. (2001). *State of the radio industry: Ownership and consolidation 2001.* Washington, DC: BIA Financial Network. Retrieved from www.bia.com
Free TV. (2002, May 9). *The Economist.* Retrieved from http://www.economist.com
Guess who's coming to dinner? (2002, May 9). *The Economist.* Retrieved from http://www.economist.com
Mathews, A. W. (2002, February 25). A giant radio chain is perfecting the art of seeming local. *The Wall Street Journal,* A1.
*Radio revenue.* (2002). Retrieved from www.rab.com
Radio services facing difficulties. (2002, August 15). Associate Press news. *The Dallas Morning News,* 12D.

## ENDNOTES

[1]Ownership limits prior to 1996 could exceed the 20-20 limitations to 24-24, if minority partners controlled the additional stations. However, very few firms qualified for this exception.

[2]In many markets, consolidation has created two to three companies that dominate the bulk of the advertising revenue in the local market. The DOJ has frowned on any mergers that would result in one company controlling more than 50% of the advertising revenue in a local market.

[3]One of the best sources for current salaries in the radio industry is the most recent edition of *Radio Station Salaries*, published annually by the National Association of Broadcasters, Washington, D.C. Salaries vary considerably by region and market size.

[4]The fee structure proposed by CARP is divided into several different categories depending on the entity broadcasting content over the Internet. For a complete review of the various fee structures, see Determination (2002).

[5]Clear Channel has had global operations for several years prior to the 1996 Act, giving them a lead on other radio companies content to function within domestic borders.

# Chapter 11

# The Economics of the Recording Industry

ERIC W. ROTHENBUHLER
*New School University*

**TOM McCOURT**
*Fordham University*

This chapter provides an overview of the recorded music industry's structure and practices. After discussing the industry's long-term performance, we examine its core services, key contingencies, and primary capitalization strategies. A second section focuses on industry structure: oligopolization, conglomeration, economies of scale, and barriers to entry. A third section examines how decision-making processes address high levels of uncertainty within the recording industry. We conclude with an analysis of events surrounding Internet music file-sharing systems and the potential benefits and problems posed by online delivery of recordings.

## OVERVIEW OF THE INDUSTRY

The recording industry may be the most pervasive, and therefore fundamental, of the entertainment industries (Vogel, 1998). Although the industry has witnessed cycles of rapid growth and relative decline throughout its history, these cycles rest on a foundation of steadily rising fortunes. A sales boom in the early-1920s peaked later in the decade, and the Great Depression nearly eliminated the industry altogether, but recording sales grew steadily in the 1940s (Ennis, 1992; Sanjek, 1988; Sanjek & Sanjek, 1991). Revenues (adjusted for inflation) leveled and declined in the early-1950s, but the advent of the rock and roll market in 1955 sent sales surging for nearly 15 years (Sanjek, 1988). Sales were flat from 1978 to 1982 (see Fig. 11.1), and much of the industry's growth in the mid-1980s and early-1990s was due to inflation; *in constant dollars*, it was not able to return to its 1978 sales levels until 1992. Figure 11.2 displays annual shipments in units (cassettes, sin-

221

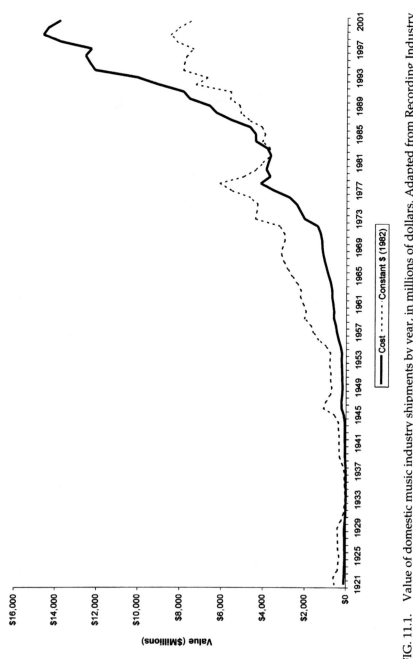

FIG. 11.1. Value of domestic music industry shipments by year, in millions of dollars. Adapted from Recording Industry Association of America (1982, 1997, 2002).

222

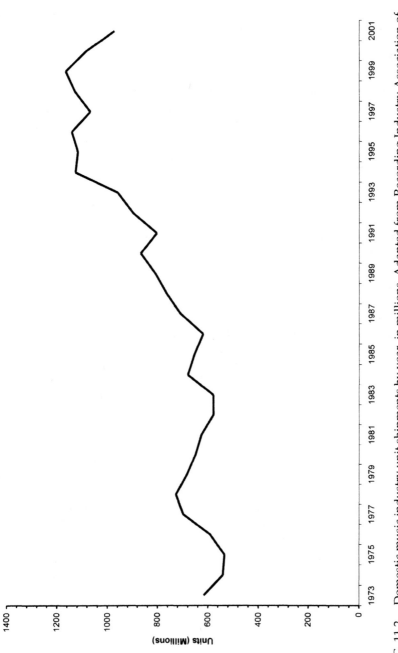

FIG. 11.2.　Domestic music industry unit shipments by year, in millions. Adapted from Recording Industry Association of America (1982, 1997, 2002).

gles, LPs, etc.) since 1973, when the Recording Industry Association of America (RIAA) began reporting these figures. Because measuring unit, rather than dollar, sales eliminates the influence of price hikes and inflation, the 1978 peak appears less precipitous than the dollar figures imply. The recording industry suffered another slump in the mid-1990s as catalog sales reached saturation and the novelty of CDs wore off. Attempts at recycling catalogs through new but inferior delivery systems (Digital Compact Cassette and Minidisc) were unsuccessful, and more entertainment alternatives, such as video games and the Internet, vied for consumer dollars.

Yet sales rose dramatically again in the late-1990s. Worldwide sales of recorded music reached approximately $34 billion in 2001, with U.S. consumers spending $114 billion on 733 million records, cassettes, compact discs (CDs), and music videos (see www.ifpi.com and www.riaa.com for latest figures). However, these figures represent a downturn from 1999, when U.S. consumers spent just over $13 billion on 870 million units. RIAA, an industry lobbying and trade group, blamed the recent downturn on unauthorized copying of CDs and sharing of music files online, whereas others cited high-retail CD prices, a lack of "superstar" releases in 2001, and reduced pressing of CD singles. Recent advances in online delivery of music have greatly unsettled the recording industry, which finds itself on the forefront of issues regarding technology and intellectual property that will significantly impact other media industries (Jones, 2000, 2002).

The cultural and economic significance of the recording industry is underscored by comparing it to other media. Table 11.1, for example, shows consumer expenditures in dollars and hours for nine media from 1985 to 2000. The time devoted to recorded music grew steadily from 1985, exceeding every medium but television. However, this figure leveled off after 1995, as the popularity of home video games grew and Internet use increased. Consumer spending on recorded music also grew steadily, only leveling off in the late-1990s (the trifold increase in consumer spending on television stemmed from the popularity of satellite TV and rising cable prices). Today music competes with interactive electronic entertainment for audiences, and the sounds, sights, and attention demands of video games and Internet surfing may provide a greater cultural unifier among teenagers than popular music (a trend exacerbated by the recording industry's niche marketing practices). Despite these challenges, recordings remain an important part of the matrix of global economics and culture.

## Key Contingencies

*Manufacturing and Distribution.*    The recording industry revolves around the manufacture and distribution of products such as records, tapes, and CDs . The infrastructure surrounding these products includes

## TABLE 11.1
## U.S. Consumer Media Expenditures

| | 1985 | 1990 | 1995[a] | 1996[b] | 1997 | 1998 | 1999 | 2000 | 2001 |
|---|---|---|---|---|---|---|---|---|---|
| | *(Hours Per Person)* | | | | | | | | |
| Television[c] | 1530 | 1470 | 1580 | 1563 | 1548 | 1551 | 1588 | 1640 | 1661 |
| Recorded Music | 185 | 235 | 288 | 292 | 270 | 283 | 290 | 264 | 238 |
| Daily Newspapers | 185 | 175 | 166 | 192 | 189 | 185 | 183 | 179 | 177 |
| Magazines | 110 | 90 | 113 | 125 | 125 | 125 | 124 | 121 | 119 |
| Books | 80 | 95 | 101 | 123 | 118 | 120 | 121 | 111 | 109 |
| Home video[d] | 15 | 42 | 49 | 34 | 33 | 36 | 39 | 46 | 56 |
| Box Office | 12 | 12 | 12 | 12 | 13 | 13 | 13 | 13 | 13 |
| Video Games[e] | | | 22 | 25 | 36 | 43 | 61 | 75 | 78 |
| Consumer Internet | | | 5 | 8 | 26 | 54 | 82 | 106 | 106 |
| | *(Dollars Per Person)* | | | | | | | | |
| | 1985 | 1990 | 1995[a] | 1996[b] | 1997 | 1998 | 1999 | 2000 | 2001 |
| Television[c] | 42.4 | 87.9 | 125.1 | 140.4 | 154.8 | 167.4 | 181.7 | 194.6 | 210.6 |
| Recorded Music | 25.1 | 36.6 | 56.9 | 57.5 | 55.5 | 61.7 | 65.1 | 62.8 | 60.6 |
| Daily Newspapers | 45.4 | 47.6 | 52.0 | 52.9 | 52.9 | 53.4 | 53.8 | 53.4 | 54.1 |
| Magazines | 29.8 | 33.1 | 38.3 | 45.4 | 46.4 | 46.5 | 46.2 | 44.9 | 43.6 |
| Books | 43.3 | 63.9 | 70.9 | 81.0 | 80.5 | 84.2 | 89.0 | 87.3 | 86.1 |
| Home video[d] | 15.2 | 56.4 | 79.9 | 87.1 | 87.0 | 92.6 | 97.3 | 102.5 | 109.6 |
| Box Office | 21.4 | 24.4 | 25.4 | 27.1 | 28.9 | 31.3 | 33.1 | 33.4 | 39.8 |
| Video Games | | | 10.5 | 11.5 | 16.5 | 18.5 | 24.5 | 25.9 | 28.0 |
| Consumer Internet | | | 8.5 | 13.2 | 20.9 | 27.6 | 41.8 | 50.6 | 62.1 |

[a]Does not correspond to earlier data series as a result of data collection and methodology changes.

[b]Does not correspond to 1995 data in certain media segments as a result of new information on consumer behavior.

[c]Includes broadcast television and cable and satellite television.

[d]Playback of prerecorded units only.

Sources. *Veronis Suhler Stevenson Communications Industry Forecast*, 1991, 1997, 2001, and 2002 editions. Copyright Veronis Suhler.

225

manufacturing plants, warehouses, shipping, wholesale distributors, independent and chain retailers, and artists, producers, and other personnel. To that end, each of the "Big Five" record companies—Universal, Sony, EMI, Warners, and BMG—maintains its own manufacturing facilities and operates a wholesale distribution system. The demands of manufacturing have shaped the recording industry from its inception, when the ease of reproducing, handling, and storing Berliner's disks gave them key advantages over Edison's cylinders, although the latter offered superior fidelity. Similarly, although digital reproduction has been widely criticized as inferior to analog recording, the CD-manufacturing process is more reliable and has lower labor costs than that of vinyl records. CDs themselves are smaller and lighter than records, which reduces shipping costs. Production efficiency, however, is not the only issue. High CD costs vis-à-vis vinyl records stemmed in part from an initial scarcity of manufacturing plants, but as CD plants proliferated, the per-unit costs of CD manufacturing dropped below those of records (although retail CD prices continued to climb).

*Music.*    Record companies do not "create" music; instead, they obtain music from contractually bound songwriters and musicians, who (in theory) benefit from the company's distribution and promotional services. These contracts take a variety of forms. "Name" artists typically work under multiyear contracts in which the record company retains ownership of the recordings and compensates the artist through royalties on sales of their recordings—at rates ranging from 7% to 15% or even 20%, contingent on the artist's status (Fink, 1996; Hull, 1998; Weissman, 1990). In contrast, studio musicians are payed union scale for their work and retain no future financial or legal interest in the recording.

Historically, many recording artists relinquished all rights and royalties in exchange for lump-sum payments up front. Although this arrangement is today widely disparaged as unethical, contracts still favor record companies. Multiyear contracts typically consist of a series of 1-year contracts in which the record company holds the right of renewal. Funds to cover the costs of recording, promotional videos, and other services are advanced to the artist and charged against future royalties. Thus, the artist will not earn royalties from sales of a recording until enough copies have been sold to recoup these costs. Moreover, when a recording fails to recoup its initial investment, that recording's debt will be applied to any follow-up recordings the artist makes while under contract. A suit pending in California, circa. 2002, argues that this arrangement allows record companies to unfairly control the careers of artists by prolonging periods between releases and holding artists liable for albums they fail to deliver (Ordonez, 2001).

Although contracts stipulate royalties as a percentage of the income from recording sales, songwriters can earn additional royalties from publishing. These royalties stem from "mechanical rights," based on physical manifestations of the song in a CD, LP, cassette, or sheet music; and "performance rights," based on performances of a song on a record and CD, or on radio, on television, on jukeboxes, in concerts, and in advertisements. Anyone who uses a song for purposes of profit must pay royalties to publishing organizations such as ASCAP and BMI, who then distribute royalties to songwriters. Consequently, songwriters may make more money from their efforts than performers. Indeed, songwriting and publishing fees have been central to the more enduring forms of music industry subterfuge since the 1920s. Over the years, many producers, executives, and prominent disc jockeys have taken songwriting credits in return for helping to make a hit (Eliot, 1993).

*Recording.*    Before the development of magnetic tape in the 1940s, music was recorded by costly and complicated disc-cutting machines in studios owned and staffed by the major record companies. The accessibility and economies enabled by tape recording led to a boom in recording activity; Kealy (1979) estimated that the number of record companies in the United States increased from 11 to nearly 200 within the 5 years following its introduction. More recently, the proliferation of digital recording technologies has enabled musicians to produce highly sophisticated recordings independently of record companies and costly studios (Jones, 1992). The techno movement, for example, is rooted in amateur musicians creating music on computers, and digital cut and paste techniques have become mainstream, as exemplified in Beck's Grammy Award-winning *Odelay* and U2's *Pop*.

*Consumption.*    The final category of recording industry contingencies is based on three key issues. The first concerns hardware. Whatever the format, from cylinders to CDs, recording sales are dependent on consumers owning the necessary playback equipment. The "war of the speeds" between RCA's 45 and Columbia's LP in the late-1940s was an early contest over hardware compatibility, although in this case each was able to carve itself a niche in the home electronics market . The success of the CD, which raised record company profits by lowering distribution costs while providing new opportunities to recycle catalogs, was by no means foreordained—its most direct predecessor, the video laser disc, was effectively stillborn on the consumer market, and subsequent audio formats have had little success. Anticopying legislation torpedoed Digital Audio Tape (DAT) for the home market in the 1980s, and formats like Digital Compact Cassette and Minidisc failed to achieve producer expectations because they lacked a substantial value-added component for consumers. Currently SuperAudio-CD and DVD-Audio are vying to be the next major audio medium, yet each format is backed by different equipment manufacturers and has received only moderate support from record companies. Whatever their success, audio formats are now largely intended to become obsolete, so that the electronics industry can sell new hardware and the recording industry can squeeze new profits from repackaging of its catalogue. *The Eagles' Greatest Hits*, for example (currently listed as the largest selling album ever), was first released on LP in 1976, has been released in myriad formats, and has now sold more than 27 million copies.

Second, each audio technology has a reciprocal relationship with consumer musical culture. Before the record boom of the early-1920s, the music business drew revenues from ticket sales for live performances and sales of musical instruments and sheet music; piano sales in the United States increased dramatically from 1870 and peaked in 1909 (Roell, 1989). Amateur musicianship was promoted as morally uplifting, and the early phonograph industry similarly touted phonographs as "good for the children" and a means to bring the world's greatest musicians, composers, and performances "into the home" (e.g., Thompson, 1995; Welch & Burt, 1994). The development of the radio industry later helped cement habits of listening to, rather than playing, music in the home. Today, computer software programs that allow users to "remix" existing recordings or create new ones have replaced instruments in many homes. Finally, the recording industry is highly vulnerable to changes in audience interests. Taste is not "fixed;" it is plastic and highly subjective. People become weary of formulas, rendering formulas useless. Musical genres continuously proliferate and evolve in ways that are anything but well-defined, a process compounded by increasing hybridization of music in the global marketplace.

### Capitalizing on the Structure

Music promotion dates to 19th-century "song pluggers" hired by publishing companies, who sought to get songs played by vaudeville, theater, and touring orchestras in hopes of building sheet music sales. As competition for this lucrative exposure increased, promotion became a bigger, and more necessary, part of the music industry. By the 1890s, music publishers were complaining that the necessary expense of song plugging was cutting into profits (Sanjek & Sanjek, 1991). Radio further accelerated the promotional process by enabling a few orchestras in prominent network time slots to have immediate national impact on sales of sheet music and recordings (Ennis, 1992; MacDougald, 1941). Since the mid-1960s, promotion has been the single largest expense in the music industry (Hirsch, 1972; see also Dannen, 1990; Haring, 1996). Indeed, it is so integral that we may consider it as one of the industry's products. Record companies manufacture hits, positions on music charts, and popularity as much as they do recordings; hype is as important to the industry as music (Harron, 1988). The importance of promotion has at times led promoters to bribe radio gatekeepers (i.e., DJs and programming directors) to play their songs, a practice the music industry terms *payola*. Although Congressional hearings in the late-1950s attempted to position payola as the product of rock and roll and suggest that it had been effectively eliminated, neither claim was true. Payola emerged with the sheet music industry in the 1880s and continues to the present (see Boehlert, 2002; Dannen, 1990; Ennis, 1992; Segrave, 1994).

## CHARACTERISTICS OF INDUSTRY STRUCTURE

### Oligopoly

The recording industry earns the bulk of its profits from recordings at the top of the popular music charts, where the most significant expenses and logistical factors are national promotion and distribution. Both of these areas exhibit a clear record of oligopolistic control throughout the industry's history. Figure 11.3, based on data from Peterson and Berger (1975), Rothenbuhler and Dimmick (1982), and Lopes (1992), indicates control by a very few corporations, except for the period from 1956 to 1970. At the same time, the nature of this control has changed from year to year as key firms rise and decline, and on occasion the dominant firms lose control of key aspects of the industry. Although the eight largest record companies controlled nearly all of the weekly top-10 hits in the early-1950s, and the pop music charts were relatively stable and homogeneous (Peterson & Berger, 1975), the rhythm and blues charts were bubbling with new artists promoted by independent labels (Gillett, 1983; Shaw, 1974). The majors initially failed to generate rock and roll hits, and an unusually diverse group of labels, artists, and genres dominated the charts throughout the late 1950s.

Both Peterson and Berger (1975) and Rothenbuhler and Dimmick (1982) indicated a negative correlation between the concentration of industrial control and the diversity of music on the charts: The higher the degree of concentration, the lesser the variety of songs, the slower the turnover on the charts, and the fewer the number of new artists. Although the correlation is not uniformly consistent, years with greater diversity tend to feature higher overall sales. Lopes (1992) and Burnett (1992) argued that a different pattern of oligopolization emerged in the late-1980s. Although six (and later five) record companies dominated the distribution of popular music, they operated through a multilayered system of ownership or interest in a number of subsidiary labels. Although the industry returned to or even exceeded historically high levels of concentration of control, musical diversity did not seem to suffer commensurately. The major firms maintained centralized financial control while allowing their subsidiary and

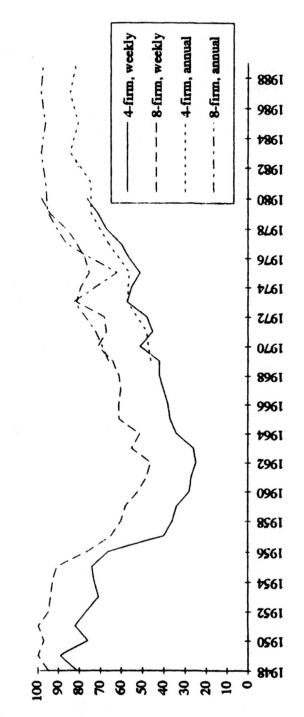

FIG. 11.3.  Percentage of the weekly and annual "Hot 100" charts controlled by the top four and top eight firms by year. Adapted from Peterson and Berger (1975), Rothenbuhler and Dimmick (1982), and Lopes (1992).

230

contracted labels to enjoy relative autonomy in making musical decisions, thus allowing for diverse product lines. The success of this strategy—maintaining music diversity and oligopolistic control simultaneously—is subject to debate. Recent research (Peterson & Berger, 1996) continues to illuminate the complex interrelationship of industrial structure and musical diversity. For example, the 1996 Telecommunications Act led to massive consolidation within the radio industry, a primary outlet for music promotion. While decision making became more centralized as radio chains grew, which added another strong influence on the standardization of music (Ahlkvist & Fisher, 2000), radio formats became increasingly diverse (although station playlists grew more circumscribed).

## Vertical Integration

The major record companies have always been vertically integrated to some extent, each owning publishing divisions, recording facilities, manufacturing plants, distribution operations, and promotional arms. In recent decades most of the majors have established record clubs for mail-order retailing, and some have invested in record store chains. Occasionally record companies have had stakes in, or have been owned by, corporations involved in the manufacture of musical instruments and audio equipment (e.g., CBS records owned Fender for several years, and, more recently, Sony purchased CBS records). Major record companies also have been owned by film studios (e.g., MGM, Warner Brothers) or developed corporate ties to the production of films, enabling increased opportunities for cross-promotion. Record companies also have had financial ties to talent and entertainment booking agencies, aiding in the supply and control of creative personnel.

Vertical integration has been one of the key forces in the major record companies' maintenance of their oligopoly status (Peterson & Berger, 1975). By controlling each step in the link between the performer and the audience, vertically integrated companies achieve four distinct advantages over their competitors. First, they increase the number of potential revenue sources. A record label that also owns a publishing company can retain the rights to its recordings and transform copyright fees from a cost to a source of income. Second, such companies can economize their use of various resources by centralizing administrative functions such as management and accounting. Third, such companies can coordinate and control their use of resources, manipulating schedules in order to maximize the performance of their offerings as a whole. Finally, through their control over the complete chain of the production process, vertically integrated companies can inhibit, or profit from, competitors' access to these goods and services. For example, a company such as Warners profits not only from the music of its subsidiary labels, but also from any label that contracts with Warners for distribution—while denying others access to its distribution and promotion machinery.

Paradoxically, vertical integration has occasionally maintained the independence of smaller companies, as exemplified by Motown Records in the 1960s. Motown's artists recorded songs written by Motown staff writers and published by Motown's publishing company. Their performances were backed by Motown staff musicians and recorded in Motown's studios by staff engineers. They were signed to Motown's artist management staff and worked through Motown's booking agency. As long as the company could keep producing hit recordings, this system produced spectacular results. By the mid-1970s, however, the hits began to dry up, and Motown was purchased by MCA in 1988.

## Conglomeration

Ties between the film and recording industries date from the advent of sound film. However, in recent years record companies increasingly have been absorbed by multinational corporations that do business across media and, in some cases (as with Universal), outside the media as well. Warner Records, through its status as a subsidiary of AOL Time Warner, is linked to cable television, the film industry, book and magazine publishing, and other media-oriented endeavors. Parent companies like Sony, Philips, and Matsushita, moreover, link record labels to other media and the home electronics market.

In addition to enabling the Big Five to vertically integrate their operations, conglomeration allows recorded music to be incorporated into the revenue streams of their parent companies. Recordings provide immediate cash flow to media conglomerates and compensate for losses on films and other properties. Record company catalogs also can generate money for decades through reissues, compilations, and licensing. Film soundtracks provide a particularly important means to promote new artists and catalog holdings. As these practices indicate, conglomerates may aggressively pursue cross-media ties to exploit the profit potential of their properties—which underscores the importance of retaining intellectual property rights through the ownership of recordings. By placing a mix of established stars and new artists from the company's roster on the soundtrack of a film, producing music videos that feature stars from the film, promoting film and recording stars on television talk shows and featuring them in magazines (all owned by the corporate parent), and selling licensed T-shirts and souvenirs in the lobbies of both movie theaters and concert venues (and, later, selling the right to use the recording to advertisers and issuing compilations) the parent corporation gains maximum exposure for their properties at minimum cost, squeezing profit from every possible use. As Frith (1988) stated:

In the music industry itself, a song—the basic musical property—represents "a bundle of rights"; income from the song comes from the exploitation of those rights, and what happened in the 1980's was that some of these (the "secondary rights" [i.e., licensing and copyright fees from other users]) became more profitable, others (the "primary rights" [i.e., selling your own records]) less so. (p. 105)

Conglomeration can also link electronics and recorded music—echoing the early decades of the 20th century, when phonograph manufacturers also produced and distributed records in order to spur sales (Kennedy, 1994; Welch & Burt, 1994). This linkage becomes particularly important as hardware divisions seek new consumer audio formats, since access to record company catalogs can provide the new format with a potential advantage over rival formats. Under situations of conglomeration, the hardware (equipment) and software (recording) divisions of a company can become not only interdependent, but strategically linked. For example, American record companies blocked the importation of DAT recorders for nearly a decade, arguing that the ability of DAT to make perfect copies of CDs would affect the sales of CDs. Despite a Congressional Office of Technology Assessment study that revealed the erroneous and self-serving nature of the record companies' arguments, their lobbying was successful—in part because the record companies were American and the importers of DAT were Japanese at a time of great economic nationalism.

The ensuing legislation, the Audio Home Recording Act of 1992, authorized consumers to make copies of digital music for personal, noncommercial use, yet prohibited serial copies. Therefore, digital recorders for the home market must incorporate Serial Copy Management System (SCMS) technology, which allows a single digital copy to be made from a digital source, but a binary code inserted into the copy makes second-generation digital copies impossible. The 1992 Act also implemented a tax on digital recorders and recording media, the revenues of which went mainly to record companies. Given the fact that audio hardware manufacturers like Sony now own record companies, they essentially pay themselves a tax.

Conglomeration and vertical integration both contribute to the effects of corporate cultures. Negus (1999) documented how corporate identity shapes decisions about artists' contracts, marketing and promotion strategies, and investments in different musical genres, with extensive and often unintended effects on industry and culture. For example, AOL Time Warner, whose holdings include magazines, cable, and Internet businesses, and whose Warner label historically has been one of the largest distributors in the record business, has tended in recent years to emphasize distribution and hardware. Music decisions, then, are delegated to others as software and content concerns. Consequently, one must be wary of overgeneralizing the benefits of corporate synergy. Divisions may often work at cross-purposes, as witnessed by developments with digital music delivery, which pitted content, distribution, and consumer electronics divisions against each other in philosophical and pragmatic terms. The *Wall Street Journal* used the example of AOL Time Warner: "To Time Warner executives producing music, the Web makes stealing pirated copies of their products far too easy. AOL, on the other hand, has grown up in a Web culture that favors the free dissemination of everything from music to movies" (Peers & Wingfield, 2000, p. B-1). Hardware divisions see a huge demand for portable music devices that download digital song files, which would require that record divisions put their catalogs on line, yet record divisions demand that portable devices and computers be prevented from playing music downloaded from the Internet without their approval.

Vivendi/Universal most clearly embodied the conglomerate faith in big media. After expanding into wireless communication systems, Vivendi (a French water treatment company) bought Universal's parent company, Seagram's, for $34 billion in 2000. Yet in early July 2002, Jean-Marie Messier, Vivendi's CEO, resigned with public admissions that the strategy had not paid off as planned. The company's productivity had not supported its stock prices and his resignation initiated a round of public discussion of whether the conglomerate experiment had come to an end (Lohr, 2002). The marriage of AOL and Time Warner was similarly rocky, sending the company's stock prices into a dive within a year of the merger.

**Economies of Scale**

Although the advantages of conglomeration to a large extent depend on a corporation's particular configuration, conglomeration and oligopoly both afford significant economies of scale. From recording to distribution to promotion, operating at high-volume offers clear advantages. The bulk of costs involved in producing and distributing a CD are fixed (although royalty rates, recording costs, and promotion budgets are "fixed" arbitrarily through negotiations or corporate policies). These first-copy costs must be spread across each unit sold, regardless of whether a given CD sells one or one million copies. As a result, selling more copies lowers the percentage of the fixed costs for each CD or tape while raising the profit margin for each unit. Put simply, the more copies that are sold, the more profits that are made on each copy.

Although economies of scale are found wherever fixed costs exist, they become most important in situations where fixed costs account for the bulk of business costs, such as the manufacture of recordings. Consider, for example, the difference between producing recordings and athletic shoes. In both cases, first copy costs include royalty rates. Recordings and shoes also involve research and development, design, production, and promotion.

Both cases also feature labor and other marginal costs: blank media and packaging for recordings; leather, rubber, and thread for athletic shoes.

However, the ratio of fixed costs to marginal costs is far higher in recordings than athletic shoes. According to Vogel's (1998) estimate, the marginal costs for manufacturing a single CD are roughly $.60 per disc. Assuming a wholesale rate of $8, roughly 93% of the record label's revenue from the sale of a CD is directed at covering first copy costs. The consequences of this figure are twofold: First, the high rate will lead to a quick payoff of those fixed costs; and second, once enough copies of the CD have been sold to cover the fixed costs, 93% of the company's revenue from each subsequent disc sold will be profit. Hence, at the breakeven point (known only to company policymakers), the marginal rate of return (i.e., profit per unit) goes up in a single huge step, whereas the overall rate of profit goes up exponentially. Nike should be so fortunate.

## Barriers to Entry

In theory the recording industry has few barriers to entry. Songwriters and performers are in oversupply, and recording technology has never been more inexpensive or accessible. Indications are that in recent years more musicians and small studios may be producing more recordings for local and regional distribution than ever before (Robinson, Buck, & Cuthbert, 1991; Slobin, 1993; Theberge, 1997). In classical, jazz, and audiophile music markets, specialized labels that market through the Internet and mail-order catalogs are common.

The big money in the recording industry, of course, is found in national and international popular music markets. Access to these markets, and opportunities to sell copies of a CD in the multiple millions, depends on both sizable amounts of capital and control of a sprawling distribution and promotion system. These factors present a huge barrier to entry. Distribution is so important that the traditional distinction between "majors" and "independents" is based on whether a company owns its own distribution system. The majors can control their own distribution, whereas independents have to contract with other companies (usually the majors themselves) for that service. This arrangement requires independent companies to share their profits with the distributor, as well as surrender some control of their own products.

The importance of the national and international markets, and the difficulty of entering them successfully, have been heightened by the growing nationalization and then internationalization of popular music since the late-1950's. At that time, radio formats in the United States varied between regions, and records often became national hits after gathering attention through local breakouts (Marsh, 1993, provided a case study). Radio formats became more nationally standardized in the 1970s, and today are nearly identical from city to city (Barnes, 1988; Fornatale & Mills, 1980; Rothenbuhler, 1985; Rothenbuhler & McCourt, 1992; 2002). National cable services such as MTV and VH-1 also are instrumental in making hits. At the same time, national record store chains, with coordinated inventories, have come to dominate retailing. In response to these trends, the Big Five have coordinated their own distribution and promotion efforts to work the whole nation as a single market. Thus the combination of vertical integration, economies of scale, and the sheer size of the distribution and promotional machinery necessary to create hit recordings has created insurmountable barriers to entry in the national and international markets for recordings. The result is the oligopolistic control of those markets by five major corporate conglomerates.

## UNCERTAINTY AND DECISION MAKING

After meeting the *break-even point* (when enough units have been sold to pay the first copy costs of recording, distribution, and promotion), a release accumulates profits at a stunning pace. Because recordings seldom reach the break-even point—Vogel (1998) estimated 1 in 10 breaks even—and yet sales of those that do become almost pure profit—the burden of financially unsuccessful albums is carried by the few that are successful. One *Thriller* (91 weeks on the chart, 37 weeks at number 1, more than 26 million copies sold by May 2002) can carry a vast quantity of unsuccessful recordings. The problem lies in recognizing the difference between the next *Thriller* and the next failure. In 1999, only 88 recordings—three tenths of 1% of all CDs issued—accounted for 25% of all record sales (Mann, 2000).

Like all manufacturers of cultural products, the recording industry faces high levels of uncertainty (cf. DiMaggio & Hirsch, 1976; Hirsch, 1972). All businesses require routine measures for prediction, planning, and control. For the recording industry, these measures are complicated by the requirements of mass manufacturing and distribution to audiences with ephemeral tastes. The recording industry's structure, therefore, is characterized by attempts to isolate and control sources of uncertainty. For example, those parts of the business that deal with creative activities or the public are organizationally isolated from those that require predictability and control (Peterson & Berger, 1971). The following section reviews additional decision-making procedures that are designed to reduce uncertainties.

### Contracts and Independent Personnel

Structured contracts comprise one strategy for managing uncertainty. Rather than supporting a staff to engage in highly uncertain activities, such as recording hit records, companies can contract with people who present themselves as specialists in these areas. These contracts may be structured so that the professional's performance is evaluated routinely, with rewards tied to specific performance criteria, and the company has the option of renewing or cancelling the contract (see Peterson & Berger, 1971). This structure has been the standard for artist contracts since rock and roll was popularized in the mid-1950s. In the more stable industrial environment preceding 1955, performers were routinely signed to a label for 5 years (Gillett, 1983). Since then, a series of five renewable 1-year contracts has become the norm (Fink, 1996; Weissman, 1990). Of course, the record company, not the artist, holds the renewal option.

In the late-1960s, contracts for independent producers, studios, and engineers became more commonplace—in part because record companies were responding to artists' demands for greater creative control. Since then, they have become the industry norm. None of the Big Five presently maintains a staff of producers and engineers (outside of classical music), although some still have company-owned studios. On the other hand, the reputation of an independent record company often is built on the sound of its producers, staff, and studios. In the 1980s independent promoters became fairly common, although no major company gave up its own promotion staff due its importance. According to more than one exposé, the primary purpose of the independent promoter system was to obtain services that were too shady, or even outright criminal, for a major corporation to ask of its own staff (Dannen, 1990; Knoedelseder, 1994). These practices have been in the news again, including Congressional testimony, in 2002.

**Track Records and Star Systems**

Another response to uncertainty of demand is to rely on track records and reputations. The recording industry's star system promotes celebrity because known performers are considered a safe investment. Bruce Springsteen, for example, remains a valuable commodity even as his style changes and sales fluctuate. Britney Spears is sold as a personality, which is a product with more predictable and controllable audience demand than the various songs on her CDs. Similarly, other personnel in the industry frequently are judged by their past performance and reputation rather than their current work. From the executives who decide which artists to sign to the producers who control the recording process, those personnel who have a reputation for producing hits inevitably will be called on for their expertise—at least until their first failure. Thus, decisions are more often based on the track records of the people involved than the merits of the project, which are more difficult to evaluate.

However, as record companies are absorbed into conglomerates, they are under increased pressure to act as efficient profit sources for their multinational parent companies and face growing quarter-to-quarter account-ability while enduring staff cutbacks. Consequently, beginning in the mid-1990s, record companies boosted short-term profits by emphasizing rapid turnover of new artists. Increased marketing and promotional costs resulted in signing fewer artists, taking fewer risks on new artists, and a greater unwillingness to sustain careers (Miller, 1997). EMI's release of the superstar Mariah Carey in 2002 after one poorly selling soundtrack album and film was a clear example. If a recording fails to generate excitement, re-sources are shifted to other projects, and the music industry increasingly emphasizes blockbusters that can be cross-promoted in other media.

## Preselection Systems and Surrogate Consumers

The music industry's products must pass through a series of stages. Songs must be recorded and published, recordings must be selected for release, the quantity of releases must be decided, a promotional budget and strat-egy must be developed, retail stores must stock the releases, and radio sta-tions and cable networks must select releases for airplay. This sequence functions as a preselection system: The items ultimately offered to consum-ers are those selected as the most likely to succeed at each preceding stage of the process (Hirsch, 1969; Ryan & Peterson, 1982). Negus (2000) pointed out that record company decision makers are more than mere gatekeepers who approve or reject completed products. Label executives, who comprise a powerful elite in the recording industry, participate in the creative deci-sions that shape recordings. Musicians, writers, producers, and engineers strive to produce successful recordings in light of the recent successes (Ryan & Peterson, 1982). However, each stage of the process is carried out by players with different positions, interests, and criteria for decision mak-ing. Songwriters want to be published, musicians want to be recorded, pro-ducers want their contracts renewed, executives want work produced on time and under budget, promoters want to devote their time to successful endeavors, radio programmers want recordings that fit their formats, and retailers want promotable recordings. Creating a hit recording requires the active participation of all of these players. The situation is further compli-cated by the fact that more products are being considered at each stage than can possibly be used. The few products that emerge at the end of the process are those that pass through filters at each stage. The preselection system of the recording industry, therefore, is very conservative.

## Overproduction and Differential Promotion

Overproduction and differential promotion are business strategies in which more products are produced than can possibly succeed in the marketplace, and promotional efforts are differentially assigned to minimize risk (Hirsch, 1972). These strategies result from the fact that the biggest investments are in promotion and distribution, which fall late in the decision-making chain (star performers may receive large recording budgets, but they ordinarily command even larger promotion budgets). Until decisions are made about substantial promotional investments, companies make smaller investments in a large number of products. This gambit provides the system with a large number of products in development at any given time. The bulk of promotional budgets then can be earmarked for products with the greatest likelihood of becoming hits, whereas the remainder are released with little or no promotion.

Because promotion budgets are the best predictors of potential hits, the preceding strategies provide a safe way to allocate the largest percentage of the total investment in a product. Only a limited number of recordings can succeed at one time; however, the record companies consistently engage in overproduction. This seemingly contradictory business practice allows record companies to cover their bets, because a major hit might emerge unexpectedly. Record companies therefore can assign the largest promotional budgets to those records predicted to be successful, and then reassign promotional money and efforts to records that begin to show promise on their own. In the latter case, promotion is used to increase the rate of return on a hit by increasing total sales, rather than creating a hit from scratch.

## THE DIGITAL REVOLUTION

The music industry (particularly the Big Five companies) faces tremendous challenges from the explosion of digital technology in the late-1990s, challenges that promise to transform every aspect of the industry. The outcome of battles over online music will create the template for industrial policies concerning online delivery of text, video, and other media, a convergence already indicated in the industrial trend to lump together writers, artists, musicians, actors, and others as content providers. The following section examines key issues in the controversy over online music and discusses some of their potential implications for the recording industry.

### The Napster Imbroglio

The earliest form of digital music delivery was the WAV standard; 3-minute songs in this format, however, required hours to download. In 1987, the Motion Picture Experts Group (MPEG, a branch of the Geneva-based International Organization for Standardization) developed new digital compression software. The most powerful version, MPEG-1 Layer 3 (MP3), could compress a 40-megabyte file to one tenth of its original size. Modem speeds also increased, and recordings could now be downloaded easily onto the hard drives of home computers. However, MP3 developed outside of the Big Five's control and offered no intrinsic protections against copying. MP3s therefore threatened the music industry by holding out the "possibility of a business model that links artists directly to consumers, bypassing the record companies completely" (Garofalo, 1999, p. 349).

Although MP3 undoubtedly will be succeeded by systems that afford greater possibilities for copy protection, it currently has a momentum that diminishes chances for the immediate adoption of a different format. The domestic recording industry claims to lose $300 million per year to pirate recordings; a report prepared for the recording industry predicted that by 2002, an estimated 16% of all U.S. music sales, or $985 million, would be lost to online piracy (Foege, 2000). The Big Five focused their mounting concerns about piracy in all formats on Napster, which was released on the Internet in August 1999. Napster functioned as a music search engine that linked participants to a huge and constantly updated library of user-provided MP3s. Its key feature was an online database of song titles and performers, searchable by keyword. Napster's brokered architecture effectively coordinated users and increased search effectiveness, and its interface was highly user-friendly. Between February and August 2000, the number of Napster users rose from 1.1 million to 6.7 million, making it the fastest growing software application ever recorded.

No sooner had Napster become a "killer app" than legal woes beset the company. The RIAA filed suit against Napster on December 7, 1999, claiming that the free service cut into sales of CDs. Their case against Napster turned on the fact that although it did not generate revenue, the service supplied users with software and provided a brokering service that managed a real-time index of available music files. This combination of products and services, the RIAA argued, effectively turned Napster into a music piracy service. Napster's defenders claimed that its users enjoyed First Amendment protection, so the state could not enforce a prior restraint on the speech of Napster's user and publishers. Its attorneys also argued that the service's "substantial, non-infringing uses" included allowing users to sample new music and "space-shift" their collections between delivery systems like CD's and hard drives (Gomes, 2000; M. Lewis, 2000).

In late-July 2000, Federal judge Marilyn Patel ordered an injunction against Napster, finding that the service was used primarily to download copyrighted music and rejecting Napster's arguments. In February 2001, a three-judge panel unanimously upheld the injunction, and Napster soon began filtering its system to block copyrighted material before shutting down altogether. Despite the RIAA's claims that Napster-driven piracy was eating into profits, recorded music sales in the United States reached an all-time high of 785.1 million units in 2000, up 4% from 1999. The RIAA claimed that sales of CD singles dropped 39% in 2000 and inferred that Napster was to blame, yet fewer CD singles were released as the industry cut production. Some market research suggests that users used Napster not primarily to "steal" music, but to sample it before purchase. Users also were drawn to the huge array of music it presented, the obscure as well as the popular—a vast catalog (including out-of-print material) that was otherwise inaccessible.

Despite Napster's defeat, Internet trading of music files continued unabated through a number of other services, which, lacking Napster's centrality, were virtually impossible to police. The recording industry has attempted to reassert its control through a variety of means, including legislation, buyouts, and digital rights management technologies. Each of these are discussed in turn.

## Legislation

The Big Five have been instrumental in recent legislation concerning intellectual property. In addition to the Audio Home Recording Act of 1992, the Digital Performance Rights in Sound Recordings Act of 1995 gave the owners of recordings (i.e., the record companies) exclusive control over their music in online web casts. In contrast, radio stations have freedom to use music as they wish after acquiring a license from songwriters' organizations . The two most important legislative acts affecting the recording industry, however, were passed in 1998: the Sonny Bono Term Extension Act and the Digital Millennium Copyright Act (DMCA). In the former, Congress, responding to industry pressure, extended copyright protection for an additional 20 years. Authored works are covered for the life of the author plus 70 years, whereas corporate-owned "works for hire," such as recordings, are covered for 95 years. Section 1201(a) of the DMCA made it illegal to circumvent copy-protection technologies; the purpose of bypass is immaterial. The DMCA essentially eliminated "fair use" provisions of the 1976 Federal Copyright Act, dismissing the tenet that we buy the right to make unlimited copies for personal use after purchasing an original copy of a recording. The DMCA also treated Internet service providers and telecommunications networks as publishers, rather than common carriers, with the intent of forcing these networks to bar their users from sharing copyrighted material (Gomes, 2001).

## Buyouts

The Big Five have privately hedged their bets through mergers and acquisitions that would allow file-sharing under their exclusive control. Shortly after the Napster decision, Bertelsmann broke ranks with the other major record companies on October 31, 2000, and announced that it would loan Napster $50 million to develop a secure file-sharing system that would "preserve the Napster experience" while compensating copyright holders. Bertelsmann was attracted by Napster's corporate identity, tangible assets, and software (including the protocol and interface). In exchange, Bertelsmann retained the right to take a 58% interest in Napster when the new service is developed (Gomes, 2000).

Bertelsmann's actions regarding Napster follow the example of the Musicbank storage locker service, which obtained licenses for content from Universal, Warner, and Bertelsmann only after granting these companies an equity stake. The case of MP3.com is also instructive in this regard. MP3.com's stock was valued as high as $63.61 before the company was hit by a barrage of copyright infringement lawsuits from artists, publishers, and record labels against its MyMP3.com storage locker. In May, 2001, 7 months after winning a $54.3 million judgment from the company, Vivendi purchased MP3.com for $372 million. (MP3.com had previously settled copyright infringement claims with the other four major record companies for $20 million each). Vivendi offered $5 per share for MP3.com's stock, which had traded for only $3.01 per share before the acquisition was announced (Sorkin, 2001). Despite its legal liabilities, MP3.com was attractive to Vivendi because it was one of the few firms with the technological infrastructure in place to operate a large-scale online distribution service.

The Big Five repeatedly used high-profile lawsuits to deter venture capitalists from providing second- and third-round funding to Internet startup companies. They then offer funding and content licenses to these startups in exchange for equity shares. The Big Five can thus acquire these operations below their fair market value and also save research and development costs. Most importantly, they can thwart the creation of independent distribution systems (McCourt & Burkart, 2003).

## Digital Rights Management

A final strategy for dealing with unauthorized digital music distribution involves Digital Rights Management (DRM) technologies, which "lock up" content through "trusted systems" in which copy protection is built into every component sold—the operating system, the artifact, and the player. An early attempt at creating a universal DRM system was proposed by the Secure Digital Music Initiative (SDMI), which was formed in December, 1998 by a consortium of record companies and hardware and software manufacturers. SDMI's 200 members included AOL, AT&T, IBM, Microsoft, Matsushita, Sony, RealNetworks, Liquid Audio, ASCAP, Intel, and Napster (no consumer or civil rights groups were represented). Based on watermarking technology, SDMI's system was intended to serve as a gate through which content must pass. The system enabled time limits on use, restricted the potential number of copies that the purchaser can make from an authenticated original, and allowed protected content to be traced back to the original purchaser.

However, development of the SDMI standard lagged far behind schedule. Its members had highly divergent and often antagonistic interests, which were aggravated by a problem intrinsic to software development: Every protection scheme can be broken. SDMI dissolved in early-2002, yet DRM may become a *fait accompli*. Such technology could become required by law, as was the case with SCMS. Or, equally likely, DRM could be imposed through agreements between hardware and software divisions of colluding companies. DRM would impose new costs on consumers by rendering existing formats and hardware obsolete. It also would defeat one of the principles of intellectual property most nettlesome to corporate interests: Although copyright is designed to cover works for a limited amount of time, the incorporation of DRM into distribution would copy-protect them forever.

## Implications for the Future

***Artists and Record Companies.***     Much has been made about the Internet's possibilities for artists to circumvent the control of record companies. The record industry rations an artist's material in marketable doses to optimize supply and demand, which is additionally problematized by the existing preselection system. Certainly, the Internet affords artists greater flexibility in presentation, as digital technology allows for infinitely varied packaging and releasing. A release could contain 1 or 100 songs, and any schedule for release is possible. Performers could release a song the day it is recorded and release collections in standard and advanced packages, akin to a "director's cut," with varied price structures. Several artists, such as Prince and Todd Rundgren, presently use a fan-based patronage model, with recordings, concert tickets, online chats and additional materials available to subscribers through a tiered pricing system. This direct availability to consumers negates the need for marketing subsidized by record companies; an artist who nets 50%, for example, on direct sales of 70,000 CDs earns more revenue than an artist who earns 10% royalties on 300,000 sales—not even counting deductions for production costs.

Record companies are likely to experience a faster diffusion of information and greater volatility of demand, as new genres and performers emerge and fade rapidly. These companies will have to maintain more flexible links with independent labels, which tend to follow new market developments more closely, and organize themselves in a more flexible fashion (Dolfsma, 2000). The Internet will also provide record companies with detailed consumer profiles and the ability to track "hits," or downloads, for individual artists. The Internet is likely to produce independence from the Big Five at the extremes, with a growing disparity between stars who cultivate their fan bases and fledgling performers who must essentially give away their recordings to promote interest. Yet promotion, which is the Big Five's *metier*, will remain particularly important as choices proliferate, and traditional marketing will still be needed to break new artists or recordings.

*Subscriptions.*    The Big Five may find a subscription model to be most lucrative, whereby users pay a flat monthly fee to access record company catalogs via computers, fixed and portable stereos, cell phones, and "Internet appliances." In April, 2001 two subscription systems were announced: Duet, a project of Universal, Sony, and Yahoo; and MusicNet (now PressPlay), comprised of BMG, Warner, EMI, AOL, and RealNetworks. Unlike onetime sales, subscriptions generate steady cash flow and provide a convenient benchmark by which to measure growth. Licensing, rather than sale, also provides a direct link between vendor and purchaser that makes it easier to enforce limitations on use. Because subscriptions usually are paid in advance, they avoid the volatility of retail sales or pay-per-play. Subscriptions can produce more revenue than would sales from infrequent users, while encouraging increased use among heavier users, and allow the provider to charge higher rates to advertisers (Meyers, 2001). These companies can also harness a growing collection of customer databases derived from Web activity to reduce marketing uncertainty and provide revenues through resale to other vendors (Gandy, 1993).

Subscriptions present new challenges, however. Prices would need to make up in volume what is lost in profitability, suggesting cost pressures and even price wars among music services. Subscriptions also would penalize chain music stores and retail outlets, which now account for 80% of sales in the popular music market. Record company consortiums may try to offer their own subscription models, but ultimately will have to license their catalogs to each other to attract the largest number of users. Yet licensing content between the Big Five invites antitrust action, and subscription services offered by combinations of the Big Five to date have been largely unsuccessful.

Running a successful subscription service would require the record companies to operate more like catalogs, magazines, or radio stations, and very little in their history has prepared them for this model. Both their infrastructure and their established methods of doing business are built on mass producing, distributing, promoting, and selling mechanical copies of recordings. Almost everything in the business is built around the number of physical copies sold. The recording industry has become adept over the years at maintaining a catalog, but attracting and holding attention via corporate branding and providing reliable service directly to consumers are all foreign ideas from another world of business.

## SUMMARY AND CONCLUSION

The music industry may be the most uncertain and volatile of the media businesses. Consumer tastes in recordings are highly ephemeral, and consumers also have more options than in most other categories. Although the industry runs in cycles, it nevertheless has been successful across its history, attracting consumer dollars and time at equivalent levels.

The industry's backbone remains the manufacturing and selling of recordings. Income from associated activities such as song publishing has always figured prominently and, due to the prevalence of corporate conglomerate structures, is probably more important today than ever before. To capitalize on its core activities the industry must address three major contingencies: assuring a supply of songwriters and performers, producing the recording itself, and obtaining the interest of an audience. The music industry therefore invests heavily in promotion to increase the rate of return on its investments.

The industry's structure is characterized by vertical integration and conglomeration, capitalizing on economies of scale, and promoting the nationalization and internationalization of the music market, all of which create barriers to entry that help a few major corporations maintain oligopolistic control. The industry manages uncertainty by strategic decision making, including hiring external parties under short-term, renewable contracts; the use of track records and star performers as more predictable investments than their music; the elaboration of a preselection system in which industry players operate as each other's surrogate consumers; and overproduction and differential promotion, in which the biggest investments are made in the safest products while many smaller investments are spread over more diverse musical products.

As with any business comparable in size to the Big Five, the overall system is as conservative as it can afford to be. Although the advent of new distribution possibilities via the Internet threaten to transform the industry, the Internet also provides an enhanced marketplace for record companies, because goods may be copied and transported over the Internet at minor cost, and unwanted goods may easily be disposed of or delisted. The supply of recordings far outstrips demand, which underscores the primacy of distribution over content, and this tendency certainly will increase as a result of the Internet. Although the Internet in theory allows both creators and distributors to bypass traditional promotional media for direct access to consumers, the Big Five's ties with other industries give them sizable cross-promotional and cross-industrial channels for marketing products online as well as

offline. Despite forecasts of their imminent doom, record companies will
continue to figure prominently in the future of recorded music.

## FURTHER READING

Alderman, J. (2001). *Sonic boom: Napster, MP3, and the new pioneers of music*. Cambridge, MA: Perseus.
Burnett, R. (1996). *The global jukebox: The international music industry*. New York: Routledge.
Fink, M. (1996). *Inside the music industry* (2nd ed.). New York: Schirmer Books.
Hull. G. P. (1998). *The recording industry*. Boston: Allyn and Bacon.
Negus, K. (1999). *Music genres and corporate cultures*. New York: Routledge.

## REFERENCES

Ahlkvist, J. A., & Fisher, G. (2000). And the hits just keep on coming: Music programming standardization in commercial radio. *Poetics, 27*, 301–325.
Barnes, K. (1988). Top 40 radio: A fragment of the imagination. In S. Frith (Ed.), *Facing the music* (pp. 8–50). New York: Pantheon.
Boehlert, E. (2002, June 25). Will congress tackle pay-for-play? *Salon*. Retrieved from http://www.salon.com/ent/feature/2002/06/25/pfp_congress/print.html
Burnett, R. (1992). The implications of ownership changes on concentration and diversity in the phonogram industry. *Communication Research, 19*, 749–769.
Burnett, R. (1996). *The global jukebox: The international music industry*. New York: Routledge.
Dannen, F. (1990). *Hit men: Power brokers and fast money inside the music business*. New York: Vintage.
DiMaggio, P., & Hirsch, P. M. (1976). Production organizations in the arts. *American Behavioral Scientist, 19*, 735–752.
Dolfsma, W. (2000) How will the music industry weather the globalization storm? *First Monday, 5*. Retrieved from http://firstmonday.org/issues/issue 5_5/dolfsma/index.html
Eliot, M. (1993). *Rockonomics: The money behind the music* (rev. ed.). New York: Citadel.
Ennis, P. H. (1992). *The seventh stream: The emergence of rock 'n' roll in American popular music*. Hanover, NH: Wesleyan University Press.
Fink, M. (1996). *Inside the music industry* (2nd. ed.). New York: Schirmer Books.
Fornatale, P., & Mills, J. E. (1980). *Radio in the television age*. Woodstock, NY: Overlook.
Frith, S. (1988). Video pop: Picking up the pieces. In S. Frith (Ed.), *Facing the music* (pp. 88–130). New York: Pantheon.
Foege, A. (2000, June 11). Record labels are hearing an angry song. *The New York Times*, BU4.
Gandy, O. (1993). *The panoptic sort: a political economy of personal information*. Boulder, CO: Westview Press.
Garofalo, R. (1999). From music publishing to MP3: Music and industry in the twentieth century. *American Music, 17*(3), 318–353.
Gillett, C. (1983). *The sound of the city: The rise of rock and roll* (rev. ed.). New York: Pantheon.
Gomes, L. (2000, July 27). Napster is ordered to stop the music. *The Wall Street Journal*, A3.

Gomes, L. (2001, May 4). Entertainment firms target Gnutella. *The Wall Street Journal*, B6.

Haring, B. (1996). *Off the charts: Ruthless days and reckless nights inside the music industry*. New York: Carol Publishing Group.

Harron, M. (1988). McRock: Pop as commodity. In S. Frith (Ed.), *Facing the music* (pp. 173–220). New York: Pantheon.

Hirsch, P. M. (1969). *The structure of the popular music industry*. Ann Arbor, MI: Institute for Social Research.

Hirsch, P. M. (1972). Processing fads and fashions: An organization-set analysis of cultural industry systems. *American Journal of Sociology, 77*, 639–659.

Hull, G. P. (1998). *The recording industry*. Boston: Allyn & Bacon.

Jones, S. (1992). *Rock formation: Music, technology, and mass communication*. Newbury Park, CA: Sage.

Jones, S. (2000). Music and the Internet. *Popular Music, 19*(2), 217–230.

Jones, S. (2002). Music that moves: Popular music, distribution, and Internet technologies. *Cultural Studies, 16*(2), 213–232.

Kealy, E. R. (1979). From craft to art: The case of sound mixers and popular music. *Sociology of Work and Occupations, 6*, 3–29.

Kennedy, R. (1994). *Jelly Roll, Bix, and Hoagy: Gennett studios and the birth of recorded jazz*. Bloomington: Indiana University Press.

Knoedelseder, W. (1994). *Stiffed: A true story of MCA, the music business, and the mafia*. New York: Harper Perennial.

Lewis, M. (2000, July 26). Judge rules against "monster;" Napster to appeal. *Webnoize*, 1. Retrieved from http://news.webnoize.com/item.rs?ID=9877

Lohr, S. (2002, July 3). Vivendi troubles reflect change in investor's hopes for big media. *The New York Times*, A1.

Lopes, P. D. (1992). Innovation and diversity in the popular music industry, 1969 to 1990. *American Sociological Review, 57*, 56–71.

MacDougald, D., Jr. (1941). The popular music industry. In P. F. Lazarsfeld & F. N. Stanton (Eds.), *Radio research, 1941* (pp. 65–109). New York: Duell, Sloan, and Pearce.

Mann, C. (2000, September). The heavenly jukebox. *Atlantic Monthly*, 39–59.

Marsh, D. (1993). *Louie Louie*. New York: Hyperion.

McCourt, T., & Burkart, P. (2003). When creators, corporations, and consumers collide: Napster and the development of on-line music distribution. *Media, Culture, and Society, 25*, 333–350.

Meyers, C. (2001). *Entertainment Industry Integration Strategies*. Unpublished report, New York University.

Miller, M. (1997, September 1). Who controls the music? *The Nation*, 12.

Negus, K. (1999). *Music genres and corporate cultures*. New York: Routledge.

Negus, K. (2000). Music divisions: The recording industry and the social mediation of cultural production. In J. Curran (Ed.), *Media organizations in society* (pp. 240–254). London: Arnold.

Ordonez, J. (2001, September 5). Musicians, record companies face off. *The Wall Street Journal*, B-5.

Peers, M., & Wingfield, N. (2000, April 18). Seeking harmony, AOL and Warner Music hit some dissonant notes. *Wall Street Journal*, B-1.

Peterson, R. A., & Berger, D. (1971). Entrepreneurship in organizations: Evidence from the popular music industry. *Administrative Science Quarterly, 16*, 97–107.

Peterson, R. A., & Berger, D. (1975). Cycles in symbol production: The case of popular music. *American Sociological Review, 40*, 158–173.

Peterson, R. A., & Berger, D. (1996). Measuring industry concentration, diversity, and innovation in popular music. *American Sociological Review, 61*, 175–178.

Recording Industry Association of America. (1982, April 5). *News from RIAA.* New York: Recording Industry Association of America.

Recording Industry Association of America. (1997). *The top ten fact book.* Washington, DC: Recording Industry Association of America.

Recording Industry Association of America. (2002). *2001 year end statistics.* Washington, DC: Recording Industry Association of America.

Robinson, D. C., Buck, E. B., & Cuthbert, M. (1991). *Music at the margins: Popular music and global cultural diversity.* Newbury Park, CA: Sage.

Roell, C. H. (1989). *The piano in America, 1890–1940.* Chapel Hill: University of North Carolina Press.

Rothenbuhler, E. W. (1985). Programming decision making in popular music radio. *Communication Research, 12,* 209–232.

Rothenbuhler, E. W., & Dimmick, J. (1982). Popular music: Concentration and diversity in the industry, 1974–1980. *Journal of Communication, 32*(1), 143–149.

Rothenbuhler, E. W., & McCourt, T. (1992). Commercial radio and popular music: Processes of selection and factors of influence. In J. Lull (Ed.), *Popular music and communication* (2nd ed., pp. 101–115). Newbury Park, CA: Sage.

Rothenbuhler, E. W., & McCourt, T. (2002). Radio redefines itself, 1947–1962. In M. Hilmes & J. Loviglio (Eds.), *The radio reader: Essays in the cultural history of radio* (pp. 367–387). New York: Routledge.

Ryan, J., & Peterson, R. A. (1982). The product image: The fate of country music songwriting. In J. Ettema & D. C. Whitney (Eds.), *Creativity and constraint: Individuals in mass media organizations* (pp. 11–32). Beverly Hills, CA: Sage.

Sanjek, R. (1988). *American popular music and its business, Vol. 3: From 1900 to 1984.* New York: Oxford University Press.

Sanjek, R., & Sanjek, D. (1991). *American popular music business in the 20th century.* New York: Oxford University Press.

Segrave, K. (1994). *Payola in the music industry: A history, 1880–1991.* Jefferson, NC: McFarland & Company.

Shaw, A. (1974). *The rockin '50s: The decade that transformed the pop music scene.* New York: Da Capo.

Slobin, M. (1993). *Subcultural sounds: Micromusics of the west.* Hanover, NH: Wesleyan University Press.

Sorkin, A. (2001, May 21). Vivendi in deal for MP3.com to lift online distribution. *New York Times,* C1.

Theberge, P. (1997). *Any sound you can imagine: Making music/consuming technology.* Hanover, NH: Wesleyan University Press.

Thompson, E. (1995). Machines, music, and the quest for fidelity: Marketing the Edison phonograph in America, 1877–1925. *The Musical Quarterly, 79,* 131–171.

U.S. Bureau of Census. (2002). *Statistical abstract of the United States* (144th ed.). Washington, DC: Author.

Vogel, H. (1998). *Entertainment industry economics* (4th ed.). Cambridge, UK: Cambridge University Press.

Weissman, D. (1990). *The music business: Career opportunities and self-defense* (rev. ed.). New York: Crown.

Welch, W. L., & Burt, L. B. S. (1994). *From tinfoil to stereo: The acoustic years of the recording industry, 1877–1929.* Gainesville: University Press of Florida.

# Chapter 12

# The Economics of the Advertising Industry

**MARY ALICE SHAVER**
*University of Central Florida*

Advertising in one form or another is centuries old. What we think of today as the advertising industry became formalized in the late 19th century with the formation of advertising agencies. In the early days, the fledgling agencies literally contracted for newspaper and magazine pages, which they then sold at a profit to businesses that wanted to reach a particular audience. These early arrangements evolved into full-service agencies that handled all areas of client advertising from research to creative execution to placement of the finished advertising in the appropriate media.

When we calculate advertising expenditures, however, the figure includes not only agency work (generally the majority of expenditures) but also advertising from businesses themselves (which may have their own in-house agency that works only for that business) and advertising placed by individuals. The finished product may be anything from a slick television or magazine ad to a specialty product. Many agencies provide full service to a client, doing everything concerning advertising and promotion. Others may be specialty—or boutique firms—that do only certain types of advertising.

Advertising expenditures for 2002 are estimated at 466.1 billion U.S. dollars (U.S.D.; Coen, 2002). The U.S. portion of that figure is just more than one half at 239.2 billion U.S.D. These 2001 figures are slightly lower than 2000 due to the sharp declines of 2001 caused by the severe economic drop worldwide. The drop in U.S. advertising in 2001 was the first time ad dollars had declined since World War II. The year 2002 is estimated to have a 2.4 % growth in the United States and a 2% growth overall in world markets (see Table 12.1).

There are two basic audiences for advertising. The first is the consumer *audience that is exposed* to the advertising through many types of media vehicles. The second are the manufacturing and service organizations who

## TABLE 12.1
### Worldwide Ad Growth Between 1990 and 2002

| Year | U.S.A Billion US$ | % Change | OVERSEAS Billion US$ | % Change | TOTAL Billion US$ | WORLD % Change |
|------|-------------------|----------|----------------------|----------|-------------------|----------------|
| 1990 | 130.0 | +3.9 | 145.9 | +11.8 | 275.9 | +7.9 |
| 1991 | 128.4 | −1.2 | 153.9 | +5.5 | 282.3 | +2.3 |
| 1992 | 133.8 | +4.2 | 165.4 | +7.5 | 299.2 | +6.0 |
| 1993 | 141.0 | +5.4 | 163.2 | −1.3 | 304.2 | +1.7 |
| 1994 | 153.0 | +8.6 | 179.0 | +9.7 | 332.0 | +9.1 |
| 1995 | 165.1 | +7.9 | 205.9 | +15.0 | 371.0 | +11.7 |
| 1996 | 178.1 | +7.9 | 212.1 | +3.0 | 390.2 | +5.2 |
| 1997 | 191.3 | +7.4 | 210.0 | −1.0 | 401.3 | +2.8 |
| 1998 | 206.7 | +8.0 | 205.2 | −2.3 | 411.9 | +2.6 |
| 1999 | 222.3 | +7.6 | 213.8 | +4.2 | 436.1 | +5.9 |
| 2000 | 243.7 | +9.6 | 220.2 | +3.0 | 463.9 | +6.4 |
| 2001* | 233.7 | −4.1 | 222.4 | +1.0 | 456.1 | −1.7 |
| 2002* | 239.3 | +2.4 | 226.8 | +2.0 | 466.1 | +2.2 |

*In current local currencies.
Source: Coen, R. (2002, January 1). Universal McCann's Insider Report.

use advertising to make contact with the audience of present and potential consumers of their goods and services. In this configuration, the advertising agency (whether a free-standing agency that serves many clients or an in-house agency that serves just its own company) becomes the facilitator. In cases such as classified advertising, the seller deals directly with the medium in placing the ads. This would be true for some—but not all—locally placed business run-of-press (ROP) advertising and it would also be true of an advertising director for a small business in which that director and perhaps a small staff take the place of an in-house agency and perform its functions for the business.

Advertising plays a particularly strong role in supporting the media in the United States. Advertising revenues pay for virtually all broadcast media, 70% to 80% of support for newspapers and an equally high percentage for magazines. Although there are subscription costs for nearly all newspapers and magazines, this revenue stream pays only a small amount of the actual costs of production and distribution. Advertising revenue also supports outdoor advertising. As yet, advertising does not play a major role in the support of Internet content, which is largely supported by the various news media. This may change in the foreseeable future. In the past decade, promotion and event marketing has taken an increasing amount of many companies' advertising budget, resulting in a loss of ad revenue in the traditional media. Direct mail has grown incrementally stronger in the past two decades, again, taking revenue from what used to be considered the major media. Taken together, direct mail and Internet have captured much of the retail business and threaten both traditional stores and marketplaces as well as challenging the traditional media placement. A look at the percentage of advertising revenue going to newspapers, for example, finds that it has dropped from 26% in 1984 to 22% in 2001. Newspapers and television are barely edging out direct marketing in percentages of advertising revenue received (see Fig. 12.1).

The picture is equally fragmented within the television industry as well. What used to be advertising revenue garnered by the three major networks has become revenue shared among many new networks. Cable, rather than national networks, has gained in this change.

When one examines the major trends in advertising today, there are two prominent challenges to the traditional patterns. The first is the move (begun as early as the 1960s with the death of many national magazines) from a mass to a niche market. The second is the successful challenge of new media to the old in terms of revenue, attention and importance.

## ECONOMISTS' VIEWS OF ADVERTISING

Until the mid-20th century, most economists discounted the role of advertising in the economy. One criticism of advertising has been that there are both inherent inefficiencies and perceived economic wastes in advertising activity. In his seminal work on monopolistic competition, Chamberlin (1933) pointed out that differing assumptions must be made for differing situations and that the advertiser may both add to and subtract from the markets of his immediate competition. By extending the market to new areas, the advertiser may increase the overall market. By taking away part of a competitor's market share, the advertiser subtracts from the competitive market. Chamberlin correctly stated that the market consists of all similar products and also of all products that could be considered (through simple consumer realization or as a result of an advertising message) as possible substitutes. He argued that selling costs are necessary to the production and distribution of goods and that they must be considered as such. He further argued that competitive theory must consider and account for all the components or the sales process. Starting in the 1940s, the economists view of heavy advertising causing concentration within industries became a standard view. This idea was adopted by John Kenneth Galbraith in the 1950s and popularized by his book, *The Affluent Society*. Other economists

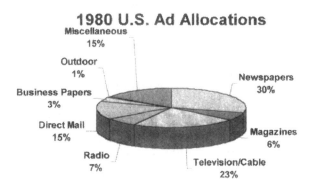

**1980 U.S. Ad Allocations**

Miscellaneous 15%
Outdoor 1%
Business Papers 3%
Direct Mail 15%
Radio 7%
Television/Cable 23%
Newspapers 30%
Magazines 6%

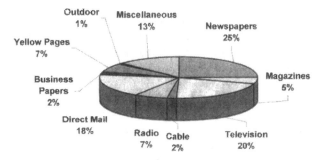

**1990 U.S. Ad Allocations**

Outdoor 1%
Miscellaneous 13%
Yellow Pages 7%
Newspapers 25%
Business Papers 2%
Direct Mail 18%
Radio 7%
Cable 2%
Television 20%
Magazines 5%

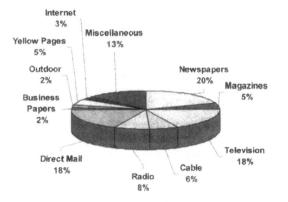

**2000 Ad Allocations**

Internet 3%
Yellow Pages 5%
Miscellaneous 13%
Outdoor 2%
Business Papers 2%
Newspapers 20%
Magazines 5%
Direct Mail 18%
Radio 8%
Cable 6%
Television 18%

FIG. 12.1.   Distribution of advertising expenditures by medium. Adapted from Coen, R. (2002, January 1). *Universal McCann's Insider Report.*

viewed advertising's role as causing concentration and competitive positioning among brands, but felt in the overall economy advertising was not of great importance because it only moved the money around brands. More recently, advertising has been viewed as a tool in generating positive competitive activity.

## STRUCTURE OF THE MARKET

The advertising industry operates in what should be termed a monopolistic competition. There are many firms but they differ in terms of reputation, service levels, location, capabilities, and size. There are some price differences as well, although the price structure is relatively common throughout the industry when specific services are compared. Unlike many businesses, the most common price structure for the advertising industry was one based upon a commission system where the client paid a (usual) 15% commission on all media buys. Hence, the larger the client and the more ambitious the advertising plan and placements, the greater the money that was paid. In recent years, there has been much criticism of this historical practice due to the very real possibility that the agency might choose the most expensive medium—typically prime time television—whether it was warranted for the strategy of the campaign and the target audience to be reached. As a result, many agencies converted to a negotiated flat price based on the actual work entailed by the job. For some jobs and in some agencies the fee basis is combined with some sort of commission for media placements, but this is becoming less common throughout the industry.

Because monopolistic competition means that the optimal price comes when product quantity yields a margin cost and when the firms involved sell products that may be differentiated from one another in several ways, the advertising industry fits best under this umbrella. However, unlike manufacturing firms, the clients or buyers of the agency production may differ from year to year as manufacturers tire of the product (the advertising) and switch to a different vendor (agency). This situation is different for firms that have their own in-house agency and for individuals who purchase advertising time and space for themselves (the latter is often classified advertising). The advertising industry fulfills the other qualifications for monopolistic competition as well: There are a large number of firms involved, entry into the business is relatively easy (although it may not be possible to compete at the highest levels due to the necessary cost and expertise demanded), and the other firms are unlikely to make retaliatory moves. The exception to this last is when a client asks several agencies to bid on a contract, but in this case, it is the client and not the competing agency that makes the initial move. The industry is competitive in the ways in which it seeks new accounts.

A tangential and important point related to the advertising industry is that outside manufacturing and service firms spend large amounts on advertising, particularly in the categories of consumer products and low-price convenience foods. It is assumed that the amount of advertising expenditure by firms is related to units sold and at what price. There are also assumed to be diminishing marginal returns on excess advertising expenditure. The problem facing those firms paying for the advertising is that it is often difficult to measure sales gains and returns directly from advertising expenditure. Advertising is essentially an information conveying business. In some cases, advertising may fail to deliver the messages in an efficient manner or to provide a return on the product (advertising messages) in the most profitable way. Some goods and services can operate without advertising (or without much advertising) because there is little to differentiate the basic consumer goods among brands. Sugar would be an example. However, low-cost and easily substitutable products tend to do a great deal of advertising in some categories. Backman (1967) pointed out that products of low cost and low risk must continually advertise to keep customers loyal. He found that soft drinks, soaps, candy, gum, and other low-financial and low-social risk products spend a greater percentage of their budgets on advertising than do more easily differentiated products.

Given similar products (the soft drink market could be an example), firms tend to advertise at a level that approximates their close competitors. When it comes to decisions regarding media buys, both the client and the agency must make decisions as to expenditure before the actual audience reach or composition can be known. In recent years, agencies have asked broadcasters for a guarantee as to audience size—and have received money back if the audience does not meet the predicted level.

## CONSOLIDATION AMONG ADVERTISING FIRMS

When one considers mergers and consolidation within the advertising industry, it is actually agency mergers and acquisitions that is meant. Although mergers began in the 1930s (Leslie 1985), it was during the 1970s, 1980s, and 1990s that activity in this area increased worldwide. Lancendorfer (2002) noted that by June 2002, with the merger of Publicis and Bcom3, the top four advertising organizations could claim more than one half of the world's gross income from advertising expenditures. During the 1990s, 69 mergers and 132 acquisitions took place (Standard Directory of Advertising Agencies; see Table12. 2).

In assessing the level of market concentration, Lancendorfer (2002) calculated the agency concentration ratios and concluded that concentration ratios have decreased from 1991 to 2001 and that the market showed an increase in competition.

**TABLE 12.2**

**Merger and Acquisition Activity Between 1991 and 2001**

| Year | Mergers | Acquisitions | Total |
|------|---------|--------------|-------|
| 1991 | 17 | 14 | 31 |
| 1992 | 12 | 19 | 31 |
| 1993 | 9 | 11 | 20 |
| 1994 | 10 | 11 | 21 |
| 1995 | 10 | 26 | 36 |
| 1996 | 0 | 1 | 1 |
| 1997 | 0 | 15 | 15 |
| 1998 | 4 | 10 | 14 |
| 1999 | 2 | 6 | 8 |
| 2000 | 2 | 1 | 3 |
| 2001 | 3 | 18 | 21 |
| Total | 69 | 132 | 201 |

Source. Standard Directory of Advertising Agencies (1991–2001). The Advertising Red Books. Reprinted with permission.

With the increased merger activity during the 1990s, the majority of U.S. advertising agencies were members of holding corporations. According to the 2001 Annual Agency Report (Ad Age), 47 U.S. agencies were part of four major holding companies. Six of these agencies were in the top 10 in U.S. billings for 2000 (see Table 12.3).

June 2002 saw the merger of two other giants—Bcom3 and Publicis. The reason for the move to conglomerate holding companies goes beyond size

**TABLE 12.3**

**Key 2001 Financial Factors for Top Four Holding Companies**

| Company | Billings Thousands US$ | Revenues Thousands US$ | EBIT Thousands US$ | Margin (EBIT/Revenue) |
|---------|------------------------|------------------------|--------------------|-----------------------|
| Interpublic | 6,727,000 | 7,005,000 | 1,192,000 | 17.72% |
| Omnicon | 6,889,406 | 968,184 | 895,385 | 13.00% |
| Publicis Groupe | 16,700,000 | 2,162,700 | 304,380 | 14.07% |
| WPP | 30,286,005 | 4,322,015 | 732,975 | 16.96% |

Source. Corporate Financial Statements.
Notes. Financials for WWP were reported in British Pounds and for Publicis Groupe in Euros. These were translated into dollars using the official Interbank rate effective 12/31/2001.

and economies of scale and scope. Individual and independent agencies cannot serve clients whose businesses would pose a conflict of interest. New and lucrative accounts may be placed in another of the conglomerate agency holdings without a conflict of interest, leaving the field open for the conglomerate to attract and bid for many more accounts.

## ECONOMIES OF SCALE AND SCOPE

Both economies of scale and economies of scope are prominent in the advertising industry. Agencies benefit from both, and the usual rule of the larger firms benefiting to a larger extent than the smaller holds for the advertising industry as well. A large agency is able to gain better contract prices on work done outside (filming, production, etc.) simply because they have a large ongoing relationship with the providers and are able to use them on products for many clients on a frequent basis. Some advertising production work is done on a contract basis with the providers being freelance operators who may work for many agencies and in many locations around the world in any given year. The larger firms are able to buy in greater quantity for all their needs and thus are in a better position to receive volume discounts. All full-service agencies are able to utilize the same creative team to develop multiple campaign messages for varying media, thereby having economies of scope. Also, teams may be developed for new clients by drawing from the same pool of talent and production services as used for longer term clients. Because of these time and cost savings and the use of one campaign theme across all media (and on occasion a product that advertises the corporation and its many products in a corporate identity campaign), both the advertising industry members and the clients they serve can attain economies of scale and scope in the area of advertising and promotion.

## HORIZONTAL–VERTICAL INTEGRATION

Advertising firms exhibit both vertical and horizontal integration. On the horizontal side, there have been increasing numbers of agency mergers and takeovers since the 1960s and continuing today. A 1986 estimate by Saatchi and Saatchi, one of the first of the larger firms that had grown from mergers, stated that the eight largest agencies controlled one fifth of the worldwide billings—up from 12% a decade before (Leslie 1995). It was during this time that many large agencies spun off the growth areas of public relations and direct mail to create new agencies for these functions. These new entities remained a part of the original agency but concentrated on specialized subcategories of the business. In this way, vertical integration was achieved. Ultimately, through multiple mergers and acquisitions, four conglomerate holding companies emerged—Interpublic (New York), Omnicom (New

York), Publicis Groupe (Paris), and WPP Group (London). Taken together, these conglomerates owned among them nearly 70 of the top 400 agencies in terms of billing (see Fig. 12.2).

## BARRIERS TO ENTRY

The controversies concerning barriers to entry and advertising do not focus on the advertising agencies or firms but rather on the manufacturers and service entities placing the advertising to gain recognition, attention, and, ultimately, brand preference and loyalty from consumers. High levels of advertising expenditure are seen as a means of advancing one's own product line, of gaining attention and as a means of gaining a high enough percentage of brand and market share to pose a formidable barrier to new firms wanting to enter the field or to established firms expanding product lines. The barriers to entry within the industry, such as they are, arise from the high reputation and worldwide experience that the larger agencies have established. It would be nearly impossible for a new entry to compete at that level. However, there are no barriers to starting an agency to serve other, smaller businesses that would be beneath the threshold of expenditure for the most prominent agencies to consider. Smaller businesses often choose smaller agencies, knowing that their lesser level of billings will not generate a high level of service at the agencies with multimillion-dollar accounts. In fact, large agencies often have a threshold of billings beyond which they will consider a client. This is a particularly relevant point if one considers the necessary avoidance of conflict of interest.

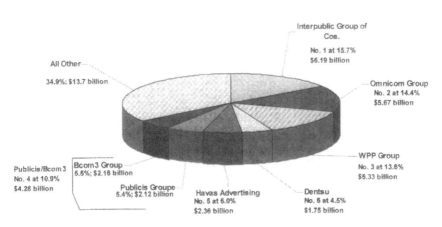

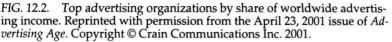

FIG. 12.2.   Top advertising organizations by share of worldwide advertising income. Reprinted with permission from the April 23, 2001 issue of *Advertising Age.* Copyright © Crain Communications Inc. 2001.

## ADVERTISING AS A CATALYST OF BARRIERS TO ENTRY

There is another aspect of barriers to entry that must be considered and that is the use of advertising as a means of setting barriers to other entrants into a given category. In the consumer markets of cosmetics and drugs, soaps, soft drinks, and other low-priced, low-risk, and easily replaceable products, the top companies hold a commanding market share and the leader will maintain that position with large advertising expenditures. Brand awareness is very high in these categories, and the manufacturers engage in high-dollar advertising expenditures in an effort to effect some brand loyalty among consumers. Given these facts, it is very difficult for a new entrant into the market to enter and compete with the established market leaders. The case may be different in a market where frequent purchase is not a factor and where information may play a more important role in the consumer decision process. Roughly 80% of new products fail each year and the vast majority of these are in areas that challenge heavy spending market leaders.

## ADVERTISING AND MARKET POWER

Related to the subject of barriers to entry is that of advertising and market power. The need for heavy advertising expenditures in a business create a differential advantage for the firms already in the market (Comanor & Wilson, 1974). Both differentiation in the products and differentiation in the mind of the consumer may exist with the latter possible even if the former is not demonstrably present. Advertising can position the leader in a field so that the public sees more difference in the product offerings than may actually exist. Actual product differentiation may be calculated by the elasticities of demand among competing products. Low elasticity indicates consumer preference for an existing brand in the marketplace. Cross-elasticities between the firms already in the market and potential entrants indicate barriers to entry (Comanor & Wilson, 1974). This view, however, is not held by all who study the advertising and economic problems. One prominent differing view has been that of market competition, which focuses on the informative properties of advertising, arguing that an informed public will seek value and demand quality. This, some argue, actually can make it possible for new firms supplying these needs to enter the field. It can also serve to lower prices. As noted earlier, the advertising market operates differently in product categories with differing frequency of purchase, differing price levels and differing risk levels.

## BASIC BUSINESS MODEL USED
## IN THE ADVERTISING INDUSTRY

If one takes the industry to mean national and global agencies, in-house agencies, and media advertising departments, there will be distinctly different models in use. The basic agency model would be of an overarching corporate structure with many different accounts each developing the strategy, audience analysis, message strategy, and advertising for a single client. The usual model has been for one group to work as a team for one client with many noncompeting clients and groups making up the agency. This model could hold true for most agencies, including global. In-house agencies might have differing groups working on segments of the account work, but all would be working for one client. In the media itself, there would be an advertising director, several managers and individual sales people or teams. The clients could be divided by category (home, travel) or by geography. The smaller the media unit, the more likely the geographical structure would be.

## REVENUE STREAMS

Again, it is necessary to distinguish between advertising agencies and the media with which the advertisements are placed. The agency earns its revenue from placing the advertisements in the media. The traditional payment for the agency has been a 15% commission on each media placement. In this model, the client pays the full amount of the placement and the agency retains 15% of the whole. From the commission, the agency takes its overhead expenses and the remainder is profit. Another model, one that is becoming more common, is that the agency charges the client a fee based on the nature and amount of the work. The agency may be paid a flat fee for the basic work and additional fees for additional work such as promotions, logo design, and the like. The client might also be charged a flat fee for the time expended on the work with the cost of production and time and space costs added. The media itself charges differing prices for time and space, depending on size or length of the advertisement, with discounts for frequency and heavy users of advertising. Service or production costs beyond the usual will garner an additional cost. Special placements and special issues will also be priced at a higher level.

## OPERATING AND NET PROFIT MARGINS

As to expenses versus revenue, the advertising expenditure level would ideally be set where the amount of advertising would most efficiently generate an acceptable amount of sales (see Table 12.3). Because measurement of the actual effects of advertising with sales cannot, in most cases, be measured in any way that would even approximate the actual impact, advertising expenditure is decided in several ways that seem arbitrary and inefficient. Some advertisers set the amount of advertising as a percentage of the last year's sales figures. Obviously this uses past figures in an attempt to predict future performance with little regard for any of the competitive and environmental issues that may cause the market for the product to fluctuate. Some advertisers attempt to forecast the amount of sales that will occur and make assumptions, often based on past performance, as to the amount of advertising it will take to generate these sales. This approach would be termed a *sales response model* (see Fig. 12.3).

Other methods are affordability—choosing the amount to spend based upon what can be spent, the competitive model—matching a competitor in the marketplace and what is termed the objective and task model in which the desired outcome is determined and the advertising budget set at a level that is believed to be capable of achieving the goals. Although this last method may be the soundest in terms of accomplishing goals and objectives, none of the methods could be said to maximize efficiency.

The product lines in the advertising business are the advertisements themselves along with special effects, special promotions, events, and other promotional activities. There may also be peripheral products such as collateral, which are materials such as point of purchase posters and specialty products.

## IMPACT OF NEW TECHNOLOGY
## ON THE ADVERTISING INDUSTRY

The emergence of the Internet provided advertisers and agencies with yet another way to reach specific niche markets with advertising messages. Agencies and major advertisers were quick to realize the benefit from the synergy of the new technological delivery system and the traditional media. Advertising strategy has long calculated the maximum number of impressions and the cross-audience reach in using a number of differing

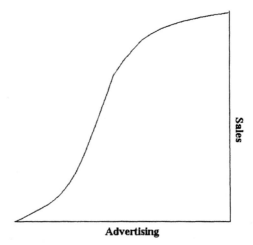

FIG. 12.3.   The S-curve sales response function.

media to deliver the same message for a client or product. Basically, advertising has been planned and purchased for the maximum effective reach (numbers of audience members who have been exposed to the message one time) and frequency (number of times the target audience has been exposed). For many products, using two or three media to deliver the same message taking advantage of the special properties of the media (radio: reminder; television: showing product and using audio and visual to increase retention of the message; newspaper and magazine: mass and niche audiences with either high-impact print ads or long ad copy; direct mail: reaching identified target audiences directly with messages developed for their profile; outdoor: large advertising with a simple message that reiterates the basic message of the campaign). What the new media added to this was both specific targeting using the profile developed by the users choices and the possibility of interactive dialog with the target. Different types of media deliver differing impact to audience members. Using two or more types of media to deliver the advertising message in more than one way has been shown to increase both understanding and retention. With the advent of new technology, more media and message synergy was possible. Although most advertisers do not feel every campaign needs to have the synergy of differing media, most do feel it is the ideal way to introduce or promote a new product. Utilizing the synergy among media in this way can provide a more compelling and involving impact upon the target audience. Although the Internet was seen at first as challenging old media, particularly direct mail, it has led the way to higher levels of service with consumers. This is seen as a particular value to retailers of direct products. However, it has proved a challenge to traditional in-store sellers.

## COPYRIGHT AND TRADEMARK

These are closely watched in the advertising industry. As with all work, an advertisement that is copyrighted cannot be used by anyone else without specific permission. Trademarks are carefully guarded, as they are a part of the brand image of a product or service. What is particularly relevant in the advertising industry is the protection of the brand and the image that has been portrayed to the consumer. Advertisements of a rival firm that are close in idea or execution to that of the registered owner are challenged. The brand image and brand equity are valuable components of the product or service sales; anything that dilutes it can take away the competitive edge and confound the image and product that has evolved through millions spent on brand advertising. Trademark law protects names, slogans, and titles. To appropriate even a part of the trademark of another brand or company is seen as unfair competition and is often challenged in court or through the advertising self-regulatory process.

# THE ADVERTISING INDUSTRY
# AND ITS IMPACT UPON SOCIETY

The relationship of advertising and society has been and is a much debated topic. The controversy arises from the classical liberal market model in which it is assumed that rational man will choose what is best for him and that competition among producers will result in the best products surviving and succeeding in the marketplace. The challenge to this is the school of thought that views advertising as manipulative and man as unable to discern the true facts within the persuasive message. Critics of advertising maintain that it causes people to buy things they do not need, that it raises prices, that it controls the market and that it dictates the values of society. Supporters of advertising counter that it raises the standard of living, lowers prices by making the market more efficient and provides information from which consumers can make purchase decisions in a rational and deliberate manner. The role of people and their individual strength in understanding the market, judging brands and ideas, and exercising his or her right of choice is central to the argument. Also central is the unsolved conundrum of whether advertising reflects the values of society or dictates them. Although the issue of the impact of advertising on both society and economics is much debated, there are no clear answers. The issues are complex and are culturally as well as economically related to the Western consumer society in which most of the resources of the world are consumed.

## FURTHER READINGS

Bagwell, K. (2001). "The Economics of Advertising, Introduction" (mimeo).
Bain, J. S. (1956). *Barriers to new competition*. Cambridge, MA: Harvard University.
Borden, N. H. (1942). *The economic effects of advertising*. Chicago: Richard D. Irwin.
Chamberlin, E. H. (1933). *The theory of monopolistic competition, a re-orientation of the theory of value*. Cambridge, MA: Harvard University.
Ekelund, R. B., & Saurman, D. S. (1988). *Advertising and the market process*. San Francisco: Pacific Research Institute for Public Policy.
Rotzoll, K. B., & Haefner, J. E. (1996). *Advertising in contemporary society*. Urbana: University of Illinois.
Tharp, M., & Jeong, J. (2001). Executive insights: The global network communications agency. *Journal of International Marketing, 9*(4).

## REFERENCES

Advertising Age's Agency Report. (2001). Crane Communications. Chicago.
Backman, J. (1967). *Advertising and competition*. New York: New York University.
Chamberlin, E. H. (1933). *The theory of monopolistic competition, a re-orientation of the theory of value*. Cambridge, MA: Harvard University.

Coen, R. (2002, January 1). *Universal McCann's Insider Report*. Retrieved from http://www.mccann.com/insight/bobcoen.html

Comanor, W. S., & Wilson, T. A. (1974). *Advertising and market power*. Cambridge, MA: Harvard University.

Interpublic annual Report for 2001 http://media.corporate-ir.net/media_files/NYS/ipg/reports/ipg_ar01.pdf

Lancendorfer, K. M. (2002). *The Effects of Mergers and Acquisitions on the Advertising Agency Industry: A Replication and Extension*. Unpublished paper.

Leslie, D. A. (1985). Global scan: The globalization of advertising agencies, concepts, and campaigns. *Economic Geography, 71*(4).

Omnicom Group. http://livedelivery.com/F/11491/_OC54727242.pdf

Publicis. http://www.finance.publicis.com/fr/60000/pdf/rapportannuel2001.pdf

Standard Directory of Advertising Agencies, National Register Publishing, 121 Chanlon Road, New Providence, NJ 07974.

WPP Group. http://www.wppinvestor.com/performance/word/prelim_01_tables.doc

# Chapter 13

# The Economics
# of Online Media

**ROD CARVETH**
*Rochester Institute of Technology*

In 1999, both Microsoft and Intel were added to the Dow Jones Industrial Index. This development symbolized a new era in which the information technology industry was officially recognized as one of the most important sectors in the U.S. economy. As the 21st century unfolds, the online industry has taken on a completely different economic as well as social status.

*Online media* (referred to hereafter as the Internet) is the result of a cross-pollination of communication technologies, offering users enhanced human communication channel functions. The versatility and interactivity of the Internet distinguishes it from other media. The Internet can deliver text, graphics, images, audio, and video at the same time, and thus can provide the functions of other mass media, such as television, radio, newspaper, magazine, and telephone. In addition, the Internet provides a continuum of interactive communication delivery ranging from one-to-one to many-to-many (Ghose & Dou, 1998), thus transforming the traditional meaning of *receiver* and *sender* in one-to-many mass mediated.

This chapter first reviews the historical development of the Internet. The chapter then moves on to an application of Michael Porter's theory of competitive strategy to the Internet, using America Online (AOL) as a case study. Finally, the chapter discusses the future role of broadband in the economics of online media.

## THE DEVELOPMENT OF ONLINE MEDIA

The rapid evolution of the Internet has been matched by a torrent of predictions about it, making it difficult to keep the medium in perspective. One way to envision the Internet, and to speculate about its future development, is to think of the Internet as part of a continuing history of online services rather than as a sudden and singular phenomenon. Here the term *online* refers generally to services that are delivered over a narrowband connection. There are three intervals of narrowband services, called (a) videotext, (b) online services, and (c) the Internet.

As argued elsewhere (Carveth & Metz, 1996), the growth of the Internet occurred in three stages. The first of these stages was initiated by the *pioneers*—mostly scientists and engineers who were concerned with the need for national security. The original network proposed and accepted was designed by individuals who had a notion of linking together computers for the sole purpose of communication. These scientists and programmers initially worked through the funding of the federal government (commissioned by the Advanced Research Projects Agency [ARPA]) to explore the possibilities of branching out a new form of technology that would enable people to work together despite great distances.

The second stage began with the arrival of the *settlers*—academics and scientists who were using the machines sharing resources and communicating with one another. Those who continually used the system began establishing comfortable communities in which interests were shared. This group of people believed that the realm of computer networking was limitless, and that there seemed to be enough room for all types of people to coexist peacefully. The primary goal for the settlers was to communicate with similar *cybernauts*—explorers who tended to be interested in technology that the mainstream population eschewed. These initial settlers saw the Internet as a public good, an expansive cyberfrontier that could be shared by all.

The third online era came with the arrival of the *people of capital*. The era had an aborted beginning in the early 1980s, but returned in the 1990s. The people of capital tried to take advantage of a new world of information, available by turning on a computer hooked up to what was called videotex—text transmitted online (e.g., over the telephone) to be displayed on a video screen (Major, 1990). Although it was not absolutely necessary to own a computer (e.g., public terminals were made available in areas such as Santa Barbara, California [Hanson, 1992]), the services provided and information available was easier to access and store with a home personal computer (PC). Despite a plethora of opportunities available, it was not until 1994 that a critical mass of consumers in the United States began to take advantage of videotext opportunities.

## The U.S. Videotex Experience

In the 1980s, marketing experts predicted that videotext would revolutionize the marketing, advertising and broadcasting industries, and become a $5-billion-a-year industry (Major, 1990). Videotex enabled customers to use a keypad to call up screens of content from a centralized database for display on a home viewing screen. It was an early example of technological convergence—combining television, the telephone, and the computer.

This hybrid technology frequently evoked notions of social and technological revolution. Videotex promised to change shopping, banking, news delivery, travel, and messaging. Many of the more optimistic predictions came from vendors offering such services.

Market researchers projected billions of dollars of revenue from equipment sales and service usage. As a result, $2.5 billion was invested in videotex. The videotex industry in the first half of the 1980s, however, generated only $400 million in revenues from 1.5 to 2 million customers. By March 1986, three U.S. videotex providers had ceased operation after consumer disinterest led to combined losses of over $100 million (Major, 1990).

The original failure of the videotex revolution could have been that early marketers of videotex were promoting a system that did not exist: Consumers lacked low-cost, user-friendly PCs and applications, consumers preferred to get news from traditional media, PCs were not widely distributed, pricing was based on the minute rather than the month, and videotex offerings were limited. As a result, videotex producers abandoned their original target of replacing traditional media and repositioned themselves as a supplemental information service provider (Major, 1990).

Another possible explanation could be that the market for videotex services was narrower than companies originally anticipated (Truet & Hermann, 1989). In this area, it is difficult to analyze the market without first understanding France Telecom's Teletel service, dubbed *Minitel*. France had long been the world leader in videotex activity, with 5 million active users of more than 15,000 different services by 1990.

Maital (1991) traced Minitel's success to three factors. First, France Telecom invested substantial tine and money designing Teletel, concentrating on long-term evolutionary planning. Second, they spent millions on a technologically advanced switching system known as Transpac, providing a more efficient cost structure of the service overall. This switching system enabled data bits to be grouped and then transferred as a "bundle" through the system, cutting the cost of sending messages and making "the cost independent of the geographical distance between the consumer and the seller" (p. 8). Third, France Telecom's monopolistic position made it possible to launch a mass-market product for which market demand did not yet exist. As Maital observed, "Who would invest massively in such terminals without first being assured of the demand for their services? The answer: A government with deep pockets, a clear purpose, and a national technology strategy" (p. 8).

By contrast, the United States government historically had none of those three requisite criteria, despite some attempts by a handful of governmental officials recommending immediate execution of a nationwide construction of electronic superhighways (Gore, 1991). Market observers attributed Teletel's success to France Telecom's farsighted planning, cost-effective service rates, and monopoly position in telecommunications. Americas initial inability to compete globally in the information services arena may be traced to the fragmentation of American telecommunications after the breakup of the American Telephone and Telegraph Co. (AT&T) monopoly (Maital, 1991). During the period from 1984 to 1990, France Telecom installed 6 million Minitel terminals in France—1 for every 10 people. Comparatively, in 1990 there were only 1.5 million subscribers to online videotex services in the United States, or 1 for every 165 people (Hawkins, 1991).

Yet another problem was the overall poor performance of videotex systems. These problems included overall economic viability of videotex, involving costs of specialized equipment and costs of communications; benefits not seen as sufficient to justify costs; a lack of industry standards with a consequent incompatibility among systems; and human social factors involving new and different ways to do things (Grover & Sabherwal, 1989). Obviously, a change in strategic orientation would be needed to repair all of these problems.

Although the launch of Prodigy in 1988 led to another round of optimistic predictions, the modest overall performance of online services dampened talk about their social impact. By 1993, three national online services, Prodigy, AOL, and CompuServe, claimed about 3 million subscribers, although Prodigy had already suffered cumulative losses of more than $1 billion.

The videotex industry began to rebound in 1990 when car manufacturers became some of the first major advertisers to tap into the videotex market (Fahey, 1990). To accommodate these new clients, Prodigy began taking steps toward making the service a mainstream advertising medium (Fahey, 1989a). Prodigy began by charging advertisers by "measured response pricing," where viewers could see teaser ads across the bottom of a screen and could access the full ad for more information (Fahey, 1989b). Although the average length of most ads was 30 screens, if a viewer accessed only 5 screens, the marketer was charged for only those 5 screens. This new method of advertising was hailed as *a no-risk medium*, because it charged on the basis of actual advertising exposure (Fahey, 1989b).

Prodigy, however, began running into trouble. General Motors Buick division reevaluated the videotex systems and decided to pull its advertisements from Prodigy, although maintaining the advertising campaign on CompuServe (Fahey, 1990). Audi renewed its contract only after serious deliberation, saying that they may have obtained a large number of leads, but the concern was whether or not they were qualified leads. Audi wanted to make sure that the Prodigy subscribers were good targets for Audi automobiles.

Such criticism evoked a strong response from Prodigy, which complained that it was "unfair for advertisers to expect videotex to provide information they don't request from other media" (Fahey, 1990, p. 54), claiming that no magazine client requires that a medium provide it delivered enough sales to justify the ad dollars. Unfortunately, although this may have been a valid argument, the fact remains that videotex advertising in 1990 was still an experiment.

By 1994, there were between 1.5 and 2 million loyal videotex users who used the various networks religiously. Nevertheless, the event that propelled explosive growth in videotex services occurred in the spring of 1994 when AOL finished its gateway onto the Internet. Since that time, growth in online services has wildly exceeded expectations.

The development of narrowband services demonstrates a pattern of progressive decentralization of the technology and content components. Videotex was a top-down model of centralized providers furnishing centralized services through a specialized terminal. The design reflected the technology of the time, but it also then emphasized centralized (i.e., transaction- and information-oriented) interactive services. These services were assumed to be desirable, but consumers were not interested; prognosticators (and suppliers) confused technological capability with market demand.

Prodigy was a centralized provider offering mostly centralized interactive services. A key component, however, changed with the use of consumers' own standards-based computers. The change in delivery device from a passive terminal to a multipurpose machine changed the assumed model for services, although Prodigy's marketers did not seem to take this fully into account. Consumers followed the pattern of text-based online services such as CompuServe and showed greater interest in electronic mail (e-mail) and bulletin boards—something for which Prodigy was architecturally and strategically unprepared.

Today, the Internet operates on a completely different model than that of the first videotex experiments. The network features decentralized content that can be created by anyone and accessed on a standardized technological platform. If the original assumption was that consumers would access online services in their homes to save time, current research suggests that consumers are more interested in using online services to produce or peruse content (web pages, e-mail, newsgroups) as a new, enjoyable way to spend time. Thus, online services have found their success through decentralization: Content is now more in the hands of users than providers, and services to communicate with others, such as e-mail and chat rooms, are highly popular.

## The Internet

As a communication medium, although the Internet constitutes one underlying communications infrastructure, it also combines within it more than one medium. At the time of ARPAnet, the medium was essentially based on the traditional, physical telephone infrastructure—with some new routing and software technologies added (Naughton, 2000).

Eventually other functions —such as e-mail in the 1970s and Usenet in the 1980s—began to evolve. Although the growth of these functions increased dramatically during the first two decades, the Internet did not become a mass medium until the advent of the World Wide Web following the introduction of hypertext (HTML) in 1989, the first web browsers (Mosaic, Netscape), and finally search engines. The growth rate of the Internet in the mid-1990s onwards increased dramatically once the Web came into being.

A number of factors contributed to the Web's explosive growth. First, the underlying technologies, infrastructure, and appliances were already widely distributed across the general population, especially the telephone system and home computers. The added costs to the economy of laying the foundation, and to the consumer of becoming connected, were relatively minimal as the Internet's "piggybacked" on what already existed.

A second reason for the Web's success is to be found in the multifunctionality of the Web and wider Internet. A user could now getting three or four new functions for the price of one—interpersonal communication, information retrieval, group conversation, shopping, etc.—from different media technologies such as e-mail, ICQ, Web, Usenet, streaming audio and video, and so forth. This technological convergence has become the rationale for the plethora of media mergers completed in the name of *synergy*. In addition, unlike radio and TV, both the Web and the Internet are profoundly interactive relatively user-friendly (Chan-Olmsted & Park, 2000). The programming that allows the user to "surf" is invisible.

Finally, largely because the Internet started as a governmental, not-for-profit endeavor, almost all content on the Web was free (and most remains so, despite some move towards a pay-per-view direction). If one compares the slower growth rates of the telegraph, telephone, cinema, and cable television, with the far faster expansion of radio, over-the-air television, and the Web (the latter does involve a relatively small, continuing charge by the service provider and the phone company), one could conclude that media without user costs (other than initial purchase of the appliance) will grow at a much faster rate than media carrying significant, continual use costs.

The reaction of older media to the Internet has taken several forms. The newspapers have felt the most threatened by the Web, and thus have been the first to respond in several ways. First, newspapers started offering their own product through the Internet but with the same "look." Second, newspapers added some new elements that fit the new medium, while keeping the original format basically intact. More recently, newspapers have sought new ways to present content, e.g. the portal with its myriad links to other pages and other sites (Chan-Olmsted & Park, 2000).

## THE ECONOMICS OF THE INTERNET

Revenue is generated in online media through three streams: service subscribership, online advertising, and pay-per-content. The focus of this next section is on Internet Service Providers (ISPs), whose revenues are derived from all three streams.

Michael Porter (1998) provided a framework that models an industry as being influenced by five forces. This model is used to better understand the industry context in which the firm operates. These forces are degree of rivalry, the threat of substitutes, the relative power of buyers, the relative power of suppliers, and barriers to entry.

### Degree of Rivalry

Firms strive for a competitive advantage over their rivals. The intensity of rivalry among firms varies across industries. Economists measure rivalry by indicators of industry concentration, such as the Concentration Ratio (CR). A high concentration ratio indicates that market share is held by a few large firms, meaning the industry is likely an oligopoly. A low concentration ratio signifies that the industry is characterized by many rivals, and is thus competitive.

The intensity of rivalry commonly is referred to as being cutthroat, intense, moderate, or weak, based on the firms' aggressiveness in attempting to gain an advantage. In pursuing an advantage over its rivals, a firm can choose from several competitive moves, including:

- Changing prices: When MSN initiated flat-fee pricing in 1996, rather than charging by the hour, other ISPs had to follow suit.
- Improving product differentiation: ISPs are constantly trying to improve features or implement innovations. For example, AOL's browser software, AOL 8.0, eliminates most "pop-up" ads, which are annoying to consumers.
- Creatively using channels of distribution: AOL is looking to position itself as a distributor of video and audio content, making it a rival to broadcast and cable television.

In addition to these competitive strategies, the intensity of rivalry is influenced by the following industry characteristics:

1. More firms in an industry increase rivalry because they must compete for the same customers and resources. If the firms have similar market share, the rivalry intensifies further.
2. Slow market growth will compel firms to fight for market share. In a growing market, firms are able to improve revenues simply because of the expanding market.

3. When total costs are largely fixed costs, the firm must produce near capacity to attain the lowest unit costs. Consequently, the firm must sell a large number of units of its product. When several companies are forced to do that, rivalry increases.
4. High storage costs or highly perishable products cause a firm to sell goods as soon as possible. If other producers are selling at the same time, competition for customers intensifies.
5. When a customer can freely switch from one product to another there is a greater struggle to capture customers.
6. If brands are not very identifiable with consumers, then rivalry is intense. On the other hand, if brand recognition is high, rivalry is lessened.
7. A diversity of rivals with different cultures, histories, and philosophies make an industry unstable. Rivalry can be intense and volatile.
8. A growing market and the potential for high profits induces new firms to enter a market and incumbent firms to increase production. A point is reached where the industry becomes crowded with competitors, and demand cannot support the new entrants and the resulting increased supply. At that point, an industry shakeout happens, with intense competition, price wars, and company failures.

## Threat of Substitutes

A threat of substitutes exists when a product's demand is affected by the price change of a substitute product. As more substitutes become available, the demand becomes more elastic since customers have more alternatives. This condition hampers a firm's ability to raise prices.

This threat of substitutes can occur at either the intra-industry or the interindustry level. An example of an intra-industry threat of substitutes would be AOL versus MSN. Both are ISPs, with similar services. The services can easily substitute for one another. An example of an interindustry threat of substitutes would be DSL (direct subscriber lines provided by phone companies) versus cable delivery of high-speed Internet access.

## Buyer Power

The power of buyers is the impact that customers have on a producing industry. In general, when buyer power is strong, the relationship to the producing industry is near to what an economist terms a monopsony—a market in which there are many suppliers and one buyer. Under such market conditions, the buyer sets the price. In reality few pure monopsonies exist, but frequently there is some asymmetry between a producing industry and buyers.

Buyers are powerful if buyers are concentrated (there are a few buyers with significant market share) or buyers purchase a significant proportion of output (such as Circuit City buying DVD players). Buyers are weak if there are significant buyer switching costs (such as going from a Windows operating system to an Apple operating system), or buyers are fragmented (such as is the case with most consumer products).

## Supplier Power

A producing industry requires labor, parts, and other supplies. This requirement leads to buyer-supplier relationships between the industry and the firms that provide it the raw materials used to create products. Suppliers, if powerful, can exert an influence on the producing industry, such as selling raw materials at a high price. Should Intel dramatically increase the price of its Pentium computer chips, that action would significantly affect online media profits.

Suppliers are powerful if they are concentrated (such as Intel's relationship to the PC industry) or there exists a significant cost to switch suppliers. Suppliers are weak if there are many competitive suppliers.

## Barriers to Entry

The possibility that new firms may enter an industry affects competition. In theory, any firm should be able to enter and exit a market. In reality, however, industries possess characteristics that protect the high profit levels of firms in the market and inhibit additional rivals from entering the market—known as a barrier to entry.

Barriers to entry are unique industry characteristics that define the industry. Barriers reduce the rate of entry of new firms, thus maintaining a level of profits for those already in the industry. From a strategic perspective, barriers can be created or exploited to enhance a firm's competitive advantage. Barriers to entry arise from several sources:

*The Government.*    Although the government generally tries to promote competition through the threat of antitrust actions, sometimes the government also restricts competition through regulation or the granting of monopolies (such as public utilities).

One example is the cable industry. The franchise to a cable provider may be granted by competitive bidding, but once a community awards the franchise a monopoly is created. Local governments were not effective in monitoring price gouging by cable operators, so the federal government has enacted legislation to review and restrict prices.

## Patents and Proprietary Knowledge

Ideas and knowledge that provide competitive advantages are treated as private property when patented, preventing others from using the knowledge and thus creating a barrier to entry.

## Asset Specificity

This term refers to the extent to which the firm's assets can be utilized to produce a different product. When an industry requires highly specialized technology or plants and equipment, potential entrants are reluctant to commit to acquiring specialized assets that cannot be sold or converted into other uses if the venture fails.

*Internal Economies of Scale.* The point at which unit costs for production are at minimum—the most cost-efficient level of production—is known as the Minimum Efficient Scale (MES). If MES for firms in an industry is known, then a firm can determine the amount of market share necessary for low-cost entry or cost parity with rivals. For example, suppose in long-distance communications roughly 10% of the market is necessary for MES. If sales for a long-distance operator fail to reach 10% of the market, the firm is not competitive.

Generally speaking, firms entering a market will face a low barrier to entry if the industry is marked by common technology, little dominant brand franchise, and easy access to distribution channels. By contrast, it is difficult to enter a market if there is patented or proprietary know-how, difficulty in brand switching, and restricted distribution channels.

*Strategies for Competitive Advantage.* Porter (1998) identified three generic strategies (cost leadership, differentiation, and focus) that can be implemented at the business unit level to create a competitive advantage. The proper generic strategy will position the firm to leverage its strengths and defend against the adverse effects of the five forces. If the primary determinant of a firm's profitability is the attractiveness of the industry in which it operates, an important secondary determinant is its position within that industry. Although an industry may have below-average profitability, a firm that is optimally positioned can generate superior returns.

A firm positions itself by leveraging its strengths. Porter (1998) has argued that a firm's strengths ultimately fall into one of two headings: cost advantage and differentiation. By applying these strengths in either a broad or narrow scope, three generic strategies result: cost leadership, differentiation, and focus. These strategies are applied at the business unit level. They are called *generic strategies* because they are not firm or industry dependent.

Cost leadership strategy requires a firm to be the low-cost producer in an industry for a given level of quality. The firm sells its products either at average industry prices to earn a profit higher than that of rivals, or below the average industry prices to gain market share. Some of the ways that firms acquire cost advantages are by improving process efficiencies, gaining unique access to a large source of lower cost materials, making optimal outsourcing and vertical integration decisions, or avoiding some costs altogether. If competing firms are unable to lower their costs by a similar amount, the firm may be able to sustain a competitive advantage based on cost leadership.

Firms succeeding in cost leadership often have (a) access to the capital required to make a significant investment in production assets (such access to capital represents a barrier to entry that many firms may not overcome); (b) skill in designing products for efficient manufacturing, for example, having a small component count to shorten the assembly process; (c) a high level of expertise in manufacturing process engineering; or (d) efficient distribution channels. A cost leadership strategy can fail if other firms can match the cost savings, which often happens with improved production and distribution technology.

A differentiation strategy calls for the development of a product or service that offers unique attributes that are valued by customers and that customers perceive to be better than or different from the products of the competition. The value added by the uniqueness of the product may allow the firm to charge a premium price for it. The firm hopes that the higher price will more than cover the extra costs incurred in offering the unique product. Because of the product's unique attributes, if suppliers increase their prices the firm may be able to pass along the costs to its customers who cannot find substitute products easily.

Firms that succeed in a differentiation strategy often possess one or more of the following: access to leading scientific research, a highly skilled and creative product development team, a strong sales team with the ability to successfully communicate the perceived strengths of the product, or corporate reputation for quality and innovation.

The focus strategy concentrates on a narrow market segment and within that segment attempts to achieve either a cost advantage or differentiation. The premise is that the needs of the group can be better serviced by focusing entirely on it. A firm using a focus strategy can often obtain a high degree of consumer loyalty, thus discouraging other firms from competing for that target.

Firms pursuing a focus strategy often have lower volumes because of their smaller target market and may lose some bargaining power with suppliers. On the other hand, what the firms lose in cost savings may be able to be passed on to their customers because close substitute products do not exist. An example of this is Apple Computer. Because Apple does not license their operating system to other computer manufacturers, customers are forced to deal with Apple.

A focus strategy allows a firm to develop a broad range of product strengths to a relatively narrow market niche. The major downsides of either strategy are that the product strengths a firm possesses may be imitated by competitors (e.g., Microsoft did with developing Windows), or the tastes and preferences of the target market may change (as they age, for example).

## Competitive Advantage

When a firm sustains profits that exceed the average for its industry, the firm is said to possess a competitive advantage over its rivals. Porter (1998) identified two basic types of competitive advantage: cost advantage and differentiation advantage. A cost advantage exists when the firm is able to deliver the same benefits as competitors but at a lower cost. A differentiation advantage exists when the firm's products deliver benefits that exceed those of competing products.

In order to develop a competitive advantage the firm must have resources (firm-specific assets) that are superior to those of its competitors and that cannot be acquired easily. Examples of these resources would be patents and trademarks, intellectual property, customer databases, corporate reputation, and brand equity. These resources make it difficult for competitors to replicate what the firm was doing and reduce its competitive advantage. Firms also have to be able to utilize its resources effectively, such as launching a new product before its competitors.

*AOL.* AOL, the largest Internet Service Provider in the world, had a relatively inauspicious beginning. In 1983, William Von Meister launched Control Video Corporation, whose primary product line was GameLine, a service that allowed subscribers to download video games onto their Atari 2600 home game machines. With the collapse of the home video-game market several months later, the GameLine service was discontinued.

Assisted by marketing director Steve Case, Von Meister began a new company called Quantum, and offered an online service for Commodore 64 computer users called Q-Link. Quantum then moved on to build proprietary online services for computer manufacturers, eventually signing up Apple, Tandy, and IBM. By 1992, the company, now renamed America Online (AOL), went public. Shortly afterward, Steve Case (only 33 at the time), was named company CEO.

By 1994, AOL had built a gateway onto the Internet. At the same time, AOL began mailing out free copies of its software, along with the promise of a free month of service. Subscribership mushroomed, and revenues skyrocketed. AOL also made some shrewd deals. For example, in early 1996, AOL entered into two major agreements designed to simplify the use of their service and make it more compatible with major software systems. Although AOL had benefitted a great deal from the popularity of the Web, many users were not impressed with its browsers that were slow during peak hours. In February 1996, AOL and Netscape announced a marketing and technology alliance. AOL agreed to license the Netscape browser for all of its services. Initially, the browser would be integrated into AOL's GNN Internet service. AOL would get some exposure on Netscape's homepage, at the time one of the most popular pages on the Web. Putting Netscape's browser into the hands of, the then, 8 million AOL subscribers would better position both Netscape and AOL in their respective battles versus Microsoft's Internet Explorer and the MSN ISP.

Then, the day after announcing the Netscape deal, AOL and Microsoft announced their own technology and marketing agreement. Microsoft's Internet Explorer would be seamlessly integrated into AOL's client software by the end of 1996. In return, AOL would be preinstalled with future versions of the Windows operating system in a folder on the desktop called *Online Services*. This move was designed to significantly reduce AOL's customer acquisition costs.

The next major move for AOL was its move to flat-rate pricing (i.e., non-metered pricing). One benefit of such a scheme is that customers are happy with it because it is simple and easy to understand, and they are not inhibited from using the system. Another benefit is that is easy to implement billing systems for flat-rate pricing plans.

A major drawback of flat-rate pricing, however, is that there are no incentives for customers to make efficient use of bandwidth. Also, because everyone pays the same flat fee, the ISP cannot assign a higher priority to those customers who are willing to pay more. Finally, there is the issue of equity in that the small volume users actually subsidize the big volume users of the network.

The other option as an ISP is to use usage-sensitive pricing. The advantage of usage- sensitive pricing is that it makes for more efficient use of the bandwidth. The drawback is that consumers do not like it.

Until October 1996, major online services such as AOL and CompuServe had a combination of flat rate (e.g., $19,95 per month) and usage-sensitive ($5.95 per hour) pricing. These pricing plans were simple to understand and implement, although sophisticated enough that users had incentives to act in the most cost-efficient manner. In October 1996, MSN began a new pricing plan to reduce customer turnover (or "churn")—$19.95 per month for unlimited access. AOL immediately responded in kind.

At the same time, AOL launched a series of marketing initiatives aimed at growing its subscriber base. AOL billed itself as "The Internet and a Whole Lot More" (one of the initial ads used the music from the classic futuristic cartoon, "The Jetsons"). AOL also promoted personalization capabilities and community strengths, and began to focus on member satisfaction and reliability. AOL's strategy was to not only get people signed up, but to get them to use the service more.

The new price structure and the aggressive advertising campaign drew many more customers to AOL than projected. The increase in customers, and the increased time each customer used AOL, placed a serious strain on its service. Many of AOL's customers found that they had long delays in being able to dial up the service. Consequently, the company invested more than $150 million to upgrade its capacity. In addition, in October 1997, AOL acquired CompuServe. The motivation for the acquisition was as much to take advantage of CompuServe's underutilized technical infrastructure, as it was to obtain new subscribers. The strategy worked: AOL's stock hit $94 a share in December 1999, and Steve Case had money to burn to look for an acquisition.

*The Merger.*     On January 10, 2000, AOL chairman Steve Case and Time Warner chairman Jerry Levin announced that they were merging their two companies—the largest corporate merger in history to that date. The two chairmen projected that AOL Time Warner—a combination of a "new" media company with an "old" media company—would produce a 30% surge in profits on $40 billion in sales in the first year alone (Dugan, 2000).

Within weeks, however, economic events foreshadowed major problems for the new company. The so-called "dot-com bubble" burst, as Internet-based companies saw earnings dive or get wiped out altogether. AOL was also affected, though because the company was the leader in online subscriptions, the effect was not initially dramatic. In fact, the combined company's stock peaked at $56.60 in May 2001.

Though governmental approval of the merger was relatively swift (final approval was made in January 2001), AOL Time Warner stock plummeted. In April 2002, the company announced a $54 billion write-down, reflecting the company's deterioration in value since the merger. It was forced to pay a $7 billion to purchase Bertelsmann's interest in AOL Europe, an obligation that came with the merger. Debt ballooned to $28 billion. In July 2002, The *Washington Post* reported alleged accounting improprieties at AOL during the months before the merger was completed, supposedly conducted to prop up AOL's earnings to support the completion of the deal. Within days, the SEC and the Department of Justice launched investigations. AOL Time Warner stock hit bottom in July 2002 at $8.70, and, at the time of this writing, is trading at slightly over $15. The stock collapse wiped out nearly $280 billion in value for the company. Why the economic debacle for AOL Time Warner?

The answer may lie in the complete shift in strategic focus for the new company. AOL made its mark largely because it employed a cost advantage strategy. By aggressively acquiring customers, the company was able to achieve unrivaled economies of scale for its Internet service. At the time of the merger, AOL had 4 times as many subscribers as its nearest rival, MSN.

By merging with Time Warner, the strategy shifted to differentiation. Now customers would get content that no other company could provide. In the abstract, the strategy appeared sound. Implementing that strategy was another matter entirely. In order for the strategy to work—to get proprietary Time Warner content to AOL subscribers—the distribution technology needed to be upgraded to broadband.

*Moving to Broadband.* At the time of this writing, AOL had slightly more than 35 million subscribers. Of those, 17.7 million U.S. subscribers pay the full $23.90 a month for AOL. Microsoft's MSN was second with more than 8 million for its own ISP (Lohr & Kirkpatrick, 2003).

In order to remain profitable in the long run, however, AOL needs to be able to make the shift to broadband. Two problems emerge, though. First, shifting to broadband could result lower profit margins for AOL due to the high cost of paying cable and phone companies for their high-speed lines. Second, it is likely that the current subscriber base for dial-up Internet access for AOL will be the customer base for broadband. In other words, AOL may cannibalize its more profitable narrowband subscriber base.

AOL and other ISPs may have to provide *value-added services*, or services that providers can charge an extra fee to use, to generate more revenues. To date, the prospects have been mixed. Online music subscriptions, which were predicted to propel broadband growth, have not filled their promise.

Unfortunately for AOL, the broadband market is growing dramatically. The number of U.S. households with broadband has jumped from 5.2 million in 2000 to 10.4 million in 2001, and is expected to reach 15.4 million in 2002, according to Jupiter Research (Emling, 2002). As this number grows, further pressure will be put on AOL to both expand its broadband subscriber base while preventing its dial-up subscribers from defecting.

Many providers offer discounts on the first 3 to 6 months of service, this may not overcome consumer sticker shock. Consumer DSL offerings grew by 10% in the second quarter of 2002, whereas the cable modem audience grew by 12% from a much larger subscriber base. Higher average prices for DSL than for cable largely explain this difference. In addition, early adopters have broadband at this point, and new strategies and messages will likely be required to entice increasingly mainstream dial-up users to broadband.

Companies pursuing new broadband users must start considering specific segments within the audience, not the audience as a whole. Thus, they need to avoid gearing offerings to generic broadband users; instead, focus on serving needs of particular segments, especially segments determined by online activities.

But luring new users to adopt broadband services is not the only challenge providers will face next year. To date, broadband service providers have benefitted from low industry-wide churn rates, mainly because consumers have shunned the high price of switching providers. Most of the churn has been involuntary, resulting from providers going out of business. Broadband service providers need to start developing subscriber retention strategies so they will not be caught short by churn as it inevitably increases in 2003. In addition, broadband marketing will have to evolve beyond selling speed, 24/7 connections, and avoiding second phone lines. Providers will need to tailor marketing strategies to specific types of consumers in order to push broadband penetration rates higher while minimizing customer churn.

## CONCLUSION

With almost universal market penetration in the 1970s, television began to undergo upheaval—not because of the reaction of other media but because of industry specific technological, content, and regulatory factors that changed the face of television: CATV, satellite TV, digital TV, etcetera. Thus, while factors external to a specific medium cause it to change, so too do internal factors.

In terms of the Internet, most of the factors creating its change are internal, not external, such as technological (XML taking over from HTML software; file swapping programs), political and regulatory (taxation legislation; variation among national laws), and especially economic (the beginning of the end of free content). Dealing with these factors will help shape the further expansion of the Internet, most likely by strengthening the financial base of surviving e-companies.

Older media will survive in the coming years but with significant changes. Although their content and function will remain recognizable, their modes of transmission and distribution will change drastically. Most newspapers will ultimately become exclusively electronic, delivered through the Internet by cable or wireless into new media appliances (PDA, e-book). Radio will continue to gravitate to the Internet, especially because that is where people will be spending more of their work and leisure time. Television is a different matter—it is unclear whether the Internet will be delivered on the TV screen, or TV programming will be streamed via a computer screen. One thing is clear: The content for these media will be distributed through the Internet.

Further, the content of older media will look similar, but will also to the Web's pull by upgrading the mode, quantity, and quality of their contents. Each medium will attempt to better serve old audiences while finding or creating new audience niches.

Finally, the future adaptation of older media to the Internet and the Web might take the form of convergence in order to provide a multifunctional, multimedia platform that can compete on equal terms with online media.

Making this possibility ever more likely is the increasing conglomeratiz-ation of the media world, with each corporation owning radio and TV sta-tions as well as print newspapers and magazines (e.g., Rupert Murdoch's News Corporation or AOL Time Warner). In short, older media do not nec-essarily have to adapt individually to the threat of the new medium. They can do so together. Thus, it's unlikely that traditional media may disappear, though some media may morph into something else (e.g., the print news-paper becoming an electronic newspaper).

As the Internet captures a wider (and younger) audience, the medium threatens the future existence of older media because the audience will not be open (or even able) to "consume" in the traditional fashion. Thus, the threat of a new medium lies in the change in the way content is consumed and perceived. Can newspapers hold the attention of adults in 2020 brought up in a 1990s sensory environment in which 10 seconds of concen-tration is a long time? In short, the real technological threat of the new me-dium may be psychological—the ways older media are processed and used may be transformed by changing deep-rooted patterns of thought and con-sumption.

At the present, the Internet just passed 50% market penetration in the U.S. It is now at a crossroads. Some scenarios suggest that convergence and synergy will allow online media to sentence technologies such as broad-casting and magazines to the Island of Misfit Media. Given the recent diffi-culties with companies attempting such convergence and synergy (e.g., AOL Time Warner), this does not appear to be happening soon.

## FURTHER READING

McKnight, L., & Bailey, J. (Eds.). (1997). *Internet economics*. Cambridge, MA: MIT Press.
Negroponte, N. (1995). *Being digital*. New York: Knopf.
Stoll, C. (1995). *Silicon snake oil: Second thoughts on the information highway*. New York: Doubleday.

## REFERENCES

Carveth, R., & Metz, J. (1996, Spring). Frederick Jackson Turner and the democrati-zation of the electronic frontier. *The American Sociologist*, 72–90.
Chan-Olmsted, S. M., & Park, J. S. (2000). From on-air to online world: Examining the content and structures of broadcast TV stations' web sites. *Journalism & Mass Communication Quarterly, 77*(2), 321–340.
Dugan, I. (2000, January 12). AOL's stock falls, cutting value of deal. *Washington Post*, A01.
Emling, S. (2002, May 4). AOL's push to rev up Net service faces hurdles. *Atlanta Journal-Constitution*, 1F.
Fahey, A. (1989a, May 29). Prodigy opens videotex to outside creative work. *Adver-tising Age*, 31.

Fahey, A. (1989b, October 23). Prodigy sets trade, consumer ads. *Advertising Age*, 16.

Fahey, A. (1990, January 20). Car makers plug into PCs. *Advertising Age*, 54.

Ghose, S., & Dou, W. (1999). Advertising, marketing, and consumer behavior. *Communication Abstracts, 22*(1), 77–86.

Gore, A. (1991). Infrastructure for the global village. *Scientific American, 265*(3), 150–153.

Grover, V., & Sabherwal, R. (1989, June). Poor performance of videotex systems. *Journal of Systems Management*, 31–36.

Hanson, G. (1992, January 27). Making waves via computers. *Insight, 6*(11), 32–33.

Hawkins, D. (1991, March). Videotex markets, applications, and systems. *Online*, 97–100.

Lohr, S., & Kirkpatrick, D. D. (2003, May 30). Technology: Microsoft to pay AOL $750 million. *New York Times*, A 1.

Maital, S. (1991, November). Why the French do it better. *Across the Board*, 7–9.

Major, M. (1990, November 12). Videotex never really left, but it's not all there. *Marketing News*, 2–3.

Naughton, J. (2000, July 17). Click your mouse and vote. *New Statesman, 129*, 29–31.

Porter, M. E. (1998). *Competitive advantage of nations*. New York: Free Press.

Truet, B., & Hermann, M. (1989, July 10). A skeptic's view of videotex. *Telephony*, 26–27.

# Glossary

**Above the line:** A term used in motion picture and television budgets that refers to the artistic expenses of a production. Above the line workers include producers, directors, writers, actors; other above the line expenses include the purchase of rights to a story or script.

**Acquisition:** The purchase of operating assets or stock of one company by another firm. Distinct from a merger or consolidation in that the selling company typically continues to exist following the transaction.

**Amortization:** Accounting procedure that gradually reduces the cost value of a limited life or intangible asset through periodic charges to income.

**Archives:** Archives are organizations that collect and store material of historic and cultural significance. In the case of motion picture and television archives the Library of Congress has taken the lead in encouraging legislation that facilitates the development and maintenance of public archives for these media.

**Asset:** Anything having commercial or exchange value that is owned by a business, institution, or individual.

**Back end revenue:** Back end revenue is part of a hybrid model for pricing advertising, where cost-per-thousand or cost-per-point is discounted at the front end, and anticipated revenue for transactions on a given media channel is shared between the advertiser and television network at the back end. Hybrid models allow the buyer and the seller of advertising to share the risk that the campaign will succeed or fail.

**Balance sheet:** Financial report also called statement of condition or financial position showing the status of a company's assets, liabilities and owner's equity on a given date.

**Barriers to entry:** Real or imagined costs that act to prevent firms from entering a particular industry.

**Barter syndication:** Barter is a form of syndication in which the cost of programs to stations and cable program services is reduced in return for reserving several commercial availabilities within the program for use by the provider of the program.

**Below the line:** A term used in budgeting and planning motion picture and television production. Below the line workers include such specialists as set carpenters, camera operators, grips, gaffers, sound mixers, and other technicians required by a production. Below the line expenses include costs of film, lease of production equipment and other facilities.

**Blind bidding:** An unethical and illegal practice in the distribution of motion pictures, it requires theater operators to bid on productions that they were not allowed to preview prior to their bid.

**Block booking:** An unethical and illegal practice in the distribution of motion pictures it requires theater operators to commit to presentation of a set or "block" of productions of unknown value in order to show one or more productions of unquestioned value.

**Bond:** Any interest-bearing or discounted government or corporate security that obligates the issuer to pay a specified sum of money at specified times and to repay the principal amount of the loan at maturity.

**Book value:** (1) Value at which an asset is carried on the balance sheet. For example, a piece of manufacturing equipment is put on the books at its cost when purchased. Its value is then reduced each year as depreciation is charged to income. (2) Net asset value of a company's securities calculated as total assets minus intangible assets minus current and long-term liabilities and any equity issues that have a prior claim.

**Capital expenditure:** Outlay of money to acquire or improve capital assets such as buildings and machinery.

**Capital structure:** Corporation's financial framework, including long-term debt, preferred stock, and net worth. It is distinct from financial structure in that it includes additional sources of capital such as short-debt, accounts payable, and other liabilities.

**Capital asset pricing model:** Sophisticated model of the relationship between expected risk and expected return. It says that the return on an asset or security is equal to the risk-free return such as that on a short-term Treasury security plus a risk premium.

**Capitalization ratio:** Analysis of a company's capital structure showing what percentage is debt, preferred stock, common stock, and other equity.

**Cartel:** A formal or informal arrangement of companies that attempt to eliminate competition between themselves by agreeing to common prices, quality standards, advertising and the like.

**Cash flow:** In a larger financial sense an analysis of all the changes that affect the cash account in a given accounting period. In investments, refers to the cash generated from operations and may be defined as EBIT, EBITDA, Free Cash Flow, or other variations of net income plus non cash expenses. The sum of retained earnings and depreciation provision made by firms. As an indicator of revenue remaining after all direct expenses have been deducted, it is the source of internally generated long-term funds available to the firm.

**Common stock:** Units of ownership of a public corporation. Owners typically are entitled to vote on the selection of directors and other important matters as well as to receive dividends on their holdings. In the event that a corporation is liquidated, the claims of secured and unsecured creditors and owners of bonds and preferred stock take precedence over the claims of those who own common stock.

**Comparable sales:** Those firms, which are comparable in size, location, and profitability, that have been sold lately. As they are like the firm under consideration, they should have similar values.

**Comparative advantage:** The situation that exists when market forces allocate a nation's resources to those industries where it is relatively most productive, especially in terms of keeping costs low.

**Competition:** Rivalry of buyers and sellers with and among themselves in a market. The term also refers to a market structure in which many buyers and sellers of the product compete.

**Competitive advantage:** The situation that exists when a nation or firm holds an industrial advantage over others. Competitive advantage considers not only the costs of production, product quality, product features, but new product innovation as well.

**Concentration of market power:** A situation where the top firms in an industry collectively control the vast majority of industry sales or assets. It is usually measured by the cumulative market shares of the four to eight largest firms.

**Concentration ratio:** The proportion of industry sales concentrated within selected numbers of firms, typically 4, 8, and 20.

**Concentration:** The degree to which the largest companies in the same product and geographic market control the economic activities of that market.

**Concept:** In the planning and preparation of a broadcast program or cereals a concept is a brief statement of the main idea. It is particularly useful in research to determine the value of program proposals.

**Conglomerate:** A large corporation composed of companies in a variety of businesses.

**Consent decree:** A negotiated settlement of an antitrust case before a judgment is rendered. No admission of guilt is implied by such a settlement nor may it be the foundation for assessing damages to injured parties.

**Consolidation:** A type of merger in which both companies cease to exist after the transaction and an entirely new corporation is formed that retains the assets and liabilities of both companies.

**Cost per point (CPP):** Cost per point is a method of evaluating media efficiency and represents a ratio based on how much it costs to buy one rating point, or one percent of the population in an area being evaluated. The common formula is: CPP equals the cost of advertising schedule purchased divided by Gross Rating Points (GRPs).

**Creamskimming:** To take the most desirable and valuable part of a business, akin to skimming cream off the top of milk bottles prior to pasteurization.

**Cultural discount:** The variations in a product's value as it moves into international markets based on consumer preferences in different cultures.

**Default:** Failure of a debtor to make interest or principal payments or to meet some other provision of a bond indenture.

**Deficit financing:** A situation where the costs of production (including normal profits) are not fully covered by payments, forcing producers to either sacrifice normal profits or cross-subsidize operations from revenues derived in other areas.

**Depreciation:** Amortization of fixed assets, such as plant or equipment, so as to allocate the cost over their depreciable life.

**Distribution deal:** A financial arrangement for the production of a broadcast program or series or of a motion picture. A distribution deal commits the producer to making the finished production available to a stipulated channel of distribution, such as network broadcast, cable program service, or videocassette. In return, the distribution channel benefitting from these arrangements provides a part of the financing of the production.

**Duopolies:** Market structures in which there are two sellers of a product.

**EBITDA:** Earnings before depreciation, amortization, interest, and taxes are paid.

**Economies of scale:** Declining levels of average cost accompanying greater expansion of product output and optimal use of plant and equipment. Cost advantages associated with the increasing size of firms.

**Equity:** Ownership of a company arising from purchasing shares or stock or building the enterprise from scratch.

**Excess profits:** Profit over and above normal profits.

**Exclusivity:** A provision of syndication contracts that guarantees that a program purchased by a station or cable program service will not also be available to its competitors within the same national runs covered by the contract.

**Expected value:** Precisely the mean value of the distribution function. It provides an estimate of average value when the true value is unknown.

**Externalities:** Factors that can influence the value of goods, or affect an exchange, but that are not ordinarily considered as part of the market for that good. An example might be the desire of a purchaser to gain the prestige of being a publisher.

**Fair market value:** The expected value of a property under normal conditions. What the typical buyer, or seller, would price a property at.

**Financial interest in syndication:** A set of federal rules that limit the ownership of programs presented first by a broadcast network. In general, the network on which the program or series is first presented in prime time may participate in ownership only under very restricted conditions such as foreign distribution.

**First-run (original) syndication:** These are programs and series produced especially for the syndication.

**Fixed costs:** Costs that do not vary when output is increased or decreased.

**"Frame of mind" value:** The dimensions of reputation, familiarity, and popularity bestowed upon a production by patronage of an audience.

**Free cash flow:** Earnings after interest and taxes minus capital expenditures plus depreciation and amortization.

**Goodwill:** In acquisition accounting, going concern value in excess of book value.

**Gross domestic product:** The sum total of all goods and services produced in the United States in 1 year.

**Gross rating point (GRP):** A gross rating point is a unit of measurement of advertising audience size equal to one percent of the total potential audience universe. GRP measures the exposure of one or more TV programs or commercials without regard to multiple exposure of the same advertising to individuals. A GRP is the product of media reach times exposure frequency.

**Highly leverage transaction (HLT):** A merger or acquisition predicated on the use of borrowed funds to finance a portion of the transaction resulting in a company that has substantially more debt than is typical for the industry. See also *leveraged buyout.*

**Holding company:** Organizational entities that form umbrella structures linking independent advertising agencies.

**Income forecasting method:** A procedure used by accountants and management of broadcast stations and cable program services to estimate the value of a proposed purchase from syndication. It can also be used to estimate the worth of programs or series already under contract from syndication.

**Independent producer:** A producer of motion pictures or television programs who operates a production business separate from a motion picture studio, network. program service, or distribution organization.

**Investment bank:** A firm acting as an agent that serves as an intermediary between an issuer of securities and the investing public. Additional services include client advisement and the provision of broker-dealer security trading.

**Joint operating agreement:** A business relationship allowed under law that provides newspapers with an exemption to antitrust law. Under a joint operating agreement two separately owned newspapers combine business operations while maintaining separate news and editorial operations.

**Junk bond:** Bond with a speculative grade credit rating from Standard & Poor's and Moody's rating services.

**Knowledge communities:** Also called expert communities. A geographic cluster of companies and professionals working in a single industry or area of expertise. The development of a knowledge community encourages innovation and industry development by assisting in the rapid exchange of ideas among professionals working on similar problems.

**Lead-in index:** A value calculated from audience measurements that reflects the demonstrated ability of a television program to capture and/or enlarge the audience of the program that immediately precedes it in the broadcast schedule.

**Leverage:** Debt in relation to equity in a firm's capital structure.

**Leveraged buyout:** Takeover of a company using borrowed funds. Most often, the target company's assets serve as security for the loans taken out by the acquiring firm, which repays the loans from the cash flow of the acquired company.

**Limited series:** A production intended for presentation on one or more of a small number of days. A limited series may include from two to any number of episodes but is usually not planned for presentation on a once a week basis or for periods of time greater than a few weeks.

**Marketing concept:** A core principle emphasizing the centrality of consumer need satisfaction in marketing products and services.

**Media conglomerate:** A corporation that deals in several (seemingly unrelated) media business.

**Merger:** A combination of two companies either through a pooling of interests, where the accounts are combined; a purchase, where the amount paid over and above the acquired company's book value is carried on the books of the purchaser as goodwill; or a consolidation, where a new company is formed to acquire the net assets of the combining companies. A legal process whereby two or more firms consolidated into one corporation.

**Monopolistic competition:** The condition that exists in a market where there are many sellers but the products cluster and within each genre of product sellers compete to differentiate their products. A market structure in which a number of competing sellers of similar, but differentiated, products exist.

**Monopoly:** A market structure in which a single seller of a product exists and controls the market, often resulting in restraint of free trade.

**Monopsony:** A monopoly from the buyer's (rather than the seller's) perspective.

**Multiples:** A "quick and dirty" way of estimating fair market value, based on a multiple of some indicator of firm size or profitability.

**Multiplex:** A movie theater complex with several auditory with a common lobby.

**National Association of Television Program Executives (NATPE):** A professional association of television program directors and program managers. The annual meeting of the association has become the principal meeting at which programs and series for syndication are bought and sold.

**National run (also simply called *run*):** The presentation of a motion picture or television program or series to a national audience one time. The audience is deemed "national" in industry practice if presented once in any city. The second presentation in any city begins a second national run.

**Natural monopolies:** Monopolies that occur not because of acts of competitors but because scale economies and other factors make a single producer most efficient and drive others from the market.

**Network:** The simultaneous transmission of a program by two or more stations or systems, interconnected by wire or satellites; it also refers to organizations that provide a continuous flow of such programs to prearranged groups of stations or systems that are affiliates.

**Normal profits:** The rate of return on invested capital for entrepreneurs that provides sufficient compensation to them to invest their scarce time and funds in the enterprise rather than switch to another one; also referred to as the opportunity cost of entrepreneurship.

**Off-network series:** A television series originally presented on network television in prime time that has subsequently become available for syndication.

**Oligopoly:** A market structure composed of a few very large and powerful firms that control an industry. The higher the market concentration, the stronger/tighter the oligopoly. A market structure in which competition exists among a small number of sellers of similar products.

**Operating profits:** That profit which would be earned if no resources were diverted to expansion or reinvestment (retained earnings). The same as **EBTT.**

**Opportunity cost:** The economic value of the next best alternative to what one is currently doing.

**Package:** A collection of films or programs that are sold as a unit in syndication.

**Pay-in-kind securities:** Fixed income securities, typically bonds, that meet interest payments through the issuance of like securities in the principal amount of the payment in lieu of a cash payment. Similar to a common stock paying a dividend in common stock.

**Piracy:** The unauthorized reproduction and distribution of copyrighted products.

**Present value:** Value today of a future payment or stream of payments, discounted at some appropriate compound interest or discount rate. For example, the present value of $100 to be received 10 years from now is about $38.55, using a discount rate equal to 10% compounded annually.

**Price discrimination:** A market situation in which sellers find it possible and profitable to separate two or more markets for its product or service and charge a different price in each of the markets. In the movie business the first market is the theaters (or theatrical window) and the others (cable TV, home video, and over-the-air TV) are referred to as the ancillary markets.

**Price/earnings ratio (P/E):** The price of a stock divided by the earnings of the company.

**Prime time:** Hours of peak viewing for a broadcast network or station or cable program service. Although other hours may be designated as prime by a broadcaster, practice has become uniform that in the Eastern and Pacific time zones, for example. prime time on weekdays is from 7 p.m. until 11 p.m. local time.

**Prime-time access rule (PTAR):** A rule adopted by the FCC in 1971, PTAR provides that the commercial television networks may not program for their affiliates more than three of the week night block of 4 prime-time hours. In addition, in the top 50 television markets local network affiliates may not schedule off-network programming in the daily hour of prime time that they program.

**Prime-time alternative:** Prime-time alternatives are purchased by independent television stations hoping to attract audience from affiliates during prime time, by network affiliates that intend to preempt network programs with less audience appeal and by cable channels wishing to win audiences from broadcast television stations during prime time.

**Private placement:** The sale of securities directly to a limited number of institutional investors. A private placement need not be registered with the S.E.C.

**Product differentiation:** The process whereby a company differentiates itself or its products from those of its competitors.

**Public goods:** Goods that can be consumed by one user without diminishing the quantity of the product available to others.

**Publishing:** For the purposes of this book, the term **publishing** referred specifically to the book industry; consumer and business periodicals; electronic databases and CD-ROM products; and miscellaneous publishing (e.g., directories, annuals, newsletters, loose-leaf reporting services, etc.).

**Pure competition:** A marketplace characterized by four conditions: (a) homogeneity of product, (b) smallness of each buyer or seller to the market, (c) absence of artificial restraints, and (d) mobility of resources.

**Reality-based programs and series:** Television programs or series comprised of material from reality, such as biography, history, nature, science, or extraordinary experiences of ordinary citizens.

**Rerelease:** A motion picture term, it refers to presentations of a motion picture several years after initial release of a theatrical film.

**Residuals:** Payments to above-the-line workers in motion pictures and television for second and subsequent presentation of the productions) to which they contributed.

**Rough:** A relatively crude or unfinished version of a program or series. Roughs are used to give potential purchasers and investors an audiovisual impression of a finished program or series.

**Scale economies:** Cast savings that result when long-run average costs decline as output and plant size increase.

**Self-sufficiency:** The condition in which a firm is totally reliant on itself for its supply of inputs into the production or distribution process. Widespread self-sufficiency indicates significant vertical integration.

**Shared monopoly:** When a cartel arrangement is so stable and successful that the several firms operate in unison as if a single monopolist controlled the industry.

**Significantly viewed cable-imported television signal:** A television station presented in the market of a local over-the-air television station by cable If the imported station duplicates some programs of the local telecaster, cable is usually required to black out or not present, the program on the imported signal that duplicates the local outlet. If, however, audience measurement within the market indicates that there is a consistently significant audience for the imported station's signal within the counties covered by the local station, then a local station may not use FCC rules to protect its programs against duplicated programming from the "significantly viewed" station.

**Speculative presentations:** Presentations prepared by advertising agencies in order to attract new business clients.

**Stages of production:** Product is said to flow through several stages from its earliest origins as raw material through various manufacturing, distribution, and wholesaling levels until its final appearance as a retail consumer product. Each successive stage adds complexity and value to the product.

**Strip (strip scheduling):** A practice in scheduling television programs in which the programmer schedules the same program at the same time on Consecutive days.

**Studio:** A motion picture business which produces theatrical films and/or television programs and series. Studios develop and maintain a lot (outdoor sites for shooting films and television), property and setting shops and warehouses, film processing laboratories, film and related equipment.

**Superstation:** An independent TV station sent via satellite to distant cable markets.

**Supplier:** A firm which provides programs or series to a television network, cable program service, or syndication.

**Syndicated research services:** Companies that collect information on media audiences and product usage that is sold to advertisers, advertising agencies, and the media.

**Syndication exclusivity (syndex):** Rules reinstituted in January 1991 requiring cable systems to black out or substitute other programs for, syndicated programs brought into the local market by cable from distant television stations. The syndics blackout is required only for those syndicated programs under exclusive syndication to a local television station in the cable system's area and after application to the cable system by the local broadcast station involved.

**Syndication:** The sale of rights to present broadcast programs or series or motion pictures to individual television stations and cable program services.

**Syndicator:** A firm offering television programs or series or cable program services for syndication.

**Tax shelter:** Methods used by investors to legally avoid or reduce tax liabilities. Legal shelters include the use of depreciation of assets such as plant and equipment and the amortization of goodwill as operating expenses.

**Up-front money:** Funds provided to a producer in advance of production of television programs or series.

**Use of proceeds:** A statement made by an issuing company in an offering prospectus as to how the capital being raised is to be spent.

**Utility:** A basic concept of economic value, based on the notion that goods are desired because they are somehow useful. Utility is derived as an indicator of "usefulness."

**Variable costs:** Costs that vary as the amount of output increases. Labor and materials are commonly variable costs.

**Vertical integration:** The situation where a company occupies adjacent stages of production in an industry, thereby removing this stage either partially or wholly from access by outside companies (depending on the level of self-sufficiency).

**Zero coupon security:** Security that makes no periodic interest payments but instead is sold at a deep discount from its face value. The buyer of such a bond receives the rate of return by the gradual appreciation of the security that is redeemed at face value on a specified maturity date.

# Author Index

## A

Ahlkvist, J. A., 231, *246*
Albarran, A. B.,170, 196, 206, 207, 208, 211, 212, 213, *219*
Alderman, J., *246*
Alexander, A., 3
Ambler, T., *147*
Auletta, K., 151, *170*

## B

Backman, J., 254, *262*
Bagdikian, B. H., 70, 80, 81, 83, 111, 123, 124, 130, *145*
Bagwell, K., *262*
Bailey, J., *281*
Bain, J. S., *262*
Baker, C., 77, 81, *83*
Bales, B., *173*
Barnes, K., 236, *246*
Batra, R., 141, *145*
Becker, B. W. 137, *145*
Beebe, J. H., *170*
Benjaminson, P., 110, *124*
Berger, D., 229, 231, 236, 237, 247, *248*
Berkowtiz, H., 185, *191*
Bezjian-Avery, A., 144, *145*
Blackstone, E. A., 203, *206*
Boehlert, E., 229, *246*
Bogart, Dave, 128, *145*
Borden, H. H., *262*
Bowman, G. W., 203, *206*
Brody, J., 110, 111, 121, *124*
Bryon, C., 136, *145*
Buck, E. B., 235, *248*
Bulkeley, W. M., 215, *219*

Burkart, P., 242, *247*
Burnett, R., 229, *246*
Burt, L. B. S., 228, 233, *248*
Busterna, J. C., 80, 83, 122, *124*

## C

Calder, B., 144, *145*
Carnevale, D., 215, *219*
Carveth, R., 3, 49, 66, 265, 266, *281*
Cassey, J., 216, *219*
Castells, M., 166, *170*
Chamberlin, E. H., 251, *262*
Chambers, T., *173*
Chan-Olmstead, S. M., 270, *281*
Clurman, R., 136, *145*
Coen, R., *263*
Collins, R., 153, 161, *170*
Comanor, S. W., 258, *263*
Compaine, B. M., 80, 83, 193, 203, 206, *219*
Corden, W. M., 111, 113, *124*
Corn-Revere, R., *49*
Crawford, G., 189, *191*
Cuthbert, M., 235, *248*

## D

Daly, C., 127, *145*
Dannen, F., 228, 229, 237, *246*
Dertouzous, J. N., 115, 120, 122, 124, *125*
DiMaggio, P., 236, *246*
Dimmick, J., 196, 206, 229, *248*
Dolfsma, W., *246*
Dou, W., 265, *282*
Downey, K., 155, *170*

# Subject Index

CPSIA information can be obtained at www.ICGtesting.com
Printed in the USA
LVOW10s1257090115

422139LV00012B/266/P